An Introduction to the Study of Shakespeare

Hiram Corson

Alpha Editions

This edition published in 2019

ISBN : 9789353953300

Design and Setting By
Alpha Editions
email - alphaedis@gmail.com

AN

INTRODUCTION

TO THE STUDY OF

SHAKESPEARE.

BY

HIRAM CORSON, LL.D.,

PROFESSOR OF ENGLISH LITERATURE IN THE CORNELL
UNIVERSITY.

BOSTON:

D. C. HEATH & CO., PUBLISHERS.

1899.

EL

PREFACE.

THE present work is an attempt to indicate to the student some lines of Shakespearian study which may serve to introduce him to the study of the Plays as plays. No one line is carried out to any extent; but enough is presented, it is hoped, to enable the student, with the additional aid of such easily accessible sources as are noted, to extend the several lines of study indicated.

The commentaries presented on Romeo and Juliet, King John, Much Ado about Nothing, Hamlet, Macbeth, and Antony and Cleopatra, aim chiefly to present the points of view which are demanded, *me judice*, for a proper appreciation of Shakespeare's general attitude toward things, and his resultant dramatic art. The moral spirit with which he worked, as distinguished from a moralizing spirit, it is all-important to appreciate. His Plays surpass all those of the contemporary dramatists in their moral proportion — in the harmony which they exhibit with the eternal fitness of things — in their truthfulness in respect to the fatalism of overmastering passion. Herein consists their transcendent educating value. To come into the fullest possible sympathy with this moral proportion, with this harmony and truthfulness, should be the highest aim of Shakespearian culture.

The textual study of the Plays is abundantly provided for by numerous annotated editions, such as Rolfe's, Hudson's, the Clarendon Press, etc. These scholarly editions will not soon be superseded by others having the same general purpose.

HIRAM CORSON.

CONTENTS.

AN INTRODUCTION TO THE STUDY
OF. SHAKESPEARE.

INTRODUCTION.

———

ON the verso of the title-page, and facing the first page of the
Preface, of James Orchard Halliwell-Phillipps's "Outlines of
the Life of Shakespeare," is a woodcut, representing the scattered
bits of foundation wall which remain of Shakespeare's house, in
Stratford-upon-Avon, known as New Place. In the opening of
the Preface, the author remarks, with a touch of pathos, "the
remains of New Place, a partial sketch of which is engraved on
the opposite leaf, are typical of the fragments of the personal history of Shakespeare which have hitherto been discovered. In this
respect the great dramatist participates in the fate of most of his
literary contemporaries, for if a collection of the known facts relat-
ing to all of them were tabularly arranged, it would be found that
the number of the ascertained particulars of his life reached at
least the average. . At the present day, with biography carried to
a wasteful and ridiculous excess, and Shakespeare, the idol not
merely of a nation but of the educated world, it is difficult to
realize a period when no interest was taken in the events of the
lives of authors, and when the great poet himself, notwithstanding
the immense popularity of some of his works, was held in no general reverence. It must be borne in mind that actors then occupied an inferior position in society, and that in many quarters even
the vocation of a dramatic writer was considered scarcely respec-
table. The intelligent appreciation of genius by individuals was
not sufficient to neutralize in these matters the effect of public
opinion and the animosity of the religious world ; all circumstances
thus uniting to banish general interest in the history of persons con-

nected in any way with the stage. This biographical indifference continued for many years, and long before the season arrived for a real curiosity to be taken in the subject, the records from which alone a satisfactory memoir could have been constructed had disappeared. At the time of Shakespeare's decease, non-political correspondence was rarely preserved, elaborate diaries were not the fashion, and no one, excepting in semi-apocryphal collections of jests, thought it worth while to record many of the sayings and doings, or to delineate at any length the characters, of actors and dramatists, so that it is generally by the merest accident that particulars of interest respecting them have been recovered."

But meagre as our knowledge remains of the external life of Shakespeare, after all the untiring researches of the last, and more especially of the present century, we, nevertheless, thanks to those researches, possess a kind of knowledge quite as desirable as any knowledge of his personal history, desirable as that is — more so than that of any other great author in the world's literatures. The material for this knowledge was collected by Dr. C. M. Ingleby, and published in 1874, in a volume entitled "Shakespeare's Centurie of Prayse; being materials for a history of opinion on Shakespeare and his works, culled from writers of the first century after his rise," that is, from 1591, the 27th year of the poet's life, to 1693. These materials are far more abundant than any who have not made a special study of the subject, and who hold the traditional opinion that little or nothing has been delivered of Shakespeare by his contemporaries, and the two generations immediately succeeding his death, would be apt to suppose. The Index to Authors cited, contains 116 names; many of them being those of prominent writers of the period covered by the work. Several additions have been made to these, in the 2d edition, revised by Lucy Toulmin Smith, and published by the New Shakspere Society, 1879. The "Centurie of Prayse" furnishes "both positive and negative evidence as to the estimation in which Shakespeare was held by the writers of the century during which his fame was germinating; viz., 1592-1693. . . . The testimonies bear witness

to *subjective* opinions, preparing the way for the *objective* judgment which has seated Shakespeare on the throne of poets."

We really know more of Shakespeare than we know of any other
author of the time, either in English or in European literature, *who
was not connected with state affairs.* The personal history of a
mere author, and especially of a playwright, as a dramatic author,
whatever his ability, was frequently called, with no influence at
Court, was not considered of sufficient importance to be recorded
in those days, when the Court was everything, and the individual
man without adventitious recommendations, was nothing.

Already in 1598, when Shakespeare was but 34 years of age, a
clergyman, Francis Meres, educated at the University of Cambridge, in a work entitled " Palladis Tamia," ranked Shakespeare
with the greatest poets and dramatists of Greece and Rome. He
would hardly have done this if Shakespeare was so obscure and so
little estimated at the time as to cause such a judgment as he
expresses, to be laughed at. Meres, as his book shows, was a man
of great scholastic learning; and scholastic learning in those days
meant a reverential estimate of the great classics of Greece and
Rome. •

Higher still is the testimony to his greatness borne by Ben
Jonson, in his lines in the 1st Folio : —

*To the memory of my beloved, the Author Mr. William Shake-
speare: and what he hath left us.*

> *To draw no enuy* * (Shakespeare) *on thy name,*
> *Am I thus ample to thy Booke, and Fame :*
> *While I confesse thy writings to be such,*
> *As neither* Man, *nor* Muse, *can praise too much.*
> *'Tis true, and all mens suffrage. But these wayes*
> *Were not the paths I meant vnto thy praise:*

---

* "'To draw no envy,' etc., certainly does not mean what the editor of
Brome's " Five New Plays," 1659 (To the Reader, p. 4), imputes to it; as if
Ben thought to lower Shakespeare by extravagantly praising him. He meant

For seeliest Ignorance on these may light,
  Which, when it sounds at best, but eccho's right;
Or blinde affection, which doth ne're aduance
  The truth, but gropes, and vrgeth all by chance;
Or crafty Malice, might pretend this praise,
  And thinke to ruine, where it seem'd to raise.
These are, as some infamous Baud, or Whore,
  Should praise a Matron. What could hurt her more
But thou art proofe against them, and indeed
  Aboue th' ill fortune of them, or the need.
I, therefore will begin. Soule of the Age!
  The applause! delight! the wonder of our Stage!
My Shakespeare, *rise; I will not lodge thee by*
  Chaucer, *or* Spenser, *or bid* Beaumont *lye*
A little further, to make thee a roome: *
  Thou art a Moniment, without a tombe,
And art aliue still, while thy Booke doth liue,
  And we haue wits to read, and praise to giue.
That I not mixe thee so, my braine excuses;
  I meane with great, but disproportion'd Muses: †
For, if I thought my iudgement were of yeeres,
  I should commit thee surely with thy peeres,
And tell, how farre thou didstst our Lily *out-shine,*
  Or sporting Kid, *or* Marlowes *mighty line.*
And though thou hadst small Latine, *and lesse* Greeke, ‡

---

to say, that while Ignorance, Affection, or Malice, by excessive, indiscriminate, or unjust praise, would be sure to provoke the detraction of Envy, 'these ways were not the paths I meant unto thy praise'; for he could with full knowledge and strict impartiality award him the higbest praise that could be expressed." — Dr. Ingleby, in his "Shakespeare's Centurie of Prayse."

* "'I will not lodge thee,' etc., refers to Basse's lines, and means that he will not class Shakespeare with Chaucer, Spenser, and Beaumont, because he is out of all proportion greater than they — men 'of yeeres' or 'for an age.' Nor will he praise him by declaring how far he excelled Lily, Kid, and Marlow. Shakespeare, indeed, like them (yet beyond them), was for the age in which he flourished; but he was also for all time, and not *of* an age." — Dr. Ingleby, in his "Shakespeare's Centurie of Prayse." † Poets.

‡ "*And though thou hadst,*' etc. Here *hadst* is the subjunctive. [?] The

From thence to honour thee, I would not seeke
For names; but call forth thund'ring Æschilus,
Euripides, *and* Sophocles *to vs,*
Paccuuius, Accius, *him of* Cordoua *dead,*
To life againe, to heare thy Buskin tread,*
And shake a Stage: Or, when thy Sockes† were on,
Leaue thee alone, for the comparison
Of all, that insolent Greece, *or haughtie* Rome
sent forth, or since did from their ashes come.
Triümph, my Britaine, *thou hast one to showe,*
To whom all Scenes‡ of Europe *homage owe.*
He was not of an age, but for all time!
And all the Muses *still were in their prime,*
When like Apollo *he came forth to warme*
Our eares, or like a Mercury *to charme!*
Nature her selfe was proud of his designes,
And ioy'd to weare the dressing of his lines!
Which were so richly spun, and wouen so fit,
As, since, she will vouchsafe no other Wit.
The merry Greeke, *tart* Aristophanes,
Neat Terence, *witty* Plautus, *now not please;*
But antiquated, and deserted lye
As they were not of Natures family.
Yet must I not giue Nature all: Thy Art,
My gentle Shakespeare, *must enioy a part.*

---

passage may be thus paraphrased: 'Even if thou hadst little scholarship, I would not seek to honour thee by calling thee, as others have done, Ovid, Plautus, Terence, etc., *i.e.*, by the names of the classical poets, but would rather invite them to witness how far thou didst outshine them. Ben does not assert that Shakespeare had 'small Latin and less Greek,' as several understand him, though doubtless, compared with Ben's finished scholarship, Shakespeare's was small; but, that the lack of that accomplishment could only redound to Shakespeare's honour, who could be Greek or Roman, according to the requirements of the play and the situation." — Dr. Ingleby, in his "Shakespeare's Centurie of Prayse."

* Buskin, by metonymy, for Tragedy.
† Sockes, by metonymy, for Comedy.
‡ Scenes, dramatic Stages.

For though the Poets *matter, Nature be,*
 His Art, doth giue the fashion. And, that he,*
Who casts† to write a liuing line, must sweat,
 (such as thine are) and strike the second heat
Vpon the Muses anuile: turne the same,
 (And himselfe with it) that he thinkes to frame;
Or for the lawrell, he may gaine a scorne,
 For a good Poet's *made, as well as borne.*
And such wert thou. Looke how the fathers face
 Liues in his issue, euen so, the race
Of Shakespeares *minde, and manners brightly shines*
 In his well torned, and true-filed lines:‡
In each of which, he seemes to shake a Lance,§
 As brandish't at the eyes of Ignorance.
Sweet Swan of Auon! *what a sight it were*
 To see thee in our waters yet appeare,
And make those flights vpon the bankes of Thames,‖
 That so did take Eliza,¶ *and our* Iames!
But stay, I see thee in the Hemisphere
 Aduanc'd, and made a Constellation there!
Shine forth, thou Starre of Poets, *and with rage,***
 Or influence, chide, or cheere the drooping Stage;
Which, since thy flight frō hence, hath mourn'd like night,
 And despaires day, but for thy Volumes light.

---

* Man. † Casts (in his mind), thinks, purposes.

‡ "As Epius Stolo said, that the Muses would speake with Plautus tongue, if they would speake Latin: so I say that the Muses would speak with Shakespeares *fine filed* phrase, if they would speake English." — Francis Meres, "Palladis Tamia," 1598.

§ An evident play on the name of Shakespeare. So in Thomas Bancroft's "Two Bookes of Epigrammes, and Epitaphs," 1639, No. 119, *To Shakespeare:*

"Thou hast so us'd thy *Pen,* (or *shocke thy Speare*)
That Poets startle, nor thy wit come neare."

‖ *Bankes of Thames,* on which the Globe Theatre stood.

¶ Eliza, Queen Elizabeth.

** *Rage* and *influence* are used here in their astrological senses: *chide* and *cheere* refer, respectively, to *rage* and *influence.*

Ben Jonson was not a man given to excessive praise of others : he was, in fact, very chary of his praise, as great egotists generally are ; and he was the greatest egotist of his time. He certainly would not have indulged in praise, however sincerely he could have done so, which would have been regarded as merely perfunctory and conventional. The lines have a ring of unquestionable sincerity. And they are remarkable lines. Every time I read them, they seem more remarkable then they ever did before. The line, " He was not of an age, but for all time," has been generally understood to express Shakespeare's universality. But what is properly meant by universality, is, perhaps, not always understood. Ruskin has noted it as "a constant law that the greatest men, whether poets or historians, live *entirely in their own age,* and that the greatest fruits of their work are gathered *out of their own age.* Dante paints Italy in the 13th century; Chaucer, England in the 14th ; Massaccio, Florence in the 15th ; Tintoretto, Venice in the 16th ; — all of them utterly regardless of anachronism and minor error of every kind, but getting always *vital truth* out of the vital *present.* If it be said that Shakespeare wrote perfect historical plays on subjects belonging to the preceding centuries, I answer, that they *are* perfect plays just because there is no care about centuries in them, but a life which all men recognize for the human life of all time ; and this it is, not because Shakespeare sought to give universal truth, but because, painting honestly and completely from the men about him, he painted that human nature which is, indeed, constant enough, a rogue in the 15th century being, *at heart,* what a rogue is in the 19th and was in the 12th ; and an honest or a knightly man being, in like manner, very similar to other such at any other time. And the work of these great idealists is, therefore, always universal ; not because *it is not portrait,* but because it is *complete* portrait down to the heart, which is the same in all ages : and the work of the mean idealists is *not* universal, not because it is portrait, but because it is *half* portrait, — of the outside, the manners and the dress, not of the heart. Thus Tintoret and Shakespeare paint, both of them, simply Venetian and English nature as they saw it in their time, down to the root; and it does for *all* time; but as for any care to cast themselves into the particular ways and tones of thought, or custom, of past time in their historical work, you will find it in neither of them, nor in any other perfectly great man that I know of."

We may take Ben Jonson's estimate of Shakespeare, not only as perfectly sincere on his part, but as representing the opinion of the great poet by the best judges of the time.

Mr. Gerald Massey, in his "Secret Drama of Shakespeare's Sonnets," etc. 1872, p. 528, remarks that, "Harvey's lusty *réveille* and Ben Jonson's eulogy notwithstanding, it is quite demonstrable that Shakespeare's contemporaries had no adequate conception of what manner of man or majesty of mind were amongst them. We know him better than they did."

That, perhaps, though said with so much assurance, is questionable. The fact must not be overlooked, however ungracious it may be to the patient and laborious delvers in Shakespearian lore, that much of the study devoted to Shakespeare, in these days, consists largely of a peeping and botanizing that are really not essential to a full appreciation of his dramatic power, which is, after all, *the one great thing needful.* There is reason to believe that there are many mere scholars at the present day, whose Shakespearian learning, extensive and thorough as it may be, in respect to editions, and texts, and readings, and the commentary which, during the last hundred and fifty years and more, has gathered around Shakespeare, as the desert sands around the Egyptian sphinx, does not help them much to a higher appreciation of this power; other things being equal, they would have quite as much without it. I would not depreciate this kind of learning; "may it mix with men and prosper!" but, in many cases, it does not justify scholars, when passing opinions on the contemporary appreciation of Shakespeare, in saying, as Mr. Massey says, that the men of his time had no adequate conception of what manner of man or majesty of mind were amongst them, and that we know him better than they did. He should have stated in what respects we know him better than they did. In some respects we do. That he was not appreciated in certain directions as he is now, is undeniable; but that he was even *popularly* appreciated, in his own day, in a *dramatic* direction, and that, too, to an even fuller extent than he is now, is equally undeniable. It is not improbable that the people who attended the Globe Theatre, even the inferior sort, were more susceptible, got more of the real thing, than the ordinary attendants of theatres in our days, when so much, too, is addressed to the eye which was not so addressed in Shakespeare's time, but had to be *imagined.* Now our stage carpentry leaves nothing to be imagined. We shut off imagination in earliest childhood, in having our children's dolls made to squeak when they are squeezed, and to say *mamma,* and to creep along the floor, moved by a wound-up spring in the stomach. The rag doll was much better, as it gave scope to a child's imagination, and children loved it more on that very account.

There must have been very superior acting in Shakespeare's time. And the great impersonator, in his own time, of the leading characters in his Plays, Richard Burbadge, the poet's life-long friend, must have had his valuable guidance in his impersonations. And these impersonations must have been adequately appreciated. There are abundant evidences of a general susceptibility, in the times of Shakespeare, hardly inferior to that which the Greek people must have possessed in the best days of their drama; a susceptibility which the growth of general and "useful" knowledge, and a more rigid conventionalism in society, have done much to deaden.

It is quite impossible that any contributions can be made to our present knowledge of the external life of Shakespeare: and with that limited knowledge we must rest content; especially as an infinitely better knowledge is within our reach. We can drop the questions as to what Shakespeare did as a boy and a young man; as to whether he were a butcher-boy, or a schoolmaster, or a lawyer's clerk, or what not. How his soul must have been attuned, is an infinitely higher question — a question, too, which can be answered with greater certainty than can the other and less important questions as to how he was *outwardly* occupied as a boy and a young man. It is a question, in fact, which can be absolutely answered. "The soul," says George H. Calvert, in his 'Shakespeare : a biographic æsthetic study,' "while laying the foundations of greatness, keeps its own counsel ; and what it had been doing and preparing is only revealed by the completed work. The Tempest, and Lear, and Julius Cæsar tell us, and tell us with the peal of resounding clarions, that Shakespeare was a wonderful child, and from them, and only from them, can this be learnt ; so that we now know about the child William what his own father and mother had no inkling of" (pp. 25, 26).

Much has been said of the *impersonality* of the Plays. They are, indeed, wonderfully impersonal in one sense, namely, that each and every character speaks and acts from the standpoint of his own personality ; but they are, at the same time, the most autobiographical compositions, in the very highest sense of the word, that have ever been produced. No one who has communed with them for years, can have any doubt of this ; can doubt that the *benign aura* exhaled from all the Plays was infused into them from the glorious nature of. their author — a nature more fully in harmony with the soul of things than has ever been exhibited by any other of the sons of men of whom we have record.

It has been well said, and the idea has been eloquently expanded, by Whipple, that "the measure of a man's individuality is his creative power ; and all that Shakespeare created, he individually included." *

Could we have possibly known more of the real man Shakespeare, the *real man*, more of that *immanent* something, that mystery of personality, that "innermost of the inmost, most interior of the interne," as Mrs. Browning designates the mystery of

---

* See "The Literature of the Age of Elizabeth." By Edwin P. Whipple, Boston : 1869. pp. 36 *et seq.*

personality, of "the hidden Soul," — which is projected into, and constitutes the soul of the plays — could we, I say, have possibly known more of this, than we know from his Plays, even if he had written for us his own biography, as Alfieri, or St. Augustine, or Goethe, wrote his, or even if he had had a Boswell to record his life as minutely as "sleek wheedling James" recorded Samuel Johnson's? Could we, indeed, have known as much of the real man as we now know? Would not a full record of the man's outer life, with all the short-comings, distortions, obliquities, and imperfections of judgment, and prejudices in one direction and another, which, as a human production, would necessarily have marked it, even if it had been written by a personal and intimate friend, and that friend the best conditioned to appreciate him, have tended rather to obscure the real man, as he is breathed forth from the Plays and the Sonnets, than to reveal him more distinctly? There can be but little doubt that such would have been the result.

Shakespeare came into the world at a time the most favorable in human history for the exercise of great dramatic genius. No great genius was ever more favored than he by the circumstances of time and place. " His was an age full of dramatic elements ; rich in character and passion ; one of transition from old to new conditions of society, and containing the peculiarities of both ; one in which all the depths of human nature had just been stirred, and its strongest passions revealed ; and in which society had not yet arrived at that calm uniformity of manners which has, perhaps, weakened our sympathy with the expression of strong passion." *

But these favoring circumstances did not make the *genius* of Shakespeare ; that was something entirely independent of them. They only stimulated it into activity, and determined the mode of its manifestation. The physiology, so to speak, of great works

---

* "The Influence of Foreign Literature on English Literature." By Rev. James Byrne, M.A. (Dublin Afternoon Lectures on Literature and Art. 3d Series.)

of genius, can be explained, to some extent, by the circumstances of time and place — but not their essential life. *That* must come from the personality of the author ; and that personality is a mystery which philosophy cannot reach.

Favored as Shakespeare was by the circumstances of his time, he, in spite of mere scholarship and learning, was the best *educated* man that ever lived ; and by "best educated," should be understood, that his faculties, intellectual and spiritual, especially the latter, and all that enter into a personality, had the fullest, and freest, and most harmonious play. Of no man in the history of the race can it be said that he attained to a completer command of his faculties than did Shakespeare. And this is why it may be said that he was the best educated man that ever lived, and most completely realized De Quincey's definition of a great scholar : "not one who depends simply on an infinite memory, but also on an infinite and electrical power of combination ; bringing together from the four winds, like the angel of the resurrection, what else were dust from dead men's bones, into the unity of breathing life."

> " He of a temper was so absolute,
> As that it seemed, when nature him began,
> She meant to show, all that might be in man." *

Out of this complete nature proceeded that ethical system, that sense of moral proportion, which all the Plays exhibit more or less distinctly.

Shakespeare understood the meaning of true education as compared with mere learning ; and it appears that he came to this understanding very early. He no doubt voiced his own convictions in Love's Labor's Lost, A. I. Sc. i. 55–93. Biron asks :

What is the end of study? let me know.
  King. Why, that to know, which else we should not know.
  Biron. Things hid and barr'd, you mean, from common sense?
  King. Ay, that is study's godlike recompense.

---

* Drayton's " The Barons' Wars," ed. of 1619.

Biron. Come on then; I will swear to study so,
To know the thing I am forbid to know:
As thus, — To study where I well may dine,
  When I to feast expressly am forbid;
Or, study where to meet some mistress fine,
  When mistresses from common sense are hid:
Or, having sworn too hard-a-keeping oath,
Study to break it, and not break my troth.
If study's gain be thus, and this be so,
Study knows that, which yet it doth not know:
Swear me to this, and I will ne'er say, no.
  King. These be the stops that hinder study quite,
And train our intellects to vain delight.
  Biron. Why, all delights are vain; and that most vain,
Which, with pain purchas'd, doth inherit pain:
As, painfully to pore upon a book,
  To seek the light of truth; while truth the while
Doth falsely blind the eyesight of his look:
  Light, seeking light, doth light of light beguile:
So, ere you find where light in darkness lies,
Your light grows dark by losing of your eyes.
Study me how to please the eye indeed,
  By fixing it upon a fairer eye;
Who dazzling so, that eye shall be his heed,
  And give him light that it was blinded by.
Study is like the heaven's glorious sun,
  That will not be deep-search'd with saucy looks:
Small have continual plodders ever won,
  Save base authority from others' books.
These earthly godfathers of heaven's lights,
  That give a name to every fixed star,
Have no more profit of their shining nights,
  Than those that walk, and wot not what they are.
Too much to know is, to know nought but fame;
And every godfather can give a name.

Shakespeare must have felt his superiority to the merely learned
men with whom he came in contact, and must soon have discovered that *he* drank from fountains of which they knew nothing.

It is because he was the best educated man that ever lived that he is the greatest of the world's human teachers, and will continue such until a greater than he shall arise. When that will be, is, perhaps, more remote than the time which Ruskin fixed for another Turner. A young Scottish art-student of his, as Ruskin himself tells us, once asked him, after being praised for his work, " Do you think, sir, that I shall ever draw as well as Turner? " Ruskin replied, " It is more likely you should be made Emperor of all the Russias. There is a new Emperor every fifteen or twenty years, and, by a strange leap, and fortunate cabal, anybody might be made Emperor. But there is only one Turner in 500 years, and God decides, without any admission of auxiliary cabal what piece of clay his soul is to be put in."

In the whole history of the race, so far as we know it, there has been but one Shakespeare ; and the extent of that history will perhaps be repeated, before another appears who will recover the staff which he broke and buried certain fathoms in the earth, and the book which he drowned deeper than did ever plummet sound, when he abjured his wondrous magic.

The study of his works, in its highest form, could be made, if properly pursued, to contribute to the stimulating, strengthening, and, what is most important of all, marshalling into more or less *co-operative* action, the moral, intellectual, emotional, analytic, and synthetic powers. It is especially the *co-operative* action of all our faculties which Shakespeare demands of us, for his best appreciation, and it is in this that his *educating* power especially consists. I speak of course of a *true* study of Shakespeare, of Shakespeare as the master-*artist* of the race ; and such study means, the growing *towards*, I will not say the growing up to (that is quite impossible), the growing a little way *towards*, the manifold, complex, all-comprehensive soul-movement of the artist — a movement which carries with it, thought, emotion, imagination, fancy, humor, wit, pathos — a movement, in short, in which the entire *personality* is brought into play. This is what I mean by Shakespeare's being the *master*-artist of the race ; for no other artist, either of ancient or modern times, ever worked with such a complete and harmonious co-operation of all the powers inherent in the human soul.

" O, mighty poet!" exclaims De Quincey, at the conclusion of his subtle analysis of the art-purpose of the knocking at the gate, after Macbeth has murdered his King, " O, mighty poet! Thy works are not as those of other men, simply and merely great works of art; but are also like the phenomena of nature, like the sun and the sea, the stars and the flowers, — like frost and snow, rain and dew, hail-storm and thunder, which are to be studied with entire submission of our own faculties, and in the perfect faith that in them there can be no too much or too little, nothing useless or inert — but that, the further we press in our discoveries, the more we shall see proofs of design and self-supporting arrangement where the careless eye had seen nothing but accident."

Shakespeare was of course perfectly well acquainted with the classical unities of action, time, and place, the first only of which (action), is an absolute dramatic-art principle; the others were originally due to the constitution of the Greek drama. In The Tempest, he has strictly observed them, more strictly than they are observed in some of the ancient dramas — in "The Suppliants" of Euripides, for example, in the "Trachiniae" of Sophocles, or the "Heauton-timoroumenos" (the Self-Tormentor) of Terence. The period of time covered by The Tempest is but little more than that required for the stage performance. The time, as noted by Prospero and Ariel, is about four hours. Shakespeare has also strictly observed the unities in the Comedy of Errors. The scene is confined to Ephesus, and the whole time of the dramatic action is comprised in one day, ending about 5 P.M.* But in The Winter's Tale, which was composed about the same time as The Tempest (and these two Plays were probably his last), he has utterly disregarded the unities in an actual sense, but he has nevertheless

---

* See " A Time-Analysis of the Plots of Shakspere's Plays," by P. A. Daniel (Transactions of the New Shakspere Soc., 1877-9. Series I. Part II. pp. 117 *et seq.*).

moulded the heterogeneous elements of which the Play is composed, into " the unity of breathing life " — the only unity which,
in itself considered, is worth anything in Art.

A system of time and place, especially of time, that was suited
to the narrower range of the ancient drama, was not suited to the
vastly wider range of the modern romantic drama; and Shakespeare, whose genius ever rose above arbitrary law and authority,
and became law and authority to itself, had recourse to an expe-
dient, worked out a dramatic time-system of his own, and according to this system, as has been shown, he constructed most of his
Plays. It might be characterized as a system of time-perspective,
by which, when it is demanded by dramatic necessity, a long period
of time, filled with many events, is made to impress as short, and
a short period, as long. The sagacious critics to whom the discovery and exposition of this system of time-perspective were due,
were the Rev. Nicholas John Halpin (a clergyman of the English
Church, and a graduate of Trinity College, Dublin), and Professor
John Wilson (Christopher North). Each claimed the discovery
as his own, and there is no evidence that either was indebted to
the other, or to any one else. But Mr. Halpin's exposition of it,
is by far the fullest and clearest. He shows, with great subtlety,
that Shakespeare, in his Plays, realizes in its fullest potential sense,
the canon of the Roman Critic — *ut pictora poesis* (" Ars Poetica,"
v. 361). Professor Wilson first made known what he calls his
"astounding discovery," in the 5th and 6th parts of " Dies Boreales,"
which appeared in Blackwood's Magazine for Nov. 1849, and April,
1850, applying his theory to Macbeth and Othello. Mr. Halpin
was, without question, the earlier discoverer of this system of time-
perspective, by many years; but he had made it known only to a
few friends, and did not publish his Time-Analysis of the Merchant
of Venice until after Professor Wilson's first paper appeared in
Blackwood for Nov. 1849. But he fully established the priority
of his own discovery.*

---

* See his letter addressed to the Editor of Blackwood's Magazine, dated
Dublin, Nov. 12, 1849.

The article entitled "Dramatic Time," in the "Shakespeare Key," by Charles and Mary Cowden Clarke, occupying 180 fine-type 8vo pages, presents an exhaustive collection of the passages in all the Plays which elucidate the time-scheme upon which Shakespeare worked. There is certainly no art-feature of the Plays more deeply interesting or more worthy a careful study. Professor Wilson's Double-Time Analyses of Macbeth and Othello, and Mr. Halpin's Time-Analysis of the Merchant of Venice, should first be thoroughly understood before studying the article in "The Shakespeare Key." They have been reprinted in the New Shakspere Society's Transactions, 1875–6, pp. 349–412, and edited by Dr. C. M. Ingleby.

Another feature of Shakespeare's Dramatic Art to which the student's attention should be given, and which contributes to what may be called the dramatic perspective, or in other words, constitutes the still background to what is dramatized, is the narrated element of the Plays, by which is meant all that is told or described by the characters in the Plays, instead of being scenically or dramatically represented to the audience. This feature is an extremely interesting subject of study. Of course we find such an element in all the dramatic literature of the time, and, indeed, of all time. It is unavoidable. The Romantic Drama, with its rich variety of elements, and its wide scope, especially demanded it. But no other dramatist of the time has employed this told-element with an equal artistic skill, for the reason that Shakespeare was the greatest master of dramatic perspective. In mapping out a play, he must have considered what he would bring into the foreground through dramatization, and what he would throw into the background through narration on the part of his characters. Artistic symmetry demanded this; and it was also necessary in order to secure effects which would be weakened by dramatically representing certain things. For example, in The Winter's Tale, it might be supposed that the reconciliation, toward the end of the drama, of the two kings, Leontes and Polixines (so long parted by reason of the unfounded jealousy of Leontes) and the identifying of the shepherdess Perdita as King Leontes' own daughter, should be dramatized. These incidents have great dramatic capabilities. But they are only related by eye-witnesses, in the 2d Scene of the 5th Act, the reason for which is readily noted. The reconciliation of the two kings, and the identifying of Perdita, come immediately before the *true* denouement of the drama, which we have in the 3d and last Scene of the 5th Act, where Paulina shows to the two kings, and to Perdita, Florizel, and attendants, the putative statue of Hermione, which turns out to be the living Hermione herself. A scenic representation of what is related in the penultimate scene of the Play, would be most inartistic, as it would seriously weaken the effect of the crowning incident of the drama — the reanimation and restoration to husband and daughter, of the lovely, noble, and long-enduring Hermione. But an inferior artist could hardly have resisted the temptation to represent scenically the impressive incidents which are related in the 2d Scene.

Again, in the Merchant of Venice, when Shylock learns that Jessica has run away with a Christian, and carried off two sealed bags of ducats, and a rich store of jewels, in his rage and despair, he goes about the streets of Venice followed by hooting boys. If all this were *scenically* represented, instead of being *described*, as it *is* by Salanio, in a dozen lines, in the 8th Scene of the 2d Act, it would weaken Shylock's appearance in the next Scene but one, the 1st of the 3d Act, where he meets with Salanio and Salarino, and, after they go out, is driven almost to desperation by the news which Tubal brings him. Furthermore, the poet must have felt that, in representing scenically what Salanio describes, he would be heaping too much indignity on the leading character of the Play, in advance of the main business of the action. The poor fellow is treated badly enough as it is. But if he had been in the hands of almost any other dramatist of the time, that dramatist would probably have made the most possible out of the incidents which are merely related in Shakespeare's Play, and thus kept in the background. We should have had, most likely, a scene in which poor

Shylock was pelted by the hooting boys with sticks and stones, and insulted with outrageous epithets.

Shakespeare's use of narration in his Dramas, has been treated by Professor Delius, in two Papers read before the New Shakspere Society, and published in its Transactions for 1875-6. He traces what he calls the Epic or Narrative elements, in about 25 of the Plays, and shows their artistic bearings, and also how, in some cases, they were determined by the nature of the stage properties in Shakespeare's day, and the necessities of the theatre. A careful study should be made of these two papers. They will help to a new insight into the poet's workmanship. It is more important, far more important, to get at the secrets of the poet's dramatic effects, at the skilful management of the dramatic action than it is to study the Plays as embodying philosophic ideas. They should not be studied as closet plays, but as plays written *expressly* for representation on the stage. When we read them, we should read them with the stage before the mind's eye ; otherwise we read them from a standpoint other than the artist's own. If we regard them as *arenas* for philosophical disquisition, as some commentators have done, we do not treat them fairly, because we lose sight of their real character.

Another means of effective expression, most skilfully employed in the Plays, is *Contrast*, of which Shakespeare was a great master, and of which he was evidently fond.

The extent to which the high and the low, the great and the little, the noble and the base, the sad and the merry, are brought together in the Plays, shocked and disgusted some of the earlier critics, both English and French (Thomas Rymer and Voltaire, for example), who could not sufficiently free their minds from classical and from merely conventional standards, to appreciate aright the artistic management of the heterogeneous. The bringing together of such diverse material, is, in itself, easy enough to do ; but to subject it all to the dominancy of a great idea and a profound feeling, is the work of the master-artist, who lives for all and in all — whose heart is the heart of the world — who sustains a sympathetic relationship with all things — the force and richness of whose inner life assimilate all the forms of human activity around him.*   In this respect no modern poet comes nearer to Shakespeare than does Robert Browning.   And in the Prologue to his "Ferishtah's Fancies," written September 12, 1883, in his 72d year, he has expressed, with a wonderful touch, what is as applicable to the varied ingredients of a Play of Shakespeare, as to the "Fancies" which it is meant to characterize.

Shakespeare surpasses all other dramatists, both of ancient and modern times, in the natural evolution of his dialogue — the natural evolution — the way in which one speech depends on, and is evolved out of a preceding speech.   It is quite unnecessary to give special examples of this.   They can be found wherever one happens to open the Plays.   This natural evolution of the dialogue indicates how completely the poet identified himself with his scenes.   And with what skill little intervals are filled up with side-dialogues !   For example : in Julius Cæsar, A. II. Sc. i. 86-112, the conspirators, Cassius, Casca, Decius, Cinna, Metellus Cimber, and Trebonius, call upon Brutus, before the day breaks.   After Cassius has presented his companions to Brutus, who welcomes them all, he entreats a word aside with Brutus.   While they whisper apart, Decius says to the others : "Here lies the east ; doth not the day break here?   *Casca.* No.   *Cinna.* O, pardon, sir, it doth ; and yon gray lines, that fret the clouds, are messengers of day.   *Casca.* You shall confess that you are both deceived.   Here, as I point my sword, the sun arises ; which is a great way growing on the south, weighing the youthful season of the year.   Some two months hence, up higher towards the north he first presents his fire ; and the high east stands, as the Capitol, directly here."

---

* In connection with this subject, see Mr. Hales's Paper on the Porter Scene in Macbeth, New Shakspere Society Transactions, 1874, p. 262; and *Contrasting Scenes* in the "Shakespeare Key," by Charles and Mary Cowden Clarke, pp. 50, 51.   The Scenes noted are, Henry VIII., A. V. Sc. iii.; Romeo and Juliet, A. IV. Sc. v. 96 *et seq.;* Macbeth, A. II. Sc. iii. 1-45; Hamlet, A. V. Sc. i.; Othello, A. III. Sc. i.; Antony and Cleopatra, A. V. Sc. ii. 241-281.

The private conference over, Brutus turns to the others and says : " Give me your hands all over, one by one." etc.

How simple, and as a matter of course, all this seems ! And yet it demanded a perfect identification on the part of the poet with his characters — their situations and their circumstances.

The side-dialogue may be regarded, too, as indicating the con-spirators' deep sense of what they have entered upon ; and they endeavor to persuade themselves that they are calm and self-pos-sessed under it, by their off-hand talk, during the conference of Brutus and Cassius, about where lies the east and the direction of the Capitol. This talk on ordinary matters, at a time of great import, is not unlike the minute observation which attends a great intensity of feeling.*

Thomas De Quincey, in his Life of Shakespeare, contrasts Shakespeare's dialogue with that of the French and the Italian drama (perhaps a little too strongly, as is his wont) : "Among the many defects and infirmities of the French and of the Italian drama, indeed, we may say of the Greek, the dialogue proceeds always by independent speeches, replying indeed to each other, but never modified in its several openings by the momentary effect of its several terminal forms immediately preceding. Now, in Shakespeare, who first set an example of that most important innovation, in all his impassioned dialogues, each reply or rejoin-der seems the mere rebound of the previous speech. Every form of natural interruption, breaking through the restraints of cere-mony under the impulses of tempestuous passion ; every form of hasty interrogative, ardent reiteration when a question has been evaded ; every form of scornful repetition of the hostile words ; every impatient continuation of the hostile statement ; in short, all modes and formulæ by which anger, hurry, fretfulness, scorn, impatience, or excitement under any movement whatever, can dis-turb or modify or dislocate the formal bookish style of commence-

---

* See "Crossing Speeches," in "The Shakespeare Key" : by Charles and Mary Cowden Clarke, pp. 69–73.

ment, — these are as rife in Shakespeare's dialogue as in life itself; and how much vivacity, how profound a verisimilitude, they add to the scenic effect as an imitation of human passion and real life, we need not say. A volume might be written illustrating the vast varieties of Shakespeare's art and power in this one field of improvement; another volume might be dedicated to the exposure of the lifeless and unnatural result from the opposite practice in the foreign stages of France and Italy. And we may truly say, that were Shakespeare distinguished from them by this single feature of nature and propriety, he would on that account alone have merited a great immortality."

What material for an artistic education is everywhere present in Shakespeare ! In the minutest details of his art, and in the management of the general dramatic action ! There is no clap-trap, no getting up of the unexpected and surprising, to which Dryden and his contemporaries attached so much importance, no tricky inventions. The whole organism of a play is made to serve the *soul* of the play. And instead, too, of that *mechanical* unity of action, which the classical plays of modern times more or less exhibit, there is that higher *vital* unity which results from a dominant, all-pervading, moulding and unifying *feeling*.

THE

SHAKESPEARE–BACON CONTROVERSY.

———◦◦◦———

Lady Bab. Did you never read Shikspur?
Mrs. Kitty. Shikspur? Shikspur? Who wrote it?
— Garrick's *High Life below Stairs.*

THE question which was raised, some years ago, and which
has been discussed ever since, as to the authorship of the
Shakespeare Plays, is one which no more calls for an answer than
a question which might be raised by some bumptious quidnunc,
as to whether the Canterbury Tales were not written by John
Gower, or the Faerie Queene, by Sir Walter Raleigh, or the Dun-
ciad, by Dean Swift, or Tam O'Shanter, by some Scottish philosopher, or other.

There's not a particle of evidence to begin with, of a kind even
to raise the faintest suspicion, that William · Shakespeare of Stratford-upon-Avon, Gentleman, was not the author of the Plays and
Poems attributed to him. The question as to the authorship of
these wonderful products of dramatic genius, started with the mere
assumption that a man circumstanced as was William Shakespeare,
and with no scholastic training, could *not* have written the Plays ;
and Lord Bacon was, accordingly, selected from the many great
men of the time, as having the most august intellect, and, *ergo*, as
being the most likely to have produced the Plays. The assumption, of course, involved the idea that great *intellectual* ability, of
a signally analytic and inductive order, would, of itself, be equal
to the production of works which exhibit the most signally synthetic and intuitive order of mind which has yet been known
among men.

The *learning* which the Plays exhibit it has been thought impossible for a man in Shakespeare's position to have possessed. When the transcendent power of the Plays is considered, the learning, strictly speaking, which is secreted in them, is surprisingly little. The Plays bear more emphatic testimony than do any other masterpieces of genius, to the fact that great creative power may be triumphantly exercised *without* learning (I mean the learning of the Schools). But the knowledge and the wisdom with which they are gloriously illuminated, are the greatest possible which man has yet, in his whole history, shown himself capable of possessing — just that kind of knowledge and wisdom which Shakespeare, assuming the requisite constitutional receptivity, was most favorably circumstanced to acquire.

A notion prevails in these days of a diseased analytic consciousness that the only way to *know* in any given direction, is to make a large number of observations in that direction, and when one has, say, a flour barrel full of jottings, to turn them out on the floor, and to get down on hands and knees and sort 'em into some result !

But there is such a thing as *a direct perception of truth;* and of a kind of truth which can never be attained to by the mere grubbing and delving intellect, however great that intellect may be. This direct perception of truth is an attribute of man's spiritual nature. When a man's spiritual nature is adequately quickened, and in the requisite harmony with the constitution of things (and there can be no artistic or creative power in any one who is not to a greater or less degree, so conditioned), he takes cognizance of the workings of nature and of the life of man, *by direct assimilation of their hidden principles* — principles which cannot be reached through an observation, by the natural intelligence, of the phenomenal. He may thus become possessed of a knowledge, or rather wisdom, far beyond his conscious observation and objective experience. By direct assimilation of hidden principles, I mean, that assimilation which results from the response of spirit to spirit. All spirit is mutually attractive, as all matter is; and, if it is not

" cabined, cribbed, confined," but free in its activity, it goes forth to respond to all manifestations of spirit made through the phenomena of nature and of human life. It is this freedom of spiritual activity which distinguishes what we call genius from what is understood as mere talent. Genius finds its way, by its own light, where mere intellect would be lost in darkness.

In all other works of genius with which I am acquainted, I discover no such evidences of a direct perception of truth, as I discover in the works of Shakespeare. By a direct perception of truth, I mean, an immediate grasp of truth, without any conscious induction or deduction. Women have this direct perception, in some respects, more than men. And every great genius has united in himself the masculine and the feminine nature. And here is a remarkable fact to be noticed, in regard to Shakespeare — all the knowledge and wisdom which he was circumstanced to acquire directly from his own environment, is quite unerring : but his mere book-knowledge, wherever it appears, in his works, is more or less incorrect. Indeed, such was the creative force of the man, that all knowledge outside of the range of his own experience, he used with a grand audacity. Of the time and place of persons, and things, and events and customs, he appears to have been quite regardless. He knew that such great men as Galen, and Alexander, and Cato, once lived, that Galen was a celebrated physician, Alexander, a famous conqueror, and Cato (the Censor), an eminent patriot, and soldier, and statesman ; but he introduces them all into one of his greatest plays — perhaps the most perfect as a work of dramatic art — Coriolanus ! The period of the legendary Coriolanus, was the 5th century before Christ; his victory over the Volscians, at Corioli, being placed at 450 B.C. Alexander was born nearly 150 years later ; Cato, more than 250 years later ; and Galen, more than 600 years later !

The Winter's Tale exhibits false geography and a jolly jumble of times and events and persons. The great poet was too much occupied with his dramatic creation, to trouble himself with mere matters of scholarship. *Accordingly, Bohemia is made a maritime country (as it is, also, in the original novel, " Pandosto, or the Triumph of Time," by Robert Greene) ; Whitsun pastorals and Christian burial, and numerous other features of the Elizabethan age, are introduced into pagan times ; Queen Hermione speaks of herself as a daughter of the Emperor of Russia ; her statue is represented as executed by Julio Romano, an Italian painter of the 16th century ; a puritan sings psalms to hornpipes ; and, to crown all, messengers are sent to consult the oracle of Apollo, at Delphi, which is represented as an island !

This lovely romantic drama, which, with all this gallimaufry, invites a rectified attitude toward the True and the Sweet, was one of the latest, if not the latest, of the poet's compositions. But it doesn't appear that his indirect knowledge improved much with years.

Such examples of jumble and anachronism abound throughout the Plays.   And there is not a single Play, whatever be its time and place, which does not reflect, in every act, almost, some features of the age of Elizabeth.

Learning, indeed !   If Shakespeare hadn't possessed something infinitely better than learning (and, I would add, something infinitely better than a great analytic, inductive, deductive, and classifying intellect, such as that possessed by Lord Bacon), we should not now be enjoying such a noble dramatic heritage as we are. And if John Shakespeare had had the means to send William to Oxford or Cambridge, and William had gone through, or been driven through, the curriculum of either of these Universities, what a misfortune it might have been to mankind !   He might have been schooled in, and might afterwards have adhered to, those laws of dramatic art which, in the absence of such schooling, he rendered obsolete for all time, and, by the wonderful dramatic art which he himself developed, wrought a complete revolution in the drama.

It may be said, too, that there is nothing in the Plays to which Shakespeare could have been helped, by either of the Universities in his time, so far as his creative power was concerned.   That might have been seriously impaired. His scholarship, if he had been a University man, would have been more correct, but a more correct scholarship would not have contributed anything to the dramatic excellence of the Plays, or to the triumphant organization which they exhibit.

If Shakespeare did not write the Plays attributed to him, certainly Lord Bacon did not write them. That Bacon was one of the most august of human intellects is freely conceded. But vast as is the range of powers exhibited in his works, there is no evidence in them that he possessed the *kind* of powers required for the composition of the Shakespeare Plays. The evidence is of the strongest kind that he was strangely deficient in such powers. His spirituality appears to have been in inverse proportion to his intellectual power. And his intellectual power was not of the creative order. In fact, intellectual power, however great, cannot be, of itself, creative. It must be united with spiritual power. Bacon's mind was signally analytic, inductive, deductive, judicial; the mind which produced the Shakespeare Plays was as signally intuitive (by reason of its spiritual temperament), and as signally synthetic (taking in everything which was presented to it, in its completeness, and in all its relations).

It is universally admitted that the author of the Shakespeare Plays, whether that author were William Shakespeare, or Lord Bacon, or Sir Walter Raleigh, or Queen Elizabeth, was the greatest physiologist of human passion, of whom we have any record in human history. This, I say, is universally admitted. And he was not only the greatest physiologist of human passion, but the most *artistic* physiologist of human passion; by which I mean, that passion, in its evolution, he always presents in its relation to the constitution of things. That constitution is never violated. The power of self-assertion declines as the passion develops; and you can put your finger on the place, in any tragedy, where a great passion passes into fate, after which its subject is swept helplessly along.

Herein consists the moral proportion of the Plays, namely, that they move in harmony with the constitution of things. And this moral proportion could not have been secured by the rules of the ancients nor by any other outside rules. It was secured by the artist's deep sense of the constitution of things — by his spiritual harmony with the constitution of things.

To return from this digression, what *must* this greatest physiologist of human passion have been? Certainly, one who had, himself, a deeply passionate nature ; one, who could sympathetically reproduce within himself all the passions which are depicted in the Plays. And if all the Plays had perished, and only the Rape of Lucrece, the Venus and Adonis, and the Sonnets, had been preserved, these works would, alone, have testified to his profoundly passionate nature. Or, if all his works had been lost, with the exception of Antony and Cleopatra, this Play would have sufficiently testified to his profoundly passionate nature.

The works of Francis Bacon bear an emphatic testimony to his having been the coldest of mankind. No one, certainly, of the great Elizabethan men, who has left a sufficient record of himself, by which he may be judged, was so deficient in sympathetic warmth as Lord Bacon. And yet this man wrote Romeo and Juliet ! (See his Essay " Of Love.") This man was the creator of a Cordelia, a Desdemona, a Miranda, a Perdita, a Hermione, and, more surprising still, of a Cleopatra ! This man, we are asked to believe, wrote dramatic blank verse which has never been equalled on this earth as a manifestation of feeling and of perfect dramatic identification — verse which no mere metrical skill nor metrical sensibility, even, could have produced. But see " The Translation of certain Psalms into English Verse. By the Right Honourable Francis Lord Verulam, Viscount St. Alban," and dedicated " To his very good friend, Mr. George Herbert," who translated part of the Advancement of Learning, into Latin. (The Psalms are I, XII, XC, CIV, CXXV, CXXXVII, CXLIX.) The translation was published in 1625, in Quarto, two years after the publication of the First Folio edition of the great Plays

This doggerel, Lord Bacon thought it worth while to publish, in his 65th year, though he ignored the authorship of what are regarded as the greatest productions of human genius ! The credulity of those who are suffering from the dry rot of doubt is something wonderful.

THE

AUTHENTICITY OF THE FIRST FOLIO.

N O more authentic volume was published in the first quarter
of the 17th century than the First Folio edition of the Plays
of Shakespeare, which bears the following title :

"Mr. William Shakespeares Comedies, Histories, & Tragedies.
Published according to the True Originall Copies.   London
Printed by Isaac Iaggard, and Ed. Blount. 1623."

The colophon reads : " Printed at the Charges of W. Jaggard,
Ed. Blount, I. Smithweeke, and W. Aspley, 1623."

On the title page, on a rectangular ground, measuring 7.5 x 6.3
inches, is a portrait of the Poet, under which, on the left-hand
side, is the inscription, " Martin Droeshout sculpsit London."
Droeshout was a Dutch artist, resident, at the time, in London.
He engraved portraits of George Chapman (for his translation of
Homer), John Fox, the martyrologist, John Howson, Bishop of
Oxford, afterward Bishop of Durham, Richard Elton, Lord Mont-
joy Blount, William Fairfax, who fell at the siege of Frankendale,
in 1621, and other distinguished persons of the time. (See 3d
Var. ed. of Shakespeare, 1821, vol. 2, p. 514.)

Droeshout may never have seen Shakespeare, and may have
had to work after some poor sketch or painting, in the possession
of Shakespeare's family, or, which is more likely (as the costume
is evidently theatrical, even to the hair, which has the appearance
of a peruke), after some daub which had been hanging in the tir-
ing-room of the theatre, representing Shakespeare in one of his
impersonations, possibly, as has been suggested, Old Knowell, in

Ben Jonson's " Every Man in his Humour." Be that as it may, the portrait must have been a passably good likeness, or Ben Jonson, his most intimate friend, would hardly have allowed his lines " To the Reader" respecting it, to face the title-page, especially, too, as there must have been hundreds of people in London, at the time, to whom Shakespeare's face had been familiar. But all which concerns our present purpose is, that the portrait is not a "sell," but, unquestionably, an authentic, a *bona-fide* portrait, done by an engraver of whose work numerous other specimens exist, and testified to by a life-long friend, and that friend one of the most prominent of the poets and dramatists of the time, and exceedingly jealous of his own reputation.

Ben Jonson's lines 'To the Reader' are familiar to everybody who reads :

> " This Figure, that thou here seest put,
> It was for gentle Shakespeare cut;
> Wherein the Grauer had a strife
> with Nature, to out-doo the life:
> O, could he but haue drawne his wit
> As well in brasse, as he hath hit
> His face; the Print would then surpasse
> All, that was euer writ in brasse.
> But, since he cannot, Reader, looke
> Not on his Picture, but his Booke."
>
> B. I.

A large allowance must of course be made for conventional extravagance of phrase, in such cases. Similar compliments to engravers were not uncommon at the time. See notes to the Lines, in "Shakespeare's Centurie of Prayse ; . . . By C. M. Ingleby, LL.D. Second edition, . . . by Lucy Toulmin Smith," pp. 141, 142. But the important thing is the high tribute involved in the Lines, to the Poet's "wit."

Though it is outside of our present purpose, one thing must be said in defence of Droeshout, as an engraver, namely, that, judging from other portraits which exist, engraved by him, especially those of Fairfax and Bishop Howson, this of Shakespeare, as we have it in the First Folio, does not do him (the engraver) justice, evidence existing that the plate on which the portrait was engraved, was tampered with before it was used for printing the portrait as it appears in the First Folio. That evidence is afforded by a proof-impression now among the Shakespearian rarities, drawings, and engravings, possessed by James Orchard Halliwell-Phillipps,* Esq., F.R.S., at Hollingbury Copse, near Brighton, England, " that quaint wigwam on the Sussex Downs which has the honour of sheltering more record and artistic evidences connected with the personal history of the Great Dramatist than are to be found in any other of the World's libraries." Mr. Halliwell-Phillipps privately printed a Calendar of these rarities, " For Special Circulation and for Presents only." I have had the privilege of examining the above-mentioned proof-impression, and can testify to the superior delicacy and softness of the work to that exhibited by the portrait as it appears in all existing copies of the First Folio. The late F. W. Fairholt, F. S. A., in his description, given in the Calendar, of this proof-impression, minutely contrasts it with the Folio engraving, and explains how by cross-hatching and coarse dotting, the artistic merit of the plate was seriously impaired ; and the late Mr. William Smith, Director of the National Portrait Gallery, the highest authority on early engraving, after a careful examination of the proof-impression, gives it as his opinion, that " on what is technically termed proving the plate, it was thought that much of the work was so delicate as not to allow of a sufficient number of impressions being printed. Droeshout might probably have refused to spoil his work, and it was retouched by an inferior and coarser engraver."

Sed hæc hactenus. My theme is the authenticity of the First Folio.

Following the title-leaf, is the Dedication, " To the most noble and incomparable paire of brethren. William Earle of Pembroke, &c. Lord Chamberlaine to the Kings most Excellent Maiesty.

---

* Mr. Halliwell-Phillipps died on the 3d of January, 1889.

and Philip Earle of Montgomery, &c. Gentleman of his Maiesties Bed-Chamber. Both Knights of the most Noble Order of the Garter, and our singular good Lords."

It may be assumed, as a matter of course, that the privilege of dedicating the Work to two noblemen of such exalted rank and station as were the Earl of Pembroke and the Earl of Montgomery, had first to be solicited and secured by the dedicators, John Heminge and Henry Condell. It would have been a piece of unexampled audacity, in those days, for two actors to dedicate the Work to them without express permission. And it is evident from the Dedication itself, that the privilege was granted by them, not so much on account of the honor (although they no doubt esteemed it such), which the Dedication would do them, as by reason of their personal interest in Shakespeare, and of their admiration of his Plays.

From what we know of one of the dedicatees, the Earl of Pembroke, as a liberal patron of literature and the drama, and of their representatives, it may be presumed, that he generously aided in the enterprise, which must have been attended with large expense. The publication of such a magnificent volume, in those days, when there was no general reading public, and no book trade, in its present meaning, was a great undertaking, and could have been possible only with noble patronage.

The knowledge we have of these two noblemen, is abundant and entirely authentic. Anthony á Wood says of them, in his "Athenæ Oxonienses. — An exact history of all the Writers and Bishops who have had their Education in the most Antient and Famous University of Oxford, from 15 Hen. VII. A.D. 1500, to the Author's death in Nov. 1695," "William Herbert, son and heir of Hen. Earl of Pembroke, was born at Wilton in Wilts, 8 Apr. 1580, became a nobleman of New Coll. in Lent Term 1592, aged 13, continued there about two years, succeeded his father in his honours 1601, made Knight of the Garter 1 Jac. 1. and Governour of Portsmouth six years after. In 1626 he was unanimously elected Chancellor of this University [Oxford], being a great patron of learning, and about that time was made Lord Steward of the Kings Household. He was not only a great favourer of learned and ingenious men, but was himself learned, and endowed to admiration with a poetical geny, as by those amorous and not inelegant aires and poems of his composition doth evidently appear; some of which had musical-notes set to them by Hen. Lawes * and Nich. Laneare. All that he hath extant, were published with this title : Poems written by William Earl of Pembroke, etc., many of which are answered by way of repartee, by Sir Benj. Rudyard, with other poems written by them occasionally and apart. Lond. 1660. Oct. He died suddenly in his house called Baynard's Castle in London, on the tenth of Apr. in sixteen hundred and thirty . . . whereupon his body was buried in the Cath. Ch. at Salisbury near to that of his Father. See more of him in the "Fasti," among the Creations, an. 1605. He had a younger brother named Philip, who was also a nobleman of New Coll. at the same time with his brother, was afterwards created Earl of Montgomery, and upon the death of his brother William, succeeded in the title of Pembroke. . . . He also turned rebel † when the Civil Wars began in 1642, was one of the Council of State by Oliver's appointment after K. Ch. I. was beheaded," . . .

He too was Chancellor of the University of Oxford, in 1648.

Pembroke College was named after William, Earl of Pembroke. He presented to the Bodleian Library 242 Greek manuscripts which he had bought in Italy.

In the " Fasti Oxonienses " appended to the " Athenæ Oxonienses," the Earl of Pembroke is represented as " the very picture and *viva effigies* of Nobility, a person truly generous, a singular lover of learning and the professors thereof, and therefore by the Academians elected their Chancellor some years after this. . . .

---

* The leading musical composer of the time. He composed the music for Milton's Comus, and performed the combined characters of the Spirit and the shepherd Thyrsis in that drama; was one of the court-musicians to K. Charles the First.   † Wood was a hot Royalist.

His person was rather majestic than elegant, and his presence, whether quiet or in motion, was full of stately gravity. His mind was purely heroic, often stout, but never disloyal, and so vehement an opponent of the Spaniard, that when that match fell under consideration in the latter end of the reign of K. Jam. I. he would sometimes rouse to the trepidation * of that king, yet kept in favour still ; for His Majesty knew plain dealing (as a jewel in all men so) was in a Privy-Counsellor an ornamental duty ; and the same true heartedness commended him to K. Ch. I."

These two noblemen were nephews of Sir Philip Sidney, their mother being Mary Sidney, Sir Philip's sister, who married Henry, 2d Earl of Pembroke, in 1576. For her Sir Philip wrote his "Arcadia." She composed an "Elegy on Sir Philip Sidney," and a "Pastoral Dialogue in Praise of Astraea" (Queen Elizabeth). She was a Hebrew scholar, and translated a number of the Psalms into English verse, and also certain works from the French. She died in 1621. For a further account of her, see Rose's "Biographical Dictionary." She was the subject of Ben Jonson's celebrated epitaph :

> "Underneath this sable † hearse
> Lies the subject of all verse,
> Sidney's sister, Pembroke's mother.
> Death, ere thou hast slain another,
> Learn'd ‡ and fair and good as she,
> Time shall throw a dart at thee."

Lord Clarendon gives a noble portrait of the Earl of Pembroke, in his "History of the Rebellion and Civil Wars in England : "

"William, Earl of Pembroke, was next, a man of another mould and making [than the Earl of Arundel], and of another fame and reputation with all men, being the most universally beloved and esteemed of any man of that age ; and having a great office in the

---

* Ham-I.'Estrange in his "History of the reign of King Charles I." under the year 1630.　　　† V. R., "marble."　　　‡ V. R., "wise."

court, he made the court itself better esteemed, and more rever-
enced in the country. And as he had a great number of friends
of the best men, so no man had ever the confidence to avow himself to be his enemy. . . . He was master of a great fortune from
his ancestors, and had a great addition from his wife, . . . but all
served not his expense, which was only limited by his great mind,
and occasions to use it nobly.

" He lived many years about the court, before in it ; and never
by it ; being rather regarded and esteemed by King James, than
loved and favoured. After the foul fall of the earl of Somerset,
he was made lord Chamberlain of the King's house, more for the
Court's sake than his own ; and the Court appeared with the
more lustre, because he had the government of that province.
As he spent and lived upon his own fortune, so he stood upon his
own feet, without any other support than of his proper virtue and
merit ; and lived towards the favourites with that decency, as
would not suffer them to censure or reproach his master's judgment and election, but as with men of his own rank. He was exceedingly beloved in the court, because he never desired to get that
for himself, which others labored for, but was still ready to pro-
mote the pretences of worthy men. And he was equally celebrated in the country, for having received no obligations from the
court which might corrupt or sway his affections and judgment ;
so that all who were displeased and unsatisfied in the court, were
always inclined to put themselves under his banner, if he would
have admitted them ; and yet he did not so reject them, as to make
them choose another shelter, but so far suffered them to depend
on him, that he could restrain them from breaking out beyond
private resentments and murmurs.

" He was a great lover of his country, and of the religion and justice, which he believed could only support it ; and his friendships
were only with men of those principles. And as his conversation
was most with men of the most pregnant parts and understanding,
so towards any such, who needed support or encouragements,
though unknown, if fairly recommended to him, he was very lib-

eral. Sure never man was planted in a court, that was fitter for that soil, or brought better qualities with him to purify that air."

See also Lodge's "Portraits of Illustrious Personages of Great Britain," Bohn's ed., vol. 3, pp. 257–266.

The poet Daniel inscribed to the Earl of Pembroke, in 1601, his prose work, "A Defence of Rhyme." We learn from this work that Daniel pursued the study of history and poetry under the patronage of the Pembroke family, he having been brought up at Wilton, the family seat, and to the same family he appears to have been indebted for a university education.

Ben Jonson dedicated his "Catiline his Conspiracy," in the First Folio edition of his Works, 1616, to the Earl of Pembroke, in words which reflect the character of both the dedicator and the dedicatee.

"To the Great Example of Honor, and Vertue, the most noble William, Earle of Pembroke, Lord Chamberlaine, etc. My Lord, In so thick, and darke an ignorance, as now almost covers the age, I crave leave to stand neare your light : and, by that, to bee read. Posteritie may pay your benefit the honor, & thanks : when it shall know, that you dare, in these jig-given times, to countenance a legitimate Poeme. I must call it so, against all noise of opinion : from whose crude, and ayrie reports, I appeale, to that great and singular faculty of iudgement in your Lordship, able to vindicate truth from error. It is the first (of this race) that ever I dedicated to any person, and had I not thought it the best, it should have beene taught a lesse ambition. Now, it approcheth your censure [i.e., judgment] cheerfully, and with the same assurance, that innocency would appeare before a magistrate.

Your Lo. most faithfull

honorer,

Ben Ionson."

Jonson also dedicated his "Epigrammes," in the First Folio edition of his Works, to the Earl of Pembroke.

In Chapman's translation of Homer, there is a sonnet addressed to the Earl of Pembroke, in the following words : "To the learned, and most noble patron of learning, the Earl of Pembroke, etc. [Against the two Enemies of Humanity and Religion (Ignorance and Impiety) the awak't spirit of the most knowing and divine Homer calls, to attendance of our Heroical Prince, the most honoured and incorruptible heroë, the Earl af Pembroke, &c.] " *

The sonnet ends with the line, " Pure are those streams that these times cannot trouble," which reflects the reputation the Earl universally enjoyed.

As shown by Charles Armitage Brown, in his "Shakespeare's Autobiographical Poems, being his Sonnets clearly developed," etc., there is "every probability short of certainty," that by the " Mr. W. H." to whom the first edition of the Sonnets (1609) is dedicated, as their "onlie begetter," (that is, the Sonnets were born of him,†) was meant William Herbert, Earl of Pembroke. The judicial Henry Hallam remarks thereupon, in his " Introduction to the Literature of Europe," " This hypothesis is not strictly proved, but sufficiently so, in my opinion, to demand our assent."

Shakespeare's " sugred Sonnets among his private friends," are alluded to by Francis Meres, in his " Palladis Tamia," published in 1598. If these "sugred sonnets " were the same, or generally the same, as those published in 1609, it is, therefore, not unlikely, that the friendship of Poet and Patron must have extended over a period of twenty years.

The Dedication of the First Folio, it is plain to see, is not the ordinary, conventional, adulatory, meaningless dedication of the time, which was as often solicited by the dedicatee, who was short of honors, as by the dedicator, who was short of funds ; but that so distinguished had been the favor shown to Shakespeare by the Earl of Pembroke and the Earl of Montgomery, and such had been their estimation of his Plays, and such was their pre-eminence (especially that of the Earl of Pembroke) as liberal patrons of literature and the drama, that, in the words of the Dedication,

---

* The brackets are in the original title.

† " Yet be most proud of that which I compile, whose influence is thine and born of thee." Sonnet 78.

"the Volume asked to be theirs." What significant words (or are they merely words without any significance?) are the following, from the Dedication: "*But since your L. L. have beene pleas'd to think these trifles some-thing, heeretofore; and have prosequuted both them, and their Authour living, with so much favour: we hope, that (they out-living him, and he not having the fate, common with some, to be exequutor to his owne writings) you will use the like indulgence toward them, you have done unto their parent. There is a great difference, whether any Booke choose his Patrones, or finde them: This hath done both. For, so much were your L. L. likings of the severall parts, when they were acted, as before they were published, the Volume ask'd to be yours. We have but collected them, and done an office to the dead, to procure his Orphanes, Guardians; without ambition either of selfe-profit, or fame: only to keep the memory of so worthy a Friend, & Fellow alive, as was our* SHAKESPEARE, *by humble offer of his playes, to your most noble patronage.*"

The Pembrokes were of the best stock in England; and no other noble family of the time sustained more intimate relations with, and favored more liberally, literature and the drama, and their representatives, nor was better acquainted with all the literary and dramatic *circumstances* of the time. The Earl of Pembroke certainly knew more about the man Shakespeare and the authorship of the Shakespeare Plays than William Henry Smith, Delia Bacon, Nathaniel Holmes, Ignatius Donnelly, and other "unfortunate souls that trace them in their line," all of whom belong to a class of minds characterized by Dr. Ingleby: "Mix up," he says, "a quantity of matters relevant and irrelevant, and those minds will eliminate from the instrument of reasoning every point on which the reasoning ought to turn, and then proceed to exercise their constitutional perversity on the residue."

If the Earl of Pembroke had had any doubt as to Shakespeare's being the veritable author of the Plays, he was not the man to accept the dedication of them as Shakespeare's, nor to allow the statement in the Dedication that he and his brother Philip, had "*prosequuted both them and their Authour living, with so much favour.*" Again. No other author of the time knew the man Shakespeare better, sustained more intimate relations with him, nor was better acquainted with all the literary and dramatic *circumstances* of the time, than Ben Jonson. And if *he* had had any doubt, induced by the faintest whisper of suspicion in the dramatic world, as to whether Shakespeare were the veritable author of the Plays, he was the unlikeliest man in all England to lend his name, and authority, to a work of questionable authorship. We know the personal character of Ben Jonson better, perhaps, than we know that of any other man of the time. His character is to us as distinct as that of his great namesake of the 18th century. Both were characterized by a rough (I was going to say, brutal) honesty; both showed no quarter to shams; both had marvellous good opinions of themselves; and both were chary of their praises of others.

Following the Dedication is the Address of the editors, John Heminge and Henrie Condell, *To the great Variety of Readers.* The 2d paragraph of this address is notable: "It had bene a thing, we confesse, worthie to have bene wished, that the Author himselfe had liv'd to have set forth, and overseen his owne writings; * But since it hath bin ordain'd otherwise, and he by death departed from that right, we pray you do not envie his Friends, the office of their care, and paine, to have collected & publish'd them; and so to have publish'd them, as where (before) you were abus'd † with diverse stolne, and surreptitious copies,‡ maimed, and

---

* There seems to be implied here the supposition on the part of the Editors, that Shakespeare, if his life had been prolonged, would have "set forth and overseen his own writings." And there is good evidence that his death was sudden and unexpected.   † deceived.

‡ The (in most cases, no doubt) unauthorized and pirated quarto editions of Shakespeare's Plays, published during his lifetime, are referred to here. Sixteen Plays were so published, some of them in two or more editions, namely, Romeo and Juliet, Richard II., Richard III., 1 Henry IV., Love's Labour's Lost, Much Ado about Nothing, Midsummer Night's Dream, Merchant of Venice,

deformed by the frauds and stealthes of injurious impostors, that expos'd them : * even those, are now offer'd to your view cur'd, and perfect of their limbes ; and all the rest, absolute in their numbers, as he conceived thē.   Who, as he was a happie imitator of Nature, was a most gentle expresser of it.   His mind and hand went together :   And what he thought, he uttered with that easinesse, that wee have scarse received from him a blot † in his papers."

The knowledge we have of Heminge and Condell, is, as far as it

---

2 Henry IV., Henry V., Titus Andronicus, Merry Wives of Windsor, Hamlet, King Lear, Troilus and Cressida, and Pericles.   Othello was published in 1622. Eighteen Plays appeared for the first time in the Folio of 1623, for which we are indebted to Heminge and Condell, some of them being the greatest of Shakespeare's Plays, for example, Julius Cæsar, Macbeth, Antony and Cleo-patra, Coriolanus, The Tempest, The Winter's Tale.   But for their pious care, these greatest of human productions may have been lost to the world.

* *i.e.*, for sale.

† Erasure.   Ben Jonson, in his "Timber; or, Discoveries, etc.," says : "I *remember*, the Players have often mentioned it as an honour to *Shakespeare*, that in his writing (whatsoever he penn'd) hee never blotted out line.   My ánswer hath beene, would he had blotted a thousand.   Which they thought a malevolent speech.   I had not told posterity this, but for their ignorance, who choose that circumstance to commend their friend by, wherein he most faulted.   And to justifie mine owne candor, (for I lov'd the man, and doe honour his memory (on this side Idolatry) as much as any).   He was (indeed) honest, and of an open, and free nature : had an excellent *Phantsie;* brave notions, and gentle expressions : wherein hee flow'd with that facility, that sometime it was necessary he should be stop'd : *Sufflaminandus erat;* as *Augustus* said of *Haterius.*   His wit was in his own power; would the rule of it had beene so too.   Many times hee fell into those things, could not escape laughter : As when hee said in the person of Cæsar, one speaking to him; *Cæsar thou dost me wrong.*   Hee replyed : *Cæsar did never wrong, but with just cause :* and such like; which were ridiculous.   But he redeemed his vices, with his virtues.   There was ever more in him to be praysed, then to be pardoned."   Mr. Halliwell-Phillipps remarks ("Life of Shakespeare," 1848, p. 185), "If *wrong* is taken in the sense of *injury* or *harm*, as Shakespeare sometimes uses it, there is no absurdity in this line."   It is not unlikely that Ben Jonson had a hand both in the Dedication and in the Address "To the great Variety of Readers."   There can be but little doubt of this in regard to the latter.   See the "Variorum" of 1821, Vol. II. pp. 663–675.

goes, of the most authentic character, being derived from contemporary works and legal documents. They were both men of high standing in their profession, ranking, as it appears, next to Richard Burbadge, as actors. They both, especially Condell, appear to have been held in the highest esteem by their theatrical associates. Their Wills show them to have possessed considerable property, to have had strict business habits, and great uprightness of character, and to have been affectionate husbands and fathers. Shakespeare honored them along with Richard Burbadge, with an expression of his regard, in the following Item of his will :

"I gyve and bequeath . . . *to my fellowes John Hemynges, Richard Burbage, and Henry Cundell xxvi⁵ viij^d a peece to buy them ringes.*"

We learn from the First Folio edition of Ben Jonson's Works, published in 1616, that they both had parts in the following Plays, when they were first acted: "Every Man in his Humour," in 1598; "Every Man out of his Humour," in 1599; "Sejanus his Fall," in 1603; "Volpone, or the Foxe," in 1605; "The Alchemist," in 1610; "Catiline his Conspiracy," in 1611.

"In some tract, of which I have forgot to preserve the title," says Malone, in his "Historical Account of the English Stage," "he [John Heminge] is said to have been the original performer of Falstaff."

Condell had parts in a number of the Plays of Beaumont and Fletcher; in "The Captain," "Bonduca," "The Knight of Malta," "Valentinian," "The Queen of Corinth," "The Loyal Subject," and "The Mad Lover"; and he played the Cardinal in Webster's "Duchess of Malfi."

Heminge died (it is supposed of the plague) in October, 1630; and Condell, in December, 1627.*

---

* See "Memoirs of the Principal Actors in the Plays of Shakespeare." By J. Payne Collier, Esq., F.S.A.; "On the Actor Lists," 1578–1642. By F. G. Fleay, M.A. (contained in Transactions of the Royal Historical Society, Vol. IX.); John Marston's Works, ed. Bullen, Vol. I. ; "Dictionary of National Biography," edited by Leslie Stephen, Vol. XI. Art. Condell.

After the Address, in the First Folio, *To the great Variety of Readers,* come Ben Jonson's lines, already given, pp. 5–8. Then follow commendatory verses by Hugh Holland,* L[eonard] Digges,† and I. M.‡ Those by Hugh Holland, speak of "the dainty Playes, which made the Globe of heav'n and earth to ring."

Those by Leonard Digges are worthy to be quoted entire :

> Shake-speare, at length thy pious fellowes giue
> The world thy Workes : thy Workes by which, out-liue

---

* . . . "born at Denbigh, bred in Westminster School, while Camden taught there, elected into Trinity College in Cambridge, *an.* 1589, of which he was afterwards Fellow. Thence he went to travel into Italy, . . . Thence he went to Jerusalem to do his devotions to the holy Sepulcher, and in his return touch'd at Constantinople, . . . At his return into England, he retired to *Oxon ;* spent some years there as a Sojourner for the sake of the public Library, . . . He is observed by a Cambridge man [Thos. Fuller, in his Worthies of England, in Wales, p. 16] to have been no bad English, but an excellent Latin Poet, . . . He died. . . in sixteen hundred thirty and three; . . ."
　　　　— Anthony Wood's "Athenæ Oxonienses," 1721, Vol. I. p. 583.

† "Leonard Digges . . . was born in London, became a Commoner of Univ. Coll. in the beginning of the year 1603, aged 15, took the degree of Bac. of Arts, retired to the great City for the present, afterwards travelled into several Countries, and became an accomplished Person. Some years after his return he retired to his Coll. again, and upon his supplication made to the venerable Convocation, he was, in consideration that he had spent many years in good letters in transmarine Universities, actually created M. of A. in 1626. He was esteemed by those who knew him in Univ. Coll. a great Master of the English language, a perfect understander of the French and Spanish, a good Poet and no mean Orator. . . . He died on the 7th of Apr. in sixteen hundred thirty and five, . . . Several verses of his composition I have seen printed in the beginning of various Authors, particularly those before Shakespear's Works, which shew him to have been an eminent Poet of his time."—Anthony Wood's "Athenæ Oxonienses," 1721, Vol. I. p. 599.

"His translation of Claudian's Rape of Proserpine was entered on the Stationers' books, Oct. 4, 1617."—Steevens. It was printed in the same year.

‡ It is not known for whose name these initials stand. Claims have been made for John Marston, Jasper Mayne, and James Mabbe. See "Shakespeare's Centurie of Prayse," 2d ed. p. 155, and Notes and Queries, 2d S. XI. 4.

Thy Tombe, thy name must : When that stone is rent,
And Time dissolues thy Stratford Moniment,*
Here we aliue shall view thee still. This Booke,
When Brasse and Marble fade, shall make thee looke
Fresh to all Ages : when Posteritie
Shall loath what's new, thinke all is prodegie
That is not Shake-speares ; eu'ry Line, each Verse
Here shall reuiue, redeeme thee from thy Herse.
Nor Fire, nor cankring Age, as Naso said,
Of his, thy wit-fraught Booke shall once inuade.
Nor shall I e'er beleeue, or thinke thee dead
(Though mist) vntill our bankrout Stage be sped
(Impossible) with some new straine t' out-do
Passions of Iuliet, and her Romeo ;
Or till I heare a Scene more nobly take,
Then when thy half-Sword parlying Romans spake.
Till these, till any of thy Volumes rest
Shall with more fire, more feeling be exprest,
Be sure, our Shake-speare, thou canst neuer dye,
But crown'd with Lawrell, liue eternally."

See Leonard Digges's Verses, prefixed to the 1640 edition of
Shakespeare's Poems, quoted in the criticism on Much Ado
about Nothing, p. 178.

The verses by I. M., *To the memorie of Mr. W. Shake-speare,*
appear to indicate, the first two of them, that Shakespeare's death
was unexpected, and occasioned surprise. The histrionic metaphor
involved throughout the verses, is interesting :

"Wee wondred (Shake-speare) that thou went'st so soone
From the Worlds-Stage, to the Graues-Tyring roome.
Wee thought thee dead, but this thy printed worth,
Tels thy Spectators, that thou went'st but forth

---

* Here it appears that the monument in the Stratford Church had been
erected in the interval between the death of Shakespeare and the publication
of the First Folio — by order, without question, of Dr. John Hall and his wife
Susanna, Shakespeare's eldest daughter, who were appointed executors of his
last will and testament.

To enter with applause.   An Actors Art,
Can dye, and liue, to acte a second part.
That's but an Exit of Mortalitie ;
This, a Re-entrance to a Plaudite." *

---

* Latin imperative pl., " *applaud, or clap, ye,*" pronounced to the audience by the actors or the Epilogue, at the conclusion of a play.   Generally the words, *Vos valete, et plaudite,* " Farewell, and applaud," were used.   See Plays of Terence, at the end.

CHRONOLOGY OF THE PLAYS.

—◆◇◆—

I T has been a special object of Shakespearian study, of late years,
to determine, so far as it can be determined, the chronological order of the Plays, with the ulterior object of tracing the development of the poet's dramatic art, and his own individual growth ;
in other words, of studying his works in their totality, and with
reference to the personality of which they are a manifestation.
That chronological order has been settled as conclusively as it
can, perhaps, ever be, and the results toward the realization of the
ulterior object I have named, are already of the highest importance.   Of these results, Professor Dowden's "Shakspere : a
critical study of his Mind and Art," is, perhaps, the best expression.

There is, perhaps, no great author, whose growth can be more
distinctly traced through his works, than can Shakespeare's, from
the period of his apprenticeship, when he retouched and recon-
structed old plays, and tried his hand cautiously at original work
— that period being represented by such plays as the 1st, 2d, and
3d parts of Henry VI., Love's Labour's Lost, The Comedy of Errors,
and The Two Gentlemen of Verona — up to the period of his full
development and ripeness, represented by his great tragedies,
Othello, Lear, Macbeth, and Antony and Cleopatra and, finally,
the Plays now usually called Romances (characterized as they all
are by romantic elements), Cymbeline, The Tempest, and The
Winter's Tale.   Between the earliest and the latest work, is a
period of twenty-two or twenty-three years, say from 1590 or '91
to 1612 or '13 ; and the steady and healthy growth traceable

throughout this period bears testimony that the vigorous vitality of the author was maintained to the end.

The evidence which has been brought to bear upon the dates of composition of the several plays, is chiefly of three kinds : 1. That which is wholly external. 2. That which is partly external and partly internal. 3. That which is wholly internal.

Edmund Malone, the latest of the Shakespeare editors of the 18th century, first undertook systematically to settle the chronology of the Plays ; and the result of his investigations was first published in 1778, in an Essay entitled "An Attempt to ascertain the order in which the Plays of Shakespeare were written." He confined himself chiefly to the 1st and 2d kinds of evidence, namely, that which is wholly external, and that which is partly external and partly internal (meaning by the latter, "supposed allusions in the Plays, to contemporary circumstances and events "). Of the first kind are "the dates of the quarto editions of some of the Plays, entries in the Register of the Stationers' Company, and references to the Plays in contemporary books or manuscripts."

These several kinds of evidence served to reach an approximate chronological order upon which could be based the third kind of evidence, namely, that which is wholly *internal* (furnished by the verse), and which has served to rectify considerably the conclusions arrived at, from the other kinds of evidence.

It should be stated that Malone recognized the verse test, especially rhyme. He frequently alludes to it. In treating of the date of composition of Love's Labour's Lost, he notes "the frequent rhymes with which it abounds, of which, in his [Shakespeare's] early performances, he seems to have been extremely fond." To this remark he appends a long note, in which he anticipates much that has been set forth, of late years, in regard to the rhyme test. Under Romeo and Juliet, he speaks of rhyming as "a practice from which he [Shakespeare] gradually departed, though he never wholly deserted it." Under Cymbeline, he says, "The versification of this play bears, I think, a much greater resemblance to that of The Winter's Tale and The Tempest, than to any of our author's earlier plays."

The first valuable contribution to the study of the verse was a little volume, published anonymously in 1857 (the author was a Mr. Bathurst) and entitled "Remarks on the Differences in Shakespeare's Versification in different periods of his life, and on the like points of difference in Poetry generally." Though in some respects a pioneer work, it maps out, with great sagacity, the whole subject, which has since been so minutely worked up by several members of the New Shakspere Society of London.

SHAKESPEARE'S VERSE.

———◆◇◆———

WHEN Shakespeare began to write, blank verse had not yet reached, was very far from having reached, that development which adapted it to the highest dramatic purposes. It owed its earliest form to the rhyming pentameter couplet. Rhyme imparts an emphasis to the end of a verse and presents a check more or less strong, to the flowing of one verse into another. The consequence is, that, in rhymed verse, the thought is more or less obliged to move within prescribed limits. It is *sectioned off* by the metre, and pause-emphasis and pause-melody are thereby more precluded than in free blank verse. But in the earliest blank verse in the literature, Lord Surrey's translation of the 2d and 4th Books of Virgil's Æneid (about 1540), fashioned as it was, upon rhyming verse, the melody resulting from variety of pause is a *minimum.* George P. Marsh says of Surrey's blank verse, that it " is very often quite undistinguishable from common prose." But the fact is, that the reader is kept all the time too conscious of the metrical bondage to which the thought is subjected. We do not find, in the words of Milton, "the sense variously drawn out from one verse into another." It is presumed that in the material for which blank verse is a proper vehicle, there is preserved a certain equilibrium of thought and feeling, the former being more generally in the ascendant, and such material would therefore be bondaged by the cyclic movement which, to material containing a predominance of feeling over thought, would not be bondage at all but would be the movement which it would naturally seek for itself. Thought tends toward a straightforward movement — toward what the Anglo-Saxons called

forðriht spræc ; that is, forthright speech, straightforward speech ;
(that, in fact, is what our Latin word *prose* means : *prorsa oratio*,
contracted form of *proversa*, turned forward, or straightforward
speech) : * feeling must *revolve*, must return upon itself; when
strong, it is *importunate* to do so.

The following bit from the description of the serpents that
attacked Laocoön after he had hurled his spear against the side
of the wooden horse, will serve to illustrate the general character
of Surrey's blank verse.

> " Whiles Laocon, that chosen was by lot
> Neptunus priest, did sacrifice a bull
> Before the holy altar, sodenly
> From Tenedon, behold ! in circles great
> By the calm seas come fletyng † adders twaine,
> Which plied towardes the shore (I lothe to tell)
> With rered brests lift up above the seas :
> Whose bloody crestes aloft the waves were seen :
> The hinder parte swamme hidden in the flood :
> Their grisly backes were linkéd manifold :
> With sound of broken waves they gate the strand, ‡
> With gloing eyen, tainted with blood and fire :
> Whose waltring § tongs did lick their hissing mouthes.
> We fled away, our face the blood forsoke.
> But they with gate direct ‖ to Lacon ran.
> And first of all eche serpent doth enwrap
> The bodies small of his two tender sonnes :
> Whose wretched limmes they byt, and fed thereon.
> Then raught they hym, who had his wepon caught
> To rescue them, twise winding him about,
> With folded knottes, and circled tailes, his waist.
> Their scaled backes did compasse twise his neck,
> Wyth rered heddes aloft, and stretched throtes.
> He with his handes strave to onloose the knottes :
> Whose sacred fillettes all be-sprinkled were

---

* "That *prose* is derived from Lat. *uersus*, whence E. *verse*, is remarkable." — Skeat.   † floating.
   ‡ reached the shore.   § rolling.   ‖ direct path, agmine certo.

With filth of gory blood and venim rank.
And to the sterres such dredfull shoutes he sent,
Like to the sound the roring bull fourth loowes,
Which from the halter wounded doth astart,
The swarving axe when he shakes from his neck."

It will be perceived how servilely the thought moves within the limits of the metre. And an impression is got, too, of merely a *succession* of verses : a *list* of verses : they do not run into each other and form a *system ;* there's a pause at the end of each, and they resemble couplets deprived of their rhymes. There's none of the *sweep* — of the *elasticity*, to which blank verse fifty or sixty years later attained.

The Tragedy of Gorboduc, otherwise known as Ferrex and Porrex, the first three acts of which were written by Thomas Sackville, first Lord Buckhurst, appeared a little more than a score of years after Surrey's Translation of Virgil. It is the earliest English drama of any kind written in blank verse. The verse shows a considerable improvement upon Surrey's, in smoothness and in variety of pause ; but, as a general thing, the thought is metre-bound. The speeches are long and read too much as if they had been prepared beforehand by the several speakers, and the dialogue is, as a consequence, not very dramatic. The following speech of King Gorboduc to his counsellors, in the opening of Act I. Scene 2, affords a fair specimen of the general tenor of the verse. He is urging the importance of a proper training of the princes for future rule :

" My lords, whose grave advice and faithful aid
Have long upheld my honour and my realm,
And brought me to this age from tender years,
Guiding so great estate with great renown :
Now more importeth me than erst, to use
Your faith and wisdom whereby yet I reign ;
That when by death my life and rule shall cease,
The kingdom yet may with unbroken course
Have certain prince, by whose undoubted right

Your wealth and peace may stand in quiet stay :
And eke that they whom nature hath prepared,
In time to take my place in princely seat,
While in their father's time their pliant youth
Yields to the frame of skilful governance,
May be so taught, and trained in noble arts,
As, what their fathers which have reigned before
Have with great fame deriv*é*d down to them,
With honour they may leave unto *their* seed :
And not be thought for their unworthy life,
And for their lawless swerving out of kind,
Worthy to lose what law and kind them gave ;
But that they may preserve the common peace,
(The cause that first began and still maintains
The lineal course of king's inheritance)
For me, for mine, for you, and for the State
Whereof both I and you have charge and care.
Thus do I mean to use your wonted faith
To me and mine and to your native land.
My lords, be plain without all wry respect,
Or poisonous craft to speak in pleasing wise,
Lest as the blame of ill-succeeding things
Shall light on you, so light the harms also."

The movement of the verses is considerably freer than Surrey's and they are more *sequacious* — have more continuity, more *go*.

In all the early blank verse, a substitute, it would seem, was felt to be necessary, by its several writers, whose ears were accustomed to the enforcement imparted to the close of verses by rhyme. As the ear became accustomed to the absence of rhyme, and the *progress* of the verse became freer and more melodious, the strong word or syllable at the end of the line, was less solicited.

When, in tracing the development of blank verse, we come to Marlowe, we find a great advance upon all that had been previously produced. Though the thought is restricted more or less to metrical limits, there is a far greater freedom and grace of movement *within* those limits. The individual verse is more melodiously fused ; and the ear is, in consequence, more engaged with the *prog-*

ress of the verse than with its close; and this being the case, the sequence of the verses is felt to be more fluent than in the case of verses less melodious in movement and with a more strongly marked close.

Marlowe's earliest play, "Tamburlane the Great," is characterized by bombast, rant, and brag; but these are to some extent atoned for by the, at times, splendid vigor of the verse. In his best play, "Edward II.," there is more self-restraint, and we meet with verse quite equal to the verse of Shakespeare's second period of authorship.

Take, for example, the speech of young Mortimer, in regard to the king's favorite, Gaveston :

> "Uncle, his wanton humour grieves not me;
> But this I scorn, that one so basely born,
> Should by his sovereign's favour grow so pert,
> And riot it with the treasure of the realm.
> While soldiers mutiny for want of pay,
> He wears a lord's revenue on his back,
> And, Midas-like, he jets it in the court,
> With base outlandish cullions at his heels,
> Whose proud fantastic liveries make such show,
> As if that Proteus, god of shapes, appeared.
> I have not seen a dapper-Jack so brisk;
> He wears a short Italian hooded-cloak,
> Larded with pearl, and, in his Tuscan cap,
> A jewel of more value than the crown.
> While others walk below, the King and he
> From out a window laugh at such as we,
> And flout our train, and jest at our attire.
> Uncle, 'tis this makes me impatient." —A. I. Sc. iv.

Young Mortimer receives letters from Scotland informing him that his uncle is taken prisoner by the Scots; with which, when he acquaints the king, he gets simply "Then ransom him" for a reply.

> "*Y. Mortimer.* My Lord, the family of the Mortimers
> Are not so poor, but, would they sell their land,

'Twould levy men enough to anger you.
We never beg, but use such prayers as these.

*   *   *   *   *   *   *   *

The idle triumphs, masks, lascivious shows
And prodigal gifts bestowed on Gaveston,
Have drawn thy treasury dry, and made thee weak;
The murmuring commons, overstretched, break.

*   *   *   *   *   *   *   *

The haughty Dane commands the narrow seas,
While in the harbour ride thy ships unrigg'd.
Thy court is naked, being bereft of those
That make a king seem glorious to the world;
I mean the peers whom thou shouldst dearly love.

*   *   *   *   *   *   *   *

When wert thou in the field with banners spread?
But once: and then thy soldiers march'd like players,
With garish robes, not armour; and thyself,
Bedaub'd with gold, rode laughing at the rest,
Nodding and shaking of thy spangled crest,
Where women's favours hung like labels down."

In the 3d Scene of the 2d Act, Gaveston is represented as
frolicking with the king at Tynemouth. The nobles resolve on a
surprise :

"*Y. Mortimer*. I'll give the onset.
Warwick. And I'll follow thee.
Y. Mortimer. This tattered ensign of my ancestors,
Which swept the desert shore of that dead sea,
Whereof we got the name of Mortimer,
Will I advance upon this castle's walls.
Drums strike alarum, raise them from their sport,
And ring aloud the knell of Gaveston."

There is often a dashing vigor in some of young Mortimer's
speeches almost equal to that of some of the speeches of Hotspur
in 1 Henry IV., but it does not bear with it an equal weight
of thought.

Much of the verse of Marlowe's "Dido, Queen of Carthage," is very beautiful of its kind :

> " Then he unlocked the horse, and suddenly
> From out his entrails, Neoptolemus,
> Setting his spear upon the ground, leapt forth,
> And after him a thousand Grecians more,
> *In whose stern faces shined the quenchless fire,*
> *That after burnt the pride of Asĭā.*"

Æneas is urging the necessity of his leaving Carthage :

> " Let my Phænissa grant and then I go.
> Grant she or no, Æneas *must* away;
> Whose golden fortune, clogged with courtly ease, .
> Cannot ascend to Fame's immortal house,
> Or banquet in bright Honour's burnished hall,
> Till he has furrowed Neptune's glassy fields,
> And cut a passage through his topless hills."

But the garment is at best slightly too big for the thought.

> "*Dido.* Æneas, I'll repair thy Trojan ships,
> Conditionally that thou wilt stay with me,
> And let Achates sail to Italy :
> I'll give thee tackling made of rivelled gold,
> Wound on the barks of odoriferous trees,
> Oars * of massy ivory, full of holes,
> Through which the water shall delight to play;
> Thy anchors shall be hewed from crystal rocks,
> Which, if thou loose, shall shine above the waves;
> The masts whereon thy swelling sails shall hang,
> Hollow pyramides of silver plate :
> The sails of folded lawn, where shall be wrought
> The wars of Troy, but not Troy's overthrow.
> For ballace, empty Dido's treasury;
> Take what ye will, but leave Æneas here.
> Achates, thou shalt be so newly clad,

---

* Dissyllabic.

As sea-born nymphs shall swarm about thy ships,
And wanton mermaids court thee with sweet songs,
Flinging in favours of more sovereign worth
Than Thetis hangs about Apollo's neck,
So that Æneas may but stay with me."

The play contains single lines of great grace ; such as

" The air is clear, and southern winds are whist."

But Marlowe's thought, even when freest, rarely transgresses the bounds of metre, and the *dramatic* capabilities of blank verse are consequently but imperfectly realized in his Plays.   But within those bounds, his thought has a remarkable ease and grace of movement.

Great as is the praise due to Marlowe's blank verse, it is certainly not entitled to that bestowed upon it by an able writer in *The Cornhill Magazine,* vol. xv. p. 622.   The merits he attributes to it are rather those of Shakespeare's blank verse, in its highest *recitative* form, as exhibited in 1 Henry IV.   The passages he selects from Doctor Faustus, Edward the Second, Tamburlane, and the Jew of Malta, do not support his eulogies.   After giving a specimen of the blank verse of the tragedy of Gorboduc, by Sackville and Norton, he says : " Mr. Collier, in his ' History of Dramatic Poetry,' mentions two other plays written in blank verse, but not performed on the public stage, before the appearance of Marlowe's ' Tamburlane.'   It is to this tragedy that he assigns the credit of having once and for all established blank verse as the popular dramatic metre of the English.   With this opinion all students who have examined the origin of our theatrical literature will, no doubt, agree.   But Marlowe did not merely drive the rhymed couplet from the stage by substituting the blank verse of his contemporaries : he created a new metre by the melody, variety, and force which he infused into the iambic, and left models of versification, the pomp and gorgeousness of which Shakespeare and Milton alone can be said to have surpassed.   The change which he operated was so thorough and so novel to the playwrights as well as the playgoers of his time, that he met with some determined opposition. Thomas Nash spoke scornfully of 'idiot art masters, that intrude themselves to our ears as the alchemists of eloquence, who (mounted on the stage of arrogance) think to attract better pens with the swelling bombast of bragging blank verse.' In another sneer he described the new measure as 'the spacious volubility of a drumming decasyllabon'; while Robert Greene, who had written many wearisome rhymed dramas, talked of making 'verses jet on the stage in tragical buskins, every word filling the ear like the fa-burden of Bow bell, daring God out of heaven with that atheist, Tamburlan, or blaspheming with the mad priest of the Sun.' But our 'licentiate iambic' was destined to triumph. Greene and Nash gave way before inevitable fate, and wrote some better plays in consequence.

"Let us inquire what change Marlowe really introduced, and what was his theory of dramatic versification. He found the ten-syllabled heroic line monotonous, monosyllabic, and divided into five feet of alternate short and long. He left it various in form and structure, sometimes redundant by a syllable, sometimes deficient, enriched with unexpected emphases and changes in the beat. He found no sequence or attempt at periods; one line succeeded another with insipid regularity, and all were made after the same model. He grouped his verse according to the sense, obeying an internal law of melody, and allowing the thought contained in his words to dominate over their form. He did not force his metre to preserve a fixed and unalterable type, but suffered it to assume most variable modulations, the whole beauty of which depended upon their perfect adaptation to the current of his ideas. By these means he was able to produce the double effect of variety and unity, to preserve the fixed march of his chosen metre, and yet, by subtle alterations in the pauses, speed, and grouping of the syllables, to make one measure represent a thousand. Used in this fashion, blank verse became a Proteus. It resembled music, which requires regular time and rhythm; but, by the employment of phrase, induces a higher kind of melody to rise above the common and prosaic beat of time. Bad writers of blank verse, like Marlowe's predecessors, or like those who in all ages have been deficient in plastic energy and power of harmonious modulation, produce successions of monotonous iambic lines, sacrificing all the poetry of expression to the mechanism of their art. Metre with them ceases to be the organic body of a vital thought, and becomes a mere framework. And bad critics praise them for the very faults of tameness and monotony which they miscall regularity of numbers. It was thus that the sublimest as well as the most audacious of Milton's essays in versification fell under the censure of Jonson."

The best form of Marlowe's verse may be said to have been the *ground*, the *tune*, the plain song, on which Shakespeare raised his future dramatic descants.* But he first got the plain song to perfection before he raised any descants thereupon. He first learned to move with freedom and grace within the limits of five measures. But here the misconception must be guarded against that Shakespeare's development as an artist proceeded from form to spirit. His verse, it is plain to see, developed in certain directions. But the change of form which it gradually underwent, from first to last, barring certain conventionalities, was not by imposition of the foreign hand, — was not superinduced. Its development was not so much *ab extra* as *ab intra*. When we consider that in some of his earliest plays, sentiment predominates over thought, the poetic over the dramatic, we must admit that the verse of these plays, (the more or less conscious imitation of his predecessors and cotemporaries, and the traditional demands of the theatre, perhaps, being sufficiently taken into account,) is quite as organic as that of his latest, *so far as the spirit that moulds it is concerned.* It was because the *man* Shakespeare, in the later period of his career,

---

* " Shakespeare's metre was a free offspring of the ear, owing little but its generic form to his predecessors and contemporaries." Halliwell-Phillipps's " Outlines of the Life of Shakespeare," 5th ed. p. 204.

had grown, spiritually, intellectually, and morally — had grown in self-knowledge and in world-wisdom, — had taken the measure of those proportions by which the moral elements of the world are balanced, — and, more than all, had reached a fuller capability of dramatic identification, the fullest ever reached by man, — that the language-shaping of his latest plays differs so materially from that of his earliest plays. It is not so much the difference between the work of an apprentice and the work of a master (though it must be admitted that he had to serve an apprenticeship, like the rest of mortals), as it is the difference between genius in the bud and genius in full bloom. The student of his verse must not therefore reason after the theory of evolution, as it is often understood in these days, but must reason in a directly opposite direction, namely, from pre-existent spirit to form. "Every spirit makes its house," says Emerson, "and we can give a shrewd guess from the house to its inhabitant." And Spenser, in his Hymn in Honor of Beauty, says :

"Of the soul, the body form doth take ;
For soul is form, and doth the body make."

It may be stated in a general way that the development of Shakespeare's verse proceeds from the *recitative* to the *spontaneous,* and in accordance with this development, it at first moves obediently within metrical limits, gradually gaining in melody and grace until it reaches the highest possible freedom of movement within those limits, and realizes its fullest dramatic capabilities ; it then gradually transgresses them more and more until, in the latest plays, The Winter's Tale, Cymbeline, and The Tempest, it is often but slightly other than rhythmical prose — an unbroken pentameter measure not being returned to sufficiently often to be felt as a standard. For it should be distinctly understood (it has not been by a great many writers of blank verse), that however cunningly varied the pause may be, variety ceases to be variety when the standard pentameter measure is wandered from to such an extent that it is no longer in the feelings even as a sub-consciousness.

Suppose that twenty or more consecutive verses were broken thus (the three dots at the ending of some of the verses indicating that those verses run on into the following) :

The pause-melody would be quite annulled, for the pentameter *standard* would cease to be in the feelings. Effective variety there would be none, for the simple reason that there would be nothing varied from. Milton understood this, and always acted upon it. There is no other blank verse in the literature, in which the *pause-melody* constitutes so large a feature as it does in Milton's. And it will be found to be due to his skilful management of the pentameter standard.

Masson remarks that " the most frequent Cæsura * in Milton's Blank Verse is at the end of the third foot (*i.e.*, generally after the sixth syllable, though it may occasionally be after the seventh, or even after the eighth) : *e.g.*, —

---

* By ' Cæsura ' he means, as he explains above, " the pause attending the conclusion of a period, or of some logical section of a period, when that pause occurs anywhere else than at the end of a line."

" And took in strains that might create a soul
Under the ribs of Death." ‖

" In Vallombrosa, where the Etrurian shades
High overarched embower." ‖

" Prone on the flood extended long and large
Lay floating many a rood." ‖

" Dropt from the zenith, like a falling star,
On Lemnos, the Ægean isle." ‖

This, I think, is also Shakespeare's favorite Cæsura. Next in frequency in Milton is the Cæsura after the second foot (generally the fourth syllable) : *e.g.,* —

" A thousand demigods on golden seats
Frequent and full." ‖

After these two, but a long way after them, the most common are the Cæsura in the middle of the third foot (generally after the fifth syllable), and that in the middle of the fourth foot (generally after the seventh syllable) : *e.g.,* —

" shapes and forms,
The heads and leaders thither haste where stood
Their great Commander." ‖

" Lay vanquished, rolling in the fiery gulf
Confounded, though immortal." ‖

Considerably less frequent still is the Cæsura after the completed fourth foot (generally the eighth syllable) ; and still more rare, though occasional, are the Cæsuras at the middle of the second foot (generally after the third syllable) and after the first completed foot (generally the second syllable) : —

" Anguish and doubt and fear and sorrow and pain
From mortal or immortal minds. ‖ Thus they "

" For now the thought
Both of lost happiness and lasting pain
Torments him. ‖ Round he throws his baleful eyes."

" And now his heart
Distends with pride, and hardening in his strength,
Glories : ‖ for never since created man "

Very rare indeed is the Cæsura in the middle of the fifth foot (*i.e.*, after what is generally the ninth syllable) ; but there are instances :

" Were it a draught for Juno when she banquets,
I would not taste thy treasonous offer. ‖ None
But such as are good men can give good things."

Hardly to be found at all is the Cæsura after the first syllable or in the middle of the first foot ; but this may pass as an instance :

" The Ionian Gods, of Javan's issue held
Gods : ‖ yet confessed later than Heaven and Earth."

Cowper, in the Preface to his translation of the Iliad, after speaking of the greater difficulty of writing blank verse than rhymed verse, adds : " He [the poet] in order that he may be musical, must exhibit all the variations, as he proceeds, of which ten syllables are susceptible ; between the first syllable and the last there is no place at which he must not occasionally pause, and the place of the pause must be perpetually shifted."

But he omits to say one very important thing, without which variation of pause will not result in pause-melody, but in metrical chaos ; namely, that *an unbroken pentameter measure must be returned to sufficiently often for it to be felt as a standard.*

I would say here, by the way, that Milton often secures what might be called an *emphasis* melody, by the variation of the positions of the emphatic syllables. It will be found that there are four *chief* places in his verse where the logical emphasis falls, namely, the 4th and 8th, and 6th and 10th syllables of the verse. If the emphasis falls on the 4th, the next generally falls on the 8th ; if on the 6th, then on the 10th. Frequently in connection with the 6th and 10th, it also falls on the second.

The opening lines of the " Paradise Lost" afford a good illustration of this :

> " Of Man's first disob*e*dience, and the fru*i*t
> Of that forb*i*dden tree, whose m*o*rtal taste
> Brought d*ea*th into the w*o*rld, and all our w*o*e,
> With loss of *E*den, till one gr*ea*ter Man
> Rest*o*re us and reg*ai*n the blissful s*ea*t,
> Sing, heavenly M*u*se, that on the s*e*cret top
> Of *O*reb, or of S*i*nai, didst insp*i*re
> That sh*e*pherd, who first t*au*ght the chosen s*ee*d,
> In the beg*i*nning how the h*ea*vens and earth
> Rose out of Ch*ao*s : or, if S*i*on hill
> Delight thee m*o*re, and Siloa's br*oo*k that flow'd
> Fast by the *o*racle of G*o*d, I thence
> Invoke thy *ai*d to my adventurous song,
> That with no m*i*ddle flight int*e*nds to soar
> Ab*o*ve the Aonian m*ou*nt, while it purs*u*es
> Things *u*nattempted y*e*t in prose or rh*y*me."

The emphatic syllables are indicated by the italicized vowels. The following exhibits the emphasis scheme as to locations of the emphasized syllables in the several verses :

```
∪ — ∪ — ∪ 6̲ ∪ — ∪ 10̲
∪ — ∪ 4̲ ∪ — ∪ 8̲ ∪ —
∪ 2̲ ∪ — ∪ 6̲ ∪ — ∪ 10̲
∪ — ∪ 4̲ ∪ — ∪ 8̲ ∪ —
∪ 2̲ ∪ — ∪ 6̲ ∪ — ∪ 10̲
∪ — ∪ 4̲ ∪ — ∪ 8̲ ∪ —
∪ 2̲ ∪ — ∪ 6̲ ∪ — ∪ 10̲
∪ 2̲ ∪ — ∪ 6̲ ∪ — ∪ 10̲
∪ — ∪ 4̲ ∪ — ∪ 8̲ ∪ —
∪ — ∪ 4̲ ∪ — ∪ 8̲ ∪ —
∪ — ∪ 4̲ ∪ — ∪ 8̲ ∪ —
∪ — ∪ 4̲ ∪ — ∪ 8̲ ∪ —
∪ — ∪ 4̲ ∪ — ∪ 8̲ ∪ —
∪ — ∪ 4̲ ∪ — ∪ 8̲ ∪ —
∪ 2̲ ∪ — ∪ 8̲ ∪ — ∪ 10̲
∪ 2̲ ∪ — ∪ 6̲ ∪ — ∪ 10̲
```

But the most effective epic movement is inadequate to the demands of the freest dramatic movement, to which metrical restraint must, at times, entirely give way, as it does in those scenes of Shakespeare's Plays, wherein the completest dramatic identification is reached. The verse is verse only to the eye, not to the ear.

In the First Folio, we meet with sets of broken verses which editors have taken the pains to arrange into pentameter measure. But what is gained thereby? Nothing more than that it is made verse to the eye; the effect upon the ear is of course not changed. The sections of blank verse might all be printed as separate lines. There would, in fact, be some advantage in so doing. The recurrence of the unbroken pentameter measure could thus be better exhibited to the eye.

To return. The development of Shakespeare's verse proceeds from the recitative to the spontaneous.

Any one who will read aloud two or three of the earliest plays, and two or three of the latest (and he need not be particular about their being the very earliest or the very latest), will find that the former ask a quite different elocution from that of the latter. The elocution of the former, whatever may be any one's habits as a reader, will naturally run more or less into the *recitative* style of expression — will be such as a reader is apt to give to matter previously prepared; the elocution of the latter will, as naturally, *dwell* more upon the thought, as if it, the thought, were having its genesis in the mind, at the time of its expression.

In the composition of some of the earlier Plays, sentiment with the poet, was, as I have said, often predominant over thought — his mood was often more poetic than dramatic — and he had, in consequence, the tune, the plain song, more in his feelings; later, when sentiment was to a considerable extent displaced by thought, when the poetic mood yielded almost entirely to dramatic identification, the plain song was sunk in the descants.

It is not, indeed, necessary to read *entire* plays of the poet's earliest and latest workmanship to feel this; a few passages taken

at random from the verse-portions of the plays, will suffice, so
marked is the difference of the language-shaping, and yet it is
felt to be the language of one and the same mind, but the same
mind under different attitudes. Again : the gradual and regular
changes which Shakespeare's language-shaping underwent, must
have wrought changes in the stage-elocution — which changes
may, in turn, have had a reactionary effect upon his latest style.
At the first great outburst of the Drama, in the reign of Elizabeth,
the stage-elocution must have been more or less of the recitative
style, and inflated withal. This is inferable from the versification
which preceded Shakespeare's ; and there was no doubt a traditional style, dating far back, which had to be counteracted to some
extent, before the way was open for the effective, natural, and
deliberate style which, there is evidence, Richard Burbadge must
have practised. In " A Funeral Elegy on the death of the famous
Actor, Richard Burbadge, who died on Saturday in Lent, 13th of
March, 1618," it is said of his elocution, that " not a word did fall
Without just weight to ballast it withal."

We learn from this Elegy (there is, however, some question as
to its genuineness *), the interesting fact that Burbadge played
twelve parts in Shakespeare's Plays, namely Shylock, Richard III.,
Prince Henry, Romeo, Henry V., Brutus, Hamlet, Othello, Lear,
Macbeth, Pericles, and Coriolanus. And he may have played
others. The long and intimate relationship which existed between
Shakespeare and Burbadge, must have resulted in a mutual advantage. The one wrote better plays, perhaps, in having such an
actor to impersonate the principal characters, and the other had
his best powers brought into play and developed in having such a
dramatist to provide him with such characters. It would be interesting to know to what extent the excellences of one were
reflected upon those of the other. It can be safely inferred that
their mutual obligations must have been considerable.

* See " Shakespeare's Centurie of Prayse : by Dr. C. M. Ingleby." 2d
edition, p. 132.

Contemporaneously with the Recitative form of Shakespeare's blank verse, rhymes more or less abound, and they gradually diminish with the progress of the verse toward the spontaneous, more dramatic form. In the Recitative period, sentiment with the poet was often predominant over thought, his mood was more poetic than dramatic, and he had, in consequence, the tune, the plain song, more in his feelings. The metre of this plain song is, as a general thing, marked by a strong word or syllable in the 5th foot, upon which the voice can and must press ; and this marking of the metre, is, *under certain emotional conditions,* enforced by rhyme.

In Love's Labor's Lost there are about 1100 rhyming verses ; in A Midsummer Night's Dream, about 900 ; in Romeo and Juliet, about 500 ; in Richard II., over 500. In the intermediate period between the more decidedly recitative, and the more decidedly spontaneous, periods, rhymes keep gradually diminishing ; and in the latest period of the poet's work, they are used very sparingly, and for some special purpose — for the rounding off of a scene, etc. In Cymbeline, there are about 100 ; in Coriolanus and in Antony and Cleopatra, about 40 ; in The Tempest, but 2 ; and in The Winter's Tale, there are none at all, except those in the Chorus which introduces the 4th Act ; and it's questionable whether this Chorus was written by Shakespeare.

Though the proportion of rhyming to blank verses may indicate the *period,* whether recitative or spontaneous, to which a play belongs, rhyme is, however, only one of a number of phenomena which have to be taken into account, in determining approximately the place of a play in the chronological order. And this can be said with equal truth, and without exception, of all other tests.

Of two early Plays, the fact that one contains 100, or 200, or even 300 rhymes, more or less than the other, the whole number of verses in each play being taken into account, is, of itself, no evidence that it came before, or followed, the other in composition. Though Shakespeare appropriated conventional forms of language, he never servilely subjected his mind and feelings to them; and his using more rhymes or less rhymes in one early play than in another, would depend upon the pitch of the poetic or dramatic key in which it happened to be written. Every reader of A Midsummer Night's Dream must feel that rhyme is an inseparable adjunct to the speeches of those persons of the Drama who are in its main current — if adjunct that can be called which, in this play, particularly, is so organic an element of the language-shaping. Sometimes the feeling under which the verse moves reaches out after a double rhyme:

> " The will of man is by his reason sway'd;
> And reason says you are the worthier maid.
> Things growing are not ripe until their season:
> So I, being young, till now ripe not to reason; "
>   — A. II. Sc. ii. 111–114.

And in one case, the rebounding pitch of the speaker's feelings, or spirits, exhibits itself in a repetition of the same rhyme through a number of successive verses:

> " Be kind and courteous to this gentleman;
> Hop in his walks and gambol in his eyes;
> Feed him with apricocks and dewberries,
> With purple grapes, green figs and mulberries;
> The honey-bags steal from the humble-bees,
> And for night-tapers crop their waxen thighs,
> And light them at the fiery glow-worm's eyes,
> To have my love to bed and to arise;
> And pluck the wings from painted butterflies
> To fan the moonbeams from his sleeping eyes —
> Nod to him, elves, and do him courtesies."
>   — A. III. Sc. i. 167–177.

Now if rhyme, at the outset of his career, had been a mere matter of *adoption* with the poet, and he had employed it simply because he liked it, it wouldn't be of much account in gauging the poetic pitch of a play. But as it is employed in A Midsummer Night's Dream, the reader must feel that it is *essential*

to the poetic pitch of the play. The poet, with a more dramatic
purpose, might have previously written a number of plays on a
lower poetic key, and have used, in consequence, fewer rhymes.
It is quite certain that he did previously write such plays. That
he could not have written a more dramatic play at the time he
composed A Midsummer Night's Dream, is not for a moment to
be supposed.

Rhyme, by itself, must be, as he employs it, a somewhat un-
reliable chronological test except in determining whether a play
be an early or a late one.

The place of a pause or a break in a verse has some relation to the current of the feeling. The ordinary comma-pause
doesn't make much difference in the movement of a verse, one
way or another ; but where a sentence closes within a verse, with a
complete foot, the break is more marked than where it closes with
the light syllable of the iamb, the next sentence beginning with
the heavy syllable.   In the latter case, the feeling of the *current*
of the verse is more or less sustained, though there is a close in
the thought, as the following verses from Romeo and Juliet show :

O, where is Rom*eo*? *Saw* you him to day?

Well, in that hit *you miss :* she'll not be hit
With Cupid's ar*row* ; *she* hath Dian's wit,

A man, young la*dy* ! *la*dy, such a man

You are a lov*er* ; *bor*row Cupid's wings,

She is the Fairies' mid*wife* ; *and* she comes

And sleeps *again*. This is that very Mab

This being the case, we should expect *a priori* the pauses or
breaks to be more frequently after the light syllables, in the more
smoothly flowing verses of the recitative form of Shakespeare's
verse ; and so I have found them to be, in going over a number
of Plays having this form of verse. It may be said that the place
of the pause is determined, more or less, by the verse-sense of the

poet, at the time of his writing. When his verse-sense is strong,
the pauses coming after the light syllable of an iamb will predominate ; as his verse-sense goes down, so to speak, there will be
an increase in the pauses after complete feet.

In King John, Richard II., Parts I. and II. of Henry IV., and
Henry V., the dates of whose composition range about from 1596
to 1599, the recitative form of verse reaches its highest degree of
freedom, vigor, and *sweep*, and realizes its fullest dramatic capabilities. The best blank verse in these plays, presents a strong
contrast to that of the poet's earliest plays, Love's Labor's Lost,
for example.

Take as a fair specimen of the blank verse of the latter play,
the speech of the Princess, wherein she commissions Boyet to
secure for her a personal conference with the King (A. II. Sc. i.
13–34) :

> " Good Lord Boyet, my beauty, though but mean,
> Needs not the painted flourish of your praise :
> Beauty is bought by judgment of the eye,
> Not uttered by base sale of chapman's tongues :
> I am less proud to hear you tell my worth
> Than you much willing to be counted wise
> In spending your wit in the praise of mine.
> But now to task the tasker : good Boyet,
> You are not ignorant, all-telling fame
> Doth noise abroad, Navarre hath made a vow,
> Till painful duty shall outwear three years,
> No woman may approach his silent court :
> Therefore to's seemeth it a needful course,
> Before we enter his forbidden gates,
> To know his pleasure : and in that behalf,
> Bold of your worthiness, we single you
> As our best-moving fair solicitor.
> Tell him, the daughter of the King of France,
> On serious business craving quick dispatch,
> Importunes personal conference with his grace :
> Haste, signify so much ; while we attend,
> Like humble-visag'd suitors, his high will."

Contrast with this speech the following speech of King John to Hubert, A. III. Sc. iii, in which he intimates to Hubert his wish to have the little prince put out of the way. The thought keeps on the wing, so to speak, through 19 verses, and the verse exhibits a union of strength, lightsomeness, and elasticity. There is perhaps no passage, in any earlier play, in which the blank verse has attained to such a *sweep* as it has in this passage.

The nineteen lines to which I allude, begin with the words

"If the midnight bell."

Hubert says: "I am much bounden to your majesty"; and the King replies:

"Good friend, thou hast no cause to say so yet.
 But thou shalt have; and creep time ne'er so slow,
 Yet it shall come for me to do thee good.
 I had a thing to say, — but let it go.
 The sun is in the heaven, and the proud day,
 Attended with the pleasures of the world,
 Is all too wanton and too full of gawds
 To give me audience. If the midnight bell
 Did, with his iron tongue and brazen mouth,
 Sound on into the drowsy race of night;
 If this same were a churchyard where we stand,
 And thou possessed with a thousand wrongs,
 Or if that surly spirit, melancholy,
 Had bak'd thy blood and made it heavy, thick,
 Which else runs tickling up and down the veins,
 Making that idiot, laughter, keep men's eyes
 And strain their cheeks to idle merriment,
 A passion hateful to my purposes,
 Or if that thou couldst see me without eyes,
 Hear me without thine ears, and make reply
 Without a tongue, using conceit alone,
 Without eyes, ears, and harmful sound of words;
 Then, in despite of brooded watchful day,
 I would into thy bosom pour my thoughts.
 But, ah, I will not! — yet I love thee well;
 And, by my troth, I think thou lov'st me well."

There's a moral significance in the suspended construction of the language. The mind of the dastard king hovers over the subject of the ungodly act, and dares not alight upon it; and the verse in its uncadenced movement admirably registers the speaker's state of mind.

Another example of the freedom attained in the recitative form of Shakespeare's verse, and of the dramatic capabilities realized by it, is afforded by the speech of Hotspur, in the 3d Scene of the 1st Act of 1 Henry IV. He has been charged with refusing to give up the prisoners taken at Holmedon. Northumberland says to the king:

> " Those prisoners in your highness' name demanded,
> Which Harry Percy here at Holmedon took,
> Were, as he says, not with such strength denied
> As is delivered to your majesty:
> Either envy, therefore, or misprision,
> Is guilty of this fault, and not my son."

It will be observed that of the 41 verses of which Hotspur's speech is composed, but two or three run into the verses following them; and yet there's very little impression of metrical restraint upon the language.

> " My liege, I did deny no prisoners,
> But, I remember, when the fight was done,
> When I was dry with rage and extreme toil,
> Breathless and faint, leaning upon my sword,
> Came there a certain lord, neat, trimly dress'd,
> Fresh as a bridegroom; and his chin new reap'd,
> Show'd like a stubble-land at harvest home;
> He was perfumed like a milliner:
> And 'twixt his finger and his thumb he held
> A pouncet-box, which ever and anon
> He gave his nose, and took't away again; —
> Who, therewith angry, when it next came there,
> Took it in snuff: — and still he smiled, and talk'd;
> And, as the soldiers bore dead bodies by,
> He call'd them — untaught knaves, unmannerly,

To bring a slovenly unhandsome corse
Betwixt the wind and his nobility.
With many holiday and lady terms
He question'd me; among the rest, demanded
My prisoners, in your majesty's behalf.
I then, all smarting with my wounds being cold,
To be so pester'd with a popinjay,
Out of my grief and my impatience,
Answer'd neglectingly I know not what;
He should, or he should not; — for he made me mad
To see him shine so brisk, and smell so sweet,
And talk so like a waiting-gentlewoman
Of guns and drums, and wounds (God save the mark!)
And telling me the sovereign'st thing on earth
Was parmaceti, for an inward bruise;
And that it was great pity, so it was,
That villanous salt-petre should be digg'd
Out of the bowels of the harmless earth,
Which many a good tall fellow had destroy'd
So cowardly; and but for these vile guns,
He would himself have been a soldier.
This bald unjointed chat of his, my lord,
I answer'd indirectly as I said;
And I beseech you, let not his report
Come current for an accusation
Betwixt my love and your high majesty."

In the 1st Scene of the 4th Act, Hotspur says, alluding to the King,

" Where is his son,
The nimble-footed madcap Prince of Wales,
And his comrades, that daff'd the world aside,
And bid it pass?"   •
                                        ❀

Sir Richard Vernon replies:

" All furnish'd, all in arms;
All plumed like estridges that with the wind
Bate it like eagles having lately bathed;
Glittering in golden coats like images;

As full of spirit as the month of May,
And gorgeous as the sun at midsummer,
Wanton as youthful goats, wild as young bulls.
I saw young Harry, with his beaver on,
His cuisses on his thighs, gallantly arm'd,
Rise from the ground like feathered Mercury,
And vault it with such ease into his seat,
As if an angel dropp'd down from the clouds,
To turn and wind a fiery Pegasus,
And witch the world with noble horsemanship."

A passage like this may be regarded as the climax of the free-dom of movement and the bounding vigor which Shakespeare's blank verse reached in its *recitative* form — that form, to repeat, in which *the normal pentameter measure of the verse determines more or less the orbit of the thought.* When it reached this vigor-ous, and, at the same time, buoyant metrical movement, the poet had realized the extreme dramatic capabilities of this form of blank verse. But for the freest movement of his dramatic thought in its fullest maturity, he passed beyond the recitative form of blank verse into that which I have named the *spontaneous*, the most obvious characteristics of which, are :

1st. The metre is sunk more or less,

a. Through the weakness of the word receiving the 5th ictus of the verse.

b. By a looser melodious fusion of the verse, and by a more arbitrary use of pauses and breaks.

2d. Extra end-syllables crop out more and more, as the *recita-tive* form of verse is departed from.

And first :

The Metre is sunk more or less, *a. Through the weakness of the word receiving the 5th ictus of the verse.*

As the poet advances in dramatic identification, the metre of his blank verse yields more and more to the movement of the thought. The firmest resting place for the voice, in the more markedly recitative style, is the accented syllable or word of the

5th foot; in the spontaneous style, this syllable or word is frequently the lightest on which the voice can press, and sometimes this place in the verse is occupied by a proclitic particle on which it cannot press at all, but must move on into the succeeding verse.

The normal metre is thus, at times, more or less lost to the feelings, and only the foot rhythm of the language is felt. In The Winter's Tale verses frequently end with such atonic or proclitic words as *a, are, and, as, but, if, nor, or, of, for, the, to, which, with :*

Temptations have since then been born to's : for

And his pond fish'd by his next neighbor (by
Sir *Smile,* his neighbour :)

A lip of much contempt, speeds from me, and

Which puts some of us in distemper ; but

Which must be ev'n as swiftly follow'd as

Turn then my freshest reputation to

By each particular star in heaven and

I know not : but I'm sure 'tis safer to

Still neighbour mine. My ships are ready and

I will respect thee as a father if

You'll kiss me hard, and speak to me as if

Freed and enfranchised ; not a party to
The anger of the king nor guilty of

They should not laugh if I could reach them, nor

Which contradicts my accusation and

Which to deny concerns more than avails ; for as

Mine own, nor any thing to any, if

Of celebration of that nuptial which

Which does mend nature, change it rather, but

Most incident to maids; bold oxlips and

Hides not his visage from our cottage, but

Resolv'd for flight: now were I happy if

There's no disjunction to be made, but by

She is as forward of her breeding as

That heirless it hath made my kingdom; and

Might thus have stood begetting wonder, as

Fled from his father, from his hopes, and with

The father of this seeming lady and

My evils conjured to remembrance, and

b. By a looser melodious fusion of the verse, and by a more arbitrary use of pauses and breaks.

When feeling or sentiment is in the ascendant over the dramatic, its plastic or unifying power is manifested in a closer and more melodious fusion of the verse — the pauses and breaks are made with more reference to the standard measure of the verse, that is, they do not occur in such a way as to cause the standard to be sunk in the varied measures. But take the following speech from Cymbeline, A. III. Sc. ii. 50–70, and note how the melody fusion of the verses is reduced, and how the standard measure of the verse is sunk in the varied measures.

Imogen learns that her husband is at Milford-Haven, and is eager to go to him there:

"O, for a horse with wings! Hear'st thou, Pisanio?
He is at Milford-Haven: read, and tell me
How far 'tis thither. If one of mean affairs
May plod it in a week, why may not I
Glide thither in a day? then, true Pisanio, —
Who long'st, like me, to see thy lord; who long'st, —

O, let me bate, — but not like me — yet long'st,
But in a fainter kind : — O, not like me ;
For mine's beyond beyond — say, and speak thick, —
Love's counsellor should fill the bores of hearing,
To the smothering of the sense — how far it is
To this same blessed Milford : and by the way
Tell me how Wales was made so happy as
To inherit such an haven : but, first of all,
How we may steal from hence, and for the gap
That we shall make in time, from our hence-going
And our return, to excuse : but first, how get hence.
Why should excuse be born or ere begot?
We'll talk of that hereafter. Prithee, speak,
How many score of miles may we well ride
'Twixt hour and hour? "

2d. *Extra end-syllables crop out more and more, as the recitative form of verse is departed from.*

As used by Fletcher, extra end-syllables are but little more than
a mere mannerism, that is, they are not to any extent, organic —
are not occasioned by the movement of the thought or feeling.
Their origin may perhaps be attributed partly to Italian influence,
and as employed by Fletcher they may have been largely a mere
adoption — an adoption which became, in time, more or less a
mere habit. The dramatic capabilities of the double ending are
therefore not realized, to any extent, in Fletcher's verse, by reason
of the over-frequency of its occurrence.

Shakespeare made use of the conventional in other things than
forms of language ; he, indeed, absorbed all that was conventional
in the literature of his age ; but such was the force and plastic
power of his genius, that he always infused into conventional forms
a new soul — he translated them from the conventional into the
organic ; the formal becomes smoothed down into spontaneous
grace. He is the freest of all authors from mannerisms, and that
is one reason why (although the habitual student of his works
comes, in time, to feel what is Shakespearian and what is not), he
cannot be imitated with any success ; there is not that in his dic-

tion which the imitator generally lays hold of — an evidence of the organic character of his language-shaping. For to the degree that expression is organic, does imitation become difficult, which generally lays hold on mannerisms and mere excrescences. The organic can be reproduced only to the extent that the formative spirit has a palingenesis in another mind.

Shakespeare's extra end-syllables were something more than an adoption with him ; * and it becomes important in the study of his verse to determine to what extent they are conventional and to what extent they are organic, or inseparable from the expression of certain modes of feeling and of mind movement.

This may be said in a general way, that what is true of his use of rhyme is equally true of his use of extra end-syllables — they are employed when sought for — when the feeling, so to speak, reaches out for them. And of two given plays, if one has a considerable number of extra end-syllables more than another, it is not a legitimate inference that it was composed after the other ; unless it be assumed that the use of extra end-syllables was a mere habit that grew upon the poet, in each succeeding Play, in the later period of his workmanship. But no one who reads Shakespeare with due faith in the organic significance, in general, of his language-shaping, would assume anything of the kind. He

---

* " The temperate introduction of lines with the hypermetrical syllable has often a pleasing effect, but during the last few years of the poet's career, their immoderate use was affected by our dramatists, and although, for the most part, Shakespeare's metre was a free offspring of the ear, owing little but its generic form to his predecessors and contemporaries, it appears certain that, in the present instance [Henry VIII.], he suffered himself to be influenced by this undesirable fashion." — Halliwell-Phillipps's "Outlines of the Life of Shakespeare," 5th ed. p. 204.

In the " Illustrative Notes," p. 586, No. 258, the author adds : " Shakespeare probably wrote verse as easily as prose, and very few species of dramatic metre had then taken an absolute form by precedent. Even if it had been otherwise, the metrical ear, which, like that for music, is a natural gift, must, in his case, have revolted from a subjection to normal restrictions."

would seek rather to penetrate to the moulding spirit resident within the forms, and to discover why in one play that moulding spirit reached out oftener after extra end-syllables than it did in the other. If he succeed in doing this, or think he has succeeded, he may not indeed have a clue to the priority or subsequence of one of two or more plays, but he will have a new assurance of the flexibility of the poet's spirit, and an increased faith in the organic nature of his forms.

Extra end-syllables are not, indeed, confined to the spontaneous form of his verse — they occur often where the recitative form is in the ascendent.

In Hamlet's first soliloquy, A. I. Sc. ii. 129–158, beginning,

" Oh, that this too too solid flesh would melt,"

the effect of the additional light syllables which occur both at the end of, and within the verses, is readily felt as an organic effect — they express the rebound of the speaker's impulsive feeling :

" Oh, that this too too solid flesh would melt,
Thaw, and resolve itself into a dew :
Or that the Everlasting had not fixt
His canon 'gainst self-slaughter. O God, O God!
How weary, stale, flat, and unprofitable
Seems to me all the uses of this world !
Fie on't ! oh fie, fie, 'tis an unweeded garden
That grows to seed : things rank and gross in nature
Possess it merely. That it should come to this !
But two months dead ! Nay, not so much, not two :
So excellent a king, that was to this
Hyperion to a Satyr : so loving to my mother,
That he might not beteem the winds of heaven
Visit her face too roughly. Heaven and Earth
Must I remember? Why she would hang on him,
As if encrease of appetite had grown
By what it fed on ; and yet within a month —
Let me not think on't — Frailty, thy name is woman ! —
A little month, or ere those shoes were old

With which she followed my poor father's body,
Like Niobe, all tears, — why she, even she, —
(O Heaven! a beast that wants discourse of reason,
Would have mourn'd longer) married with my uncle,
My father's brother, but no more like my father
Than I to Hercules. Within a month?
Ere yet the salt of most unrighteous tears
Had left the flushing of her galled eyes,
She married! O, most wicked speed, to post
With such dexterity to incestuous sheets!
It is not, nor it cannot come to good.
But break my heart, for I must hold my tongue."

In the soliloquy, "To be or not to be," the additional light
syllables impart a *reflectiveness* of tone to the language :

" To be or not to be, that is the question :
Whether 'tis nobler in the mind to suffer
The slings and arrows of outrageous For*tune,*
Or to take arms against a sea of trou*bles,*
And by opposing end *them :* "

I fancy that Shakespeare must sometimes have heard some of
the speeches of his characters independently of the thoughts expressed, and that he fashioned them after the sound that was in
his mind.

Although the particular effects of the extra end-syllables cannot
always be set forth, every one who is susceptible to verse, must
feel more or less their organic character, in Shakespeare's verse.

There is often an effective mingling of verses having extra end-
syllables with verses having the normal ending on accented syllables. The soliloquy of Gloster with which the play of Richard III.
opens, is a good illustration of this.

The extra end-syllable has an agreeable effect when it crops out
after a succession of smooth verses, as in the 4th verse of this
soliloquy :

" Now is the winter of our discontent
Made glorious summer by this sun of York :

> And all the clouds that lour'd upon our house
> In the deep bosom of the ocean bur*ied*."

In the four following verses of the soliloquy (28–31), there is an effective alternation of the normal and of extra-syllable endings :

> " And therefore, since I cannot prove a lov*er*,
> To entertain these fair well-spoken days,
> I am determinéd to prove a vill*ain*
> And hate the idle pleasures of these days."

While with Shakespeare the extra end-syllable is more or less organic, and imparts a liveliness to the verse, with Fletcher it is often a cold, monotonous mannerism.

.

DISTINCTIVE USE OF VERSE AND PROSE
IN SHAKESPEARE'S PLAYS.

———◦◦◦———

NO writer has exhibited the power which "the great protago-
nist in the arena of modern poetry" has exhibited, of marshalling words, of stimulating language to its utmost capacity, and
moulding it into the "infinite variety" of organic form demanded
by all the possible attitudes of the mind and the sensibilities. I
say *organic* form ; for, although he adopted, at the outset, as the
general tenor of his language, forms employed by his predecessors
and contemporaries, yet, such was the plastic power of his mind
and feelings over them that they, the forms, were gradually brought
more and more under easy submission and became more and more
organic, or, in other words, inseparable from the thought and emotion embodied therein. He was the first to mingle, organically, in
dramatic composition, blank verse and rhyming verse, and prose.
These are all found in harmonious union, often within the limits of
a short scene. He may never have defined to his own mind, the
peculiar and legitimate functions of each of these modes of language-shaping, but he must have had the nicest and most reliable
feeling as to their use. He passes from blank verse to rhyme and
from rhyme to prose, and back again to blank verse, and the reader
feels all the while, generally, perhaps without thinking so, that it's
the most natural thing in the world to do. The *rationale* and the
morale of the varied phases which his verse presents at different
periods of his career, it is often difficult to determine ; but it is
not so difficult to note the distinctive use of the two grand divis-
ions of language-shaping, Prose and Verse, throughout all the
Plays. In the first place, all the dramatis personæ *that are not*

drawn into the higher movements of thought and feeling, are, generally, made to speak in straightforward prose. (This, however, is
not so true of the earlier Plays as it is of the later. Shakespeare's
nice sense of the peculiar domains of Verse and Prose was gradually developed along with other developments, one of the most
important of which was humour.* As Dowden says, " Had Shakspere written the play [Richard II.] a few years later, we may
be certain that the gardener and servants (A. III. Sc. iv.) would
not have uttered stately speeches in verse, but would have spoken
homely prose, and that humour would have mingled with the
pathos of this scene. The same remark may be made with reference to the subsequent scene, in which his groom visits the dethroned King in the Tower." And even the leading persons of
the drama, in situations demanding no idealization of language,
speak often in prose. Hamlet speaks in verse to his mother, to
his bosom friend Horatio, to the majestic ghost of his father, and
in his soliloquies ; but to the old chancellor Polonius whom he
despises, to the time-serving courtiers, to the players, and in the
scene with the grave-diggers, he speaks in the most off-hand prose.
But in this last scene, when his mind turns to the great Roman, he
speaks then not only in verse but in rhymed verse :

> " Imperious Cæsar, dead and turn'd to clay,
> Might stop a hole to keep the wind away:
> O, that the earth which kept the world in awe,
> Should patch a wall t'expel the winter's flaw ! "

A character like Falstaff, speaks, of course, in prose. Great
and various as are the possibilities by which Falstaff's actual self
is backed, his higher faculties are always under the cloud of
sensual indulgence ; and like all sensualists, his mind never rises
above considerations of self — never reaches that *pitch* of thought
and feeling which demands a rhythmical and metrical form of

---

* See " Dowden's Shakspere: his Mind and Art." Chap. vii. " The Humour
of Shakspere."

language. He *affects* indeed, such a form, in A. II. Sc. iv., of
1 Henry IV. :

"*Fal.* Well, thou wilt be horribly chid to-morrow when thou
comest to thy father : if thou love me, practise an answer.

Prince. Do thou stand for my father, and examine me upon
the particulars of my life.

Fal. Shall I ? content : this chair shall be my state, this dagger
my sceptre, and this cushion my crown.

Prince. Thy state is taken for a joined-stool, thy golden sceptre
for a leaden dagger, and thy precious rich crown for a pitiful bald
crown !

Fal. Well, an the fire of grace be not quite out of thee, now
shalt thou be moved. Give me a cup of sack to make my eyes
look red, that it may be thought I have wept ; for I must speak in
passion, and I will do it in King Cambyses' vein.

Prince. Well, here is my leg.

Fal. And here is my speech. Stand aside, nobility.

Hostess. O Jesu, this is excellent sport, i' faith !

Fal. Weep not, sweet queen, for trickling tears are vain.

Hostess. O, the father, how he holds his countenance !

Fal. For God's sake, lords, convey my tristful * queen ;
        For tears do stop the flood-gates of her eyes.

Hostess. O Jesu, he doth it as like one of these harlotry players
as ever I see ! "

This is all the metrical language which Falstaff utters, except
the two verses addressed to King Henry V., in 2 Henry IV., A. V.
Sc. v. 42 and 50 :

"*Fal.* God save thy grace, King Hal ! my royal Hal ! . . .

Chief Justice. Have you your wits ? Know you what 'tis you
speak ?

Fal. My King ! my Jove ! I speak to thee, my heart !

King. I know thee not, old man : fall to thy prayers ; . . ."

An interesting transition from prose to verse, is shown in the
3d Scene of the 1st Act of The Merchant of Venice. While Bas-

---

* Trustfull : Qq., Ff.

sanio is negotiating with Shylock for a loan of three thousand ducats, for three months, for the repayment of which Antonio is to be bound, the talk is in business-like prose, and quite unimpassioned except in Shylock's speech in reply to Bassanio's proposal that he dine with him and Antonio :

"Yes, to smell pork ; to eat of the habitation which your prophet, the Nazarite, conjured the devil into. I will buy with you, sell with you, talk with you, walk with you, and so following ; but I will not eat with you, drink with you, nor pray with you."

This speech, by the way, coming just before the entrance of Antonio, serves well as a transition to the language-shaping which follows. When Antonio comes in, against whom he has long borne bitter grudges for wrongs done him, real or imaginary, Shylock's feelings are intensified, and the language is at once moulded into metre, the pulse of which rises highest in the following speech :

> "Signior Antonio, many a time and oft,
> In the Rialto, you have rated me
> About my moneys and my usances :
> Still have I borne it with a patient shrug ;
> For sufferance is the badge of all our tribe.
> You call me misbeliever, cut-throat dog,
> And spet upon my Jewish gaberdine,
> And all for use of that which is mine own.
> Well then, it now appears you need my help :
> Go to, then ; you come to me, and you say,
> ' Shylock, we would have moneys : ' you say so ;
> You, that did void your rheum upon my beard,
> And foot me, as you spurn a stranger cur
> Over your threshold — moneys is your suit.
> What should I say to you?   Should I not say,
> ' Hath a dog money?   Is it possible
> A cur should lend three thousand ducats?'   Or
> Should I bend low, and in a bondman's key,
> With bated breath and whispering humbleness,
> Say this :
> ' Fair sir, you spet on me on Wednesday last ;

You spurn'd me such a day ; another time
You call'd me dog ; and for these courtesies
I'll lend you thus much moneys.' "

Antonio's reply is the highest-pulsed speech which *he* utters, in
the scene ; and then Shylock tones down, and an agreement in
regard to the loan is finally arrived at.

The scene is rounded off with two rhymes :

> " *Antonio.*   Hie thee, gentle Jew.   [*Exit* SHYLOCK.
> The Hebrew will turn Christian : he grows kind.
> *Bassanio.* I like not fair terms and a villain's mind.
> *Antonio.* Come on : in this there can be no dismay ;
> My ships come home a month before the day."

A remarkable illustration, one of the most remarkable, perhaps,
in Shakespeare, of changes in language-shaping adapted to the
varied pitch of thought and feeling, is afforded by the 3d Scene of
the 1st Act of Othello, wherein the Moor, accused by Brabantio
of having won his daughter Desdemona by love-potions and
witchcraft, makes his defence before the Duke and Senators of
Venice, and tells the story of his courtship.

When he addresses the Senators, he employs language indicative of a self-sustained dignity, but free from the least touch of
arrogance. There is a certain weight imparted to the movement
of the verse by a more than usual correspondence of the rhythmical ictus with the logical emphasis. The double-endings which
occur, " masters," " daughter," " offending," "battle," " patience,"
" deliver," " magic," impart a certain decisiveness of tone ; the
breaks in the verse, too, come after complete feet : .

> " Most potent, grave, and reverend signiors,
> My very noble and approved good masters,
> That I have ta'en away this old man's daughter,
> It is most true ; true, I have married her :
> The very head and front of my offending
> Hath this extent, no more.   Rude am I in my speech,

> And little blest with the soft phrase of peace;
> For since these arms of mine had seven years' pith,
> Till now some nine moons wasted, they have used
> Their dearest action in the tented field;
> And little of this great world can I speak,
> More than pertains to feats of broil and battle;
> And therefore little shall I grace my cause
> In speaking for myself. Yet, by your gracious patience,
> I will a round unvarnish'd tale deliver
> Of my whole course of love; what drugs, what charms,
> What conjuration and what mighty magic —
> For such proceeding I am charged withal —
> I won his daughter."

When Othello speaks of his courtship, the stateliness of the verse is somewhat reduced, and his speech is characterized by an ingenuousness of tone to which the movement of the verse is admirably adapted:

> " Her father loved me; oft invited me;
> Still question'd me the story of my life,
> From year to year, the battles, sieges, fortunes,
> That I have pass'd.
> I ran it through, even from my boyish days,
> To the very moment that he bade me tell it;
> Wherein I spake of most disastrous chances,
> Of moving accidents by flood and field,
> Of hair-breadth scapes i' the imminent deadly breach,
> Of being taken by the insolent foe
> And sold to slavery, of my redemption thence
> And portance in my travels' history:
> Wherein of antres vast and deserts idle,
> Rough quarries, rocks and hills whose heads touch heaven,
> It was my hint to speak, — such was the process;
> And of the Cannibals that each other eat,
> The Anthropophagi and men whose heads
> Do grow beneath their shoulders. This to hear
> Would Desdemona seriously incline:
> But still the house-affairs would draw her thence:

Which ever as she could with haste dispatch,
She'ld come again, and with a greedy ear
Devour up my discourse : which I observiug,
Took once a pliant hour, and found good means
To draw from her a prayer of earnest heart
That I would all my pilgrimage dilate,
Whereof by parcels she had something heard,
But not intentively : I did consent,
And often did beguile her of her tears,
When I did speak of some distressful stroke
That my youth suffer'd.   My story being done,
She gave me for my pains a world of sighs :
She swore, in faith, 'twas strange, 'twas passing strange,
'Twas pitiful, 'twas wondrous pitiful :
She wish'd she had not heard it, yet she wish'd
That heaven had made her such a man ; she thank'd me,
And bade me, if I had a friend that loved her,
I should but teach him how to tell my story,
And that would woo her.   Upon this hint I spake :
She loved me for the dangers I had pass'd,
And I loved her that she did pity them.
This only is the witchcraft I have used :
Here comes the lady ; let her witness it."

At the close of his story, Desdemona enters.   To the question of her father, " Do you perceive in all this noble company Where most you owe obedience ? " she replies in blank verse, which has the directness of prose ; the rhythmus, too, is kept down, and the whole is raised just so much above prose as is necessary to express the daughter's respect for the father — the closeness of their relationship not allowing a form of language any more elevated than what she employs.   The additional light syllables which occur at the end of some of the verses, (and there are two within the verse, before breaks, " respect | you ; " " your daugh | ter : ") serve to neutralize somewhat the rhythmical effect :

" My noble father,
I do perceive here a divided duty :

> To you I am bound for life and education ;
> My life and education both do learn me
> How to respect you ; you are the lord of duty :
> I am hitherto your daughter : but here's my husband,
> And so much duty as my mother show'd
> To you, preferring you before her father,
> So much I challenge that I may profess
> Due to the Moor my lord."

The first three lines of Brabantio's reply in which he gives up the case, are not distinguishable from prose ; and their off-hand movement serves to express the grieved old man's submission to the state of things.

> " God be with you ! — I have done. —
> Please it your grace, on to the state affairs ;
> I had rather to adopt a child than get it."

When he addresses the Moor, his speech is slightly elevated and decided in movement, which latter feature is helped by the mono-syllabic words :

> " Come hither, Moor :
> I here do give thee that with all my heart,
> Which, but thou hast already, with all my heart
> I would keep from thee. For your sake, jewel,
> I am glad at soul I have no other child ;
> For thy escape would teach me tyranny,
> To hang clogs on them. I have done, my lord."

Of the Duke's speech in reply, the first three lines are scarcely verse at all, and their prose effect is helped by the extra end-syllables of the words " sentence," " lovers," " favour." With such an introduction, the sententious character of the rest of the speech is more brought out. It has a marked rhythmical movement, and the metre is enforced by rhyme, and one of the rhymes is rendered more emphatic by being a double rhyme, — *ended, depended.* In addition thereto, each couplet constitutes a sentence composed of two balanced members, and each member makes a distinct verse :

" *Duke.* Let me speak like yourself, and lay a sentence
Which, as a grise or step, may help these lovers
Into your favour.
When remedies are past, the griefs are ended
By seeing the worst, which late on hopes depended.
To mourn a mischief that is past and gone
Is the next way to draw new mischief on.
What cannot be preserved when fortune takes,
Patience her injury a mockery makes.
The robb'd that smiles steals something from the thief;
He robs himself that spends a bootless grief."

Brabantio, with a bitterness of spirit, retorts in the same sententious, markedly rhythmical, and strongly rhymed language. But as indicating that he is completely done with the case, his speech ends with a line of pure prose : " I humbly beseech you, proceed to the affairs of state : "

" So let the Turk of Cyprus us beguile;
We lose it not, so long as we can smile.
He bears the sentence well, that nothing bears
But the free comfort which from thence he hears;
But he bears both the sentence and the *sorrow*,
That, to pay grief, must of poor patience *borrow*.
These sentences, to sugar or to gall,
Being strong on both sides, are equivocal:
But words are words; I never yet did hear
That the bruised heart was pierced through the ear.
I humbly beseech you, proceed to the affairs of state."

The Duke's speech which follows is in the most straightforward prose, which is felt to be the only proper medium of a plain matter-of-fact order to his general :

"The Turk with a most mighty preparation makes for Cyprus. Othello, the fortitude of the place is best known to you ; and though we have there a substitute of most allowed sufficiency, yet opinion, a sovereign mistress of effects, throws a more safer voice on you : you must therefore be content to slubber the gloss of your new fortunes with this more stubborn and boisterous expedition."

Othello replies in blank verse whose movement expresses the
in procinctu state of the brave soldier's mind :

> " The tyrant custom, most grave senators,
> Hath made the flinty and steel couch of war
> My thrice-driven bed of down : I do agnize
> A natural and prompt alacrity
> I find in hardness ; and do undertake
> These present wars against the Ottomites.
> Most humbly therefore bending to your state,
> I crave fit disposition for my wife,
> Due reference of place and exhibition,
> With such accommodation and besort
> As levels with her breeding."

To draw the line between the domains of prose and verse, is not
easy.   But Shakespeare's works afford perhaps the best material
for determining those domains, when the critic shall appear whose
art vision is clear enough

> " to watch
> The Master work, and catch
> Hints of the proper craft, tricks of the tool's true play,"

and to penetrate to the laws underlying his use of these forms of
language. This should be said, however, that Shakespeare adopted
verse as the general tenor of his language, and therefore expresses
much in verse that is within the capabilities of prose ; in other
words, his verse constantly encroaches upon the domain of prose,
but his prose can never be said to encroach upon the domain of
verse.

The nearest approach to it, perhaps, is in the prose speech
of Hamlet, A. II. Sc. ii. . . . " this goodly frame, the earth,
seems to me a sterile promontory ; this most excellent canopy,
the air, look you, this brave o'erhanging firmament, this majesti-
cal roof, fretted with golden fire, why, it appears no other thing to
me than a foul and pestilent congregation of vapours. What a

piece of work is a man! how noble in reason! how infinite in faculty! in form and moving how express and admirable! in action, how like an angel! in apprehension how like a god! the beauty of the world! the paragon of animals!"

There are two characteristics of the material of legitimate verse (characteristics which are the result of the very feeling which produces verse), by which it is especially differentiated from prose material, namely, the general concreteness and the imaginative imputation which it exhibits, resulting from the intense sympathy which animates great poets. The concrete is, so to speak, the vernacular language, the indispensable medium, wherethrough poetic passion is manifested, which, when intense, must needs radiate into numerous images furnished by nature and by human life. These images may be regarded as the harmonies into which the melody or rhythmus of his thought is ever tending to run, and the more impassioned this melody or rhythmus, the greater the necessity thus to expand itself.

When Macbeth tells his wife that a dreadful deed shall be committed before nightfall, the intensity of his feelings at the time radiates into imagery and epithet which are beyond what the most impassioned prose could sustain :

> " Ere that the bat hath flown
> His cloister'd flight; ere to black Hecate's summons,
> The shard-borne beetle with its drowsy hums
> Hath rung night's yawning peal, there shall be done
> A dead of dreadful note.
> *Lady M.* What's to be done?
> *Macb.* Be innocent of the knowledge, dearest chuck,
> Till thou applaud the deed. — Come, seeling night!
> Skarf up the tender eye of pitiful day,
> And with thy bloody and invisible hand
> Cancel and tear to pieces that great bond
> Which keeps me pale! — Light thickens and the crow
> Makes wing to the rooky wood :
> Good things of day begin to droop and drowse,
> Whiles night's black agents to their preys do rouse. —

Thou marvell'st at my words : but hold thee still ;
Things bad begun make strong themselves by ill : "

It is through his epithets and his metaphors that a great poet
reveals the intensity of his sympathies, the depth of his spiritual
insight, and his recognition of the moral aspect of things.   If he
takes in only their familiar and general outlines, and their more
prominent features, his epithets will, as a consequence, be commonplace ; they will be stock epithets, embodying only the popular idea.   If his sympathies are feeble, he will not think *in* and
by and *through* his figures, but he will hitch them on to his thought
and sentiment.   In regard to a poet's use of epithets, it may also
be remarked, that his all-embracing sympathy, and the tendency
of his imagination to imbue all things with feeling, will often
cause him to transfer an epithet from the word whose idea it properly qualifies, to another to which it is logically inapplicable, but
which is thus brought more within the embrace of the sympathies ;
for example :

" Leak'd is our bark,
And we, poor mates, stand on the *dying* deck,
Hearing the surges threat : " — T. of A. IV. ii. 20.

" He only lived but till he was a man ;
The which no sooner had his prowess confirm'd
In the *unshrinking* station where he fought,
But like a man he died." — Macbeth V. viii. 42.

A signal example of how Shakespeare raised prose material into
glowing and luxuriant poetry, is afforded by the description in Antony and Cleopatra (A. II. Sc. ii. 196–231), given by Enobarbus to
Agrippa, of Cleopatra's sailing down the Cydnus to meet Antony,
the circumstances of which, Shakespeare derived from North's
Plutarch.*   (See Commentary on Antony and Cleopatra, in this
volume.)

---

* "This version, called by Warton Shakespeare's 'storehouse of learned
history,' was made by Sir Thomas North.   The translation was made, not from
the original Greek, but from a French version by Jaques Amyot, bishop of

Superior as is Shakespeare's verse to that of all his dramatic contemporaries, and they all, with very few exceptions, wrote verse of great vitality,* his prose is not less superior to all English prose, produced in every department of literature down to, and many years subsequent to, his time. The prose of Bacon's Essays would probably first occur to many as bearing the palm of highest excellence reached at the time it was produced. But it is cramped and rugged in comparison with Shakespeare's best prose. Take, for example, the 2d Scene of the 5th Act of The Winter's Tale, ll. 1-121. As dramatic prose, this has a corresponding excellence with the blank verse of the 2d Scene of the 1st Act of The Tempest, beyond which dramatic blank verse has never gone. If Shakespeare did not write this prose in The Winter's Tale, Bacon certainly did not.

" *Enter* AUTOLYCUS *and a* Gentleman.

Aut. Beseech you, sir, were you present at this relation?

1 *Gent.* I was by at the opening of the fardel; heard the old

---

Auxerre. It was first published in 1579, the dedication to Queen Elizabeth being dated Jan. 6, and his address to the Reader Jan. 24, 2d edition 1595. Other editions appeared in 1603, 1612, 1631, 1656, and 1676. A selection from the Lives in North's Plutarch which illustrate Shakespeare's Plays, has been edited with notes, etc., by the Rev. Walter W. Skeat, London, 1875."

* "What it was that happened to the English ear after that [the Elizabethan era] I know not; perhaps I may have abandoned my own too exclusively to their music and become insensible or intolerant to what succeeded; but for more than a hundred years the art of writing anything but the heroic couplet seems to have been lost, which couplet, I confess, it costs me almost an heroic effort to read; and when our verse ceased to clank this chain, it rose into lyrical movements of some force and freedom, but to me it seems never to have recovered the subtle and searching power and consonantal pith which it lost in that fatal eighteenth century, when our language itself was dethroned and levelled. The blank verse of Young and Cowper in the last century, or (with the exception of occasional passages) of Southey and Wordsworth in this, is, to my mind, no more like that of the better Elizabethans than a turnpike road is like a bridle path, or a plantation like a forest." — From letter of Henry Taylor to Sir John Herschel, Aug. 26, 1862 (" Correspondence of H. T., edited by Edward Dowden," pp. 243, 244).

shepherd deliver the manner how he found it : whereupon, after a little amazedness, we were all commanded out of the chamber ; only this methought I heard the shepherd say, he found the child.

Aut. I would most gladly know the issue of it.

1 *Gent.* I make a broken delivery of the business ; but the changes I perceived in the king and Camillo were very notes of admiration : they seemed almost, with staring on one another, to tear the cases of their eyes ; there was speech in their dumbness, language in their very gesture ; they looked as they had heard of a world ransomed, or one destroyed : a notable passion of wonder appeared in them : but the wisest beholder, that knew no more but seeing, could not say if the importance were joy or sorrow ; but in the extremity of the one it must needs be.

Enter another Gentleman.

Here comes a gentleman that haply knows more : The news, Rogero ?

2 *Gent.* Nothing but bonfires : the oracle is fulfilled ; the king's daughter is found : such a deal of wonder is broken out within this hour, that ballad-makers cannot be able to express it.

Enter a third Gentleman.

Here comes the lady Paulina's steward ; he can deliver you more. How goes it now, sir ? this news, which is called true, is so like an old tale, that the verity of it is in strong suspicion : has the king found his heir ?

3 *Gent.* Most true ; if ever truth were pregnant by circumstance ; that which you hear you'll swear you see, there is such unity in the proofs. The mantle of queen Hermione's, her jewel about the neck of it, the letters of Antigonus found with it which they know to be his character, the majesty of the creature, in resemblance of the mother, the affection of nobleness, which nature shows above her breeding, and many other evidences, proclaim her, with all certainty, to be the king's daughter. Did you see the meeting of the two kings ?

2 *Gent.* No.

3 *Gent.* Then have you lost a sight, which was to be seen, cannot be spoken of. There might you have beheld one joy crown another, so and in such manner, that it seemed sorrow wept to take leave of them; for their joy waded in tears. There was casting up of eyes, holding up of hands; with countenance of such distraction, that they were to be known by garment, not by favour. Our king, being ready to leap out of himself for joy of his found daughter, as if that joy were now become a loss, cries, 'Oh, thy mother, thy mother!' then asks Bohemia forgiveness; then embraces his son-in-law; then again worries he his daughter, with clipping her; now he thanks the old shepherd, which stands by, like a weather-bitten conduit of many kings' reigns. I never heard of such another encounter, which lames report to follow it, and undoes description to do it.

2 *Gent.* What, 'pray you, became of Antigonus, that carried hence the child?

3 *Gent.* Like an old tale still; which will have matter to re-hearse, though credit be asleep, and not an ear open. He was torn to pieces with a bear: this avouches the shepherd's son; who has not only his innocence (which seems much) to justify him, but a handkerchief and rings of his that Paulina knows.

1 *Gent.* What became of his bark, and his followers?

3 *Gent.* Wracked the same instant of their master's death, and in the view of the shepherd: so that all the instruments which aided to expose the child, were even then lost, when it was found. But, oh the noble combat that 'twixt joy and sorrow was fought in Paulina! She had one eye declined for the loss of her husband, another elevated that the oracle was fulfilled: she lifted the princess from the earth, and so locks her in embracing, as if she would pin her to her heart, that she might no more be in danger of loosing.

1 *Gent.* The dignity of this act was worth the audience of kings and princes; for by such was it acted.

3 *Gent.* One of the prettiest touches of all, and that which

angled for mine eyes (caught the water, though not the fish), was, when at the relation of the queen's death, with the manner how she came to it, (bravely confessed, and lamented by the king,) how attentiveness wounded his daughter; till, from one sign of dolour to another, she did, with an 'alas!' I would fain say, bleed tears; for, I am sure, my heart wept blood. Who was most marble there changed colour: some swooned, all sorrowed: if all the world could have seen 't, the woe had been universal.

1 *Gent.* Are they returned to the court?

3 *Gent.* No: the princess hearing of her mother's statue, which is in the keeping of Paulina, — a piece many years in doing, and now newly performed by that rare Italian master, Julio Romano; who, had he himself eternity, and could put breath into his work, would beguile nature of her custom, so perfectly he is her ape: he so near to Hermione hath done Hermione that they say one would speak to her and stand in hope of answer: thither, with all greediness of affection, are they gone; and there they intend to sup.

2 *Gent.* I thought she had some great matter there in hand; for she hath privately, twice or thrice a day, ever since the death of Hermione, visited that removed house. Shall we thither, and with our company piece the rejoicing?

1 *Gent.* Who would be thence that has the benefit of access? every wink of an eye, some new grace will be born: our absence makes us unthrifty to our knowledge. Let's along.

[*Exeunt* Gentlemen."

THE LATIN AND THE ANGLO-SAXON ELE-MENTS OF SHAKESPEARE'S ENGLISH, AND THE MONOSYLLABIC VOCABULARY,

IN THEIR RELATIONS TO THE INTELLECTUAL, THE EMO-TIONAL, AND THE DRAMATIC.

THE peculiar domains of the Latin and the Anglo-Saxon elements of the English language have been sufficiently defined by numerous writers well qualified for the task. Thomas De Quincey has distinguished these domains, in his Essay on Wordsworth's Poetry, with his characteristic sagacity and rare faculty of discrimination : " The gamut of ideas," he says, " needs a corresponding gamut of expressions ; the scale of the thinking, which ranges through *every* key, exacts, for the artist, an unlimited command over the entire scale of the instrument which he employs. Never, in fact, was there a more erroneous direction than that given by a modern rector of the Glasgow University to the students, — viz., that they should cultivate the Saxon part of our language, at the cost of the Latin part. Nonsense ! Both are indispensable ; and, speaking generally without stopping to distinguish as to subjects, both are *equally* indispensable. Pathos, in situations which are homely, or at all connected with domestic affections, naturally moves by Saxon words. Lyrical emotion of every kind, which (to merit the name of *lyrical*) must be in the state of flux and reflux, or, generally, of agitation, also requires the Saxon element of our language. And why? Because the Saxon is the aboriginal element ; the basis, and not the superstructure ; consequently, it comprehends all the ideas which are natural to the heart of man, and to the elementary situations of life. And, although the Latin often furnishes us with duplicates of these ideas, yet the Saxon or monosyllabic part has the advantage of precedency in our use and knowledge; for it is the language of the nursery, whether for rich or poor, in which great philological academy, no toleration is given to words in '*osity*' or '*ation.*' There is, therefore, a great advantage, as regards the consecration to our feelings, settled, by usage and custom, upon the Saxon strands, in the mixed yarn of our native tongue. And, universally, this may be remarked — that, whenever the passion of a poem is of that sort, which *uses, presumes,* or *postulates* the ideas, without seeking to extend them, Saxon will be the 'cocoon' (to speak by the language applied to silkworms), which the poem spins for itself. But, on the other hand, when the motion of the feeling is *by* and *through* the ideas, where (as in religious or meditative poetry — Young's, for instance, or Cowper's) the pathos creeps and kindles underneath the very tissues of the thinking, there the Latin will predominate; and so much so, that, whilst the flesh, the blood, and the muscle, will be often almost exclusively Latin, the articulations only, or hinges of connections, will be Anglo-Saxon."

So unperverted were Shakespeare's instincts, so almost infallible, in the use of words, that the general vocabulary of a Play, or even the special vocabulary of a speech, is a quite reliable indication of the key in which it is pitched. Troilus and Cressida, for example, is the most intellectual of Shakespeare's Plays; — the wisdom with which it preëminently abounds, may be characterized as the wisdom of the intellect,* rather than the wisdom of the heart; and its intellectual character might be almost guessed by

---

* Dryden, who "corrected" the Troilus and Cressida, says of it in his Preface, "The Tragedy which I have undertaken to correct, was, in all probability, one of his [Shakespeare's] first endeavors on the stage"! Further on he says it was composed "in the Apprenticeship of his writing." On which Dr. John K. Ingram remarks, "How any person of moderate discernment could suppose that play, so full of knowledge of the world and all the fruits of ripe reflection, to have been the work of a very young man, I confess, passes my comprehension."

its Latin vocabulary alone. I have not taken the pains to estimate the percentage of its Latin vocabulary over that of other
plays ; but every reader of the Play must notice that this vocabu,
lary is signally more extensive than in a play with so large an ele
ment of homely pathos, for example, as is in King Lear.

The Anglo-Saxon element of the English language is largr /
monosyllabic ; and the part which monosyllabic words play in
Shakespeare's diction, is one that it is important to take accc,unt
of, in a study of his language-shaping as organically connected
with thought and feeling.

(It will be found that deep feeling of every kind expresses itself
through, and, indeed, attracts to itself, the monosyllabic words of
the language ; not only because such words are, for the most part,
Anglo-Saxon, and therefore more consecrated to feeling than to
thought, but because the staccato effect which can be secured
through them rather than through dissyllabic and trisyllabic words,
subserves well the natural movement of impassioned speech. Take,
for example, this passage from the Song of Deborah and Barak,
5th chapter of Judges, 27th verse : " At her feet he bowed, he
fell, he lay down : at her feet he bowed, he fell : where he bowed,
there he fell down dead."

The three following lines from Julic.'s speech to the Friar
(Romeo and Juliet, IV. 1. 84–86), afford a good example of
monosyllabic effect ; and the extra end-syllable of the the third
line, adds to the effect :

> " Or bid me go into a new-made grave,
> And hide me with a dead man in his shroud ;
> Things that to hear them told, have made me tremble ; "

And the following speeches :

> " *Montague.* . . . Hold me not, let me go.
> *Lady M.* Thou shalt not stir one foot to seek a foe."
> — R. and J. I. i. 72, 73.

When Juliet entreats to delay her marriage with Paris, her
mother replies :

" Talk not to me, for I'll not speak a word :
Do as thou wilt, for I have done with thee."
                                   — A. III. Sc. v. 204, 205.

In the speech of Martha to Jesus, John xi. 21, 22, "Lord, if thou hadst been here, my brother had not died. But I know, that even now, whatsoever thou wilt ask of God, God will give it thee," how much the feeling of the speaker is subserved by the monosyllabic words in which the speech is uttered !

When Una, in the Fairie Queene, meets with Archimago, in the disguise of the Red-Cross Knight, whom to find, she has wandered many a wood, and measured many a vale, weeping she addresses him, thinking him to be indeed her own true knight :

" Ah, my long lacked Lord,
Where have ye bene thus long out of my sight?
Much feared I to have bene quite abhord,
Or ought have done, that ye displeasen might,
That should as death unto my dear heart light :
For since mine eie your joyous sight did mis,
My chearefull day is turnd to cloudless night,
And eke my night, of death the shadow is ;
But welcome now, my light, and shining lamp of blis ! "

76 words, of which 72 are Saxon. The Saxon vocabularly alone, *as* Saxon, subserves the feeling of the speaker ; but how much in addition thereto the *utterance* of the feeling is subserved by the monosyllabic words ! Take especially the 2d verse of the stanza ;

"Where have ye bene thus long out of my sight?"

Note the staccato effect of the monosyllabic words, "So downe he fell," which are repeated four times in the 54th Stanza, of Canto XI. Book 1 of the Faerie Queene. The stanza occurs in the description of the slaying of the Dragon by the Red-Cross Knight :

" *So downe he fell*, and forth his life did breath,
That vanisht into smoke and cloudes swift ;
So downe he fell, that th' earth him underneath

Did grone, as feeble so great load to lift ;
So downe he fell, as an huge rocky clift,
Whose false foundacion waves have washt away,
With dreadfull poyse is from the mayneland rift,
And rolling downe great Neptune doth dismay :
So downe he fell, and like an heaped mountain *lay*."

The first verse is all monosyllabic. The final monosyllabic
word " lay," after the dissyllabic words " heapéd mountain," is
effective. So in Paradise Lost, Book X. vv. 541, 542 :

" down their arms,
Down fell both spear and shield ; down they as fast ; "

Note the prayerful tone imparted to the 2d and 3d Stanzas of
the Introductory Poem to Tennyson's " In Memoriam," by the
monosyllabic words of which, with one exception, they are entirely
composed. The exception is the word ' madest,' which is used
three times ; and even this word is monosyllabic without the
inflection. But being here a dissyllable, and being also the key
word of the stanza, it is isolated into prominence. It also ends
the stanza, and this fact gives it additional prominence :

" Thine are these orbs of light and shade ;
Thou madest Life in man and brute ;
Thou madest Death ; and lo, thy foot
Is on the skull which thou hast made.

Thou wilt not leave us in the dust ;
Thou madest man, he knows not why ;
He thinks he was not made to die ;
And thou hast made him : thou art just."

The same prayerful tone could not have been secured through
Latin dissyllabic words. In the two stanzas there are but 3 words,
not Anglo-Saxon in origin, "orbs," " brute," "just " — 3 words out
of 61.

No living poet has woven his song to such an extent as Tennyson has done, out of the Saxon vocabulary. " In Memoriam "

exhibits, perhaps, a greater percentage of Saxon words than any other poem of the same extent, in the literature, since the days of Chaucer; and this is largely owing to the genuine, unaffected feeling in which the subtlest conceptions are steeped. The 103d section, beginning " On that last night before we went From out the doors where I was bred," may be cited as an exámple of perfect poetic diction, simple, and almost as direct and free from inversion and involution, as the most unadorned and straightforward prose. Of the 381 words which it contains, 342 are Saxon, and but 39 of Latin, Greek, or other origin; 322 are monosyllabic; the 11th stanza is purely monosyllabic with the exception of the Latin word, " silence.")

King Lear, the homliest in its pathos, of all the Plays of Shakespeare, abounds in striking examples of staccato effect, secured through monosyllables :

> " Go tell the duke and's wife I'ld speak with them,
> Now, presently : bid them come forth and hear me,
> Or at their chamber-door I'll beat the drum
> Till it cry sleep to death."— A. II. Sc. iv. 112–115.

> " If you do love old men, if your sweet sway
> Allow obedience, if yourselves are old,
> Make it your cause ; send down, and take my part ! "

> " O sides, you are too tough ;
> Will you yet hold? How came my man in the stocks? "
> —A. II. Sc. iv. 187–189 ; 194, 195.

> " You see me here, you gods, a poor old man,
> As full of grief as age ; " . . .   —A. II. Sc. iv. 269, 270.

> " I will have such revenges on you both
> That all the world shall — I will do such things —
> What they are, yet I know not, but they shall be
> The terrors of the earth. You think I'll weep ;
> No ; I'll not weep : . . . .
> O fool, I shall go mad ! "— A. II. Sc. iv. 274–280 ; 283.

> " Blow, winds, and crack your cheeks ! rage ! blow ! "— A. III. Sc. ii. 1.

" My wits begin to turn.
Come on, my boy : how dost, my boy? art cold? "

"Poor fool and knave, I have one part in my heart
That's sorry yet for thee." — A. III. Sc. ii. 66, 67 ; 72, 73.

" No, I will weep no more. In such a night
To shut me out! Pour on ; I will endure.
In such a night as this !" . . .

" Your old kind father, whose frank heart gave you all, —
O, that way madness lies ; but let me shun that ;
No more of that." — A. III. Sc. iv. 17–19 ; 20–22.

" *Edg.* What will hap more to-night, safe 'scape the king !
Lurk, Lurk." — A. III. Sc. vi. 113, 114.

" *Corn.* . . . Upon these eyes of thine I'll set my foot.
Glou. He that will think to live till he be old,
Give me some help ! " — A. III. Sc. vii. 67–69.

" *Alb.* You are not worth the dust which the rude wind
Blows in your face." — A. IV. Sc. ii. 30, 31.

" *Lear.* Ha ! Goneril, with a white beard ! They flattered me
like a dog, and told me I had white hairs in my beard ere the
black ones were there. To say ' ay ' and ' no ' to every thing that
I said ! 'Ay' and 'no' too was no good divinity. When the
rain came to wet me once and the wind to make me chatter ;
when the thunder would not peace at my bidding ; there I found
'em, there I smelt 'em out. Go to, they are not men o' their
words : they told me I was every thing ; 'tis a lie, I am not ague-
proof." — A. IV. Sc. vi. 96–104.

" *Lear.* O, ho, are you there with me? No eyes in your head,
nor no money in your purse? Your eyes are in a heavy case, your
purse in a light : yet you see how this world goes." — A. IV. Sc. vi.
143–146.

" Thou know'st, the first time that we smell the air,
We wawl and cry. I will preach to thee : mark.

When we are born, we cry that we are come
To this great stage of fools.   This's a good block.
It were a delicate stratagem, to shoe
A troop of horse with felt: I'll put't in proof;
And when I have stolen upon these sons-in-law,
Then, kill, kill, kill, kill, kill, kill!"—A. IV. Sc. vi. 178–186.

"*Lear.* You do me wrong to take me out o' the grave:
Thou art a soul in bliss; but I am bound
Upon a wheel of fire, that mine own tears
Do scald like molten lead."

"*Cor.* Sir, do you know me?"

"*Lear.* You are a spirit, I know.   When did you die?"

"*Cor.* Still, still, far wide!"—A. IV. Sc. vii. 45–50.

"*Lear.* I know not what to say.
I will not swear these are my hands: let's see;
I feel this pin prick."—A. IV. Sc. vii. 54–56.

"*Lear.* No, no, no, no!   Come, let's away to prison:
We two alone will sing like birds i' the cage:
When thou dost ask me blessing, I'll kneel down
And ask of thee forgiveness: so we'll live,
And pray, and sing, and tell old tales, and laugh
At gilded butterflies, and hear poor rogues
Talk of court news; and we'll talk with them too,
Who loses and who wins, who's in, who's out;
And take upon us the mystery of things,
As if we were God's spies: and we'll wear out,
In a wall'd prison, packs and sects of great ones
That ebb and flow by the moon."—A. V. Sc. iii. 8–19.

"Wipe thine eyes;
The good-years shall devour them, flesh and fell,
Ere they shall make us weep: we'll see 'em starve first.
Come."—A. V. Sc. iii. 23–26.

"*Lear.* Howl, howl, howl, howl!   O, you are men of stones:
Had I your tongues and eyes, I'ld use them so

That heaven's vault should crack. She's gone forever!
I know when one is dead and when one lives;
She's dead as earth. Lend me a looking-glass;
If that her breath will mist or stain the stone,
Why, then she lives." — A. V. Sc. iii. 258–264.

"*Lear.* And my poor fool is hang'd! No, no, no life!
Why should a dog, a horse, a rat, have life,
And thou no breath at all? Thou'lt come no more,
Never, never, never, never, never!
Pray you, undo this button: thank you, sir.
Do you see this? Look on her, look, her lips,
Look there, look there!"   [*Dies.*
     — A. V. Sc. iii. 306–312.

No other than a monosyllabic vocabulary, and that vocabulary, too, the Saxon vocabulary of every-day life, would serve so effectually to express the homely pathos involved in the two last speeches.

Observe the effect secured by the monosyllabic words, in the following passage from King John, A. III. Sc. iii. They serve to convey the impression of a close confidence. The King is speaking to Hubert and hesitates to declare openly his wish to have the little prince Arthur put out of the way. To the speech of Hubert, "I am much bounden to your majesty," the King replies:

"Good friend, thou hast no cause to say so yet,
 But thou shalt have; and creep time ne'er so slow,
 Yet it shall come for me to do thee good.
 I had a thing to say, but let it go."

The entire speech, of which these are the opening lines, is a wonder of metrical movement. The sense is kept suspended through twenty-one verses, though the mind and ear are promised here and there, a descent which is nevertheless withheld, till we come to the lines, "I would into thy bosom pour my thoughts: But, ah, I will not! yet I love thee well; And, by my troth, I think thou lov'st me well."

Observe how the abruptness of strong feeling is subserved by the monosyllabic words in the following passage from the same play, A. IV. Sc. iii. Salisbury says to the Bastard,

> " Stand by, or I shall gall you, Faulconbridge."

The Bastard replies in great anger,

> " Thou wert better gall the devil, Salisbury:
> If thou but frown on me or stir thy foot,
> Or teach thy hasty spleen to do me shame,
> I'll strike thee dead. Put up thy sword betime;
> Or I'll so maul you and your toasting-iron,
> That you shall think the devil is come from hell."

And a little further on, in the same Scene, when the Bastard expresses to Hubert his suspicions that he (Hubert) has killed the young Prince, note the staccato effect of the monosyllabic words of which some of the clauses are entirely composed.

The Bastard says:

> " Here's a good world!   Knew you of this fair work?
> Beyond the infinite and boundless reach
> Of mercy, *if thou didst this deed of death*,
> Art thou damn'd, Hubert."

The effect of the staccato movement of the clause, "if thou didst this deed of death," is enforced by the lengthened movement of what immediately precedes:

> " Beyond the infinite and boundless reach of mercy,
> If thou didst this deed of death,
> Art thou damn'd, Hubert.
> *Hub.* Do but hear me, sir.
> *Bast.* Ha! I'll tell thee what;
> Thou'rt damn'd as black, — nay, nothing is so black;
> Thou art more deep damn'd than Prince Lucifer:
> There is not yet so ugly a fiend of hell
> As thou shalt be, *if thou didst kill this child*."

Note the effect of the monosyllabic words, in the oft-repeated " I'll have my bond," in Shylock's speech to Antonio (Merchant of Venice, A. III. Sc. iii.) ; they suggest, as Charles and Mary Cowden Clarke say, in their "Shakespeare Key," the bark of the ' dog' he taunts Antonio with having called him :

> " *I'll have my bond;* speak not against my bond :
> I have sworn an oath that *I will have my bond.*
> Thou call'dst me dog before thou hadst a cause ;
> But, since I am a dog, beware my fangs. . . .
> *Antonio.* I pray thee hear me speak.
> *Shylock. I'll have my bond;* I will not hear thee speak :
> *I'll have my bond;* and therefore speak no more. . . .
> I'll have no speaking : *I will have my bond.*"

In the following speech of Constance (King John, A. III. Sc. iv.), the iteration of the monosyllabic words, " I am not mad," and the additional monosyllabic vocabulary, subserve well the expression of her passionate grief :

> " *Pand.* Lady, you utter madness, and not sorrow.
> *Const.* Thou art not holy to belie me so ;
> I am not mad. This hair I tear is mine ;
> My name is Constance ; I was Geffrey's wife ;
> Young Arthur is my son, and he is lost :
> I am not mad, — I would to heaven, I were !
> For then, 'tis like I should forget myself :
> O, if I could, what grief should I forget ! —
> Preach some philosophy to make me mad,
> And thou shalt be canonized, cardinal ;
> For, being not mad, but sensible of grief,
> My reasonable part produces reason
> How I may be deliver'd of these woes,
> And teaches me to kill or hang myself :
> If I were mad, I should forget my son ;
> Or madly think a babe of clouts were he.
> I am not mad, too well, too well I feel
> The different plague of each calamity.

It will also be found that the more violent feelings of anger, hate, detestation, scorn, etc., in addition to their attracting to themselves the monosyllabic words of the language, express themselves on the abrupt vowels of words ; while the gentler feelings of love or admiration or of the beautiful, express themselves on the prolongable vowels.

Examples of special effect secured by emphasis on abrupt vowels, abound throughout the Tragedies and Histories. Take for example the following speeches of Gloster, in Richard III. A. I. Sc. iii. 103 *et seq.*, in which he replies to Elizabeth, queen to Edward IV., and to Queen Margaret, widow of Henry VI. :

" *Queen Eliz.* My Lord of Gloster, I have too long borne
Your blunt upbraidings and your bitter scoffs;
By heaven I will acquaint his majesty
Of those gross taunts that oft I have endur'd. . . .

   Enter QUEEN MARGARET, *behind, where she remains.*

Small joy have I in being England's queen.
 Queen Marg. And lessen'd be that small, God, I beseech him!
Thy honor, state, and seat is due to me.
 Gloster (*in anger*). Whăt! thrĕat you me with tĕlling of the King?
Tĕll him, and spare nŏt: *look*, what I have said
I will avouch in prĕsĕnce of the King ; . . .
 Queen Marg. Out, devil! I remember them too well.
Thou kill'dst my husband Henry in the Tower,
And Edward, my poor son, at Tewksbury.
 Gloster. Ere you were queen, ay, or your husband King,
I was a păck-horse in his great affairs : . . .
To royalize hĭs blood I spent mine own.
 Queen Marg. Ay, and much bĕtter blood than his or thine.
 Gloster. In all which time, you and your husband Grey,
Were făctious for the house of Lancaster ; —
And, Rivers, so were you. —Was not your husband
In Margaret's battle at Saint Alban's slain?
Let me put in your minds, if you forget,
What you have been ere this, and what you are ;
Withal, what I have been, and what I am."

The italicized vowels in Gloster's speeches should be uttered with a strongly percussive force. An extra effect is secured through the words "telling" and "Tell," by carrying the voice (after uttering the abrupt vowel, *ĕ*, with a percussive force) through a wide upward interval on *l* in "telling," and a wide downward interval on *l* in "Tell"—the latter having a haughtily defiant effect. The staccato effect secured through the monosyllabic words in the three last lines, "Let me put in your minds," etc., subserves well the highly wrought feelings of the speaker.

Good examples occur throughout the quarrel scene between Brutus and Cassius, in Julius Cæsar, A. IV. Sc. iii.

ROMEO AND JULIET.

IN Romeo and Juliet, Shakespeare's first tragedy, we have what
has been well called the lyric melody of passion. In the poet's
growth, this lyric melody of passion is gradually developed into
what Dowden calls 'the orchestral symphony of emotion which
envelops us when we approach King Lear.'

There is a sentence in King Lear which might serve as a motto
to the Tragedy of Romeo and Juliet. The King of France says
to Burgundy, after Cordelia has been cast off by her father:

> " My lord of Burgundy,
> What say you to the lady? Love's not love
> When it is mingled with regards that stand
> Aloof from the entire point." — A. I. Sc. i. 242.

That is, Love's not love when it is mingled with considerations
that stand aloof from the main point of affection. True love
ignores all such considerations. Or a portion of the 116th Sonnet
would serve as an appropriate motto :

> " Let me not to the marriage of true minds
> Admit impediments. Love . . .
> . . . is an ever-fixed mark,
> That looks on tempests and is never shaken ;
> *   *   *   *   *   *   *   *
> Love's not Time's fool, tho' rosy lips and cheeks
> Within his bending sickle's compass come ;
> Love alters not with his brief hours and weeks,
> But bears it out even to the edge of doom."

In Romeo and Juliet, love is represented as entirely divorced
from all considerations which stand aloof from the entire point —

from the main point of affection. And there is not in the play any *vicarious* condemnation of such divorcement; I mean by vicarious condemnation, that which is uttered by a character in the place of the poet himself. There *is* a moderation enjoined upon Romeo by Friar Laurence; but all that he says is said *in propria persona,* and not vicariously. Love becomes the agency for developing a pair of young and exquisitely organized human beings into heroic manhood and heroic womanhood. And tragic as are, or may be regarded, the consequences of their love, their devotion unto death not only completes their lives, but effects a reconcilement of the bitterly hostile houses which they represent. As the Prologue expresses it, their " misadventured piteous overthrows do with their death bury their parents' strife, which but their children's end nought could remove."

This, Shakespeare's first tragedy, it is all important to regard from the right standpoint, as it can be taken as illustrative of the poet's characteristic mode of presenting strong passion, — a mode which may best be called Shakespearian. In Ben Jonson's Comedies, his characters are often personifications rather than personalities — personifications of autocratic moods or humors. He has been called a dramatic Dickens. Again, we see in other dramatists, a predetermination to elucidate the effects of some mastering passion, or of some social principle. In the case of Shakespeare the critic is likely to go astray, if he see such predeterminations; is likely to ascribe an undue place, in his creative work, to the conscious understanding, and to moral verdicts on the part of the poet. I cannot but think that critics have gone more astray in this respect, in their treatment of Romeo and Juliet, simple as is the melody of the passion, than in the treatment of almost any other play. They have, with but few exceptions, attributed to Shakespeare the predetermination in this play, of exhibiting the bad, the fatal consequences of violent, unrestrained passion : and the importance of moderation — of observing the golden mean between too much and too little ; and in accordance with this view, they have regarded Friar Laurence as the poet's

own spokesman, put into the play for the special purpose of vicariously giving voice to the moderate and the prudential. Such a
mode of proceeding may be necessary to dramatists of an inferior
order, whose work moves under the condition of a *notion* of some
kind. But Shakespeare's plays, *none* of them, move under such
condition. He chose the subject of Romeo and Juliet for its
passionate capabilities; he is the artistic physiologist of human
passions. And by artistic physiologist I mean, that he treats the
passions under the condition of the moral constitution of things,
but not as a moralist.

Shakespeare is always especially happy in the opening scenes of
his Plays. They generally strike the keynote of the whole dramatic
action. Romeo and Juliet is no exception to this. Furthermore,
the opening scene is, of itself, a sufficient refutation of much of the
commentary on the play, which ascribes, as we shall see further on,
the misadventured piteous overthrows of the two lovers, to *subjective* causes — to causes existing within themselves — to the immod-
erateness, the rashness, the impetuosity, of their loves, rather than
to *objective* causes — to the ancient grudge between the "two
households, both alike in dignity," which, in the words of the
Prologue, "break to new mutiny, where civil blood makes civil
hands unclean."

If the misadventured piteous overthrows of the two lovers were
primarily due to subjective causes, and the mutual hatred of their
families were only a secondary cause, the poet would hardly have
opened the play with the angry contention in the streets, between
the servants of the households, which has to be suppressed by the
Prince of Verona, the representative of the state. When the fight
is at its hottest, —

> "*Enter old* CAPULET, *in his gown; and Lady* CAPULET.
>
> *Cap.* What noise is this? Give me my long sword, ho!
> *La. Cap.* A crutch, a crutch! Why call you for a sword?
> *Cap.* My sword, I say! Old Montague is come,
> And flourishes his blade in spite of me.

Enter old MONTAGUE *and Lady* MONTAGUE.

Mon. Thou villain Capulet! Hold me not, let me go.
La. Mon. Thou shalt not stir one foot to seek a foe.

Enter PRINCE, *with his train.*

Rebellious subjects, enemies to peace,
Profaners of this neighbour-stained steel, —
Will they not hear? — what, ho! you men, you beasts,
That quench the fire of your pernicious rage
With purple fountains issuing from your veins,
On pain of torture, from those bloody hands
Throw your mistemper'd weapons to the ground,
And hear the sentence of your moved prince.
Three civil brawls, bred of an airy word,
By thee, old Capulet, and Montague,
Have thrice disturb'd the quiet of our streets,
And made Verona's ancient citizens
Cast by their grave beseeming ornaments,
To wield old partisans, in hands as old,
Canker'd with peace, to part your canker'd hate;
If ever you disturb our streets again,
Your lives shall pay the forfeit of the peace.
For this time, all the rest depart away:
You, Capulet, shall go along with me;
And, Montague, come you this afternoon,
To know our farther pleasure in this case,
To old Free-town, our common judgment place.
Once more, on pain of death, all men depart."

If the commentary on the play is correct, which ascribes the
sorrows of the two lovers to their own characters (and it constitutes by far the largest portion of that commentary), then this
opening scene is not in Shakespeare's manner; and even if judged
by an absolute standard, it is artistically faulty — the most artistically faulty of all the opening scenes of his Plays. But, as I
understand the play, Shakespeare, in this opening scene, strikes the
keynote of the whole dramatic action — which dramatic action is
due entirely to the outward circumstances with which the lovers

are to be brought into a fatal conflict — and strikes it loudly ; emphasizes the intensity of the hatred between the Capulets and the Montagues — a hatred which interferes with public peace and public security, and demands the interposition of the highest authority of the commonwealth.

In this state of things, the two lovers are placed, the one a Montague and the other a Capulet ; and their mutual love is of that completely absorbing character that it sets at defiance all outward considerations and obstacles which oppose its course — a course of true love which, it can at once be seen, can*not* run smooth, but will be kept in violent, boiling agitation until it ends in the repose of the grave.

This, then, is the dramatic situation : two lovers, whose souls are completely absorbed in each other, are brought in conflict with a hatred which has existed between their two families for many generations, and which time has not softened, but rather intensified. For, at the period when the play opens, the ancient grudge of the "two households, both alike in dignity," is dramatically presented to us as broken out into new mutiny, and things are at their worst.

Romeo is first presented to us in love with an obdurate fair, named Rosaline, who will give no ear to the young man's suit ; and the next important points to be considered are, the character and the artistic significance of this first love. There is danger of an essential misunderstanding of it — a misunderstanding which has been encouraged by some of the leading critics of the play — by most of the leading critics of the play, and which Mrs. Jameson, in her "Characteristics of Shakespeare's Women," has most strongly set forth. She calls Romeo's first love a "visionary passion"; represents him as "the thrall of a dreaming, fanciful passion," after the style of the fantastic school of gallantry.

Romeo's first love being so understood, its introduction into the play is wholly superfluous — it is merely an intrusion, an excrescence ; and more than that : Romeo, in being first introduced as a merely conventional lover, with a *visionary* passion, after the style of the fantastic school of gallantry, would be too much lowered in our estimation, would forfeit too much our respect for him, to be, afterwards, with Juliet, the representative of the power and the triumph of love, which it is certainly the purpose of the play poetically to idealize.

Ulrici, in his "Shakespeare's Dramatic Art," after setting forth his view of the *destructive excess* of the passion of the lovers, Romeo and Juliet, and after representing Romeo as carried away, as it were, by some malignant and irresistible impulse, adds : " In order to *throw out this caprice in a still stronger light,* Shakespeare introduces him to us in a *dreamy passion* for Rosaline." Which is about equivalent to saying that Shakespeare does his extreme best to render Romeo unworthy of our respect. According to Ulrici, he is a better subject for comedy than for a deep tragedy.

Kreyzig, in his "Vorlesungen über Shakespeare," says : "We make the acquaintance of Romeo at the critical period of that not dangerous sickness to which youth is liable." He calls it " that love lying in the eyes of early and just blooming manhood, that humorsome, whimsical 'love in idleness,' that first, bewildered, stammering interview of the heart with the scarcely awakened nature. Strangely enough," he says, " objections have been made to this 'superfluous complication,' as if down to this day, every Romeo had not to sigh for some full-blown Junonian Rosaline, nay, for half a dozen Rosalines, more or less, before his eyes open upon his Juliet." That's true enough. But this fact doesn't answer the objections which, strangely enough, he says, have been made to this superfluous complication. The objection stills holds good when all that is said against it is, that it's a common thing for a young man to have an early love before he finds his Juliet. Well, it's a common thing for a child to have the measles, or the mumps ; but an artist would not introduce a child into a play and represent it as having the measles, or the mumps, unless he had some artistic purpose in so doing. Let us look for the "proof of design and self-supporting arrangement" which are everywhere found in Shakespeare.

Shakespeare never adopts anything from his original without making it *organic* — that is, an element of the action of his drama. What he adopts may be in the original story an excrescence ; but it becomes in the play a part of its organic vitality. This is as true of Romeo's first love as of any adoption in any of the Plays. He found it in the old story, but he did not retain it merely because it was there. That can be said with perfect assurance. If it had not suited his purpose, he could easily, and would, have eliminated it. His power of rejecting was as great as his power of appropriating. He did both with equal judgment and skill. And he was quick to detect the dramatic capability of this first love when he met with it in the old story.

We find, on referring to the original of Romeo and Juliet, namely, the old English poem, by Arthur Brooke, entitled "The Tragicall Historye of Romeus and Iuliet," published in 1562, that Shakespeare has modified, in two important particulars, what Brooke says of this first love ; and we can see by this modification, his dramatic purpose. [For the history of the old story, its various forms, etc., see Mr. P. A. Daniel's Introduction to his edition of Romeus and Iuliet, by Arthur Brooke, and "Rhomeo and Iulietta," by William Painter, published by the New Shakspere Society, in 1875. That Brooke's Poem was Shakespeare's original, is conclusively shown by the Editor.]

In Brooke's poem, Romeo, after repeated failures to make any impression upon the heart of the fair maid he loves, is represented as thinking to leave Verona and to try if *change of place* might change away his ill-bestowed love. He reflects :

> " Perhaps mine eye once banished by absence from her sight,
>   This fire of mine, that by her pleasant eyes is fed,
>   Shall little and little wear away, and quite at last be dead."
>
> vv. 86-88.

Here Romeo, although he is represented as loving deeply, has not so entirely surrendered his individuality, but that he retains considerable power of asserting his selfhood. There's a portion

of himself, a pretty big portion, we must suppose, belonging to
himself. The absorption of his individuality in one of the opposite sex is not complete. Again, when his friend who, in the play
is called Benvolio (he is nameless in the poem, as is also the obdurate fair one), when his friend advises him to turn his eyes in
other directions, and endeavor to seek out "some one of beauty,
favor, shape, and lovely carriage," upon whom to bestow his
heart, and thus forget his present love,

> " The young man's listening ears received the wholesome sound,
> And Reason's truth yplanted so, within his head had ground;
> That now with healthy cool ytempered is the heat,
> And peacemeal wears away the grief, that erst his heart did fret; "
>
> vv. 141–144.

and he plights to his friend a solemn oath that, at every feast by
day, and banquet by night, at church, at games in open street,
and everywhere he would resort where ladies were accustomed to
assemble. All this is strong and conclusive evidence that, as a
lover, he was not so very far gone. The poem then goes on to
relate how Romeo went to a banquet given by the Capulets, and
there fell in love with Juliet, just as in the play. It will be observed, in the first place, how the play follows the poem in a
general way, and in what important particulars it departs from
it; and those departures bear testimony to the poet's dramatic
purpose.

Romeo in the play presents a strong contrast, as the lover of
Rosaline, to the Romeo of Brooke's poem. In the play his absorption is so complete that he has no power to assert, in the
least, his selfhood, as he does in the poem. The gentleness of
his nature, the dramatist has also emphasized. He is presented
in strong contrast with the fiery Tybalt, and with the general dis-
cordant spirit around him. Tieck says, "in good fortune, as in
bad, he is violent and rough." But he says this in the service of
his theory. The play certainly does not so represent him.

Romeo's first love is represented in A. I. Sc. ii. 123–244. In

the speeches of Benvolio and old Montague, we have evidence
only of a genuine, all-absorbing passion, not a fanciful one.   His
love has been a thing too sacred to allow him even to speak of
the object of it, to his parents and closest friends.   His father
neither knows, nor can learn of him, the secret of his grief.   The
advice of his friend, Benvolio, to give liberty to his eyes, and to
examine other beauties, calls forth a response quite different from
that in the poem to the same kind of advice.   In the poem we
read :

> " To his approved friend, a solemn oath he plight,
>   At every feast ykept by day, and banquet made by night,
>   At pardons in the church, at games in open street,
>   And everywhere he would resort where ladies wont to meet."
>
> vv. 145–148.

Romeo's response in the play to his friend's advice (A. I. Sc. i.
231–244), is quite of another tune :

> " *Ben.*   Be rul'd by me, forget to think of her.
>   *Rom.*   O teach me how I should forget to think.
>   *Ben.*   By giving liberty unto thine eyes ;
> Examine other beauties.
>   *Rom.*   'Tis the way
> To call hers, exquisite, in question more :
> These happy masks, that kiss fair ladies brows,
> Being black, put us in mind they hide the fair :
> He that is strucken blind, cannot forget
> The precious treasure of his eyesight lost :
> Show me a mistress that is passing fair,
> What doth her beauty serve, but as a note
> Where I may read who pass'd that passing fair?
> Farewell : thou canst not teach me to forget.
>   *Ben.*   I'll pay that doctrine, or else die in debt."

In the poem, the nameless object of Romeo's first love does
not appear at the banquet of the Capulets : and Romeo goes to it
to seek out a new beauty.   In the play, Rosaline is included in
Capulet's invitation, and called " my fair niece Rosaline " ; and it

is entirely in the hope of seeing *her* that Romeo, having read for the servant the names of those invited, decides to go to the entertainment, though it's a perilous thing to do, to go uninvited to the house of his mortal enemy.

Romeo, be it understood, is presented to us in the play, as a representative of a most refined and exalted sexual love — a love which finally develops him into full manhood. And his constitutional fitness for such a love is first shown us through his unrequited love for Rosaline. And when he is first presented to us, he is suffering " the pangs of disprized love." Byron says " Man's love is of man's life a thing apart, 'Tis woman's whole existence." But this characterization of man's love will not suit Romeo's ; for he has been raised up especially by the poet to exhibit sexual love in its most refined, exalted, and exalting form. If his first love had been even partially requited ; if the object of that first love had been *incapable,* suppose, of *fully* requiting his love, but had requited it to the extent of her power of loving, he would not have been justified in transferring it, even if he had transferred it upon one capable of fully requiting it. But it was wholly *un*requited. This the poet has emphasized ; and thus unmistakingly indicated that the soul of Romeo is *free* to accept a response from another soul, when that response comes. *And it can be true to itself only by so doing.* It is evident, too, that the poet's purpose is that Romeo's soul shall be brought just to that temper which renders its response to a kindred soul, spontaneous and immediate. When he meets with Juliet, his love is something other than what is generally signified by love at first sight. It is of a more spiritual character. And that more spiritual character is largely due, we must suppose, to his previous subjective state, induced by his unrequited love.

The next feature of the play which it is important to note, is Juliet's situation and surroundings, before she meets with Romeo.

The 3d Scene of the 1st Act indicates, was meant to indicate, the imperfect sympathy, or rather *no*-sympathy, which her two closest companions, almost her only companions, her mother and her nurse, had with the young girl's most secret being; which secret being when it is revealed by her love for Romeo, must, we are assured, before that love was awakened, have had a strong consciousness of this imperfect or *no*-sympathy, on the part of the mother and nurse, and of all around her, and must have been ready for an immediate and full response to the first kindred and sympathetic soul she should meet with. In the preceding scene, to the inquiry of the County Paris, "But now, my lord, what say you to my suit?" Capulet replies, "My child is yet a stranger in the world; she hath not seen the change of fourteen years." This indicates the seclusion in which she had been kept up to this time. But it does not necessarily indicate that her soul has been without cravings for sympathy such as those around her were incapable of affording. In the 3d Scene, Lady Capulet's idea of marriage is revealed to us, as is also that of the gross-minded nurse. Marriage is to both a mere arrangement, and has nothing to do with the *souls* of those entering into this arrangement. Lady Capulet says, "Tell me, daughter Juliet, how stands your disposition to be married?" She knows her daughter's heart has not gone out toward any one; but what of that? It is about time, she thinks, she were married. "Younger than you," she continues, "here in Verona, ladies of esteem, are made already mothers: by my count, I was your mother much upon these years, that you are now a maid. Thus then, in brief: The valiant Paris seeks you for his love." The nurse interposes, "A man, young lady! lady, such a man, as all the world — why, he's a man of wax."

Lady Capulet, as is evident from a following speech, expects her daughter to give an immediate answer in regard to her marrying a man whom she has never seen: "What say you? can you love the gentleman?" And then after expatiating merely upon his personal appearance, she says, with some impatience (Juliet, as we must suppose, not having shown a very warm interest in this to her unknown fine gentleman), "speak briefly, can you like of Paris' love?" Juliet, who hitherto has known only submission to the wishes of mother and nurse, replies, "I'll look to like, if looking liking move." This little speech sufficiently indicates that whither her heart goes, there will follow her hand, and not elsewhere. Of Juliet's aptitude for a deep all-absorbing love, a love "that looks on tempests and is never shaken," we have no other intimation, previous to her meeting with Romeo. But any stronger intimation would be objectionable ; and the poet has accordingly given us only this slight hint, that Juliet is not disposed to marriage for its own sake, and that to her, marriage can be honorable only on a true ethical basis.

The two other lines which she utters in connection with the line just quoted, it is important to note :

> " But no more deep will I endart mine eye
> Than your consent gives strength to make it fly."

They indicate the point from which to estimate Juliet's transition, through the developing, strengthening, exalting power of love, from mere submissive femineity to self-sustained, self-asserting, heroic, and triumphant womanhood.

She and Romeo meet at the Capulet masquerade, and such is their previous preparedness for each other, that " a single word, a single look, a single touch, have joined two hearts in a moment and forever."

The heart of each

> " Responds, as if with unseen wings,
> An angel touched its quivering strings ;
> And whispers, in its song,
> 'Where hast thou stayed so long!'"

To adapt a simile in Tennyson's " Princess," as the lily folds all her sweetness up, and *slips* into the bosom of the lake, so Juliet folds herself and slips into Romeo's bosom, and is lost in him.

In the loss of themselves in each other, Romeo and Juliet find themselves. But with Romeo, the finding of self in the loss of self, is not so immediately complete as it is with Juliet. And it is dramatically just that Romeo should not be so suddenly freed from self-consciousness as is Juliet. A man is rarely so suddenly

freed from self-consciousness in love as is a woman. We have this
exhibited in the garden scene which follows — the 2d Scene of
the 2d act — the most nearly flawless, in its composition, of the
entire play. It should be noted that the imagery indulged in,
sometimes passing into the fanciful, is nearly all in Romeo's
speeches; such for example as:

> " Two of the fairest stars in all the heaven,
> Having some business, do intreat her eyes
> To twinkle in their spheres till they return.
> What if her eyes were there, they in her head?
> The brightness of her cheek would shame those stars,
> As daylight doth a lamp; her eyes in heaven
> Would through the airy region stream so bright,
> That birds would sing and think it were not night."

Juliet is direct, straightforward, as if possessed with a deep
sense of what she has entered upon.

Shakespeare makes the progress of occurrences which follow
the marriage much more rapid than in the original poem, where
we are told,

> " The summer of their blisse, doth last a month or twain;
> But winter's blast with speedy foot, doth bring the fall again.
> Whom glorious fortune erst had heavéd to the skies,
> By envious fortune overthrown, on earth now groveling lies.
> She paid their former grief with pleasure's doubled gain,
> But now for pleasure's usury, tenfold redoubleth pain."

vv. 949–954.

The poem then goes on to relate a new outbreak, in the general
course of outbreaks, of bloody hostilities, "the morrow after
Easter day," Tybalt being chosen as the leader of the Capulets.
Romeo, walking with his friends, comes upon the scene, and
endeavors to allay the strife,

> " to part and bar the blows
> As well of those that were his friends, as of his deadly foes."

vv. 1005, 1006.

Tybalt, without provocation, furiously attacks Romeo, who tells him he does him wrong, as his purpose is only to part the fray, and that not dread but other weighty cause stays his hand — the weighty cause being his marriage with Tybalt's cousin Juliet, a fact which Tybalt does not know of. Tybalt is deaf to reason, and forces Romeo to defend himself. The result is that

" Our Romeus thrust him thro' the throat, and so is Tybalt slain."
                                                        v. 1034.

In the play, there's a modification of what is given in the poem in the conduct and construction of the action, — a modification which it is important to note, as it is in the service of the exhibition of Romeo's character — his gentleness and his honorableness are strongly brought out by the modification. Tybalt is the evil genius of discord set over against Romeo, the loving and the beloved. In the poem, Tybalt does not, as in the play, figure at the masquerade : he is not even alluded to as being there. In the poem, a month or twain after the marriage of the lovers, which has been kept a secret, he attacks Romeo when the latter attempts to allay the strife, simply because he is a Montague, not from any special offence. But in the play, Tybalt, previous to his fatal encounter with Romeo, is specially enraged against him, for his bold and, as he regards it, insulting intrusion at the masquerade : hearing there Romeo's voice, he says :

" This, by his voice, should be a Montague : —
Fetch me my rapier, boy : — What ! dares the slave
Come hither, cover'd with an antic face,
To fleer and scorn at our solemnity?
Now, by the stock and honour of my kin,
To strike him dead I hold it not a sin.
    Cap. Why, how now, kinsman? wherefore storm you so?
    Tyb. Uncle, this is a Montague, our foe ;
A villain, that is hither come in spite,
To scorn at our solemnity this night.
    Cap. Young Romeo, is't?
    Tyb. 'Tis he, that villain Romeo.

Cap. Content thee, gentle coz, let him alone,
He bears him like a portly gentleman ;
And, to say truth, Verona brags of him
To be a virtuous and well-govern'd youth :
I would not for the wealth of all this town,
Here in my house do him disparagement :
Therefore be patient, take no note of him :
It is my will ; the which if thou respect,
Show a fair presence, and put off these frowns,
An ill-beseeming semblance for a feast.
     Tyb. It fits, when such a villain is a guest ;
I'll not endure him.
     Cap.   He shall be endur'd.
What, goodman boy ! I say, he shall : Go to ;
Am I the master here, or you? go to.
You'll not endure him ! God shall mend my soul —
You'll make a mutiny among my guests !
You will set cock-a-hoop ! you'll be the man !
     Tyb. Why, uncle, 'tis a shame.
     Cap.   Go to, go to ;
You are a saucy boy : — Is't so indeed?
This trick may chance to scathe you — I know what.
You must contrary me ! — marry, 'tis time —
Well said, my hearts ! — You are a princox ; go
Be quiet, or — More light, more light ! for shame !
I'll make you quiet ; What ! — Cheerly, my hearts !
     Tyb. Patience perforce with wilful choler meeting
Makes my flesh tremble in their different greeting.
I will withdraw : but this intrusion shall,
Now seeming sweet, convert to bitter gall."   [*Exit.*

In the play, the heat of the day on which Romeo and Juliet
are married is not yet over, when Tybalt, brooding upon the in-
sult conceived the previous night at the ball, meets with Romeo's
friends, Mercutio and Benvolio (A. III. Sc. i. 40). The personal
encounter which soon follows takes the place of the general fray
we have in the poem, a month or twain after the marriage. In
comparing the play with the poem, we are helped to see, but it
is plain to see without such outside help, at what special pains,

pains which have gone for nothing with some commentators, the poet was, to exhibit the sweetly gentle character of Romeo (and he has a true manly valor, withal; he's no coward), and perfectly to justify his slaying of Tybalt. There's not the slightest rashness in the act. What he does he does when forbearance ceases to be a virtue. Tieck says, without any authority whatever from the play, that "in good fortune as in bad, he is violent and rough." But as Skottowe has noted, it not appearing enough to the dramatist, that Tybalt, as in the poem, should be the unprovoked aggressor, or that Romeo's self-command should only be overcome by repeated insults, he adds the aggravation of Mercutio's murder — a murder due, also, to Romeo's coming between them, with the good intention of parting them. Romeo has patiently endured Tybalt's treatment of himself, by reason of his marriage with Juliet, his love for her being reflected upon her kinsman; but when his friend Mercutio is slain in his behalf, and the furious Tybalt comes back again, he exclaims: "Alive! in triumph! and Mercutio slain! Away to heaven, respective lenity" (that is, the lenity he has thus far shown, out of regard to his relationship to Tybalt, by his marriage with Juliet), "and fire-eyed fury be my conduct now" (that is, conductor or guide)! "Now, Tybalt, take the villain back again, that late thou gavest me."

Under the circumstances, the poet could not have preserved to us the requisite respect for Romeo, in any other way. He also emphasizes Romeo's gentle forbearance and honorable conduct, through what Benvolio is made to relate of the affair to the Prince (A. III. Sc. i. 157–180). The point to be especially noted is, that the cause of what proves such a misfortune to Romeo lies *outside of himself,* and is not at all attributable, as most commentators attribute it, to Romeo's own character. He and Juliet are "star-crossed lovers." That's the important thing to note. And if it is not sufficiently noted, if the lovers, in themselves considered, are regarded as responsible for their misfortunes, an entirely false understanding of the play must be the result. The poet's dramatic purpose demanded that Romeo's character should be, throughout, such as not in the least to damage that purpose, which, I repeat, is, to exhibit the moral energy induced by an all-absorbing love in conflict with the most adverse circumstances. All the calamities to which that love is subjected are represented as due, exclusively due, to objective, outside causes.

Before the sad sentence of banishment imposed upon Romeo by the Prince is known to her, comes Juliet's lovely Epithalamium (A. III. Sc. ii.), the fullest signification of which depends on a proper understanding of "runaway's eyes," in the 6th line :

> " Spread thy close curtain, love-performing night,
> That runaway's eyes may wink, and Romeo
> Leap to these arms, untalk'd of and unseen."

No *crux criticorum* in all the plays of Shakespeare has occasioned such an amount of commentary as has this. But I think it should be considered as put forever at rest, by the explanation of N. J. Halpin, as given in the 2d volume of "The (old) Shakespeare Society's Papers," 1845. He has shown with entire conclusiveness from ancient mythology, and from contemporary epithalamic and other erotic poems, that "runaway" means Cupid : who, in reference to his runaway propensity, was called by the Greeks δραπετης δραπετίδας, of which the English runaway is an exact translation, and by the Latins, *fugitivus, profugus, vagus ;* and by the English, truant, deserter, wanderer, vagrant, vagabond, runagate.

"Assuming this interpretation established," says Halpin, "we arrive at the full hymeneal meaning of the passage ; which, stripped of its conventional diction, appears to be this : Secrecy is essential to our safety. Let the day, therefore, depart, and let Night spread her curtain around, and let not Cupid discharge his ministry of lighting-up the bride-chamber. If (as painted by some) he have eyes, let them wink — *i.e.,* be darkened ; for we have need of darkness, that the interview, being invisible, may be untalked-of : and we have no need of light, because lovers can see by their own beauties. If, however (as depicted by others), he be blind, it is all as it should be : his blindness agrees with that darkness, for the sake of which the presence of night is so desirable.

"The passage, . . . should be printed and pointed thus:

> " 'Spread thy close curtain, love-performing Night!
> That Run-away's eyes may wink, and Romeo
> Leap to these arms untalked-of and unseen.
> Lovers can see to do their amorous rites
> By their own beauties: or, if Love be blind —
> It best agrees with Night.'

"And now it may be asked, how comes Juliet so conversant with the topics and diction of this class of poetry: and why, on this occasion, does she pour out her heart in its language?

"In answer to the first we may observe, that the nuptial pageant had, at that time, become common and popular in England. Our scene, it is true, lies in Italy; but it matters little whether the Italians observed the same custom or not; for Shakespeare gives to every country the manners of his own; and, on this cosmopolitan principle, he has (in common with some of his dramatic contemporaries) given proof of the habitual occurrence of such festivities in his time, by celebrating with the nuptial mask the marriage of some of his heroines.

"From the prevalence of the practice, then, it is to be assumed that Juliet had witnessed the bridal ceremonies of many of her young companions, and, like other noble persons of the day, ' expressed a most real affection ' to the parties by taking a character in the mask. Thus might she have caught up the topics and language appropriated to this species of poetry: and hence may be inferred her familiarity with thoughts and expressions not likely, in any other way, to have obtained entrance into the mind of an innocent and unsophisticated girl of fourteen years of age.

"And why (in the second place) does she harp upon this string on the present occasion?

"Alas, poor Juliet! who is there that, in the concomitant circumstances, does not see the reason? It is her bridal day; but, a bridal without its triumphs. . . .

" Her marriage is clandestine. She can have no hymeneal mask. No troops of friends led her to the church, nor followed her to the banquet. No father — no mother — gave away her hand. No minstrel sung her nuptial hymn ; and the hour that should conduct her all glorious to the bride-chamber finds her alone, unfriended, without countenance, without sympathy. Is it any wonder, then, that the absence of those festive rites, which, under happier auspices, would have given splendour to her nuptials, should recall them to her imagination, and — with the vision — bring vividly to her memory the sentiments appropriated to such occasions, and the very turn of expression which they had habitually acquired ? Nay, is it not of the very essence of our nature, that, pacing that solitary chamber, while the twilight was thickening into darkness, and the growing silence left the throbbings of her heart audible, she should brood over the impassioned imagery of the Bridal Song, and give it a half unconscious utterance ? Poor Juliet ! She had nobody to sing this song for her. It bursts spontaneously from her own lips.

" I cannot but think that this view invests the passage with a melancholy charm, unsurpassed in its pathos by any situation in the whole range of the drama, except, perhaps, that of Iphigenia at the sacrificial altar. It is scarcely possible, indeed, that it can ever again awaken emotions so intense as it must have kindled in the days of Elizabeth and James ; because its language does not call up in our minds the same associations as in the minds of our ancestors. The Hymeneal Mask has vanished from our customs, and its idiom has become a dead letter. To us the language is not a suggestion, but a study : to them it was fraught with a peculiar significance, and every image was coupled with an every-day reality. The very opening lines — so essentially epithalamic — must have conjured up, to an auditory in whose ears the phraseology was as ' familiar as household words,' the whole ' pride, pomp, and circumstance ' of honored wedlock ; and they would have instinctively imagined the magnificent and joyous solemnities that should have blessed the union of the only daughter of **the** rich and noble Capulet with the only son of the no less noble and wealthy Montague. But what was the scene before their eyes? Where was the bridal escort? where the assembled friends of 'both their houses'? where the crowd of gay and gallant youths who should have homaged the beauty of the bride — and where, oh, where, the maidens that were her fellows to bear her company? Of all the customary pageant, but one solitary figure — the figure of the bride herself — is to be seen. All is solitude, and darkness, and silence. But one sound breaks the unnatural stillness — the voice of that sweet, lonely girl, who — like the young bird timidly practising, in the unfrequented shade, the remembered song of its kindred — 'sits darkling' in her sequestered bower, and eases her impassioned heart in snatches of *remembered song*, which, in *her* mind, too, are associated with her situation.

"And what a song it is ! — sweet as the nightingale's that

> " 'Nightly sings on yon pomegranate tree ; '

and ardent as when in Eden,

> " 'the amorous bird of night
> Sung Spousal ; and bid haste the evening Star
> On his hill-top to light the bridal lamp : '

but it is sad and ominous withal ; and, to the auditor familiar with its import, as portentous and melancholy as the fatal descant which, in poets' ears, preludes the departure of the dying swan."

The decree of banishment (III. i. 192–200), the epithalamic monologue of Juliet (III. ii. 1–31), the return of the Nurse with the sad news, which she communicates to Juliet in a torturing manner (III. ii. 36–143), the attempted consolation of Romeo, by the Friar (III. iii. 1–80), the message and ring from his love, brought to the Friar's cell by the Nurse, and the arrangement for the meeting of the lovers at night (III. iii, 81–175), the fixing of the day by Capulet, of Juliet's marriage to Paris (III. iv.), Romeo's departure for Mantua (III. v. 1–59), all follow in rapid succession, without any intervals, from the slaying of Tybalt in the afternoon till the early dawn of the next day, when the lovers part, uttering the sweetly-sad dialogue poem, in which they question whether it be the nightingale or the lark, they hear, and whether the light which is in the sky, be the light of the coming day. Their hearts are filled with dire forebodings, and shrink with an intuitive anticipation of the stroke of doom. As Romeo descends, Juliet says:

> " Art thou gone so? my lord, my love, my friend !
> I must hear from thee every day in the hour,
> For in a minute there are many days:
> O, by this count I shall be much in years
> Ere I again behold my Romeo!
>   *Rom.* Farewell ! I will omit no opportunity
> That may convey my greetings, love, to thee.
>   *Jul.* O, think'st thou we shall ever meet again?
>   *Rom.* I doubt it not ; and all these woes shall serve
> For sweet discourses in our time to come.
>   *Jul.* O God ! I have an all-divining soul;
> Methinks I see thee, now thou art below,
> As one dead in the bottom of a tomb :
> Either my eyesight fails, or thou look'st pale.
>   *Rom.* And trust me, love, in my eye so do you:
> Dry sorrow drinks our blood. Adieu, adieu! "
>   [*Exit* ROMEO.

The pangs of separation from Romeo which Juliet has to suffer, alone and without sympathy from father, mother, or nurse, are followed immediately by even a severer trial, but a trial which nerves her soul to the greatest intensity, and gives it all the moral courage demanded by the trying situation. She who but three days before was the submissive girl, with all her capabilities still quiescent, saying to her mother when the subject of marriage was first broached to her,

> " no more deep will I endart mine eye
> Than *your* consent gives strength to make it fly,"

passes with one bound, as it were, into a self-sustained, heroic womanhood.

When Lady Capulet tells her the "joyful tidings" that "early next Thursday morn, the gallant, young, and noble gentleman, the County Paris, at St. Peter's Church, shall happily make her there a joyful bride," all the woman and all the wife rise within her and assert themselves, and she replies :

> " Now, by St. Peter's church, and Peter too,
> He shall not make me there a joyful bride.
> I wonder at this haste ; that I must wed
> Ere he that should be husband comes to woo.
> I pray you tell my lord and father, madam,
> I will not marry yet ; and, when I do, I swear,
> It shall be Romeo, whom you know I hate,
> Rather than Paris. These are news indeed !
> *La. Cap.* Here comes your father ; tell him so yourself,
> And see how he will take it at your hands."

This spiritually desiccated father, who is incapable of any sympathy with the young girl's feelings, severs, by his grossly brutal treatment of her, on this occasion, the last ties which should bind her to him, as a daughter. When he goes out, the poor girl turns to her mother for sympathy, but she proves herself equally insensible and heartless, replying merely to her daughter's passionate entreaty,

> " Talk not to me, for I'll not speak a word :
> Do as thou wilt, for I have done with thee."

To the old nurse she then appeals for comfort and counsel. But what comfort and counsel can come from such a mass of earthiness and grossness, to one who has been lifted above all temporal considerations ? The old idiot urges that Paris is "a lovely gentleman ! Romeo's a dishclout to him : " etc.

She now stands alone, and she has the inward resources to do so, and "stands upright as the palm-tree in a realm of sand." To the nurse, to whom she has made a last appeal for sympathy, without receiving any, she calmly says, " Go, counsellor, thou and my bosom henceforth shall be twain. — I'll to the friar, to know his remedy ; if all else fail, myself have power to die." To the dear old sympathetic friar she goes, at whose cell, before she can unburden her heart to him, she first has to undergo the additional affliction of meeting Paris. But she proves herself quite equal to respond to what are to her empty words from a man to whom marriage is but a social arrangement, quite distinct from " the love of wedded *souls*." When she is rid of him, her pent-up feelings burst out upon her only friend ; but above these feelings towers the *will* to do whatever desperate thing he may propose.

To the Friar's words :

> " Hold, daughter; I do spy a kind of hope,
> Which craves as desperate an execution
> As that is desperate which we would prevent.
> If, rather than to marry county Paris,
> Thou hast the strength of will to slay thyself,
> Then is it likely, thou wilt undertake
> A thing like death to chide away this shame,
> That cop'st with death himself to 'scape from it ;
> And, if thou dar'st, I'll give thee remedy."

She replies :

> " O, bid me leap, rather than marry Paris,
> From off the battlements of yonder tower ;
> Or walk in thievish ways ; or bid me lurk
> Where serpents are ; chain me with roaring bears ;
> Or hide me nightly in the charnel-house, ·
> O'er-cover'd quite with dead men's rattling bones,
> With reeky shanks, and yellow chapless skulls ;
> Or bid me go into a new-made grave,
> And hide me with a dead man in his shroud ;
> Things that, to hear them told, have made me tremble ;
> And I will do it without fear or doubt,
> To live an unstain'd wife to my sweet love."

The Friar then proposes a desperate remedy, which she is at once ready to accept, and the means by which she and Romeo are to be reunited :

"Hold, then; go home, be merry, give consent
  To marry Paris: Wednesday is to-morrow;
To-morrow night look that thou lie alone,
Let not thy nurse lie with thee in thy chamber:
Take thou this vial, being then in bed,
And this distilled liquor drink thou off:
When, presently, through all thy veins shall run
A cold and drowsy humour; for no pulse
Shall keep his native progress, but surcease.
No warmth, no breath, shall testify thou liv'st;
The roses in thy lips and cheeks shall fade
To paly ashes; thy eyes' windows fall,
Like death, when he shuts up the day of life;
Each part, deprived of supple government,
Shall stiff, and stark, and cold, appear like death:
And this borrow'd likeness of shrunk death
Thou shalt continue two-and-forty hours,
And then awake as from a pleasant sleep.
Now when the bridegroom in the morning comes
To rouse thee from thy bed, there art thou dead:
Then (as the manner of our country is,)
In thy best robes uncover'd on the bier,
Thou shalt be borne to that same ancient vault,
Where all the kindred of the Capulets lie.
In the mean time, against thou shalt awake,
Shall Romeo by my letters know our drift;
And hither shall he come; and he and I
Will watch thy waking, and that very night
Shall Romeo bear thee hence to Mantua.
And this shall free thee from this present shame,
If no inconstant toy, nor womanish fear
Abate thy valour in the acting it.

    Jul. Give me, give me! O, tell not me of fear.

    Fri. Hold; get you gone, be strong and prosperous
In this resolve: I'll send a friar with speed
To Mantua, with my letters to thy lord.

    Jul. Love give me strength! and strength shall help afford.
Farewell, dear father!"

Returning home, she makes her submission to her father, who is overjoyed at her supposed obedience. To his ugly speech, as she enters,

> " How now, my headstrong ! Where have you been gadding?"

She replies :

> " Where I have learn'd me to repent the sin
> Of disobedient opposition
> To you and your behests, and am enjoin'd
> By holy Laurence to fall prostrate here,
> To beg your pardon : pardon, I beseech you !
> Henceforward I am ever ruled by you."

Under the trying circumstances, this speech is not to be condemned as deception on the part of Juliet, but should be regarded as in obedience to a higher principle than truthfulness to a parent who would wrong the *soul* of his child.

Capulet, in his high glee, resolves that the knot shall be knit up to-morrow morning ; that's Wednesday, a day earlier than he before settled upon. In his mind, the whole city is much bound to the reverend holy friar, for bringing about such a happy result. He can hardly contain himself :

> " Go, nurse, go with her : we'll to church to-morrow.
>   [*Exeunt* JULIET *and Nurse.*
> *La. Cap.* We shall be short in our provision :
> 'Tis now near night.
>   *Cap.* Tush, I will stir about,
> And all things shall be well, I warrant thee, wife :
> Go thou to Juliet, help to deck up her ;
> I'll not to bed to-night ; let me alone ;
> I'll play the housewife for this once. What, ho !
> They are all forth. Well, I will walk myself
> To County Paris, to prepare him up
> Against to-morrow. My heart is wondrous light,
> Since this same wayward girl is so reclaim'd."

The nurse attends Juliet to her chamber. Lady Capulet enters to know whether her help is needed. Juliet replies :

> " No, madam ; we have cull'd such necessaries
> As are behoveful for our state to-morrow :
> So please you, let me now be left alone,
> And let the nurse this night sit up with you,
> For I am sure you have your hands full all
> In this so sudden business.
>
>   *La. Cap.*   Good-night :
> Get thee to bed and rest, for thou hast need."
>
>   [*Exeunt Lady* CAPULET *and Nurse.*

Juliet is now left alone with her own soul, and the soliloquy which she utters bears testimony to her moral energy :

> " *Jul.* Farewell ! — God knows when we shall meet again.
> I have a faint cold fear thrills through my veins,
> That almost freezes up the heat of life :
> I'll call them back again to comfort me.
> Nurse ! — What should she do here ?
> My dismal scene I needs must act alone. —
> Come, vial. —
> What if this mixture do not work at all ?
> Shall I be married to-morrow morning ?
> No, no ; — this shall forbid it : — lie thou there. —
>
>   [*Laying down a dagger.*
>
> What if it be a poison, which the friar
> Subtly hath minister'd to have me dead,
> Lest in this marriage he should be dishonour'd,
> Because he married me before to Romeo ?
> I fear it is : and yet, methinks, it should not,
> For he hath still been tried a holy man.
> How if, when I am laid into the tomb,
> I wake before the time that Romeo
> Come to redeem me ? there's a fearful point !
> Shall I not then be stifled in the vault,
> To whose foul mouth no healthsome air breathes in,
> And there die strangled ere my Romeo comes ?
> Or, if I live, is it not very like,

> The horrible conceit of death and night,
> Together with the terror of the place, —
> As in a vault, an ancient receptacle,
> Where, for these many hundred years, the bones
> Of all my buried ancestors are pack'd ;
> Where bloody Tybalt, yet but green in earth,
> Lies fest'ring in his shroud ; where, as they say,
> At some hours in the night spirits resort ; —
> Alack, alack, is it not like, that I,
> So early waking, — what with loathsome smells
> And shrieks like mandrakes' torn out of the earth,
> That living mortals, hearing them, run mad ; —
> O, if I wake, shall I not be distraught,
> Environed with all these hideous fears ?
> And madly play with my forefathers' joints ?
> And pluck the mangled Tybalt from his shroud ?
> And, in this rage, with some great kinsman's bone,
> As with a club, dash out my desperate brains ?
> O, look ! methinks I see my cousin's ghost
> Seeking out Romeo, that did spit his body
> Upon a rapier's point : — stay, Tybalt, stay ! —
> Romeo, I come ! this do I drink to thee."
>   [*She throws herself on the bed.*

Mrs. Jameson says, in concluding her long article on Juliet, " with all her immense capacity of affection and imagination, there is *a deficiency of reflection and of moral energy* " ; and this characterization is reiterated by other critics. To impute a deficiency of moral energy to this Shakespearian ideal of moral energy, is something surprising. Her moral energy approaches the sublime, when she takes the sleeping potion, *her imagination having first called up all the horrors of the charnel-vault.* But her moral energy is equal to the encountering of even these. She has, indeed, great fear ; but *our interest is in her superiority to it.* Heroism implies fear. And the poet had an artistic purpose in making her call up, as she does, these horrors, namely, to emphasize her moral energy, to bring into bold relief her will power. Some critics understand that she takes the potion when she loses herself in fright. If that were true, the whole play would be ruined. Where could the dramatic interest come from? If Juliet does not belong to herself at the time she takes the potion, all dramatic interest in the act is gone. It has no more dramatic interest than has the leaping of a maniac from a third-story window. But actresses often fail to bring out distinctly the idea of the superiority of Juliet's *will* power and moral energy, to her dread imaginings. Some leave no doubt as to their delirium, just before taking the potion.

Lord Lytton, in his strongly favorable article on Miss Anderson's Juliet, in *The Nineteenth Century*, December, 1884, after pronouncing her acting of a portion of the soliloquy as not only excellent, but surprisingly excellent, remarks : " As the soliloquy advances, the acting degenerates. She rises, rushes about the stage, rants, screams, loses all dignity, all pathos, becomes theatrical, conventionally tragic, wholly ineffective, and ruins the sentiment of the scene by a painful relapse under the tyranny of the worst traditions of the English stage." *

The scene which follows, the 4th of the 4th Act, is one of those scenes so frequent in Shakespeare's Plays which, by their commonplaceness and even, sometimes, vulgarity, serve to deepen the impressions of the sad and the tragic. In the 5th Scene, the Nurse finds Juliet dead, as is supposed, in her chamber, and clamorous selfish lamentation follows. In the midst of it, Friar Laurence and Paris, with musicians, enter. The Friar subordinates what, under the circumstances, he must regard as an inferior principle, to a superior, and speaks as one knowing nothing more of the case than the rest, and silences the clamor.

> " Peace, ho, for shame ! confusion's cure lives not
> In these confusions. Heaven and yourself
> Had part in this fair maid ; now heaven hath all,
> And all the better is it for the maid ;
> Your part in her you could not keep from death ;
> But heaven keeps his part in eternal life.

---

* Lord Lytton's article is reprinted in " Shakesperiana," January, 1885, Vol. II. No. xiii. pp. 1–22.

> The most you sought was her promotion;
> For 'twas your heaven, she should be advanc'd:
> And weep ye now, seeing she is advanc'd —
> Above the clouds, as high as heaven itself?
> O, in this love, you love your child so ill,
> That you run mad, seeing that she is well : *
> She's not well married that lives married long ;
> But she's best married that dies married young.
> Dry up your tears, and stick your rosemary
> On this fair corse ; and, as the custom is,
> In all her best array bear her to church :
> For though some † nature bids us all lament,
> Yet nature's tears are reason's merriment."

And when Capulet, Lady Capulet, Paris, and Friar go out, the dialogue between Peter and the musicians summoned to poor Juliet's marriage serves, as did the scene following Juliet's taking of the potion, to deepen the impression of the sad occasion. Who can fail to be impressed with the grimness of such contrasting scenes ? They are a feature of Shakespeare's dramatic art which was quite new to the world, and which especially shocked the classical critics of the last century. But criticism has taken a higher stand, and approvingly recognizes in such scenes, the bitter irony which humanity everywhere presents.

(See " Contrasting Scenes," pp. 50 and 51, in "The Shakespeare Key." By Charles and Mary Cowden Clarke ; and " On the Porter in Macbeth." By J. W. Hales. The New Shakspere Society's Transactions. 1874. pp. 255–269.)

The end of the 4th day of the Play has now been reached, and the 5th is entered upon at Mantua (A. V. Sc. i.). " The lively and cheerful images of this [Juliet's epithalamic] soliloquy are in striking contrast with the situation of the speaker, and serve to heighten the pity with which we anticipate the fate of the lovely

---

* "We use to say the dead are *well."* — *Antony and Cleopatra,* A. II. Sc. v. 32.

† The reading of *Qq. and F.*[1]   Most editions substitute " fond," *i.e.*, foolish.

and unconscious victim. By a similar resort to this *lightning be-fore death*, the poet has, at a later period of the action, skilfully filled the mind of his hero with happy dreams and joyful presages, which throw the approaching catastrophe into deep and dark-shadowed relief."

> " *Rom.* If I may trust the flattering truth of sleep,
> My dreams presage some joyful news at hand :
> My bosom's lord sits lightly in his throne ;
> And all this day, an unaccustom'd spirit
> Lifts me above the ground with cheerful thoughts.
> I dreamt, my lady came and found me dead : —
> Strange dream, that gives a dead man leave to think ! —
> And breathed such life with kisses in my lips,
> That I revived, and was an emperor.
> Ah me ! how sweet is love itself possess'd,
> When but love's shadows are so rich in joy !

> *Enter* BALTHASAR.

> News from Verona ! — How now, Balthasar?
> Dost thou not bring me letters from the friar?
> How doth my lady? Is my father well?
> How fares my Juliet? That I ask again ;
> For nothing can be ill, if she be well.
>   *Bal.* Then she is well, and nothing can be ill :
> Her body sleeps in Capels' monument,
> And her immortal part with angels lives.
> I saw her laid low in her kindred's vault,
> And presently took post to tell it you :
> O, pardon me for bringing these ill news,
> Since you did leave it for my office, sir.
>   *Rom.* Is it even so? then I defy you, stars ! — "

As the poet indicated the point where Juliet attained to self-poised, self-reliant womanhood, in her one short sentence to the Nurse, to whom, when father and mother failed in sympathy, she appealed for comfort and received none, " Go, counsellor, thou and my bosom shall be henceforth twain," so he has also indicated the point where Romeo attains to self-poised, self-reliant manhood, in the short sentence, "*then I defy you, stars!*"   From this point, Romeo is completely master of himself—nothing outside of himself can sway his purpose : which purpose is, as he expresses it, over the supposed dead body of Juliet, "to shake the yoke of *inauspicious stars* from his world-wearied flesh." This explains "Then I defy you, stars ! "

He continues his speech to Balthasar :

> "Thou know'st my lodging : get me ink and paper,
> And hire post-horses; I will hence to-night.
>   *Bal.* I do beseech you, sir, have patience;
> Your looks are pale and wild, and do import
> Some misadventure.
>   *Rom.*   Tush, thou art deceived;
> Leave me, and do the thing I bid thee do.
> Hast thou no letters to me from the friar?
>   *Bal.* No, my good lord.
>   *Rom.*   No matter: get thee gone,
> And hire those horses: I'll be with thee straight.
>   [*Exit* BALTHASAR.
> Well, Juliet, I will lie with thee to-night."

He buys a poison of an apothecary, and sets off immediately for Verona.   In the 2d Scene of the 5th Act, we learn how Friar John, who was sent by Friar Laurence with a letter to Romeo, informing him of his plans for his reunion with Juliet, was prevented from delivering it.   As soon as Friar John returns with the letter, Friar Laurence resolves to go at once to the tomb of the Capulets, to be on hand when Juliet awakes.   But the good man arrives too late.   Before he enters the churchyard, Romeo has opened the tomb, with mattock and wrenching iron, has fought with and slain Paris, has taken the poison, and is already dead, having, in the conclusion of his soliloquy over the supposed dead body of his Juliet, given expression to what the poet is at the pains to emphasize throughout the Play, but which some commentators have closed their eyes to, namely, that Romeo and Juliet are "star-crossed lovers"—that their sorrows are due to objec-

tive outside causes, and not at all to causes existing within themselves. "O here," says Romeo,

> "Will I set up my everlasting rest,
> And shake the yoke of inauspicious stars
> From this world-wearied flesh. — Eyes, look your last!
> Arms, take your last embrace! and lips, O you
> The doors of breath, seal with a righteous kiss
> A dateless bargain to engrossing death! —
> Come, bitter conduct, come, unsavoury guide!
> Thou desperate pilot, now at once run on
> The dashing rocks thy sea-sick weary bark!
> Here's to my love! — [*Drinks.*]   O, true apothecary!
> Thy drugs are quick. — Thus with a kiss I die."

Even Ruskin, one of the most careful of readers, says, alluding
to Romeo's forcing open the vault, "the wise and entirely brave
stratagem of the wife is brought to ruinous issue by the reckless
impatience of her husband." But even here he cannot be charged
with reckless impatience. He is unacquainted with the friar's
plan and has been informed by Balthasar that Juliet is dead and
that her body has been placed in the vault of the Capulets — and
he of course believes her dead when he opens the vault.

Juliet is, however, throughout the play, more purely heroic than
Romeo. She's the true hero of the play. There's an interesting
passage in Ruskin's "Sesame and Lilies (of Queens' Gardens),"
as to the superiority of Shakespeare's heroines to his heroes.
He asserts, indeed, in his bold way, that "Shakespeare has no
heroes; — he has only heroines."

The poet has brought the gentleness (not rashness) of Romeo,
in his encounter with Paris, into the same bold relief as in his
encounter with Tybalt. What a contrast the two present, of the
genuine and the conventional!

Paris's self-consciousness and self-complacency are shown even
when he strews flowers upon Juliet's tomb:

> "Sweet flower, with flowers thy bridal bed I strew;
> O woe, thy canopy is dust and stones,

Which with sweet water nightly I will dew,
Or, wanting that, with tears distilled by moans."

One is disposed to read these lines with a lisp, and to slur
the *r's.*

Paris observes the etiquette of bereavement. He's a nice
young man, *he* is, who wouldn't neglect any of the conventional
proprieties of life for the world. But such nice young men, and so
conventionally correct and proper, Juliets generally don't take to.

It seems almost a mistake to call the play a tragedy, as it has
such a triumphant ending — triumphant in regard to the lovers
themselves, and triumphant, inasmuch as the hostile families join
hands in peace over the dead bodies of the lovers. The very
funeral vault, which is the scene of their final acts, acts which
seal their eternal devotion, is invested with a poetic charm, and
filled with a poetic fragrance.

The Prince says, as he stands with the heads of the two families and their attendants, in front of the monument of the Capulets, before the day has dawned, and with the beautiful bodies of
the lovers before him :

" Capulet ! — Montague !
See, what a scourge is laid upon your hate,
That heaven finds means to kill your joys with love !
And I, for winking at your discords too,
Have lost a brace of kinsmen : — all are punish'd.
    Cap. O brother Montague, give me thy hand.
This is my daughter's jointure, for no more
Can I demand.
    Mon.   But I can give thee more :
For I will raise her statue in pure gold ;
That whiles Verona by that name is known,
There shall no figure at such rate be set,
As that of true and faithful Juliet.
    Cap. As rich shall Romeo by his lady lie ;
Poor sacrifices of our enmity ! "

THE COMMENTARY ON ROMEO AND JULIET.

———◦◦◦———

THE critics, English, German, and French, have, with but few exceptions, attributed to Shakespeare the predetermination, in this Play, of exhibiting the bad, the fatal consequences of violent, unrestrained passion : and the importance of moderation — of observing the golden mean between too much and too little ; and in accordance with this view, they have regarded Friar Laurence as the poet's spokesman — put into the play for the special purpose of vicariously giving voice to the moderate and the prudential. Such a mode of proceeding may be necessary to dramatists of an inferior order, whose work moves under the condition of a *notion* of some kind. But Shakespeare's Plays, *none* of them, move under such condition. He chose the subject of Romeo and Juliet for its passionate capabilities ; he is the artistic physiologist of human passion ; and having strong in himself the healthiest moral sensibilities, his penetrative, plastic intellect manipulated his material with such artistic skill that the dramatic result was a vivid and beautiful poem, bodying forth " the power and the triumph of love." (The leading object of a literary and artistic education should be, to take in the concrete and the personal as a direct, immediate language, not an indirect, a mediate language which has to be translated into the *notional* before it means anything. But such is the set of the general mind in these days, learned and unlearned, that the concrete and the personal are, more or less, like a foreign language which has to be translated into the more familiar language of the intellect, of the abstract and the *notional*.)

What is put into the mouth of the good Friar Laurence, rather than expressing, as many of the leading commentators understand it, the designed *moral* of the Play, offsets, in the way of sober philosophy, what Shakespeare must have regarded as nobler than a sober philosophy, — namely, a love which, under the wholly adverse circumstances by which it was beset, was destined to a tragic issue ; but that tragic issue had itself an issue which devotion unto death on the part of the lovers, alone could have brought about.   This is explicitly set forth in the Prologue, which is the best key to the Play, whether furnished by Shakespeare himself or not.   It is omitted in the Folios.   In the 1st Quarto it consists of but 12 lines, and is evidently not a true rendering of the original.   The form in which it is now always printed is that of the 2d Quarto of 1599.   It contains no charge against the lovers of "rashness," "imprudence," "want of proper restraint," and the like, to which the sorrows and death of the lovers are attributed by so many commentators.

> " Two households, both alike in dignity,
>   In fair Verona, where we lay our scene,
>   From ancient grudge break to new mutiny,
>   Where civil blood makes civil hands unclean.
>   From forth the fatal loins of these two foes
>   A pair of *star-crossed* lovers take their life ;
>   Whose misadventur'd piteous overthrows
>   Doth with their death bury their parents' strife.
>   The fearful passage of their death-mark'd love,
>   And the continuance of their parents' rage,
>   Which, but their children's end, nought could remove,
>   Is now the two hours' traffic of our stage ;
>   The which if you with patient ears attend,
>   What here shall miss, our toil shall strive to mend."

Nothing about fatal rashness on the part of the lovers ; the causes of their piteous overthrows are all objective (outside of themselves), not subjective (within themselves).   This is the most important point to recognize at the outset of the study of

the play. And it's important in itself, as it involves a true understanding of the poet's dramatic art — while the view, so generally
entertained (by critics), that the ardent love which is the subject
of the drama, is presented as something to be condemned for its
violent excess, involves a false understanding of the poet's dramatic art. As indicating the general drift of criticism on the
Play, in regard to the lovers, I shall cite a number of passages
(some of them of considerable length) from critics of high authority. I do this to show that I'm not *gratuitously* insisting on
what many an unsophisticated reader, on what most unsophisticated readers, would regard as a thing of course.

And first Dr. Gervinus, in his "Shakespeare Commentaries":
". . . in the midst of the world," he says, "agitated by love and
hatred, he [Shakespeare] has placed Friar Laurence, whom experience, retirement, and age, have deprived of inclination to
either. By him, who, as it were, represents the part of the chorus
in this tragedy, the leading idea of the piece is expressed in all fulness, an idea that runs throughout the whole, namely, that excess
in any enjoyment however pure in itself, transforms its sweet into
bitterness, that devotion to any single feeling however noble, be-
speaks its ascendency; that this ascendency moves the man and
woman out of their natural spheres; that love can only be a companion to life, and cannot fully fill out the life and business of the
man especially; that, in the full power of its first rising, it is a
paroxysm of happiness, which according to its nature cannot continue in equal strength; that, as the poet says in an image, it is a
flower that

    " ' Being smelt, with that part cheers each part;
    Being tasted, slays all senses with the heart.'

[Friar Laurence says this in his own person : Shakespeare doesn't
say it.]

"These ideas," he goes on to say, "are placed by the poet in
the lips of the wise Laurence in almost a moralizing manner, with
gradually increasing emphasis, as if he would provide most cir-
cumspectly that no doubt should remain of his meaning."

That is, Shakespeare set about driving firmly into our heads, and clinching, this wonderful moral of moderation. If that's the purpose of the play, it ought to be entitled Much Ado about Nothing. What an ado to enforce so little ! And that little, what the whole human race has known since the Flood, and no doubt knew before the Flood.

It is no more the purpose of the play to teach moderation, than it is the purpose of a violent rain-storm which beats down the farmer's crops, and washes away the garden beds, to teach moderation ; or than it is the purpose of a freshet on the Ohio River which destroys life and property, to teach the importance of moderation. What professorial nonsense ! The student whose mind is set on moral didacticism, and insists on it, should study some other author than Shakespeare. The moral platitudes of Tupper's Proverbial Philosophy would suit him better.

Shakespeare nowhere in his works shows himself nervously anxious that his meaning in the abstract be correctly understood. *It is not the abstract which he is occupied with.* If he *did* so show himself, he would not be the great dramatist he is : for that would imply that he was occupied overmuch with the *notional,* to the detriment of the concrete vitality of his art. And it is *because* the real creative energy of the poet was ever dominant, in the composition of his Plays, that theories which no man can number have been raised, as to his meanings, by minds with a predominant *notional* drift. Such minds are not brought into requisite sympathy with the creative energy, and therefore occupy themselves with picking nice little moral pebbles out of the stream of that creative energy.

(What a lovely moral was that which the laborious student of Homer, alluded to somewhere by De Quincey, extracted, after much patient investigation, from the Iliad ! " Keep the peace, gentlemen, you see what comes of fighting ! ")

To continue with Gervinus : " Friar Laurence utters these ideas of the poet in his first soliloquy, under the simile of the vegetable world with which he is occupied, in a manner merely *instructive* and as if without application ; he expresses them *warningly*, when he unites the lovers, at the moment when he assists them, and finally he repeats them *reprovingly* to Romeo in his cell, when he sees the latter undoing himself and his own work, and he predicts what the end will be."

"Nought," says the holy man in the first of these passages (A. II. Sc. iii. 17–30),

> " Nought so vile that on the earth doth live,
> But to the earth some special good doth give ;
> Nor aught so good, but, strain'd from that fair use,
> Revolts from true birth, stumbling on abuse.
> Virtue itself turns vice, being misapplied,
> And vice sometime's by action dignified.
> Within the infant rind of this weak flower
> Poison hath residence, and medicine power :
> For this, being smelt, with that part cheers each part,
> Being tasted, slays all senses with the heart.
> Two such opposed kings encamp them still
> In man as well as herbs, — Grace and rude Will ;
> And where the worser is predominant,
> Full soon the canker death eats up that plant."

This soliloquy, be it understood, is uttered by the good friar *before he knows anything of the loves of Romeo and Juliet.* It gives expression to his prudential, golden-mean philosophy, just such a philosophy as such a man would be expected to hold and practise, and to advocate. If it could be shown that it was meant by the poet to have a direct bearing upon the loves of Romeo and Juliet, it could be condemned as an artistic defect, in its being thus brought in before the Friar has knowledge of their loves. But Gervinus remarks on the soliloquy : "We see plainly, that these two qualities [meaning " grace " and " rude will "] which make Romeo a hero and a slave of love ; in happiness with his Juliet he displays his ' grace,' in so rich a measure, that he quickly triumphs over a being so gifted ; in misfortune he destroys all the charm of these gifts through the ' rude will,' with which Laurence reproaches him.

In the second of the passages pointed out, Romeo, on the threshold of his happiness, challenges love-devouring death to do what he dare, so that he may only call Juliet his ; and in warning reproof, Friar Laurence tells him, in a passage which the poet has first inserted in his revision of the play, applying the idea of that straining of the good from its fair use (A. II. Sc. vi. 9–14) :

> " ' These violent delights have violent ends
> And in their triumph die, like fire and powder
> Which as they kiss consume. The sweetest honey
> Is loathsome in his own deliciousness
> And in the taste confounds the appetite.
> Therefore, love moderately ; long love doth so.' "

Now, in the first place, the poet could not have made the friar, in accordance with his own character, say other than what he does, on this occasion ; and, in the second place, the friar has taken a great deal upon himself, in uniting in marriage the representatives of two powerful houses, between whom a fierce hostility has long raged. He is, of course, very anxious about the possible consequences, notwithstanding that he hopes, as he expresses it at the end of the 3d Scene of the 2d Act,

> "this alliance may so happy prove
> To turn the household's rancour to pure love."

His prudential character, accordingly, comes fully to the front. He is *himself*, and not a chorus, not a personified emanation of the poet, as Gervinus makes him, contrary to Shakespeare's almost unvarying dramatic art. Shakespeare doesn't trouble himself about interpreting abstractly his own work to us. Friar Laurence offsets, it is true, the ardency of the lovers, just as he may also be said to offset the general violent state of things around him. Shakespeare is a great master of contrast, and it is one of the most effective agencies of his dramatic art, as it is, indeed, one of every form of art — " as fundamentally necessary as symmetry, moderation, or congruity." *   (See " Shakespeare Key," pp. 50, 51.)

---

* Blackie, " On Beauty," p. 149.

To continue a moment longer with Gervinus. After the last quotation given, "These violent delights have violent end," the friar goes on to say (A. III. Sc. iii. 122–134) :

> " Fie, fie, thou shamest thy shape, thy love, thy wit;
> Which, like a usurer, abound'st in all, .
> And usest none in that true use indeed
> Which should bedeck thy shape, thy love, thy wit :
> Thy noble shape is but a form of wax,
> Digressing from the valour of a man ;
> Thy dear love sworn, but hollow perjury,
> Killing that love which thou hast vowed to cherish ;
> Thy wit, that ornament to shape and love,
> Misshapen in the conduct of them both,
> Like powder in a skilless soldier's flask,
> Is set a-fire by thine own ignorance,
> And thou dismember'd with thine own defence."

"With this significant image," Gervinus continues, "we see Romeo subsequently rushing to death, when he procures from the apothecary the poison by which the trunk is

> " ' discharged of breath
> As violently, as hasty powder fir'd
> Doth hurry, from the fatal cannon's womb.' "

On this simile, Gervinus remarks : "Thrice has the poet [no, not the poet, but the good, moderate Friar Laurence] with this same simile, designated the inflaming heart of this love, which too quickly causes the paroxysm of happiness to consume itself and to vanish, and he could choose no moral aphorism, which with such simple expressiveness could have demonstrated *the aim of his representation*, but just this image alone."

Ulrici, in his " Shakespeare's Dramatic Art : and his relation to Calderon and Goethe," after speaking of love as " the noblest and most exalted privilege that man enjoys," continues : " But even because it *is* in its nature thus eminently noble and sublime, does love become, so soon as it attaches itself to the finiteness of passion and desire, and so long as it remains unpurified from earthly dregs, a fatally destructive force, whose triumphs are celebrated amid ruin and death.   It is even because it is in its true essence of a celestial origin, that it hurries along, with demoniacal and irresistible energy, all who misuse its godlike gifts, and who, plunged in the abyss of self-forgetfulness, lavish all the riches of a heavenly endowment on the lowly sphere of their earthly existence. It is in such a light that Romeo is presented to us at the very opening of the piece.   The faculty of loving, which pervades his whole being, and which is assigned to him in so eminent a degree, instead of being refined and spiritualized by its sexual object and passion, becomes merged in passionate yearning and desire.   He thus becomes the slave of the very power whose master he ought to be.   Accordingly, at the very opening of the piece, he appears carried away by it, as it were, by some malignant and irresistible influence, and hurried along at its caprice.   In order to throw out this caprice in a still stronger light, Shakespeare introduces him to us in a dreamy passion for Rosaline.   Involuntarily, and as it were, mechanically, is he precipitated, out of his fancy for Rosaline, into the deeper and mightier passion for Juliet.   Two hearts made for each other, combine at first sight, into indissoluble unity ; the force of nature, being allowed free course, overcomes at once all the barriers of custom and circumstance.   As the lightning has already struck before a man can say it lightens, so, in their hearts a blazing flame has been quickly and irresistibly kindled, whose destroying might both feel and suspect without the power or even the wish to oppose it.   In both there is the same excess of inflammable matter; even Juliet possesses the same rich abundance of love — the divine gift in its largest measure ; and with her, too, the mighty waters all hurry to the same point, and thus, instead of diffusing fertility and blessing, they do but rise above their bed to scatter death and desolation around.   Both are high-born, richly gifted, and noble of nature ; both have earth and heaven within their bosoms ; but they pervert their loveliest and noblest gifts into sin, corruption, and evil ; they mar their rare excellence by making idols of each other, and fanatically sacrificing all things to their idolatry."

In the next paragraph he characterizes their love as "This passionateness — this *fatal vehemence* of love," etc.

Here we have the same general idea as that set forth by Gervinus, only it is even more strongly put.

And even Coleridge says: "With Romeo his *precipitate change of passion,* his hasty marriage, and rash death, are all the effects of youth."

The cold and judicial Hallam, in his "Introduction to the Literature of Europe," represents Juliet as "a child, whose intoxication in loving and being loved whirls away the little reason she may have possessed." He further says: "It is however impossible, in my opinion, to place her among the great female characters of Shakespeare's creation."

Well, that may be. But Juliet realizes all that the great poet aims after, dramatically — a lyric melody of passion, not an orchestral symphony of emotion such as some of his later great plays exhibit.

Further on Hallam says:

"It seems to have formed part of his [Shakespeare's] conception of this youthful and ardent pair that they should talk irrationally. The extravagance of their fancy, however, not only forgets reason, but wastes itself in frigid metaphors and incongruous conceptions; the tone of Romeo is that of the most bombastic commonplace of gallantry, and the young lady differs in being only one degree more mad. The voice of virgin love has been counterfeited by the authors of many fictions: I know none who have thought the style of Juliet would represent it."

Here the idea is again, that of *rashness, lightheadedness, unreasonableness,* and their attendant follies. Hallam shows himself here quite unfit to be a judge in such matters. He would no doubt have preferred the diplomacy of love-making which we are entertained with in some of the many fictions to which he refers. Would the play, could the play, possess such a charm for the cultivated world, if these critics are right? Two rash, giddy-headed lovers, flinging themselves into destruction — a subject for the greatest love poem in the world !   It is preposterous.

Maginn, in his " Shakespeare Papers," says : " Romeo leaves all to the steerage of Heaven, — *i.e.,* to the heady current of his own passions ; and he succeeds accordingly."

He gives as the moral of the play, two lines from Juvenal (Sat. x. 365, 366) :

> " Nullum numen habes, si sit prudentia ; nos te
> Nos facimus, Fortuna, deam, cœloque locamus." *

Alfred Mézières, in his " Shakespeare, ses Œuvres et ses Critiques," remarks : " The philosophy of the Friar is but *the judgment which the poet pronounces from the background of the tragedy.* When the Friar speaks, we seem to hear the reflections which the *poet is making aloud to himself* as the play comes from his creative hands.   [As if the Poet hadn't anything better to do than that !]   Under the garb of the monk, Shakespeare communicates to us the results of *his personal experience,* and the *conclusions* to which the spectacle of the world has led him.   [What a moral observer he must have been !]   He was profoundly versed in the study of human nature ; he knew its weaknesses, its contradictions, its impatient desires, its rashness attended by boundless hope and followed by utter despair, its misfortunes whether merited or self-provoked ; he knew the self-deception man so often practises ; all this he knew, and yet the knowledge never lessens his indulgence, or his sympathy for his fellow-creatures."   What a kind, charitable fellow he was !   Here we have the Friar again as Chorus, and Shakespeare, not as dramatist, occupied with giving life, but as a moralist giving us the results of his personal experience, and the conclusions to which the spectacle of the world has led him, from a moral point of view !

---

* " Thou hast no deity, O Fortune, if there be prudence ; but thee we make a goddess, and place in heaven."

" It is but natural," says Taine, " that such love should be followed by supreme calamities and fatal resolves. Ophelia becomes insane, Juliet kills herself, and that the insanity and the suicide are inevitable every one feels."

Tieck, in " Dramaturgische Blätter " (Vol. I. p. 256, Breslau, 1826), says :

"Romeo's temperament is, on the whole, much more gloomy than Juliet's ; in the garden-scene his soul lights up, but in good fortune as in bad, he is violent and rough." That's just what he is not. There are no epithets less appropriate to Romeo than *violent* and *rough*. " This vigorous manhood which so easily oversteps the bounds of mildness and tenderness, harming both itself and others, and losing all moderation and restraint when enraged, this it is that in real life enkindles such manifold passions and suffers so deeply and powerfully. This exuberance of life, sooner or later, in one way or another, involves in ruin both itself and the object of its idolatry ; and *this lesson Friar Laurence constantly preaches to the rash youth. . . .*" Further on he says : "The tragic fate lies in the *character* of Juliet, and especially of Romeo. . . . He must, Juliet must, perish ; the necessity lay *in their very natures.*"

No, the necessity lay in the circumstances with which they were beset. The necessity was objective.

" I am inclined to think," he adds, "that *the rôle of Friar Laurence the Poet wrote for himself ;*" etc.

Mrs. Jameson, in concluding her long article on Juliet, remarks :

" With all this immense capacity of affection and imagination, there is *a deficiency of reflective and of moral energy* arising from previous habit and education ; and the action of the drama, while it serves to develop the character, appears but its natural and necessary result. ' Le mystère de l'existence,' said Madame de Staël to her daughter, ' c'est le rapport de nos erreurs avec nos peines.' "

In this passage, as in all the others cited, the calamitous course and fatal end of the heroine's love, are attributed to subjective causes — to defect of character and impropriety of conduct. The inference, too, may be drawn from most of them, that if the lovers had only understood the *diplomatic style* of love, things might have gone better with them. Such criticism degrades the Play to a piece of prudential didacticism, of which Friar Laurence is the mouth-piece. The dear old man is himself, and lives his own life ; and that may be said of all Shakespeare's characters. The lovers are themselves and live their own lives. The former is not a mere personification of moderation and prudence placed beside the latter as personifications of rashness and imprudence, in order to bring these qualities into bold relief, and to impress us with a sense of what bad things they are, and how dire their consequences may be. Shakespeare, it is true, makes the Friar condemn the ardency of the lovers, but he condemns it *in propria persona.* That's quite a different thing from saying that the play, as a play, is designed to condemn it.

Bodenstedt, of all the German commentators, comes the nearest, I think, to a correct view of the case. In the Introduction to his translation of Romeo and Juliet, 1868, he says :

"The maxims and sentences of Friar Laurence are so general that they hardly admit of application to special cases, and least of all do they justify the opinion of various commentators that the Poet intended in them to bring fully out the leading thoughts of this tragedy. 'Passion gives power,' says the Poet, and he makes the calm, moderate wisdom of Father Laurence give way to the passion of Romeo, not the reverse. Indeed, could we for a moment imagine the ardor of the young lovers changed or cooled by the persuasive breath of the Friar's lips, our interest in Romeo and Juliet would be extinguished instantly. But that interest is increased when the Friar gives the benediction of the Church to the tie woven by the purest and noblest passion."

I have dwelt thus long on this one point, because I consider it a most important one — *the* most important, as upon it a true estimate and appreciation of the Play, as a whole, depends. A true estimate and appreciation of Shakespeare's mode of dramatization depend upon it. The views I have cited, of Gervinus,

Ulrici, and other commentators, in regard to the moral of the Tragedy, lead the student to an essential misunderstanding of the Play and also of the Shakespearian treatment of passion, in general. Shakespeare is not a moralist, in the small sense of the word ; and he hadn't a drop of missionary blood in his veins ; in the composition of his Plays, he always had higher business in hand than playing the part of a moralist or missionary ; but he exhibits everywhere the profoundest moral spirit.

It cannot, indeed, be said that Shakespeare ever has a direct moral purpose. His direct purpose is always a dramatic one. He is the dramatist — the dramatist transcendently and exclusively. His morals are morals in the flesh, and the interpretation or formulation of them, by critics, must vary according to the great variety of individual attitudes, of individual modes of thinking — of individual modes of feeling.

Shakespeare in his treatment of passion, of every kind, however violent that passion may be, always exhibits it under the condition of Eternal Law ! It is in this that the moral proportion which so characterizes his Plays, from the earliest to the latest, consists. That Eternal Law cannot be run against with impunity. But this is exhibited concretely, implicitly, not explicitly. Shakespeare was wholly taken up, in Romeo and Juliet, with the dramatic exhibition of the passion of pure youthful love. He is the naturalist who traces for us its inception, its progress, its final triumph over all obstacles ; and finally its regenerating power over those who endeavored to obstruct its clear and rapid current.

KING JOHN.

SHAKESPEARE wrote ten English historical Plays, in eight of which the historical connection is preserved; namely, Richard II., Henry IV., Parts 1 and 2 Henry V., Henry VI., Parts 1, 2, 3, and Richard III., which includes the reigns of Edward IV. and Edward V., and ends with the death of Richard, and the proclamation of Henry, Earl of Richmond, as king. After Richard is slain by Richmond, Lord Stanley says to the latter:

> " Courageous Richmond, well hast thou aquit thee.
> Lo, here, this long-usurpéd royalty,
> From the dead temples of this bloody wretch,
> Have I pluck'd off, to grace thy brows withal;
> Wear it, enjoy it, and make much of it."

With the accession of Richmond, as Henry VII., ended the Wars of the Roses. Henry's reign is passed over by the dramatist, as wanting, perhaps, in dramatic interest.

The next, and the last in historical order, is the play of Henry VIII., in the conclusion of which, Cranmer, Archbishop of Canterbury, in a long speech, at the baptism of the Princess Elizabeth, prophesies the prosperity, and happiness, and glory of her reign. The play is thus brought down quite as near to the poet's own time as was perhaps permissible.

The break in the series of the historical plays between the earliest, King John, and Richard II., is partly supplied by some events of the intervals which are referred to in the play of Henry V.

King John and Henry VIII. may be regarded, as Schlegel remarks, as the Prologue and the Epilogue to the other eight. King

John strikes the keynote of the whole series, that keynote being, *nationality*. And Shakespeare wrote these historical plays at a period in English history, when the sense of nationality was deeper than it had ever been before, or, perhaps, has ever been since; and when the national genius had reached its greatest intensity, as is sufficiently shown by the wonderful literary products of the period alone. Shakespeare appeared at the most favorable time in England's history, at the most favorable time, indeed, in the world's history, for the production of a great drama. It is questionable whether there will ever again come a time as favorable.

King John was first printed, so far as is known, in the Folio of 1623. It was composed in 1595 or 1596. There was an earlier play, entitled "The Troublesome Raigne of John King of England, with the discovery of King Richard Cordelions base son (vulgarly named The Bastard Fawconbridge) : also the death of King John at Swinstead Abbey, London, 1591."

The "Troublesome Raigne" was reprinted in 1611, with "written by W. Sh.," on the title-page, and again in 1622, by a different bookseller, with "written by W. Shakespeare" on the title-page. Its author is not known. Pope supposed it to be the work of Rowley; but there are no grounds for such supposition. When it was first printed, in 1591, Shakespeare was 27 years of age, and had not yet come into notice. But in 1611, when the play was reprinted, his plays were in great demand, both on the stage and in print; and the bookseller, it may be supposed, in order to help the sale, slyly put "written by W. Sh." on the title-page, and the bookseller who got out the next edition, in 1622, took advantage of this, and filled out the name.

Dr. Ingleby, in his "Shakespeare, the Man and the Book," Part 2, p. 190, says that Shakespeare's King John "is the result of *filling in a skeleton* taken from the 'Troublesome Reign,' some of the infilling being but a recast or revision of the old phraseology." This does not give a fair idea of the relation of Shakespeare's play to the old play. It is more correct to say that Shakespeare went to the old play for his history, instead of going to Holinshed's

"Chronicles," whence, it appears, he derived most of his knowledge of English and Scottish history. The whole life and spirit of his King John was original with himself.

The old play was written in the service of the Reformation, the reign of King John affording abundance of material, when moulded by a strong partisan spirit (which the author, whoever he was, certainly had), for emphasizing what he regarded as the evils of papal rule, and its antagonism to a vital nationality. Its violent partisan spirit, though entirely inconsistent with a true artistic spirit, and its appeals to the vulgar antagonisms of the groundlings, must have secured for it a great popularity at the time when it first appeared. Of this violent partisan spirit there's not a trace in Shakespeare's play.

In the old play, the ransacking of the monasteries by Faulconbridge is brought dramatically forward, and the scene in which it is presented is the most scurrilous in the play. Philip enters leading a friar, and ordering him to show where the Abbot's treasure lies. The poor friar, after some pathetic entreaties, shows Philip the Abbot's chest,

> "That wanteth not a thousand pound
> In silver and in gold."

Philip commands, "Break up the coffer, Friar." The friar does his bidding, and fair Alice, the nun, is found in the chest, who prays Philip to spare the friar, adding that

> "If money be the means of this,
> I know an ancient nun,
> That hath a hoard these seven years,
> Did never see the sun."

A not very elegant colloquy follows, which ends with Philip's ordering the nun to show him to the other chest.

> "*Nun.* Fair sir, within this press, of plate and money is
> The value of a thousand marks, and other things, by gis;
> Let us alone, and take it all, 'tis yours, sir, now you know it."

Philip orders the friar to pick the lock. The result is that Friar Laurence is found within. Another not very elegant colloquy follows. The nun cries "*Peccavi, parce me.*" A friar entreats Philip :

> " Absolve, sir, for charity,
>   She would be reconciled.
>   *Phil.* And so I shall: sirs, bind them fast,
>   This is their absolution,
>   Go hang them up for hurting them,*
>   Haste them to execution."

Then the poor Friar Laurence interposes a speech, interlarded with very bad Latin. He concludes :

> " *Exaudi me, Domine, sivis me parce*
>   *Dabo pecuniam, si habeo veniam.*
>   To go and fetch it, I will dispatch it,
>   A hundred pounds sterling, for my life's sparing."

Now, for all this dramatization of the ransacking of the monasteries of which I've given the merest outline, Shakespeare substituted four lines of *statement* only. Cardinal Pandulph, the Pope's legate, in his speech counselling the Dauphin to invade England, says :

> " The bastard Faulconbridge
>   Is now in England, ransacking the church,
>   Offending charity." — A. III. Sc. iv. 171–173.

And in the 2d Scene of the 4th Act, the Bastard enters to King John, and, to the King's inquiry, " Now, what says the world to your proceedings," replies,

> " How I have sped among the clergymen,
>   The sums I have collected shall express."

---

* For hurting them, *i.e.*, as a protection against hurting them. So in Chaucer's " Sir Thopas," " an habergeoun for percinge of his herte," *i.e.*, as a protection against the piercing of his heart; and in " Piers the Plowman," Passus VI. 62, " for colde of my nailles," as a remedy against cold of my nails; Passus I. 24, " for myseise," as a remedy against misease or discomfort.

One other example must be given of Shakespeare's suppression of the anti-Romish spirit, as it's exhibited in the old play. In the old play, the repast of the King, in the garden of Swinstead abbey, and his poisoning by a monk, with the connivance of his abbot, are dramatized. The monk tasting the King's drink, with the historic cry of "Wassell," dies, remarking aside, "If the inwards of a toad be a compound of any proof—why, so: it works." The Bastard stabs the abbot, and the King dies after some long and very strongly anti-papal speeches in which he prophesies that out of his loins shall spring a kingly branch whose arms shall reach unto the gates of Rome, and with his feet tread down the strumpet's pride, that sits upon the chair of Babylon.

There's nothing of all this in Shakespeare's play. The poisoning of the King is simply *told* by Hubert, to the Bastard in A. V. Sc. vi. To the Bastard's inquiry "What's the news?" Hubert replies:

> " The King I fear is poisoned by a monk;
> I left him almost speechless, and broke out
> To acquaint you with this evil, that you might
> The better arm you to the sudden time,
> Than if you had at leisure known of this."

In the next scene, in which the King dies, he utters not a word against the papacy.

The fierce partisan spirit of the old play has no place in Shakespeare's. Shakespeare's play is filled throughout with the spirit of Elizabethan England's defiance to the foreigner and the Pope — but to the Pope *as* a foreign power, rather than on religious grounds. That's the point to be observed. It is a national, patriotic, not a religious spirit, or rather not a religion spirit which informs his play. He understood too well the true function of dramatic art, to make religion, whether Roman Catholic, or Protestant, or any other, the *informing* spirit of his play.

The speech of Faulconbridge which concludes the play, voices the spirit of the whole :

" This England never did, nor never shall,
Lie at the proud foot of a conqueror,
But when it first did help to wound itself.
Now these her princes are come home again,
Come the three corners of the world in arms,
And we shall shock them. Nought shall make us rue,
If England to itself do rest but true."

This speech pronounced on the stage, as it no doubt was, within seven or eight years after the destruction of the Spanish Armada, must have produced a powerful effect, intense as was then the sense of nationality.

Commentators have gone to King John for proof that Shakespeare was a Protestant. It might be shown, by other plays, with as much certainty, that he was a good Catholic. But it cannot be shown that he was either one or the other. He was too great an artist to obtrude his own personal religious belief. One thing is quite evident, namely, that he was in spirit a true Christian — so true a Christian that he was perfectly tolerant.

I have said that Shakespeare went to "The Troublesome Raigne" for his history, in the composition of King John, and not to Holinshed's "Chronicles." His play turns on what is entirely unhistorical; or, if not entirely unhistorical, on what went for nothing with John's barons, namely, the defect of his title to the crown, and the exclusion of the rightful heir, his elder brother Geffrey's son, Arthur, and the supposed murder of that son, in order to maintain unsurped power.

Shakespeare's opening scenes must always receive special attention, in studying the dramatic action of his Plays, as in them the keynote of the whole action is usually and distinctly struck.

In the first 43 lines of King John, the entire action of the play is presented in germ.

"*Enter* KING JOHN, QUEEN ELINOR, PEMBROKE, ESSEX, SALISBURY,
and others, with CHATILLON.

K. John. Now say, Chatillon, what would France with us?
Chat. Thus, after greeting, speaks the king of France,

In my behaviour, to the majesty,
The borrow'd majesty, of England here.

Eli. A strange beginning ; — borrow'd majesty !

K. John. Silence, good mother ; hear the embassy.

Chat. Philip of France, in right and true behalf
Of thy deceased brother Geffrey's son,
Arthur Plantagenet, lays most lawful claim
To this fair island, and the territories ;
To Ireland, Poictiers, Anjou, Touraine, Maine :
Desiring thee to lay aside the sword,
Which sways usurpingly these several titles ;
And put the same into young Arthur's hand,
Thy nephew and right royal sovereign.

K. John. What follows if we disallow of this?

Chat. The proud control of fierce and bloody war,
To enforce these rights so forcibly withheld.

K. John. Here have we war for war and blood for blood,
Controlment for controlment ; so answer France.

Chat. Then take my king's defiance from my mouth,
The farthest limit of my embassy.

K. John. Bear mine to him, and so depart in peace :
Be thou as lightning in the eyes of France ;
For ere thou canst report I will be there,
The thunder of my cannon shall be heard :
So, hence ! Be thou the trumpet of our wrath,
And sullen presage of your own decay.
An honourable conduct let him have : —
Pembroke, look to't : Farewell, Chatillon.

[*Exeunt* CHATILLON *and* PEMBROKE.

Eli. What now, my son? have I not ever said,
How that ambitious Constance would not cease,
Till she had kindled France and all the world,
Upon the right and party of her son?
This might have been prevented, and made whole,
With very easy arguments of love ;
Which now the manage of two kingdoms must
With fearful bloody issue arbitrate.

K. John. Our strong possession, and our right for us.

Eli. Your strong possession much more than your right ;

> Or else it must go wrong with you and me:
> So much my conscience whispers in your ear;
> Which none but Heaven, and you, and I shall hear."

We have seen that the Play on its political side quite ignores the facts of history. So, on the personal side, there is an ignoring, to a greater or less degree, of the characters, as represented by history, of some of the dramatis personæ ; and this is especially so in the case of Constance and Arthur, who must be estimated independently of history, and almost as purely fictitious. We must not inquire of history what manner of woman Constance was — we must consider exclusively what she is in the play. And the same may be said of Arthur. Again, as I read the play, I see a purpose throughout to intensify the injustice, and crime, and baseness of John's usurpation, through the characters given to Constance and Arthur. In the First Scene, ll. 31–34, Elinor says of Constance :

> "What now, my son? have I not ever said
> How that ambitious Constance would not cease,
> Till she had kindled France and all the world,
> Upon the right and party of her son?"

And in A. II. Sc. i. 117, when King John says to King Philip of France,

> " Alack ! thou dost usurp authority,"

and Philip replies,

> " Excuse, it is to beat usurping down,"

Elinor interposes,

> " Who is it thou dost call usurper, France ? "

To which question Constance replies,

> " Let *me* make answer, — thy usurping son."

And then Elinor flings at her charges of adultery and guilty ambition, which she knows to be false :

> "Out, insolent ! thy bastard shall be king,
> That thou mayst be a queen and check the world ! "

These words have, I think, misled many commentators; and they have made ambition the ruling motive of Constance.

It is not safe to take the opinions which hostile characters in Shakespeare's Plays, and sometimes characters which are not hostile, are made to express of each other, as opinions which must go for anything in our estimation of the characters; quite as unsafe as it sometimes is in real life to judge of people by what we hear others say of them. In Shakespeare's Plays, what characters say must often be taken as representing themselves rather than others. This is especially true in the case of Elinor. We don't learn what others are from what she says of them; we certainly don't learn what manner of woman Constance really is; but we learn a great deal of what *she* is.

It will be shown in the chapters on the tragedy of Macbeth, that even what Lady Macbeth says of her husband, in the speech she utters, after reading his letter informing her of his having been saluted by the witches, "Hail, king that shalt be," indicates a wrong estimate of him, and that that wrong estimate she herself is made aware of, further on in the play. She gets new knowledge of him after he has "done the deed" and become King. But upon this speech of Lady Macbeth, much false interpretation of Macbeth's character has been based; and much false interpretation has been reflected from it upon herself. But I do not mean, of course, to say that we must never take the opinions of other characters into our estimates of particular characters; for Shakespeare often makes the speeches of other characters reveal a character as distinctly as it is revealed by what that character says and does in his or her own person. Such speeches emphasize it, so to speak. This is especially the case in The Winter's Tale, where our estimation of the noble Hermione is deepened by the opinions expressed of her by all about the Court. What I would say, is, that we must be careful, and not make hasty inferences from the speeches of other characters, in regard to any particular character, and must test the reliableness of those speeches by what that particular character is made to say and do.

To continue this digression a little further: when we apply this rule to Macbeth, I think we must come to the conclusion, after tracing his career from beginning to end, that he was *not*, as Lady Macbeth represents him, " too full o' the milk of human kindness to catch the nearest way "; that he was *not* " without the illness which should attend ambition "; that what he " would highly," he would *not* " holily," if it were necessary; that he *would* " play false," as well as " wrongly win." And that Lady Macbeth discovered her mistake, in regard to the real character of her husband, is afterwards made as clear as her own words and acts can make it; and, in consequence of that discovery, remorse, which had been held in abeyance while her ambition, which was *chiefly* for him (as I shall show), was predominant, got full sway, and she sank under it. Shakespeare knew that " *Nemo repente fuit turpissimus*," and he knew, too, that wives sometimes overestimate and sometimes underestimate, their husbands, just as they do now.

No careful reader of the play of King John, will, I am assured, take Elinor's accusations as at all representing the poet's dramatic purpose in Constance. The old Elinor is the political genius and guide of her son John, " an Ate, stirring him to blood and strife," as Chatillon describes her in the play (A. II. Sc. i. 63), and we must not look for the truth from *her*, in regard to Constance, whom she charges with seeking the throne for her son, only with the ambitious design of ruling herself and kindling all the world. But what Constance says of Elinor (A. II. S. i. 174–190), we can take as the truth in regard to the old queen mother.

What Ulrici says of Constance and Arthur is wide of the mark. I don't find in this German critic much evidence of insight into Shakespeare's dramatic motives, though he has ranked high as a Shakespearian critic. This is what he says, and all that he says:

" As to the fortunes of Constance and Arthur, although they are primarily but an episode in the life and character of John [that is not correct, for they constitute an inseparable part of the main action], yet it is with great significance that they *appear to*

be thus interwoven with the history of the state. The instruction
they furnish forms a pendant to the general lesson of the piece ;
for they teach us [Ulrici's interest is always directed to the didactic,
in a play, rather than to the dramatic action], for they teach us
that nothing in history more invariably meets its due punishment
than *weakness* and *passion* — *those hereditary failings of the female
character.* Women ought not to interfere in history, for history
demands action, and for that they are constitutionally disqualified."

It's a pity Ulrici could not have had a John Ruskin to teach
him what he sets forth, somewhat strongly, to be sure, in his
"Sesame and Lilies," in regard to Shakespeare's heroines. Ulrici
goes on :

"The haste and impatience with which Constance labors to
establish her son's rights . . . justly involves him as well as herself
in ruin. Arthur, therefore, although preserved by the compassion
of Hubert, must nevertheless perish. Had his mother but had the
prudence to wait until he could himself have asserted his own
rights by his own arm, and *when alone he could have possessed a
perfect title,* he could have gained for himself and her what law-
fully belonged to them."

Constance labors, he says, to *establish* her son's rights. But the
play throughout *assumes* that those rights *are* established ; and
the point upon which the whole play turns is, that her son has
been unjustly deprived of them. In history, Arthur's rights were
not established, and John was not regarded by his disaffected
barons in the light of a usurper, but of a tyrant. But the critic
of Shakespeare's play has nothing to do with authentic history ;
he has to do with the play, in itself considered. What are the
poet's postulates and assumptions, is the question to be asked.
Ulrici repeats the same mistake further on in the passage I've
quoted : "If Arthur's mother had had the good sense to wait
until he could himself have asserted his own rights by his own arm,
and when alone he could have possessed a perfect title," etc.

Such criticism as that is on a level with Gustav Rümelin's, on
Romeo and Juliet, in his "Shakespearestudien," which I may cite

here as, along with Ulrici's on King John, a good specimen of a species of criticism which interests itself in everything in a play of Shakespeare, except its own independent dramatic vitality.

Rümelin says : " Why does not Juliet simply confess that she is married already, and confront the consequences with the heroism of her love? Why does she not flee? She comes and goes unhindered, and even the Friar's plan accomplished no more than that instead of starting for Mantua from her father's house, she would have to start from the neighboring churchyard. Why does she not feign sickness? Why is not Paris induced to withdraw by being informed that Juliet is already wedded to another? Why does not the pious Father fall back upon the obvious excuse that as a Christian priest he would not marry a woman while her first husband was still living?" etc., etc.

Verily, there is not evident in such criticism, "that God-given power vouchsafed to us Germans alone before all other nations," to use Professor Lemcke's expression, in his boastful assertion of the superiority of German Shakespearian criticism to all others in the world.

These, it is true, are not, by any means, fair specimens of German criticism. Yet, we must remember, that Ulrici has ranked high among Shakespearian critics in Germany, and that his " Ueber Shakespeare's dramatische Kunst u. sein Verhältniss zu Calderon u. Goethe," first published in Halle, in 1839, was held, and is still held, in high estimation.

Of Constance, Gervinus says : " *Ambition* spurred by maternal love, maternal love goaded by ambition and womanly *vanity*, these form the distinguishing features of this character, features out of which, from the adversity of fate, that *raging passion* is developed, which at last shatters the soul and body of the *frail* woman." Further on he speaks of " her *coarse* outbursts against Elinor " ; and represents her as " the female counterpart to Richard II., who, imperious in prosperity, was speedily lost in adversity " ; " she plays with her sorrow in *witty* words and similes " ; " the *violent-natured* woman bursts forth with scornful hatred against Austria, after he has become faithless."

Is this the Constance as she is understood by the unphilosophical but sympathetic reader, with no critical theories to maintain? I think not.

The play, let me repeat, turns upon the usurpation of John and the consequent murder of Arthur, the rightful heir. The usurpation is *assumed* — the validity of Arthur's title to the crown is *assumed*, and this assumption on the part of the dramatist must not be lost sight of, authentic history to the contrary notwithstanding. It cannot then be said that Constance is ambitious for the crown, either for her son's sake or for her own sake. What she claims and contends for, and agonizes for, is her son's rights, of which he has been basely deprived. Even the queen mother, Elinor, is made, as we have seen, to express to John her sense of the usurpation, in the opening scene, after Chatillon, the ambassador from Philip of France, has gone from the royal presence. What she afterwards says to Constance should go for nothing in the case. She says what she does as a matter of course.

Faulconbridge adheres firmly to John throughout the play; but he is made to reveal, very distinctly, in his speeches, his secret sense of the injustice done to Arthur. He knows that John is a usurper; he knows that he is compounded of baseness, injustice, and treachery; but so long as he has possession of the throne, whether that possession be just or unjust, he is to him the impersonation of the state, to whom loyalty is due.

Shakespeare, it is evident, made Faulconbridge voice the feelings of the English people, *in his own time*, against foreign interference in church and state. The speeches in which he gives expression to the "self-dependent life and self-sufficing strength inherent in the nation," must have been particularly agreeable to the audiences at the Globe Theatre, the attempt made but seven or eight years before, by the then richest and mightiest of European powers, to invade England and impose upon her the Roman Catholic religion, having resulted in one of the most disastrous defeats in all history.

To return to Constance and Arthur: Constance appears only in

A. II. Sc. i. and A. III. Sc. i. and iv. Arthur appears in A. II. Sc. i., A. III. Sc. i., ii., and iii., A. IV. Sc. i. and iii. These scenes evidence with an entire conclusiveness, I think, that Shakespeare's dramatic purpose in Constance was to exhibit *outraged maternal affection*, independently of any ambition on her part. For her to show personal ambition for the crown, would mar the artistic symmetry and the whole moral tone of the play. We shall see that there is not a single speech of hers which indicates directly or by implication, any personal ambition. She is "oppressed with wrongs" done to her beloved Arthur, whom the poet, in the service of his art, represents as possessing all those charms of person and all those qualities of mind and heart which intensify a mother's affection and devotion.

In comparing Shakespeare's Arthur with the Arthur of the old play, we can easily see the dramatic purpose which determined the poet in making him what he does. And Augustine Skottowe well remarks: "The maternal distress of Constance, in the old play, is clamorous and passionate, vindictive and contumelious. The hand of Shakespeare tempered her rage into vehemence, attuned her clamour to eloquence, and modulated her coarse vindictiveness into a deep sense of gross injuries and undeserved misfortunes."

From the accounts we have of Mrs. Siddons's impersonation of Constance, it appears that she made strong-willed ambition her ruling motive, rather than maternal affection. The impersonation, in the last generation, by Miss Helen Faucit, now Lady Martin, the wife of Sir Theodore Martin, the biographer of the Prince Consort, appears to have been a truer one than that of Mrs. Siddons. From the dramatic criticism of the time (1843 and later) we learn that maternal tenderness and affection alone motived and informed her impersonation.

The situation in A. III. Sc. i., which has been led up to by the marriage of the Dauphin and Blanch, is, perhaps, unsurpassed as a dramatic situation, in all Shakespeare. To Constance, when, deserted and betrayed, she stands alone in her despair, amid her false friends and her ruthless enemies, Mrs. Jameson applies, most appropriately, the image of the mother eagle, wounded and bleeding to death, yet stretched over her young in an attitude of defiance, while all the baser birds of prey are clamoring around her eyrie. The noble Bastard, whose heart seems to be always in the right place, feels deeply the injustice of the act of the two kings:

> "Mad world! mad kings! mad composition!
> John, to stop Arthur's title in the whole,
> Hath willingly departed with a part,
> And France, whose armour conscience buckled on,
> Whom zeal and charity brought to the field
> As God's own soldier, rounded * in the ear
> With that same purpose-changer, that sly devil,
> That broker, that still breaks the pate of faith,
> That daily break-vow, he that wins of all,
> Of kings, of beggars, old men, young men, maids, . . .
> That smooth-faced gentleman, tickling Commodity,
> Commodity, † the bias of the world," etc.

There's a sort of reflex action induced in his mind, which causes him to slander himself. After representing self-interest as the bias of the world, he continues:

> "And why rail I on this Commodity?
> But for because he hath not woo'd me yet:
> *   *   *   *   *   *   *   *
> Well, whiles I am a beggar, I will rail
> And say there is no sin but to be rich;
> And being rich, my virtue then shall be
> To say there is no vice but beggary.
> Since kings break faith upon Commodity,
> Gain be my lord, for I will worship thee."

All this is pure self-slander, as his subsequent disinterested and magnanimous acts and words show.

---

* whispered.   † Profit, self-interest.

The league entered into by the two kings (first proposed by the besieged citizens of Angiers), A. II. Sc. i., is severed by Pandulph, the Pope's legate, who demands of John, why, against the authority of the Church, he keeps Stephen Langton, chosen archbishop of Canterbury, from that holy see. To this demand John returns a defiant answer (A. III. Sc. i. 147–160). The legate, thereupon, by the power that he has, declares him "curs'd and excommunicate," and commands Philip, on peril of a curse, to let go the hand of the arch-heretic, and raise the power of France upon his head, unless he submit himself to Rome. The consequence is, that Philip, after begging the Cardinal, under the circumstances, to devise some other means, and after being entreated by Constance, Austria, and Lewis, to submit to the Cardinal, and by Elinor and Blanch, to stand fast, falls off from John (though he is manifestly not convinced by the argument of the legate that it is his duty to do so), and hostilities are resumed. The French forces are worsted; they lose Angiers, and Arthur is taken prisoner by John, and conveyed to England. This gives a turn to, and complicates, things at home which will prove fatal to John. He is now forced, by circumstances resulting from the capture of Arthur, to play a losing game within his own kingdom. His fears as to the young and interesting captive, whose misfortune wins the sympathies of the courtiers and the people, drive him to measures for his own safety which deprive him of all chance of safety. He passes, irresistibly, into the power of an avenging fate. The dramatic situation, at this stage of the play, is in Shakespeare's best tragic manner. The moral baseness of John, which seals his doom, may be said to be gathered up, and exhibited in its extreme intensity, in the scene with Hubert, the 3d of the 3d Act, in which he intimates to Hubert his wish to have the little prince put out of the way: and in the 2d Scene of the 4th Act, where he accuses the aptness of the instrument as the cause of the suggestion. I would call special attention to the last 19 verses of John's long speech (A. III. Sc. iii. 30–50), beginning, "If the midnight bell." The thought keeps on the wing through all these 19 verses. There is a moral significance in the suspended construction of the language. The mind of the dastard king hovers over the subject of the ungodly act and dares not alight upon it ; and the verse, in its uncadenced movement, admirably registers the speaker's state of mind :

> " If the midnight bell
> Did, with his iron tongue and brazen mouth,
> Sound on into the drowsy race of night ;
> If this same were a church-yard where we stand,
> And thou possessed with a thousand wrongs,
> Or if that surly spirit, melancholy,
> Had bak'd thy blood and made it heavy, thick,
> Which else runs tickling up and down the veins,
> Making that idiot, laughter, keep men's eyes,
> And strain their cheeks to idle merriment,
> A passion hateful to my purposes,
> Or if that thou could see me without eyes,
> Hear me without thine ears, and make reply
> Without a tongue, using conceit alone,
> Without eyes, ears, and harmful sound of words ;
> Then, in despite of brooded watchful day,
> I would into thy bosom pour my thoughts ;
> But, ah, I will not ! yet I love thee well ;
> And, by my troth, I think thou lov'st me well."

The loveliness of Arthur is the most fully exhibited in the scene with Hubert, the 1st of the 4th Act, where he entreats Hubert to spare his eyes. The pathos of the situation is pushed to the verge of the painful. The highest art was demanded here to keep the treatment of the subject within the domain of the beautiful. And it is so kept.

I need not trace the dramatic action further. From the point reached, to the end, there are no new movements. King John is now in a current which he cannot stem, and will be swept helplessly along to the bitter end.

Shakespeare is always true to the fatality of overmastering passion of every kind. To the extent that his characters forfeit the power of self-assertion, do they become subject to fate, and are swept along by circumstances. This, of course, is a universal, an obvious, a self-evident, truth ; but it is a truth which the inferior sort of dramatists do not always observe, in their treatment of great passions, and their work is, in consequence, wanting in moral proportion.

The dramatists of the Restoration period do not observe it ; and whatever mechanical symmetry they attain to, in their plays, true moral proportion is wanting. The dramatic criticism of that period, Rymer's, for example, shows that the moral proportion of Shakespeare's plays was but little recognized. This is shown, too, by the *rifacimenti* of some of his plays which were perpetrated by Dryden, Davenant, Tate, and others. Tate's Lear is a signal example. Poetic justice meant something other with these dramatic carpenters, than the justly poetic.

MUCH ADO ABOUT NOTHING.

———•◦•———

M UCH ADO ABOUT NOTHING appeared for the first
time, in 4to, in 1600, with the following title : " Much
adoe about Nothing. As it hath been sundrie times publikely
acted by the right honourable, the Lord Chamberlaine his seruants. Written by William Shakespeare. London. Printed by
V. S. for Andrew Wise, and William Aspley. 1600."

The word "nothing" appears to have been pronounced in
Shakespeare's day, "noting"; and in A. II. Sc. iii. 57, there's a
play on the two words. Balthasar says :

> "Note this before my notes ;
> There's not a note of mine that's worth the noting."

To which Don Pedro replies :

> " Why, these are very crotchets that he speaks ;
> Note, notes, forsooth, and nothing."

The last word was changed by Theobald to " noting."

Richard Grant White sees the same pun in the title of the play.
"The play is Much Ado about Nothing," he says, " only in a very
vague and general sense, but Much Ado about Noting in one especially apt and descriptive ; for the much ado is produced entirely
by noting. It begins with the noting of the Prince and Claudio,
first by Antonio's man, and then by Borachio, who reveals their
confidence to John ; it goes on with Benedick noting the Prince,
Leonato, and Claudio, in the garden, and again with Beatrice
noting Margaret and Ursula in the same place ; the incident upon
which its action turns is the noting of Borachio's interview with

Margaret by the Prince and Claudio; and, finally, the incident which reveals the plot is the noting of Borachio and Conrade by the Watch." This interpretation is quite ingenious, if nothing more can be said of it. It should be added, that the *mis*-noting of Benedick by Beatrice, and of Beatrice by Benedick, is the occasion of the predominant comic feature of the play. The comedy, indeed, turns upon this *mis*-noting.

Shakespeare has, evidently, repeated this pun in The Winter's Tale, A. IV. Sc. iv. 626. Autolycus, speaking of the easy success of his knavery, says, "I could have filed keys off that hung in chains : no hearing, no feeling, but my sir's song, and admiring the *nothing* of it."

But see Ellis's "Early English Pronunciation," pp. 966–973, inclusive, where Richard Grant White's Elizabethan Pronunciation is presented. See especially on p. 971, 1st col., Ellis's opinion of the pun which White sees in the title of Much Ado about Nothing. The objections advanced by Ellis are not conclusive, especially the following : "Mr. White seeks to establish this [*i.e.*, the pun in the title of the play] by a wonderfully prosaic summary of instances, all the while forgetting the antithesis of *much* and *nothing*, on which the title is founded, with an allusion to the great confusion occasioned by a slight mistake — of Ursula for Hero — which was a mere nothing in itself. The Germans in translating it, *Viel Lärm um Nichts*, certainly never felt Mr. White's difficulty."

The last sentence, especially, doesn't strike me as particularly forcible.

The 1600 Much Ado about Nothing is one of the most correctly printed of the quarto editions of the Plays. There is no other quarto edition, so far as is known, previous to the publication of the First Folio, 1623. The text of the play, in the Folio, appears to have been taken from the Quarto. Some stage directions of interest occur first in the Folio, but as regards the text, where the Folio differs from the Quarto, it differs, according to the opinion of the "Cambridge" editors, almost always for the worse. Those editors, however, have a peculiar partiality for the quarto editions. But the differences are but slight, and the text of the play has, accordingly, presented but little difficulty to editors. *O si sic omnes!*

The date of composition is put, with almost absolute certainty, in 1599, when Shakespeare was 35 years old.

The play appears to have been a great favorite in Shakespeare's own day. Leonard Digges (the same who wrote the verses prefixed to the First Folio), in his verses prefixed to the 1640 edition of .Shakespeare's Poems, mentions this play, along with three or four others, as especially attractive to the frequenters of the theatre.

> "So have I seene, when Cæsar would appeare,
> And on the Stage at halfe-sword parley were
> *Brutus* and *Cassius :* oh how the Audience
> Were ravish'd, with what wonder they went thence,
> When some new day they would not brooke a line
> Of tedious (though well laboured) *Catiline ;* *
> *Sejanus* * too was irkesome, they priz'de more
> Honest *Iago,* or the jealous *Moore.*
> And though the Fox * and subtill Alchimist,*
> Long intermitted, could not quite be mist,
> Though these have sham'd all the Ancients, and might raise
> Their Authours merit with a crowne of Bayes,
> Yet these sometimes, even at a friends desire
> Acted, have scarce defraid the Seacole fire
> And doore-keepers : when let but *Falstaffe* come,
> *Hall, Poines,* the rest, you scarce shall have a roome,
> All is so pester'd : † let but *Beatrice*
> And *Benedicke* be seene, loe in a trice
> The Cockpit, Galleries, Boxes, all are full."

This is interesting contemporary testimony to the popularity of the play, and also to that of other plays of Shakespeare over Ben Jonson's best plays.

---

* Plays by Ben Jonson.   † jammed.

When we turn to the old stories upon which Shakespeare based his plays, we get, perhaps, a deeper impression of his essential originality than we should were the plots wholly his own, whatever might be their merits as plots. We are brought, in this way, to a deeper sense of the workings of the inner spirit which subjected all its appropriations to its own creative purpose. We see that the work grew from what the workman had within himself, and not merely from following what others had done before him. We see that the old story has been less worked into, than employed as the scaffolding of, his dramatic structure. A signal illustration of this is afforded by The Winter's Tale. Any one who has read this play with an adequate appreciation of its dramatic merits, must, on turning to the novel on which it was founded ("Pandosto, or the Triumph of Time," otherwise called "Dorastus and Fawnia," by Robert Greene), be struck with the admirable manner in which the poet has converted materials supplied by another to his own higher purposes. The bare outline, even, of the story, he does not follow very closely. We may say that he follows it where the propulsion of his own thought and feeling bears him along in his work parallel with the original thread; but the same propulsion also carries him away from it, — an evidence that his work has its own independent principle of movement. The old story is rather the exciting cause of what afterwards follows out its own path.

The life and the main interest of Much Ado about Nothing are due to characters which, so far as we know, were entirely original with Shakespeare, namely, Benedick and Beatrice, Dogberry and Verges. The other characters have prototypes in the original story, which is found under various forms, the earliest being the tale of Ariodante and Ginevra, in the "Orlando Furioso" of Ariosto.

Sir John Harrington's translation of Ariosto appeared in 1591, but no influence of this version can be traced in the Play. A similar tale occurs in Spenser's "Faerie Queene," Book II. Canto IV. Shakespeare's original appears to have been the 22d novel of

Bandello, which had been translated into French by Belleforest, in his "Histoires Tragiques," and possibly into English. Whether Shakespeare was indebted mediately or immediately to Bandello cannot with certainty be determined. At any rate, the portion of Shakespeare's plot pertaining to Claudio and Hero most resembles the form of the story as told by Bandello, the scene of which, as is that of the Play, is laid in Messina; the father of the slandered maiden is named Lionato, and the friend of her lover, Don Piero, or Pedro.

The characters of the play who constitute its main charm are, of course, Benedick and Beatrice. And it is upon a correct understanding of the relations of these two characters to each other, that an appreciation of the comedy essentially depends. They are faintly sketched in Love's Labor's Lost, Shakespeare's first genuine play. In comparing, or rather contrasting, the two pairs of lovers, Berowne and Rosaline, and Benedick and Beatrice, we can see Shakespeare's growth, and the nature of that growth, during the interval between the composition of Love's Labor's Lost and the composition of Much Ado about Nothing.

Beatrice has a better and deeper nature than some of her critics have allowed her. While she is, as Furnivall characterizes her, "The sauciest, most piquant, sparkling, madcap girl that Shakespeare ever drew," she is also, as he adds, "a loving, deep-natured, true woman too."

The poet Campbell slanderously characterizes her as "an odious woman," "a disagreeable female character," "a tartar by Shakespeare's own showing," etc. He adds:—"I once knew such a pair [as Benedick and Beatrice]; the lady was a perfect Beatrice; she railed hypocritically at wedlock before her marriage, and with bitter sincerity after it. She and her Benedick now live apart, but with entire reciprocity of sentiments, each devoutly wishing that the other may soon pass into a better world." He contrasts her, to her great disadvantage, with Rosalind, in As You Like It. Verplanck attributes Campbell's unjust estimate of Beatrice to accidental personal associations. And this may have been the fact.

There must have been something back of these severe strictures upon Beatrice, in the poet's own matrimonial experience. Or, perhaps, the fastidious temperament which he appears to have possessed made him condemn anything outré in the female character; so that a saucy, piquant, sparkling, madcap girl, to use Furnivall's epithets, whatever might be her more substantial qualities, appeared to him, according to his standard of the proprieties, " A disagreeable female character," " a tartar," " an odious woman."

Mrs. Jameson, along with much that is justly said, says also certain things of Beatrice, which do her, I think, great injustice. In her temper, she says, there's a slight infusion of the *termagant.* She speaks of " her scornful airs," " her assumption of superiority." Her wit she thinks " less good-humored than that of Benedick." " She appears in a less amiable light than her lover " ; " with Beatrice *temper* has still the mastery." Speaking of her relations with her cousin, Hero, she says, " Beatrice asserts the rule of a master spirit." That is true enough, if it is not understood to mean that she is domineering. Again, speaking of Hero, she says, " When she has Beatrice at an advantage, she repays her with interest, in the severe, but most animated and elegant picture she draws of her cousin's *imperious character,*" etc. This is certainly an entire misconception on the part of Mrs. Jameson, and does injustice also to Hero. The allusion is to the scene where Hero speaks with Ursula, in Leonato's garden, to be overheard by Beatrice. But the gentle, negative Hero certainly doesn't mean to *pay her back.* That's not her purpose at all, as any one can easily see who reads this scene. Again : " A haughty, excitable, and violent temper is another of the characteristics of Beatrice, but there is more of impulse than of passion in her vehemence."

Mrs. Jameson recognizes the good and even noble qualities of Beatrice, but the expressions I have quoted, and others, which vein the entire surface of her essay, reveal, I think, a feeling on the part of the authoress, that the good qualities of Beatrice are so offset by bad ones, that the former are as likely to be overbalanced by the latter, as the latter by the former.

Neither Campbell nor Mrs. Jameson can prophesy much matrimonial happiness for Benedick and Beatrice. Mrs. Jameson thinks they may be *tolerably* happy, but Campbell is quite certain that Beatrice will provoke her husband to give her much and just conjugal castigation. Furnivall has a different, and I think, truer opinion of what the married life of such a pair would be. " Fancy," he says, " Beatrice playing with her baby, and her husband looking on ! Never child 'ud have had such fun since the creation of the world."

In the opening scene of the Play, the attitudes of Benedick and Beatrice towards each other are presented ; and it is plain to see to what those attitudes are due — namely, a mutual chaffing, and, on the part of Benedick, a depreciation of womankind which is irritating to Beatrice and provokes her to the defence of her sex. It will be observed that she exhibits throughout the play great sensitiveness in regard to the honor of her sex.

From a speech of Leonato to the messenger in the opening scene, we learn that Benedick and Beatrice had had wit combats previous to his going to the wars : " You must not, sir, mistake my niece : there is a kind of merry war betwixt Signior Benedick and her ; they never meet but there is a skirmish of wit between them." The messenger shows a high admiration of Benedick ; and her inquiries in regard to him, apparently so derisive, are really designed to elicit praises of Benedick which are secretly gratifying to her. When he enters, with Don Pedro, Don John, and Claudio, he begins at once his irritating raillery. To Don Pedro's remark to Leonato, " I think this is your daughter," Leonato replies, " Her mother has many times told me so." And then Benedick interposes, addressing Leonato, " Were you in doubt, sir, that you asked her? *Leon.* Signior Benedick, no ; for then were *you* a child. *D. Pedro.* You have it full, Benedick [*i.e.,* you get as good as you gave] : we may guess by this what you are, being a man. Truly, the lady fathers herself: . . .

Bene. If Signior Leonato be her father, she would not have his head on her shoulders for all Messina, as like him as she is." This speech is sufficient, Beatrice knowing the general depreciation of woman which is back of it, to cause her to retort: " I wonder that you will still [*i.e.*, ever] be talking, Signior Benedick ; nobody marks you. *Bene.* What, my dear Lady Disdain ! are you yet living?" They are both now well started in " a skirmish of wit," in which Beatrice, as is usual, gets the best of it. To Benedick's remark, "It is certain I am loved of all ladies, only you excepted : and I would I could find in my heart that I had not a hard heart ; for truly, I love none," she replies, " A dear happiness to women : they would else have been troubled with a pernicious suitor. . . . I had rather hear my dog bark at a crow than a man swear he loves me." This speech may be easily misunderstood. It *has* been misunderstood by some critics. It musn't be taken in its absolute meaning, but entirely as provoked by the speech of Benedick. The sensitive, high-strung girl resents his professed indifference to women, and her resentment is really intensified by the secret admiration she cherishes for him. In getting the better of him, in his own habitual line of raillery, she wounds his self-esteem, as is shown by what he says of her to Claudio, when all the others go out. But we feel as we do in the case of Beatrice, that what he says is emphasized by the half-conscious admiration he has of her. In reply to Claudio's praises of Hero, in which he pronounces her as, in his eye, the sweetest lady that he ever looked on, Benedick says : " I can see yet without spectacles and I see no such matter : there's her cousin, and she were not possessed with a fury, exceeds her as much in beauty as the first of May does the last of December." Having spoken of her as possessed with a fury, he can, without incurring the suspicion of any extended admiration, praise her beauty as far surpassing Hero's ; but the reader, or the spectator, is assured that his admiration goes beyond her personal charms.

In the masquerade scene, where the two next meet, Benedick is cut to the quick, and, in spite of their secret interest in each other, a barrier is raised between them which, we shall see, has to be removed by the kind interposition of their common friends. There are two courtships going on, in the masquerade scene, Don Pedro's, of Hero, in behalf of Claudio, who hasn't the courage to court Hero in his own person, and Balthazar's, of Margaret. The conversation is a mixed one, of course. We have only bits of what passes between the different pairs. First we have a bit of Don Pedro's talk with Hero; then, of Balthazar's, with Margaret; then of Ursula's, with Antonio; and then what passes between Benedick and Beatrice. "*Beat.* Will you not tell me who told you so? *Bene.* No, you shall pardon me. *Beat.* Nor will you not tell me who you are? *Bene.* Not now. *Beat.* That I was disdainful, and that I had my good wit out of the 'Hundred Merry Tales;'—well, this was Signior Benedick that said so. *Bene.* What's he? *Beat.* I am sure you know him well enough. *Bene.* Not I, believe me. *Beat.* Did he never make you laugh? *Bene.* I pray you, what is he? *Beat.* Why, he is the prince's jester; a very dull fool; only his gift is in devising impossible slanders: none but libertines delight in him; and the commendation is not in his wit but in his villainy; for he both pleases men and angers them, and then they laugh at him and beat him. I am sure he is in the fleet: I would he had boarded me." (Note the equivocal use of "fleet," which may mean the company present, a company of ships, or, the prison for insolvent debtors; "boarded" carries out the figure, "I would he had boarded me," that is, instead of you.) "*Bene.* When I know the gentleman, I'll tell him what you say. *Beat.* Do, do: he'll but break a comparison or two on me; which, peradventure not marked or not laughed at, strikes him into melancholy; and then there's a partridge wing saved, for the fool will eat no supper that night."

The effect upon Benedick of the masked interview with Beatrice, we learn from the account of it he afterwards gives to Don Pedro. She misused him, he says, past the endurance of a block. She speaks poniards, and every word stabs. He declares he wouldn't marry her even if she were endowed with all that Adam had left him before he transgressed; she would have made Hercules have turned spit, yea, and have cleft his club to make the fire too. When she enters, Benedick makes an abrupt exit, saying, "O God, sir, here's a dish I love not; I cannot endure my Lady Tongue."

Things have now come to such a pass, the pair are so shut off from each other, as it were, by their persistent wit and raillery, that only by the kind interposition of their friends can their mutual disguises be stript off. This is done by the stratagem, first proposed by Don Pedro, and heartily seconded by Leonato, Claudio, and Hero.

There are some commentators who go so far astray as to understand this stratagem as little more than a practical joke, for uniting in marriage two people, apparently so antagonistic, and so utterly unfitted to sustain to each other the relations of husband and wife. Shakespeare would certainly not have condescended to anything so small as that, whereby to excite mirth. If it were so, it would degrade the whole play. Even Mrs. Jameson speaks of the stratagem as practised upon Beatrice, as "a snare laid for her affections." If Beatrice's affections were not already enlisted, the stratagem would be silly. Don Pedro is entirely serious when he says: "I would fain have it a match, and I doubt not but to fashion it, if you three will but minister such assistance as I shall give you direction." Leonato, the uncle and guardian of Beatrice, whom he loves as deeply as he does his own daughter, replies, "My lord, I am for you, tho' it cost me ten nights' watching." He certainly doesn't understand what is about to be done, as a practical joke, to entrap his niece and Benedick into an ill-assorted marriage which would of course result in a plentiful lack of happiness. No. It is because he feels assured that Benedick and Beatrice have already a secret love for each other, notwithstanding their combats, which he calls, in the opening scene of the play, "a kind of merry war" and "a skirmish of wit," and because he feels assured that their union would be one of happiness. The other view makes an ass of Leonato. And then see what Hero says, between whom and her cousin Beatrice, there is a deep sisterly affection. After Leonato has said, " My lord, I am for you, tho' it cost me ten nights' watchings," Claudio says, " And I, my lord." Then Don Pedro turns to Hero and says, " And you too, gentle Hero? " To which she replies, " I will do any modest office, my lord, to help my cousin to a good husband." The speech of Don Pedro which follows, and which closes the scene, testifies to Benedick's noble lineage, his approved valor and con-firmed honesty.

The soliloquies of Benedick and Beatrice, after the stratagem has been practised upon each, show what their real selves are which have been hitherto disguised. Benedick's soliloquy, taken with the soliloquy which precedes the stratagem, and in which his railing against matrimony reaches its climax, has a most comic effect. Beatrice's soliloquy, which she utters after Hero and Ur-sula go out, exhibits the genuineness of her nature.

Coming forward, she says :

> " What fire is in mine ears?   Can this be true?
>   Stand I condemned for pride and scorn so much?
>   Contempt, farewell! and maiden pride, adieu!
>   No glory lives behind the back of such.
>   And, Benedick, love on; I will requite thee,
>   Taming my wild heart to thy loving hand :
>   If thou dost love, my kindness shall incite thee
>   To bind our loves up in a holy band;
>   For others say thou dost deserve, and I
>   Believe it better than reportingly."

i.e., better than on hearsay.

We have seen what has hitherto sharpened and winged the arrows shot at Benedick. She has been kept in a state of chronic *pique* at his constant satirical reflections upon, and his professed non-allegiance to, the sex whose honor she has felt herself called upon to defend. Her true self, which has all along secretly admired the solid elements of Benedick's character, has been, in conse-quence, kept in the background ; but as soon as she is made to believe that Benedick loves her, this true self comes immediately to the front. There is no transformation wrought — only a barrier has been removed which the two have co-operated to place between themselves by their sharp wit-skirmishes.

Their mutual misnoting, along with their mutual love, is what essentially constitutes the comedy of the situation. If it be understood, as it *is* understood, more or less distinctly by some critics and readers, that a transformation has been wrought in each by the similar stratagem practised upon each, the comedy of the situation is quite destroyed. At any rate, it is of a very much inferior quality, and, I would add, it is not of a Shakespearian quality.

The stratagem having been successfully carried out, the dramatic problem is, to raise them to the height required, after all that has passed, for a mutual confession of love, and, at the same time, to keep their self-respect entire. This problem the poet has, as we shall see, beautifully solved.

The unshakable faith, the deep sympathy, and the moral indignation, of which Beatrice is capable, are shown in the scene in the church, where poor Hero is so cruelly treated. Shakespeare delights in situations which serve to exhibit the moral beauty of woman ; and he has made the situation here reveal the wealth of Beatrice's soul. Though her real nature has already been distinctly shown, in her soliloquy, after she overhears her cousin and Ursula, in the garden, it is here exalted and enlarged, and no question can arise as to what manner of woman she is. After the charge has been brought against the bride by the bridegroom, at the very altar, and it has been sustained by the Prince, both of whom, as Benedick later expresses it, having the very bent of honor, the bride's own father feels constrained, from such testimony, to believe it true. Benedick interrupts his bewailing speech with " Sir, sir, be patient. For my part I am so attired in wonder I know not what to say." But Beatrice knows what to say. In spite of all the strong testimony against her cousin, in spite of the father's harshly expressed belief in her shame, Beatrice exclaims, " Oh, on my soul, my cousin is belied!" Her full, unfaltering belief in Hero's innocence is shown still more strongly by the reply she makes to Benedick's inquiry as to whether she were Hero's bedfellow the previous night. "No, truly not; although, until last night, I have this twelvemonth been her bedfellow." This frank reply, which gives strong circumstantial support to the charge against Hero, she makes fearlessly, evidently feeling that the case can bear to have the whole truth told without the least reservation, and that Hero *must* be innocent, and will finally be proved so, all testimony, direct and circumstantial to the contrary, notwithstanding. The dramatist has, with great skill and by the simplest means, made the nobleness and perfect genuineness of Beatrice's character stand out here in the strongest light.

Her testimony that Hero was not her bedfellow the previous night, confirms the father in his belief of the charge, — "makes stronger what was before barred up with ribs of iron." The good Friar Francis interposes in a speech which does honor to his heart, but which has no effect upon the wrought-up Leonato. To the question of the Friar, "Lady, what man is he you are accused of?" Hero replies, "They know that do accuse me; I know none: if I know more of any man alive than that which maiden modesty doth warrant, let all my sins lack mercy."

The Friar thereupon remarking that there is some strange misunderstanding on the part of the princes, Benedick, assured as he is that Don Pedro and Claudio "have the very bent of honor," is led to express the suspicion that the charge against Hero is all the work of Don John the bastard, "whose spirits toil," he says, "in frame of villainies." This gives a turn to things. Hero having swooned upon her father's saying "Hath no man's dagger here a point for me," in which speech, we must understand, was implied to her a belief in the charge made against her, and the princes having left her for dead, the Friar proposes a plan, which is seconded by Benedick, that her death be published, that a mourning ostentation be maintained, that mournful epitaphs be hung on the family monument, and all rites be performed that appertain unto a burial. This plan well carried out shall, he says, " on her behalf, change slander to remorse [pity] ; that is *some* good : but not for that dream I on this strange course, but on this travail look for greater birth." This greater birth he sets forth in a speech the most beautiful in sentiment and in tone, of the whole play, one of the most beautiful, indeed, in Shakespeare :

> " She dying, as it must be so maintain'd,
> Upon the instant that she was accus'd,
> Shall be lamented, pitied, and excus'd,
> Of every hearer: For it so falls out,
> That what we have we prize not to the worth
> Whiles we enjoy it ; but being lack'd and lost,
> Why then we rack the value, then we find
> The virtue that possession would not show us
> Whiles it was ours : So will it fare with Claudio :
> When he shall hear she died upon his words,
> The idea of her life shall sweetly creep
> Into his study of imagination ;
> And every lovely organ of her life
> Shall come apparell'd in more precious habit,
> More moving-delicate, and full of life,
> Into the eye and prospect of his soul,
> Than when she liv'd indeed : — then shall he mourn,
> (If ever love had interest in his liver,)
> And wish he had not so accused her ;
> No, though he thought his accusation true."

Friar Francis is, of all Shakespeare's friars, the favorite, I am sure, with readers of the Plays, though Friar Laurence, in Romeo and Juliet, commands equally our love and respect.

Leonato, urged by Benedick, in a speech which shows how he has been lifted up by the occasion and by Beatrice's exhibition of her highest self, replies, " being that I flow in grief, the smallest twine may lead me."

Very beautiful is the art with which Shakespeare has raised Benedick and Beatrice to the height required for a mutual avowal

of love, after all that has passed between them; and when Leonato and the Friar go out, and they are left alone on the scene,
we see, in the best light, what in each has been shut off, more or
less, from view, by wit and banter, and mutual misunderstanding
— mutual misnoting (to revert to the punning title of the Play).

Their preparedness for a mutual confession of love, and, on
Benedick's part, for all that will be involved in that, in relation
to righting Beatrice's cousin, is indicated, at once, in the beginning of their conference, after Leonato and the Friar go out (A.
IV. Sc. i. 257) : "*Bene.* Lady Beatrice, have you *wept all this
while?*   *Beat.* Yea, and I will weep a while longer.   *Bene.* I
will not desire that.   *Beat.* You have no reason ; I do it freely.
Bene. Surely I do believe your fair cousin is wronged.   *Beat.*
Ah, how much might the man deserve of me that would right
her !   *Bene.* Is there any way to show such friendship?   *Beat.*
A very even way, but no such friend.   *Bene.* May a man do it?
Beat. It is a man's office, but not yours." The movement of the
dialogue thus far, is very nice, all the circumstances considered.
In Beatrice's speech, "It is a man's office, but not yours," there
is nothing whatever pettish or ill-humored to be understood, nor
the slightest ingratitude for the kindly-disposed questions of Benedick.   On the contrary, it involves the most delicate consideration
for Benedick, and indicates that she has " the very bent of honor."
In the first place, their relations to each other have not gone far
enough just yet, to give Beatrice the right to make any claims
whatever upon Benedick for the righting of her deeply-injured
cousin ; and, in the second place, those who have directly wronged
her cousin, namely, Don Pedro and Claudio, are, she knows, Benedick's dearest friends.   She knows nothing yet, of course, of what
has impelled them to the charge made against Hero.   Benedick
is quick to recognize in her speech what is in the way of her making any claims upon him, and in reply says, " *I do love nothing in
the world so well as you* " : and adds, with a sense of their past
squabbling relations, " *is not that strange ?* "

The way is now opened up for Beatrice to make confession of

her love ; and this, it is evident, yet remains to be done before any claim can be made upon Benedick, — before it becomes his office to right Hero. That way she enters with a charming indirectness : "As strange as the thing I know not. It were as possible for me to say I loved nothing so well as you : but believe me not ; and yet I lie not ; I confess nothing, nor I deny nothing. I am sorry for my cousin. *Bene.* By my sword, Beatrice, thou lovest me." There seems to be implied in "by my sword," that Benedick, who is characterized by great quickness of perception, already anticipates what will be required of him, as soon as the confession of love is mutual. Beatrice replies, "Do not swear and eat it"; in which there is evidently implied her sense of the severe task it will necessarily be for Benedick to challenge either of his friends, in support of the honor of Hero. Benedick again is quick to understand, and replies, "I will swear by it that you love me ; and I will make him eat it that says I love not you." Beatrice tests him still further, though with the kindest and most - honorable feeling, by saying, "Will you not eat your word? *Bene.* With no sauce that can be devised to it. I protest I love thee." Beatrice now feels that the final word, with all that is involved in it, can be uttered, and says, "Why, then, God forgive me ! *Bene.* What offence, sweet Beatrice ? *Beat.* You have stayed me in a happy hour ; I was about to protest I loved you. *Bene.* And do it with all thy heart. *Beat.* I love you with so much of my heart that none is left to protest." Upon this Benedick at once feels that they are now all the world to each other, and that there are no outside considerations in the way of Beatrice's making any demands upon him, and abruptly says, "Come, bid me do anything for thee"; upon which Beatrice makes the unexpected and startling demand, "Kill Claudio." This speech has been made a little too much of, by critics who have regarded Beatrice as an unamiable character. She utters it the moment all obstacles are removed from her making demands upon Benedick, just as the gentlest and kindest person might use a strong expression when under the influence of deep feeling. It exhibits the intense moral indignation she has felt and still feels, by reason of her cousin's wrongs. When the command is sprung upon Benedick, his reply, notwithstanding all that he has just said, leaps spontaneously from his lips, showing the genuine and deep friendship he entertains for Claudio, and doing honor to his heart, " Ha ! not for the wide world." But he is fully assured of what his duty is as the lover of Beatrice and as a man of honor, and resolves to do it. ".Think you," he says, " in your soul the Count Claudio hath wronged Hero? *Beat.* Yea, as sure as I have a thought or a soul. *Bene.* Enough, I am engaged; I will challenge him. I will kiss your hand; and so I leave you. By this hand, Claudio shall render me a dear account. As you hear of me, so think of me. Go comfort your cousin : I must say she is dead ; and so, farewell."

Things begin to have a decidedly tragic look ; but the reader, or the spectator, knows what the actors do not know ; and the situation has for him a comic background. He knows of the villany of Don John, and that it has been discovered by the watchmen who overhear the story told by Borachio to Conrade (A. III. Sc. iii.). Leonato has the opportunity of knowing about the villany before he goes to church, Dogberry and Verges having called on him at his house to acquaint him with it ; but in his haste to be off to the marriage ceremony, he, having only learned from them that the watch " have comprehended two aspicious persons," dismisses the rude but faithful officials to make the examination themselves of the culprits.

In A. V. Sc. i. 111 *et seq.*, we see how Benedick comports himself, in challenging Claudio. In spite of their high-proof melancholy, as they call it, Claudio and Don Pedro are disposed to indulge in drollery, and their accustomed banter, with Benedick, who soon shows to them both his indisposition and his superiority thereto. He is now only the man of honor — honor backed and braced by love of Beatrice and regard for her deeply-wronged cousin.

Benedick having challenged Claudio and gone out, Dogberry,

Verges, and the Watch, enter with Conrade and Borachio, and Don Pedro and Claudio learn how their over-ready credulity has been abused, through the machinations of the Bastard, Don John. But they don't learn that Hero is alive; nor do they know this till in the last scene of the Play.

When Benedick and Beatrice again meet, Benedick assures her that he has challenged Claudio, adding " and either I must shortly hear from him, or I will subscribe him a coward." This ends the honor matter. Each can now say,

> " I could not love thee, dear, so much,
> Loved I not honor more."

Immediately upon this, their pleasantries are renewed, with a mutual understanding of them, Benedick asking her for which of his bad parts she first fell in love with him; and she asking him for which of her good parts he first suffered love for her, etc. Ursula enters and informs them of the discovery of the villany of Don John, and they go out. Lloyd remarks, Beatrice is misrepresented when actors allow to Benedick at this point, a premature success, that is, a kiss. This is reserved for the last scene, when after manful perseverance, he is victorious at last, over the banter of others and his own, and seals his success by kissing her to stop her mouth; and in first proof of self-control, she leaves to her husband the office of retort and speaks no more.

HAMLET.

———◦◦◦———

ONE of the many vexed questions to which the Tragedy of
Hamlet has given rise — a question which has, indeed,
been imposed upon the play, as a good many other questions have
been — is that of Hamlet's sanity or insanity.

There is no other of Shakespeare's dramas in which the hero
occupies so large a space, is so great a part. Hamlet is the pro-
tagonist in the tragedy ; he is, in fact, the all, the entire play. It
is this which gives the meaning to the common saying, expressive
of nothing remaining, "The play of Hamlet with Hamlet left out."
In the introduction to "The Talisman," Scott says : "'The Be-
trothed' did not greatly please one or two friends, who thought that
it did not well correspond to the general title of 'The Crusaders.'
They urged, therefore, that without direct allusion to the manners
of the Eastern tribes, and to the romantic conflicts of the period,
the title of a 'Tale of the Crusaders,' would resemble the play
bill which is said to have announced the tragedy of Hamlet, the
character of the Prince of Denmark being left out."

If Hamlet is deranged, he should be handed over for treatment
to the superintendent of an Insane Hospital — he is not a subject
for the art critic. If he is deranged, and the poet has presented
through him correct phenomena of mental disease, the play may
be regarded as a valuable contribution to pathology, but is not
entitled to a niche in the great temple of Art.

Hamlet's sanity, then, must be postulated, for it is only on such
postulate that the art critic can proceed. But here it may be
asked, cannot the insane or the diseased in any form be employed
as part of the material with which the artist works? Most cer-

tainly it can — but the idea of his work cannot centre in it — cannot be based upon it. That idea must be one of health, of reason, of harmony with the constitution of things. Insanity may be employed in a work of art just as any other form of evil, of moral obliquity, of moral darkness, is employed — but insanity, or any other form of evil, of moral obliquity, of moral darkness, must be subsidiary to sanity, to the good and the true, to moral rectitude, to moral light.

Those dramatic compositions which have exerted the greatest influence over the sympathies of men are all characterized by a large and even predominant element of moral obliquity, of moral evil, of moral darkness. Look at all the great Greek tragedies that have come down to us, at the masterpieces of the modern drama, especially those of Shakespeare. Their power might be pronounced to be almost in direct proportion to the degree in which the element of moral darkness predominates. Witness his Richard the Third, his King Lear, his Macbeth, his Othello. All these plays exert, and ever will exert, a powerful influence over the sympathies of mankind.

Now what is the attraction for the artist when he selects subjects so characterized by enormity of crime, by enormity, we might say, of the unreasonable? Is it that he loves darkness rather than light, that evil deeds constitute so large an element of his creations? And is it because men in general love darkness rather than light, that they sympathize so deeply with such themes when treated by a great master? Certainly not. The artist does not employ, and men are not interested in, moral darkness for its own sake ; this, the most depraved would not be willing to admit ; but the attractive element and the real basis of their sympathy is the light which struggles with, and is intensified by, the darkness.

A mere reproduction of nature and of human life is not the end of art, but the emphasizing and intensifying of these in a way to impress deeply and pleasurably (*i.e.*, harmoniously). And by emphasis, I mean something other than stress or strain of expression. I don't mean that at all. Where there's the greatest emphasis, in the true sense of the word, there's the *least* stress and strain of expression. It is only by emphasizing the natural, and the manifold phases of human life and character, that the poet secures a response in less susceptible souls. The great poet's soul is an Æolian harp which vibrates responsive to the faintest spiritual breathings of things; but ordinary souls are like the stiff cordage of ships which makes music only when played upon by the strongest blasts.

Now one of the most effectual means of emphasis and intensity, employed by the word or color artist is, with the one, moral darkness, with the other, physical darkness, and these, in every true art product, are subsidiary to moral and physical light. As Blackie remarks, in his lectures on Beauty, "A picture becomes a picture in the highest artistical sense, only when the forms and lights composing it are separated from the great world of form and light, of which it is a part, by a certain and very appreciable darkness." And this applies equally as well to word-painting as to color-painting. Without moral or physical darkness, there can be, in an art product, no intensity of moral or physical light.

It is the light, then, which struggles with the darkness, which is revealed and intensified by the darkness, which is the ultimate aim of all art worthy of the name; and, although darkness may constitute, as it frequently does, the largest element, yet, in every true art product, it must ever be regarded as subsidiary to the exhibition of the light.

Now, if all this is true, it might appear that Hamlet's insanity, assuming him to be insane, could be brought within the category of dark and intensifying elements. If so, we should have to look outside of him for what is intensified; it would have to centre in some one of the other characters: it could not centre in him — in the unreasonable, the unreasoning. It might be resident in a great criminal, as is the case in the tragedy of Macbeth. But Macbeth is a responsible being; and when we sympathize with him, in an art sense, we sympathize with that *force* which we recognize as the stuff out of which true greatness and nobility of charac-

ter are built. But if he were to do what he does, in a state of
insanity, of irresponsibility, of unconsciousness as to the enormity of
his crimes, he would no longer be an art subject, but a subject for
a strait-jacket. It is not in the constitution of our common nature
to sympathize with crime as crime. In the case of a great criminal
like Macbeth, our sympathy goes with him so far as he asserts his
moral freedom and no further.

Insanity, that degree, be it less or more, of mental derangement
which does away with the responsibility of a man for his acts, cannot, of itself, be artistically treated. Art is the expression of, and
must be in sympathy with, the rational and the moral constitution
of things ; and a human being can, of himself, be a subject for art
only when his reason and moral sense, however much they may be
obscured, have that degree of vitality and activity which responsibility implies and demands.

In the tragedy of Hamlet, all the other persons of the drama,
while having their own distinct and well-defined individualities,
and independent movements of their own, may at the same time
be said to exist for the exhibition of the character of Hamlet. He
is, as I have said, the all, the entire play, and in him *centres* the
idea of the play ; and accordingly — assuming the play to be a
legitimate art product, and no one certainly would deny it this
character — the *a priori* conclusion in regard to Hamlet himself
must be, that his reason and moral sense meet the demands of an
artistic treatment. If they did not, it would be hard to explain
why the play has retained its strange interest for the greatest minds
in all civilized nations for nearly three hundred years.

When the testimonies to his sanity afforded by the play are considered, the wonder is that any question was ever raised in regard
to it. These testimonies are chiefly afforded, 1, by what Hamlet
says, in a direct way, in regard to himself and his actions ; 2, by
his soliloquies (a common means with Shakespeare, as indeed it is
with all dramatists, by which his characters are made to reveal
their true selves when they wish, or are obliged, to conceal them
from others ; Edmund, in King Lear, for example, and Iago, in

Othello); and 3, by the interviews Hamlet has with his bosom friend and only confidant, Horatio.

Let us turn to these sources of evidence. And 1, what Hamlet says in a direct way, in regard to himself and his actions.

In the 5th Scene of the 1st Act, after the Ghost has appeared and made his dread revelation to Hamlet, and imposed upon him the sacred obligation of avenging his foul and most unnatural murder, the Prince prepares Horatio and Marcellus for the part he is about to act. He makes them swear by his sword, which was in fact, equivalent to swearing by the cross.

> "*Ham.* . . . And now, good friends,
> As you are friends, scholars and soldiers,
> Give me one poor request.
>   *Hor.* What is't, my lord? we will.
>   *Ham.* Never make kown what you have seen to-night.
>   *Hor.* ⎫
>   *Mar.* ⎬ My lord, we will not.
>   *Ham.* Nay, but swear't.
>   *Hor.* In faith, my lord, not I.
>   *Mar.* Nor I, my lord, in faith.
>   *Ham.* Upon my sword.
>   *Mar.* We have sworn, my lord, already.
>   *Ham.* Indeed, upon my sword, indeed.
>   *Ghost.* [*Beneath.*] Swear.
>   *Ham.* Ah, ha, boy! say'st thou so? art thou there, truepenny?
> Come on; you hear this fellow in the cellerage;
> Consent to swear.
>   *Hor.* Propose the oath, my lord.
>   *Ham.* Never to speak of this that you have seen,
> Swear by my sword.
>   *Ghost.* [*Beneath.*] Swear.
>   *Ham. Hic & ubique?* Then we'll shift for ground,
> Come hither, gentlemen,
> And lay your hands again upon my sword,
> Never to speak of this that you have heard:
> Swear by my sword.
>   *Ghost.* [*Beneath.*] Swear.

Ham. Well said, old mole! canst work in the earth so fast?
A worthy pioner! once more remove, good friends.
  Hor. Oh day and night, but this is wondrous strange!
  Ham. And therefore as a stranger give it welcome.
There are more things in heaven and earth, Horatio,
Then are dreamt of in our philosophy.
But come;
Here, as before, never, so help you mercy,
How strange or odd soe'er I bear myself,
(As I, perchance, hereafter shall think meet
To put an antic disposition on:)
That you, at such time seeing me, never shall
With arms encumber'd thus, or thus, head shake,
Or by pronouncing of some doubtful phrase,
As, 'Well, we know;' or, 'We could, and if we would;'
Or, 'If we list to speak;' or, 'There be, and if there might;'
Or such ambiguous giving out, to note
That you know aught of me: This not to do,
So grace and mercy at your most need help you,
Swear.
  Ghost. [*Beneath.*] Swear.
  Ham. Rest, rest, perturbed spirit! So, gentlemen,
With all my love I do commend me to you:
And what so poor a man as Hamlet is
May do, to express his love and friending to you,
God willing, shall not lack. Let us go in together;
And still your fingers on your lips, I pray.
The time is out of joint;— Oh cursed spite!
That ever I was born to set it right!
Nay, come, let's go together."   [*Exeunt.*
                                        —A. I. Sc. v. 140–190.

Hamlet has here already taken in the whole difficulty of the
situation — and that difficulty is an *objective* one, not a subjective.
It is not a difficulty due to Hamlet's own character. It is a difficulty *outside* of himself, as Professor Werder, in his " Vorlesungen
über Shakespeare's Hamlet," has so ably shown, in opposition to
the views of Goethe, Coleridge, and, in fact, of nearly all the
commentators.

The portion of Scene V. above quoted would seem, of itself, to be quite sufficient to explain all the apparent mental aberration which Hamlet exhibits throughout the rest of the Play.

Another example of the first kind of testimony (what Hamlet says in a direct way in regard to himself and his actions), is afforded by his speech to his mother, in the 4th Scene of the 3d Act, beginning where the Ghost enters, 102d line :

> " Save me, and hover o'er me with your wings,
>   You heavenly guards ! — What would you, gracious figure?
>   *Queen.* Alas, he's mad.
>   *Ham.* Do you not come your tardy son to chide,
> That, laps'd in time and passion, lets go by
> The important acting of your dread command?
> Oh say.
>   *Ghost.* Do not forget: This visitation
> Is but to whet thy almost blunted purpose.
> But look, amazement on thy mother sits :
> Oh step between her and her fighting soul ;
> Conceit in weakest bodies strongest works :
> Speak to her, Hamlet.
>   *Ham.*   How is it with you, lady?
>   *Queen.* Alas, how is't with you?
> That you do bend your eye on vacancy,
> And with the incorporal air do hold discourse?
> Forth at your eyes your spirits wildly peep ;
> And as the sleeping soldiers in the alarm,
> Your bedded hair, like life in excrements,
> Starts up, and stands an end.   O gentle son,
> Upon the heat and flame of thy distemper
> Sprinkle cool patience.   Whereon do you look?
>   *Ham.* On him ! on him !   Look you, how pale he glares !
> His form and cause conjoin'd preaching to stones,
> Would make them capable. — Do not look upon me ;
> Lest with this piteous action you convert
> My stern effects : then what I have to do
> Will want true colour : tears perchance for blood.
>   *Queen.* To whom do you speak this?

Ham.   Do you see nothing there?
Queen. Nothing at all : yet all that is I see.
Ham. Nor did you nothing hear?
Queen.   No, nothing but ourselves.
Ham. Why, look you there! look how it steals away!
My father, in his habit as he lived!
Look, where he goes, even now, out at the portal!
                                 [*Exit* GHOST.

   Queen. This is the very coinage of your brain :
This bodiless creation ecstasy
Is very cunning in.
   Ham. Ecstasy?
My pulse, as yours, doth temperately keep time,
And makes as healthful music. It is not madness
That I have uttered : bring me to the test,
And I the matter will re-word; which madness
Would gambol from. Mother, for love of grace,
Lay not a flattering unction to your soul,
That not your trespass, but my madness, speaks :
It will but skin and film the ulcerous place,
Whilst rank corruption, mining all within,
Infects unseen. Confess yourself to heaven;
Repent what's past, avoid what is to come,
And do not spread the compost o'er the weeds,
To make them rank. Forgive me this my virtue,
For in the fatness of these pursy times
Virtue itself of vice must pardon beg,
Yea, curb and woo, for leave to do him good.
   Queen. O Hamlet, thou hast cleft my heart in twain.
   Ham. O throw away the worser part of it,
And live the purer with the other half.
Good night: but go not to mine uncle's bed;
Assume a virtue, if you have it not.
Refrain to-night:
And that shall lend a kind of easiness
To the next abstinence: the next more easy;
For use almost can change the stamp of nature,
And master the devil, or throw him out
With wondrous potency. Once more, good night:

And when you are desirous to be bless'd,
I'll blessing beg of you. — For this same lord,

　　　　　　　　　　　　　[Pointing to POLONIUS.

I do repent; but heaven hath pleas'd it so,
To punish me with this, and this with me,
That 1 must be their scourge and minister.
I will bestow him, and will answer well
The death I gave him.　So again, good night.
I must be cruel, only to be kind;
Thus bad begins, and worse remains behind."

And before he leaves her, he enjoins upon her not to allow the King to get from her his secret : " Let him not," he says, "make you to ravel all this matter out, that I *essentially* am not in madness, but mad in craft."

Attention might be called to numerous minor items of evidence belonging to the first class.　There is one little but very significant expression used by Hamlet, in the 2d Scene of the 3d Act, 95th line, which should be noted, as it may be easily overlooked and even misunderstood.　It occurs immediately after that healthy, robust, and noble speech of Hamlet to Horatio in which we have a nice delineation of the character of his bosom friend, and a warm expression of his high estimate of it :

　　　" *Ham.* Horatio, thou art e'en as just a man
As e'er my conversation cop'd withal.
　　　Hor. O my dear lord.
　　　Ham.　　　　　　　Nay, do not think I flatter:
For what advancement may I hope from thee,
That no revenue hast but thy good spirits,
To feed and clothe thee?　Why should the poor be flatter'd?
No, let the candied tongue lick absurd pomp,
And crook the pregnant hinges of the knee,
Where thrift may follow fawning.　Dost thou hear?
Since my dear soul was mistress of my choice,
And could of men distinguish, her election
Hath seal'd thee for herself : · for thou hast been
As one, in suffering all, that suffers nothing;

A man, that fortune's buffets and rewards
Hath ta'en with equal thanks: and blest are those,
Whose blood and judgment are so well comingled,
That they are not a pipe for fortune's finger
To sound what stop she please. Give me that man
That is not passion's slave, and I will wear him
In my heart's core, ay, in my heart of heart,
As I do thee. Something too much of this.
There is a play to-night before the king;
One scene of it comes near the circumstance
Which I have told thee, of my father's death.
I prithee, when thou seest that act a-foot,
Even with the very comment of my * soul
Observe mine uncle: if his occulted † guilt
Do not itself unkennel in one speech,
It is a damned ghost that we have seen;
And my imaginations are as foul
As Vulcan's stithy. Give him heedful note:
For I mine eyes will rivet to his face;
And after we will both our judgments join
To censure of his seeming.
    Hor.   Well, my lord:
If he steal aught the whilst this play is playing,
And scape detecting, I will pay the theft."

Hereupon, the approach of the King, Queen, Courtiers, and others, is announced by a flourish, and Hamlet says to Horatio, "They are coming to the play, I *must be idle :* get you a place." That is, not "unoccupied," as the careless reader might understand it, but "foolish, light-headed, crazy," a sense in which it is

---

   * My *F*[1]. Hamlet's meaning is, "I would have thee so enter into my feelings, so identify thyself with me that, when thou seest that act afoot, even with the very comment of *my* soul, thou wilt observe mine uncle." The use of " my" also gives force to "even with the very" which has less force in the reading "thy" of the *Qq.*

   † *Occulted guilt*: "All the ancient authors of old time defined murder to be *occulta* hominis occisio, etc., when it was done in secret, so as the offender was not known; but now it is taken in a larger sense." — Coke, 3 *Instit.* cap. 7.

used in many other places in Shakespeare.* And it is worthy of
notice, that for the speech of the Queen in the Closet Scene (A. III.
Sc. iv.), and Hamlet's reply thereto, in the 2d and subsequent
Quartos, and in the Folio, beginning, "This is the very coinage
of your brain : this bodiless creation ecstasy is very cunning in.
Ham. Ecstasy? My pulse, as yours, doth temperately keep
time, and makes as healthful music : it is not madness that I have
uttered : " we have in the original Quarto of 1603, " *Queen.* But
Hamlet, this is only fantasy, and for my love forget these idle
fits. *Ham.* Idle, no mother, my pulse doth beat like yours, It
is not madness that possesseth Hamlet."

This little speech, "I must be idle," taken in connection with
the healthy, robust, and noble speech which immediately precedes
and Hamlet's conduct which immediately follows, shows that the
latter was *prepense,* and clinches the several testimonies of the
first class to purely feigned insanity. And it is not refining too
much, to see a significance in Hamlet's saying to Horatio, "Get
you a place." The court all know the close intimacy which exists
between them, and Hamlet does not consider it politic that they
sit together. And when the Queen invites him to sit by her, he
replies, "No, good mother, here's metal more attractive," and
takes his seat by Ophelia ; and Polonius, still adhering to his original opinion as to the cause of Hamlet's supposed madness, says
aside to the King, "Oh, ho ! do you mark that?"

The second kind of testimony I've named, to Hamlet's sanity,
is that afforded by the soliloquies.

The several soliloquies not only show no aberration, in any
respect, but they, on the contrary, are characterized by high and
coherent reasoning, and profound wisdom and philosophy. In
his soliloquies, Hamlet is his best interpreter. In them, his utter-
ances are, of course, entirely uninfluenced by policy or other
considerations.

The first soliloquy, which he utters before he has been informed

---

* See Schmidt, *s.v.* 3.

of the appearance of his father's ghost, "Oh, that this too too solid flesh would melt," etc., A. I. Sc. ii. 129–158, is especially interesting. "What Hamlet, — I cannot say, *has a presentiment of,* but nevertheless, what is *in* him, dark, voiceless, but yet *there,* wholly undefined, but not to be banished, and inborn, as it were, in his nature, — he does not understand, can form no idea of it, but he *feels* it ! The atmosphere of murder, which he inhales, which breathes upon him from the person of the murderer, the shuddering sense of the ghost hovering near, all that awaits him, all that stands ready at the door, all that his friends have brought to his knowledge, all that the Ghost has upon his lips to say to him ; the terror, terrible as Past and as Future, — all that is for him *here,* and is his : all this is *in* him ! *This* is the burthen which oppresses him, the immovable weight which he does not yet understand, but which he feels ! Hence the tone and coloring of this soliloquy." *

It bears testimony to Hamlet's susceptibility to the *essential* world. It is not morbidity — it is the finest healthfulness. The soliloquy is an illustration of what Longfellow expresses in his " Evangeline " :

" As at the tramp of a horse's hoof in the limitless prairie,
  Far in advance are closed the leaves of the shrinking mimosa,
  So at the hoof-beats of Fate, with sad forebodings of evil,
  Shrinks and closes the heart, ere the stroke of doom has attained it."

The next soliloquy is that which he utters, after the players have gone out (A. II. Sc. ii. 576–634), they having given him, as he expresses it, " a taste of their quality." There is strong self-rebuke in it, and self-rebuke doesn't belong to a madman. It belongs to a man with a keen moral sense, who does not, or, as is the case with Hamlet, *cannot,* under opposing circumstances (not by reason of his own nature), do the thing he would ; cannot, in a *rational* manner. And Hamlet understands the rational in the case. A man may *unjustly* rebuke himself ; and this Hamlet does in the soliloquy before us. " Pray, have people," says Werder,

---

* Karl Werder.

"no ears for the agony of a human being, which is so intolerable
that it drives him to the extremity of falling out with himself; no
appreciation of a situation in which righteous indignation, because
it cannot reach its object, turns against itself, in order to give
itself vent, and to cool the heated sense of the *impossibility* of
acting, by self-reproach and all manner of self-depreciation?"

At the close of the soliloquy, Hamlet says:

> "I have heard
> That guilty creatures sitting at a play
> Have by the very cunning of the scene
> Been struck so to the soul that presently
> They have proclaimed their malefactions:
> For murther, though it have no tongue, will speak
> With most miraculous organ. I'll have these players
> Play something like the murder of my father
> Before mine uncle: I'll observe his looks;
> I'll tent him to the quick: if he but blench,
> I know my course. The spirit that I have seen
> May be the devil: and the devil hath power
> To assume a pleasing shape; yea, and perhaps
> Out of my weakness and my melancholy,
> As he is very potent with such spirits,
> Abuses me to damn me: I'll have grounds
> More relative than this: the play's the thing
> Wherein I'll catch the conscience of the king."

Hamlet believes that an objective, veritable ghost has appeared
to him ("Shakespeare has with marked design and care guarded
the Ghost of Hamlet's father against the damaging imputation of
subjectivity"); * but the suspicion comes to him that the spirit
he has seen may be the devil, who abuses him to damn him.
This suspicion he determines to test. The play catches the conscience of the King, and Hamlet is assured that it is an honest
ghost; but (and this is the important thing to be noted) it does

---

* George H. Calvert, in his "Shakespeare: a Biographic, Æsthetic Study,"
p. 160.

not cause the King to "proclaim his malefaction," — does not have the all-important effect which Hamlet hoped it would have, as is implied in the words :

> " I have heard
> That guilty creatures sitting at a play
> Have by the very cunning of the scene
> Been struck so to the soul that presently
> They have *proclaimed their malefactions*."

Hamlet is assured by the play, of the King's guilt, and the King knows that he is in possession of his dread secret. That is all. And the way is consequently not yet open for Hamlet to act. And because he does not act, but continues to show himself "all tongue and no hand," the inference has been, as Klein humorously expresses it, in the "Berliner Modenspiegel," 1846, "that the all-powerful imagination of Shakespeare was impregnated by a miserable scholastic abstraction that has not virility enough to engender anything . . . that it was Shakespeare's design to portray in Hamlet a German half-professor, all tongue and no hand, forever cackling, and hatching nothing, like a dog wagging his tail at the sound of his own barking, whom one would fain help out of his dream, like Polonius, with a ' less art and more matter ! ' . . . that Shakespeare had in mind a pedant who perchance likes to scrawl flourishes and arabesque abstractions in the schoolroom dust, but who is found at heart to be good for nothing when summoned to action, to the business of life, instantly losing all presence of mind, darting now here and now there, bobbing now to the right and now to the left, instead of doing, trying how not to do, running from cook to tapster, from shop to shop, hoping thus, with the devil's aid, to make his hobby go, — in the end, however, bringing nothing to pass, but at the last, as at the first, hanging, silly dunce that he is, tangled in ' the nothingness of reflection ' of his own brain. It is proved also, from the Hegelian Bible, that Shakespeare was a right orthodox Hegelian, who created Hamlet in strict accordance with the orthodox doctrine of identity. It was the split between thought and action, that, according to the Hegelian idea, Shakespeare had in mind in Hamlet ! According to a ready-made category of Hegel's stamping, Hamlet was fashioned ! But let the stamp go ! How about the split? How? Why, does not every word in the play speak of this split? Does not the essence of the tragic lie in this hunting down of thought and act, this hide and seek of willing and doing, self-stinging at one moment, and then limp, languishing away into lazy melancholy? O strange, strange, supremely strange ! The tragic ? The comic, you mean ! "

There are no soliloquies in Shakespeare in which there is so perfectly natural a movement of the reflective faculty exhibited, as in that on Suicide, A. III. Sc. i., beginning at the 56th line. Hamlet puts the question at first in the simple, abstract form, " To be, or not to be : that is the question : " then, concretely, and in its moral bearing : " Whether 'tis nobler in the mind to suffer the slings and arrows of outrageous fortune, or to take arms against a sea of troubles, and by opposing end them ? " Having put the question in these two forms, he considers what it is to die : " To die : " and after reflecting a moment, he answers, " to sleep ; no more." His decision that to die is to sleep, no more than that, starts another question, whether, by a sleep we shall " end the heartache and the thousand natural shocks that flesh is heir to." In the 1st Folio, the note of interrogation is placed after " flesh is heir to," and this is as it should be.

> " and by a sleep to say we end
> The heart-ache and the thousand natural shocks
> That flesh is heir to? "

Upon which he remarks, consonantly with his present sadness :

> " 'tis a consummation
> Devoutly to be wish'd."

He then iterates to the point he has reached : " To die, to sleep."

His mind then passes to an idea suggested by " sleep " :

" To sleep: perchance to dream ! ay, there's the rub ; "

(" rub " is a term of the game of bowls, meaning a collision hin-
dering the bowl in its course ; hence, any obstacle or impediment.)

" Ay, there's the rub ; "
And why?

" For in that sleep of death *what* dreams may come,"

(" what " is the emphatic word here ; the question is, what will
be the *nature* of those dreams ?   Will they be happy, or will they
be unhappy, dreams ?)

" For in that sleep of death *what* dreams may come
When we have shuffled off this mortal coil,"

(this entanglement, turmoil of earthly life, or, it may be, this coil
of flesh, " this muddy vesture of decay,")

" For in that sleep of death *what* dreams may come
When we have shuffled off this mortal coil,
Must give us pause : "

Then the general result of this last reflection, is set forth, and
what would be the result were it not for this restraining consideration :

" there's the respect [consideration]
That makes calamity of so long life ;
For who would bear the whips and scorns of time,
The oppressors wrong, the poor man's contumely,
The pangs of *dispriz'd* love,"

so the Folio reads, and it is a better reading than " despised " of
the Qq. A disprized or undervalued love, a love that is only partially appreciated and responded to, would be apt to suffer more
pangs than a despised love :

" The pangs of dispriz'd love, the law's delay,
The insolence of office, and the spurns
That patient merit of the unworthy takes,
When he himself might his quietus make
With a bare bodkin ? "

"Quietus is the technical term for the acquittance which every sheriff or accountant receives on settling his accounts at the Exchequer. The mention of the law's delay introduced the idea of proceedings in the courts of law, which led him to think of the Exchequer. Many an accountant in that court has longed for his *quietus.*"

> "Who would these fardels bear,
> To grunt and sweat under a weary life,"

(the Folio reading and the correct reading) : the fardels are the burdens before spoken of, the whips and scorns, the oppressor's wrong, and the other evils he had specified. Having said, who would bear (the several things he specifies) he repeats, who would bear these fardels (representing all the specified ones) for the purpose of introducing the exceptive clause,

> "But that the dread of something *after* death,
> The undiscovered country from whose bourn
> No traveller returns, puzzles the will,
> And makes us rather bear those ills we *have*
> Than fly to others that we know not of ? "

It's surprising that the word *these,* before fardels, should be omitted in all the so-called critical texts, with only two or three exceptions.

> "Thus conscience does make cowards of us all ; "

"Conscience" seems to be used here in the sense of consciousness in general, private judgment, inmost thoughts.

> "Thus conscience does make cowards of us all ;
> And thus the native hue [natural color] of resolution
> Is sicklied o'er with the pale cast of thought,"

thought is care, anxiety, melancholy, whose hue is pale.

> "And enterprises of great pith and moment
> With this regard [*i.e.*, of the future] their currents turn away,
> And lose the name of action." *

---

* See "Jottings on the Text of Hamlet," p. 344 of this volume.

And then noticing Ophelia, he says :

"Soft you now! The fair Ophelia? —
Nymph, in thy orisons be all my sins remembered."

"This," says Johnson, "is a touch of nature. Hamlet, at the sight of Ophelia, does not immediately recollect that he is to personate madness, but makes her an address grave and solemn, such as the foregoing meditation excited in his thoughts."

I have dwelt thus long on this celebrated soliloquy, to show how closely and subtly *sequacious* it is. Here we have the *real* Hamlet. In the dialogue which immediately follows, with Ophelia, we have the *assumed* Hamlet, Hamlet with "an antic disposition on." It is evident that the poet advisedly brought together this closely and subtly sequacious soliloquy and his talk with Ophelia, which to her indicates that his once "noble and most sovereign reason" is now "like sweet bells jangled out of tune, and harsh," for the purpose of strongly *contrasting* the real and the assumed Hamlet. So viewed, nothing could be more dramatically proper ; nor more in Shakespeare's manner ; while nothing could be more dramatically improper, if his talk with Ophelia be regarded as indicative of real mental aberration ; even if it be shown to be scientific that a man can be the soundest, subtlest reasoner one moment, and the very next moment have his faculties all in a jumble. For Hamlet is a work of dramatic *art*, and not a scientific treatise. Some of the experts in insanity who have treated the subject of Hamlet's mental condition, have lost sight of this fact. Shakespeare is the supreme artist ; and whatever else he is, he is first and last the artist ; and he would not, could not, have made the idea of one of his greatest productions centre in a man vibrating rapidly between reason and unreason.

The last soliloquy to which I would call attention is that in the 4th Scene of the 4th Act, which Hamlet utters after meeting with and questioning the Captain whom Fortinbras has sent to greet the Danish King and to crave the conveyance of a promised march over his kingdom (ll. 9–66).

Here we have again strong self-rebuke. But it must not be explained on the theory of Hamlet's indisposition to action, much as it may appear to support that theory.*

Swinburne justly pronounces this "the supreme soliloquy of Hamlet." "Magnificent," he says, "as is that monologue on suicide and doubt . . . it is actually eclipsed and distanced at once on philosophic and on poetical grounds by the later soliloquy on reason and resolution."

The third kind of evidence against the theory of Hamlet's insanity is that derived from the interviews he has with his bosom-friend and only confidant, Horatio. In these interviews, he is uniformly rational, and his speeches are freighted with wisdom, and show a deep insight into life and its mysteries — a deep insight due to that spiritual susceptibility indicated in the 1st soliloquy, "Oh, that this too too solid flesh would melt" (A. I. Sc. ii. 129), when coming events cast their shadows upon him, and he feels their shadows ere he knows from what they are cast — a deep insight which made him cognizant of more things than are dreamt of in human philosophy, and which caused him to feel deeply, "what a piece of work is a man! how noble in reason! how infinite in faculty! . . . in apprehension, how like a god!"

And Horatio shows nowhere in the play that he at any time has the faintest suspicion of any mental aberration on the part of Hamlet. Their perfect faith in each other, to the end, is very beautiful. After Hamlet has received his death-wound from the envenomed sword of Laertes, he says: "Horatio, I am dead; Thou livest; report me and my cause aright to the unsatisfied. . . . O good Horatio, *what a wounded name things standing thus unknown, shall live behind me!*" This last anxiety of the dying Hamlet about leaving a wounded name, reflects the idea of the play so fully and, as I think, conclusively set forth by Professor Werder. Hamlet had to revenge a secret murder of which he

---

* I must refer the student to Karl Werder's interpretation of this soliloquy given in Dr. Furness's "New Variorum Edition of Hamlet," Vol. II. p. 366.

could produce no material proof, no proof that would be accepted
— only the testimony of a ghost, whose testimony no one but himself heard ; and without producing this material proof, unveiling
the secret murder, or forcing the King to a full confession, to
have assassinated the King would have been utterly irrational : as
utterly irrational as is the assumption implied in a large body of
criticism on the play that but for Hamlet's incapacity for action,
he would have killed the King. Nonsense. And there is no
evidence that Hamlet was restrained by moral scruples, that an
abhorrence of the deed restrained him. But there *is* evidence
that his *reason*, his *common sense*, restrained him. True vengeance demanded that full proof of the King's guilt should be
afforded the court and the people of Denmark ; and it was true
vengeance which was required by the Ghost and which Hamlet
sought. And now when Fate makes him the slayer of the King,
he entreats his friend Horatio, in his last moments, to set him
right before the world :

> " If thou didst ever hold me in thy heart,
> Absent thee from felicity awhile,
> And in this harsh world draw thy breath in pain,
> To tell my story."

Experts in insanity have testified to the genuineness of Hamlet's
aberration. Well, if the phenomena be such as to cause experts
to pronounce his " antic disposition " genuine insanity, what of it,
more than that Shakespeare knew the phenomena of genuine insanity, and in making Hamlet feign insanity, made the feigning
as like as possible to the real thing. If the feigning is meant to
serve any purpose at all, the more successful it is the better.

I am disposed to think that Coleridge and Goethe, by the substantially similar theories they advanced, in regard to the man,
Hamlet, contributed more, especially Goethe (as he exercised a
wider authority than Coleridge), toward shutting off a sound criticism of the play, than any other critics or any other cause. Their
dicta were generally accepted as quite final ; and many a Shake-

speare student, now living, whatever his present views may be, can remember when he so accepted them, and had not a glimmer of suspicion that in the main they *might* be wide of the mark.

Goethe's "Wilhelm Meister's Lehrjahre," which contained his celebrated criticism on Hamlet, was given to the world in 1795. But it was probably not read in England until Carlyle's translation of it appeared, in 1824, or thereabout.

Mr. Coleridge delivered his Lectures on Shakespeare in the winter of 1811–12, and for what we possess of them we are chiefly indebted to J. Payne Collier, who took short-hand notes of a portion of the Course, which extended to 17 lectures, two or three being on Milton. Philosophical criticism was then in its infancy; and Coleridge's Lectures were regarded, and in many respects justly regarded, as new revelations of Shakespeare's power, especially as an artist. Previous to that time, the *material* of Shakespeare's Plays was chiefly regarded as constituting their greatness. That he was the master-artist was hardly yet suspected.

Let us turn, for a moment, to the view taken by Goethe, of Hamlet, in his "Wilhelm Meister," Book V. I give Carlyle's translation:

"Figure to yourselves this youth, this son of princes, conceive him vividly, bring his condition before your eyes, and then observe him when he learns that his father's spirit walks; stand by him in the terrible night when the venerable Ghost itself appears before him. A horrid shudder seizes him; he speaks to the mysterious form; he sees it beckon him; he follows it and hearkens. The fearful accusation of his uncle rings in his ears; the summons to revenge and the piercing reiterated prayer: 'Remember me!' And when the Ghost has vanished, whom is it we see standing before us? A young hero panting for vengeance? A born prince, feeling himself favored in being summoned to punish the usurper of his crown? No! Amazement and sorrow overwhelm the solitary young man; he becomes bitter against smiling villains, swears never to forget the departed, and concludes with the significant ejaculation: 'The time is out of joint; O cursed spite, That ever

I was born to set it right!' In these words, I imagine, is the key to Hamlet's whole procedure, and to me it is clear that Shakespeare sought to depict a great deed laid upon a soul *unequal to the performance of it.* In this view I find the piece composed throughout. Here is an oak tree planted in a costly vase, which should have received in its bosom only lovely flowers; the roots spread out, the vase is shivered to pieces. A beautiful, pure, noble, and most moral nature, without the strength of nerve which makes the hero, sinks beneath a burden which it can neither bear nor throw off; every duty is holy to him, — this, too hard. The impossible is required of him, — *not the impossible in itself, but the impossible to him.* How he winds, turns, agonizes, advances and recoils, ever reminded, ever reminding himself, and at last almost loses his purpose from his thoughts, without ever again recovering his peace of mind."

Here, it will be observed, the difficulty of Hamlet's situation is attributed entirely to *subjective* causes: it lies within Hamlet himself. "The impossible," Goethe says, "is required of him, — not the impossible in itself, but the impossible to *him.*" All which is equivalent to saying, if Hamlet were *other* than he is, the thing could be easily enough done.

To turn now to Coleridge's view, which we shall see is substantially the same as that of Goethe. The difficulty of Hamlet's situation he attributes wholly to subjective causes. He says: " I believe the character of Hamlet might be traced to Shakespeare's deep and accurate science in mental philosophy. Indeed, that this character must have some connection with the common fundamental laws of our nature may be assumed from the fact that Hamlet has been the darling of every country in which the literature of England has been fostered. In order to understand him, it is essential that we should reflect on the constitution of our own minds. Man is distinguished from the brute animals in proportion as thought prevails over sense: but in the healthy processes of the mind, a balance is constantly maintained between impressions from outward objects and the inward operations of the intellect; — for if there be an overbalance in the contemplative faculty, man thereby becomes the creature of mere meditation, and loses his natural power of action."

Coleridge here gives an admirable description of himself; but it is not applicable to Hamlet's case. He adds the following startling statement :

"Now one of Shakespeare's modes of creating characters is, *to conceive any one intellectual or moral faculty in morbid excess, and then to place himself, Shakespeare thus mutilated or diseased, under given circumstances.*"

Macaulay more truly says, in his Article on Madame D'Arblay, that "it is the constant manner of Shakespeare to represent the human mind as lying, not under the absolute dominion of one domestic propensity, but under a mixed government, in which a hundred powers balance each other. Admirable as he was in all points of his art, we most admire him for this, that, while he has left us a greater number of striking portraits than all other drama-tists put together, he has scarcely left us a single caricature." But would not such a mode of creating character as Coleridge ascribes to him result in caricature? And in caricature only? It certainly would. That is rather Ben Jonson's mode of creating character. He personifies autocratic moods and humors, and does not, therefore, attain to complete personalities, actuated by a subtle complexity of motives, and exhibiting what Dowden calls "the mystery of vital movement."

"In Hamlet," Coleridge continues, "he [Shakespeare] seems to have wished to exemplify the moral necessity of *a due balance* between our attention to the objects of our senses and our medita-tion on the workings of our minds, — an *equilibrium* between the real and the imaginary worlds."

Is not such a view, I would ask, by the way, un-Shakespearian — that Shakespeare *wished to exemplify*, etc.? One is likely to go astray when he sees, or looks for, abstract notions operating in a play of Shakespeare.

"In Hamlet," Coleridge continues, "this balance is disturbed;

his thoughts and the images of his fancy are far more vivid than his actual perceptions, and his very perceptions, instantly passing through the *medium* of his contemplations, acquire, as they pass, a form and a color not naturally their own. Hence we see a great, an almost enormous, intellectual activity, and a proportionate aversion to real action consequent upon it, with all its symptoms and accompanying qualities. This character Shakespeare places in circumstances under which he is obliged *to act on the spur of the moment* [!] : Hamlet is brave and careless of death; but he vacillates from sensibility, and procrastinates from thought, and loses the power of action in the energy of resolve."

This is as explicit and emphatic as it can be made. The difficulty with Hamlet, according to Coleridge, is a wholly *subjective* one — "a great, an almost enormous intellectual activity" inducing "a proportionate aversion to real action." And this statement, strong as it is, is even emphasized by the statement that "Hamlet is *brave* and *careless of death.*" His bravery and his disregard of death are not sufficient to overcome his aversion to action induced by his intellectual activity — although the *call* for action has come from the spirit of an honored father, of blessed memory, who was "of life, of crown, of queen, at once dispatch'd"; who was to the one who occupies the throne, "Hyperion to a satyr!" If this is a true characterization of Hamlet, what a monstrosity he is! the greatest monstrosity to be found in all dramatic literature. And such a monstrosity, we are told, by Coleridge himself, "has been the darling of every country in which the literature of England has been fostered." Why, if an enormous intellectual activity can possibly have such dire consequences as to bind a man hand and foot, and thus to disable him from performing the most sacred duties, there should be placarded, in colossal and glaring letters, at all the corners of our streets, for all men to read, BEWARE OF AN ENORMOUS INTELLECTUAL ACTIVITY. We should shut up all our colleges and universities, for fear that many young men and young women, through the intellectual stimulant these institutions afford, might be so unfortunate as to attain to

an enormous intellectual activity. Why, in the name of everything that's reasonable, where's the dramatic interest to come
from, with such an irredeemable do-nothing for the hero of the
drama as Coleridge represents Hamlet to be? Whatever interest
such a man might have for the mental philosopher, it's the *dramatic* interest we must always look for, in a play of Shakespeare.
Shakespeare is a dramatist, and always a dramatist, not a psychol-
ogist. And we shall always find a true dramatic interest in his
plays, if we look for it aright.

Before Coleridge delivered his lectures in London, Aug. Wilh.
Schlegel had given his on Dramatic Art and Literature, in Vienna,
in 1808, which were published under the title, " Vorlesungen über
dramatische Kunst und Literatur," 1809. It was thought that Coleridge was indebted to him, by reason of certain striking similar-
ities of view. But there's no evidence of such indebtedness. The
evidence rather is that he was *not* indebted to Schlegel, and that
evidence comes from Hazlitt, who disliked Coleridge. He says :
" I myself heard the very same character of Hamlet from Coleridge before he went to Germany (that was in 1798) and when
he had neither read nor could read a page of German."

Schlegel's view of Hamlet is, in the main, that of Goethe and
Coleridge, namely, to put it in the most general way, that Hamlet's not carrying out the injunction of his father's ghost was due
to subjective causes, and not to objective obstacles. One sentence from Schlegel will be sufficient to show this. " The whole,"
he says, " is intended to show that a calculating consideration,
which exhausts all the relations and possible consequences of a
deed, *must cripple the power of acting.*" I would remark here,
by the way, that it can never be truly said of any play of Shakespeare, that, to use Schlegel's expression, " the whole is intended
to show" this, that, or the other. That would imply that his work
moves under the condition of a *notion* of some kind ; that he
started with an abstraction, and that that abstraction determined
the movement of his work. Romeo and Juliet, we are told by
a large number of prominent commentators, among them being

Gervinus, Ulrici, Coleridge, Hallam, Maginn, Mézières, Taine, Tieck, "is intended to show" the bad consequences of excess, and the importance of moderation.

Neither Goethe, Coleridge, nor Schlegel intimate, even, the *objective* theory in regard to the tragedy of Hamlet (the only theory consonant with the Shakespearian dramatic art), which Karl Werder has so elaborately developed in his "Vorlesungen über Shakespeare's Hamlet," * Berlin, 1875. Horace Howard Furness pronounces Werder's volume on Hamlet the most noteworthy that has appeared in Germany, although its main idea is found in Klein's article in the *Berliner Modenspiegel*, 1846; and George Fletcher has distinctly indicated it, in a paragraph of his criticism on Romeo and Juliet, p. 288 of his "Studies of Shakespeare," London, 1847. It is to be regretted that this sagacious critic's "Studies of Shakespeare in the play of Hamlet, with observations on the criticism and the acting of that play," announced as in preparation, at the end of the former work, never appeared. No English critic, perhaps, ever understood better the constitution of Shakespeare's Plays than did George Fletcher.

The objective theory, briefly stated, is, that the obstacles to Hamlet's carrying out the injunction of the Ghost are wholly *objective* — that he has the power of acting, plenty of it, and all other powers in an eminent degree, required for what has been enjoined upon him to do, but he cannot achieve a true revenge by simply assassinating the King. He has a secret murder to deal with; and that secret murder must first be unveiled to the court and the people, before a rational revenge is possible — before he can, in a true sense, *fulfil* the duty which has been imposed upon him by the ghost of his father.

The theory of Hamlet's *constitutional aversion to real activity*, so strongly put by Coleridge, is pushed to the absurd by a writer

---

* Dr. Horace Howard Furness has given, in his "New Variorum Edition of Hamlet," large extracts from Werder's "Vorlesungen," which embrace the entire dramatic action of Hamlet, as set forth by him. To these extracts students are referred. They are contained in Vol. II. pp. 354-371.

in the *Popular Science Monthly*, for May, 1880, pp. 60–71. His article is entitled "The Impediment of Adipose — a celebrated case," the celebrated case being that of our friend, Hamlet, who, he says, is described with one dash of the pen: "He's fat and scant of breath." This is that "unknown quantity" which confounded Schlegel, and which Goethe thought he had found in the lines:

> "The time is out of joint; O cursed spite!
> That ever I was born to set it right."

Poor Hamlet (strange that nobody ever discovered it before) is weighted down with a non-executive or lymphatic temperament. By reason of his fatness and his scantness of breath, he lacks the energizing temperament, without which the brain is but a dumb mass of latent possibilities. His procrastination is the result of his "too too solid flesh." But for that burden of adipose substance, he were simply the most active fellow in Europe. He is afflicted with a *spherical* obesity, as is indicated by his reply to the Ghost's "Remember me:" "Remember thee! Ay, thou poor Ghost, while memory holds a seat in this distracted *globe*." This obesity is also indicated in the speech of Ophelia:

> "He raised a sigh so piteous and profound
> As it did seem to shatter all his *bulk*."

We are informed in a footnote that medical men regard frequent sighing as a sign of heart disease, caused by superfluous fat. Ophelia also speaks of him as "pale as his shirt"; and paleness, the writer informs us, is a symptom of anæmic adipose. But she gives no hint that, like Falstaff, he has fallen away vilely. If such had been the case, it would have been the first thing to attract the attention of a young lady who believed one mad for the love of her. No; neither love nor lunacy has told the least on his "bulk."

In A. V. Sc. ii. 282, the King drinks "to Hamlet's better *breath*"; and the queen-mother makes the exclamation, which is taken as the keynote of this adipose theory, "He's fat and scant of breath";

and then adds, "Here, Hamlet, take my napkin, rub thy brows."
And a little further on she says, "Come, let me wipe thy face."
Can we not see, says the writer, the perspiration trickling over the
broad, heavy cheeks, as we read these lines? It was surely from
experience that he spoke of sweating and grunting under a weary
life.

Our attention is also called to the fact that when Hamlet takes
his leisurely walk in the hall, this quiet exercise goes under no
other name than a "breathing time"; and when his obesity is
considered, how apt appears his reply to Osric: "Sir, I will walk
here in the hall; if it please his majesty, this is the *breathing-time*
of day with me."

The testimony as to the torpid condition of the Prince, consequent upon his fatness, and his scantness of breath, is not yet at
an end. When Horatio says, "You will lose this wager, my lord,"
Hamlet replies, "I do not think so ; . . . I shall win at the odds.
But thou would'st not think *how ill all's here about my heart;*
but it is no matter." Just such an answer, the writer informs us,
as a person might make who was suffering from fatty degeneration ;
the consideration of the unpleasant possibilities of the duel had
brought the action of the heart almost to a standstill — the. result
of a chronic sluggish circulatory system.

The consequences of poor Hamlet's unfortunate physical condition is summed up by the writer in the following sentence : "The
fine spirit, the clear insight, the keen reader of other men's thoughts
is imprisoned in walls of adipose, and the desire for action dies
out with the utterance of wise maxims, philosophic doubts, and
morbid upbraidings of his own inertness."

Any explanation of the man Hamlet, which proceeds upon the
assumption of the theories of Goethe and Coleridge, must be as
wide of the mark as is this, though it may not be so fleshly. And
there'll be no end to such criticism until there's a general recognition among Shakespeare scholars of what constitutes the real difficulty of the situation in which Hamlet is placed, — a difficulty
entirely independent of his own intellectual and spiritual tempera-

ment, but a difficulty especially fitted to bring that temperament into the fullest play. And I would add that the reader of the tragedy whose interest is in the subjective Hamlet, rather than in the dramatic action, must recognize the fact that the subjective Hamlet — all the thoughts, and musings, and feelings, which so interest that reader — becomes doubly interesting when he knows its relation to the objective difficulty.

THE WITCH AGENCY IN MACBETH.

THE two all-important things to be considered in the Tragedy of Macbeth, are, 1, the relations of the Witches to Macbeth, and 2, the relations of Lady Macbeth to Macbeth, in his career of ambition.

The following bits of commentary express the usual understanding of the agency of the witches in Macbeth : " He is tempted," says Hazlitt, " to the commission of guilt by golden opportunities, by the instigations of his wife, and by prophetic warnings. Fate and metaphysical aid conspire against his virtue and his loyalty." "Shakespeare's witches," says Charles Lamb, " *orignate* deeds of blood, and *begin* bad impulses to men. From the moment that their eyes first meet with Macbeth's, he is spell-bound. That meeting *sways his destiny*. He can never break the fascination."

" The *first* thought of acceding to the throne," says Thomas Whateley, " is *suggested*, and success in the attempt is promised, to Macbeth by the witches ; he is therefore represented as a man *whose natural temper would have deterred him from such a design* if he had not been *immediately* tempted and strongly impelled to it."

In the first place it may be said that such views are inconsistent with the whole theory of the entire Shakespearian drama. Shakespeare never presents a character to us as *a victim of fate* at the outset. The fatalism of passion is exhibited in all his great tragedies ; but those characters through whom it is exhibited begin their several careers as *free agents*. A true dramatic interest demands this. As a great passion is evolved, it destroys more and more the power of self-assertion, and its victim is finally swept passively and helplessly along. Only free agency is dramatic.

The weird sisters represent the night side of nature, the powers of evil which are ever attracted to the soul whose elective affinities favor such attraction. The devil visits those only who invite him in. "They who lack energy of goodness," says Dowden, "and drop into a languid neutrality between the antagonist spiritual forces of the world, must serve the devil as slaves, if they will not decide to serve God as freemen."

The power of the weird sisters is nowhere in the tragedy exhibited as *absolute*, but always as *relative*. It is shown to depend upon what in a man's soul has affinities for that power. Where these affinities do not exist, their power is nought. But where they do exist, these outside evil forces are as quick to respond to them as Sin and Death in Milton's "Paradise Lost" are represented to have been. Even before the newly-created pair sinned, before the connatural forces started in them and were realized in act, Sin is made to say to Death, as they sit together within the gates of hell, "Methinks I feel new strength within me rise, wings growing, and dominion given me large beyond this deep ; whatever draws me on, or sympathy, or some connatural force, powerful at greatest distance to unite, with secret amity, things of like kind, by secretest conveyance. Thou, my Shade inseparable, must with me along. . . . Nor can I miss the way, so strongly drawn by this new-felt attraction and instinct. Whom thus the meagre Shadow answered soon : Go, whither Fate, and inclination strong, leads thee."

(It should be remarked here that Milton obeys the higher law in his grammar, as Shakespeare so often does ; "fate" and "inclination strong" not constituting a compound idea, inclination strong being fate, when not controlled, he uses with these two subjects the singular verb " leads.")

"Go, whither Fate, and inclination strong, leads thee. I shall not lag behind, nor err the way, thou leading. . . . So saying, with delight he snuffed the smell of mortal change on earth . . .

and upturned his nostrils wide into the murky air,* sagacious † of his quarry from so far."

Strikingly parallel with this representation of Sin and Death (so quick scented, so sagacious of their quarry), is the representation of the weird sisters. In their first meeting, in the opening scene of the tragedy, it is intimated that while Macbeth is serving his king, in bravely fighting his country's foes, the promptings of a regicidal ambition had already set in. The weird sisters, with whom "fair is foul, and foul is fair," scent from afar his evil propensities. They are not the first to tempt Macbeth, but Macbeth is the first to tempt them to tempt. He tempts them to stimulate *what has originated within himself.*

"ACT I.

SCENE I. — *An open place. Thunder and Lightning.*

Enter three Witches.

1 *Witch.* When shall we three meet again
In thunder, lightning, or in rain?
2 *Witch.* When the hurlyburly's done,
When the battle's lost and won.
3 *Witch.* That will be ere the set of sun.
1 *Witch.* Where the place?
2 *Witch.*   Upon the heath.
3 *Witch.* There to meet with Macbeth."

This last speech indicates that they have already experienced, to use the language of Milton's Sin, a "sympathy or some connatural force, powerful at greatest distance to unite, with secret amity, things of like kind, by secretest conveyance."

" 1 *Witch.* I come, Graymalkin.
All. Paddock calls : — Anon. —

---

* "Murky air" here means what "mirksome air" means in Spenser, "Faerie Queene," I. v. 28, infected or tainted.   It reminds of " the fog and filthy air" through which the weird sisters in Macbeth hover.

† Sagacious, quick of scent.

> Fair is foul, and foul is fair :
> Hover through the fog and filthy air."

[Witches vanish.

(The several witch scenes are all accompanied with thunder and lightning; and it should be noted here, that in no other Play has Shakespeare so represented the natural world as reflecting the moral world.)

The following passages are examples of this :

Lady Macbeth, after receiving her husband's letter, says :

> " The raven himself is hoarse
> That croaks the fatal entrance of Duncan
> Under my battlements."   — A. I. Sc. v. 39–41.

When the " gracious " Duncan, who " hath borne his faculties so meek," and Banquo, whose character throughout shows that he has kept his heart with all diligence, approach Macbeth's castle, Duncan says :

> " This castle hath a pleasant seat ; the air
> Nimbly and sweetly recommends itself
> Unto our gentle senses."

Banquo, in his reply, shows that his pure heart has made him a susceptible observer of nature :

> " This guest of summer,
> The temple-haunting martlet, does approve,
> By his loved mansionry, that the heaven's breath
> Smells wooingly here : no jutty, frieze,
> Buttress, nor coign of vantage, but this bird
> Hath made his pendent bed and procreant cradle :
> Where they most breed and haunt, I have observed
> The air is delicate."   — A. I. Sc. vi. 1–9.

In the early morning, after the Porter has admitted Macduff and Lenox to the court of the castle, and Macbeth enters, having been aroused, as they suppose, by the knocking, Lenox says, before the murder has been discovered :

" The night has been unruly : where we lay,
Our chimneys were blown down, and, as they say,
Lamentings heard i' the air, strange screams of death,
And prophesying with accents terrible
Of dire combustion and confused events
New hatch'd to the woeful time : the obscure bird
Clamour'd the livelong night : some say, the earth
Was feverous and did shake.
　　Macb.　　　　　　　　　'Twas a rough night.
　　Len. My young remembrance cannot parallel
A fellow to it." — A. II. Sc. iii. 59–67.

With reference to the same night, is the talk between Ross and
an old man, after the murder is known :

" *Old M.* Threescore and ten I can remember well :
Within the volume of which time, I have seen
Hours dreadful, and things strange ; but this sore night
Hath trifled former knowings.
　　Rosse.　　　　　　　　Ah, good father,
Thou seest, the heavens, as troubled with man's act,
Threaten his bloody stage : by the clock, 'tis day,
And yet dark night strangles the travelling lamp :
Is't night's predominance, or the day's shame,
That darkness does the face of earth intomb,
When living light should kiss it?
　　Old M.　　　　　　　　'Tis unnatural,
Even like the deed that's done. On Tuesday last,
A falcon, tow'ring in her pride of place,
Was by a mousing owl hawk'd at and kill'd.
　　Rosse. And Duncan's horses, (a thing most strange and certain,)
Beauteous and swift, the minions of their race,
Turn'd wild in nature, broke their stalls, flung out,
Contending 'gainst obedience, as they would
Make war with mankind.
　　Old M.　　　　　　'Tis said, they eat each other.
　　Rosse. They did so, to the amazement of mine eyes
That look'd upon 't." — A. II. Sc. iv. 1–20.

Macbeth says to Lady Macbeth, with reference to the murder of Banquo and his son Fleance, for which he has arranged,

> " Ere the bat hath flown
> His cloister'd flight, ere to black Hecate's summons
> The shard-borne beetle, with his drowsy hums,
> Hath rung night's yawning peal,
> There shall be done a deed of dreadful note.
> *Lady M.* What's to be done?
> *Macb.* Be innocent of the knowledge, dearest chuck,
> Till thou applaud the deed. Come, seeling night,
> Skarf up the tender eye of pitiful day;
> And, with thy bloody and invisible hand,
> Cancel and tear to pieces that great bond
> Which keeps me pale! — Light thickens; and the crow
> Makes wing to the rooky wood;
> Good things of day begin to droop and drowse;
> Whiles night's black agents to their preys do rouse.
> — A. III. Sc. ii. 40–53.

"We see," says Fanny Kemble, "the violet-coloured sky, we feel the soft intermitting wind of evening, we hear the solemn lullaby of the dark fir-forest, the homeward flight of the bird suggests the sweetest images of rest and peace ; and, coupled and contrasting with the gradual falling of the dim veil of twilight over the placid face of nature, the remote horror of 'the deed of fearful note,' about to desecrate the solemn repose of the approaching night, gives to these harmonious and lovely lines a wonderful effect of mingled beauty and terror." *

And just before the murderers surprise Banquo, the first murderer says :

> " The west yet glimmers with some streaks of day:
> Now spurs the lated traveller apace
> To gain the timely inn, and near approaches
> The subject of our watch." — A. III. Sc. iii. 5–8.

---

* *Macmillan's Magazine*, May, 1867.

The poet appears to have been so filled with the spirit of his theme, that that spirit radiated upon all the aspects of the natural world, and was reflected therefrom. " *The west yet glimmers with some streaks of day.*" In the moral world which he is representing, there are yet some glimmerings of moral light: but these glimmerings are soon to be wholly swallowed up in moral darkness. And it is to be remarked, too, that the murder of Banquo and the appearance of his ghost at the banquet, marks the point where all light goes out for both Macbeth and his queen.

To return from this digression: Shakespeare has taken pains to make clear what he meant by the weird sisters. In the soliloquy which Lady Macbeth utters, after receiving her husband's letter, she says (A. I. Sc. v. 41–51) : " Come, *you spirits that tend on mortal thoughts,* unsex me here, and fill me from the crown to the toe, top-full of direst cruelty ! make thick my blood ; stop up the access and passage to remorse, that no compunctious visitings of nature shake my fell purpose, nor keep peace between the effect and it ! Come to my woman's breasts, and take my milk for gall, you *murth'ring ministers, wherever in your sightless substances you wait on nature's mischief !* "

(" Sightless substances " : " sightless " is used objectively, in the sense of " invisible " ; " substances " means " essences " ; sightless substances, invisible essences. " Sightless " is again used in an objective sense, in A. I. Sc. vii. 23 : " Sightless couriers of the air.")

Here, in fact, is brought out what we must understand by the weird sisters. They are the impersonations of the " spirits that tend on mortal thoughts," of the " sightless substances that wait on nature's mischief," that respond to the elective affinities of man's soul. They are objective entities, to stand against which, St. Paul tells us, we must " put on the whole armor of God." " For," he says, " we wrestle not against flesh and blood, but against principalities, against powers, against the rulers of the darkness of this world." — Eph. vi. 11, 12.

As an exposition of the spiritual constitution of things, what a reality Christianity must have been to such a soul as Shakespeare's ! A reality to be confirmed by spiritual experience, not a creed to be intellectually believed. And it is quite evident to one who reads Shakespeare aright, that the Christian miracles did not trouble him very much, and that he had not to resort to the theory of a suspension of the laws of nature, nor make them acceptable to the intellect, as some theologians of the present day are trying to do, even Canon Farrar, in his " Life of Christ " (Vol. I. pp. 337 *et seq.*, of Amer. ed.).

In All's Well that Ends Well, Lafeu says (A. I. Sc. iii.) : " They say miracles are past ; and we have our philosophical persons, to make modern [*i.e.*, common, ordinary] and familiar, things supernatural and causeless.* Hence is it that we make trifles of terrors, ensconcing ourselves into seeming knowledge, when we should submit ourselves to an unknown fear. Why, 'tis the rarest argument of wonder that hath shot out in our latter times."

Gervinus remarks (Vol. II. p. 167 of his " Shakespeare Commentaries ") : " We need hardly tell our readers whom we imagine to be more and more initiated into the mind of our poet, that his spirit-world signifies nothing but the visible embodiment of the images conjured up by a lively fancy, and that their apparition only takes place with such as have this excitable imagination " [!].

The greatest poet of the race was the greatest by reason of his exceptional nearness to the essential world — his abnormal spiritual sensitiveness brought him into a more intimate relationship with invisible potencies. His soul was more closely linked with the great vital and spiritual forces of the world, and was, through this means, admitted further into Nature's *penetralia* than is permitted to the mere discursive understanding, however great the orbit in which it may move. The discursive understanding may even tend to divorce the soul from those great vital and spiritual forces,

---

* Coleridge remarks : "Shakespeare, inspired, as it might seem, with all knowledge, here uses the word 'causeless' in its strict philosophical sense; — cause being truly predicable only of *phenomena*, that is, things natural, and not of *noumena*, or things supernatural."

in whose current alone it can be conducted to the kingdom of essential truth.

In the next scene in which the weird sisters appear, the 3d of the 1st Act, as Macbeth enters with Banquo, he says : "So foul and fair a day I have not seen." The literal significance of this speech is evident enough : namely, that the day has been foul in respect to the weather, and fair in respect to the battle in which they have engaged. It has been understood, too, as referring to the varying fortune of the day of battle, before victory was finally achieved by the king's forces under Macbeth and Banquo. But which is the true literal meaning is unimportant. The important thing to be considered is, what was, no doubt, intended to be *intimated* by the speech. The same epithets are used as are used in the last speech of the witches, in the first scene : "Fair is foul, and foul is fair," and the intimation evidently intended is, that a relationship has been established, as Coleridge has noted, between the powers of evil and Macbeth's soul — a relationship, however, which *it is yet in Macbeth's power to sever.* It is important to consider this : his free agency is not yet surrendered ; and it rests with him whether he will assert it, or resign himself to their destructive influence. It is also important to consider that the establishment of the relationship has been primarily due to Macbeth himself, and not to outside influence. It has originated in his own heart. ("Keep thy heart with all diligence, for out of it are the issues of life.") Banquo is the first to notice the witches, and in his first speech to them, and in his subsequent speeches, he shows that no magnetic current has been established between them and himself. In Macbeth's speech, only his imperious nature is manifested, as he yet knows not the relations to himself of the strange beings he is addressing : "Speak, if you can, what you are ?" The "all hail" of the 3d witch, "All hail, Macbeth, that shalt be *King* hereafter !" shows that they have had a look into his mind's construction, and have discovered there what they can stimulate into regicide and moral destruction. The speech of Banquo indicates the effect of this "all hail" upon Macbeth's mind, and the *no* effect upon his own : " Good sir, why do you *start,* and seem to fear things that do sound so fair? " He starts because the future fulfilment of the secret and wicked desire of his heart has been so mysteriously proclaimed. But there's nothing within the heart of Banquo to cause *him* to start ; and he continues in words which indicate that *he* has kept his heart with all diligence. One character serves admirably as a foil to the other. " In the name of truth," Banquo continues, " are ye fantastical [*i.e.,* creatures of fantasy or imagination], or that indeed which outwardly ye show? My noble partner you greet with present grace and great prediction of noble having and of royal hope, that he seems wrapt withal." (" Present grace," " great prediction of noble having," and " royal hope " refer respectively to the 1st, 2d, and 3d " all hail " of the witches.) Banquo continues : " to me you speak not. If you can look into the seeds of time, and say which grain will grow and which will not, speak then to me, who neither beg nor fear your favours nor your hate." *

(There's certainly nothing in this demand of Banquo, in regard to himself, which supports what Schlegel calls " the *ambitious* curiosity which prompted him to wish to know his glorious descendants." The poet evidently meant the demand to indicate the *unpossessedness* (to use Coleridge's word) of Banquo's mind, which is contrasted with the *possessedness* of Macbeth's mind. He neither begs nor fears the witches' favors nor their hate.)

In reply to Banquo's command to speak to him, the witches answer : " *1st Witch.* Lesser than Macbeth, and greater. *2d Witch.* Not so happy [*i.e.,* fortunate, Latin *felix*], yet much happier. *3d Witch.* Thou shalt *get* kings, tho' thou be none : so all hail, Macbeth and Banquo ! *1st Witch.* Banquo and Macbeth, all hail ! *Macbeth.* Stay, you imperfect speakers, tell me more," etc. It is plainly indicated what is *back* of this eager insistence on the part of Macbeth, that these imperfect speakers " *stay.*" Without know-

---

* Note the respective construction : " favours " is respective to " beg," and " hate " to " fear." He neither begs their favors nor fears their hate.

ing anything of the nature or trustworthiness of the strange beings before him, he is ready to gulp all he can draw from them. "Fere libenter homines id quod volunt, credunt," says Julius Cæsar (B. G. III. 18), who rarely turns aside to express an abstract truth. "Men very readily believe what they *desire* to be true." But Macbeth's eager insistence is not at all caught by Banquo. He quietly remarks, when the witches vanish : "The earth hath bubbles, as the water has, and these are of them. Whither are they vanished ? *Macbeth.* Into the air : and what seemed corporal, melted as breath into the wind. *Would they had stayed !"* Note this last speech, *"Would they had stayed !"* He is disappointed that he has not heard more of what so deeply concerns him. But Banquo simply says, indicating that there is nothing in his own breast to be aroused by what he has heard, "Were such things here as we do speak about? Or have we eaten on the insane root that takes the reason prisoner?" But Macbeth, wholly absorbed and *inflamed* by what he has heard, continues, without replying to what Banquo has just asked, "Your children shall be kings." Note, too, that Banquo makes nothing of Macbeth's saying, "your children shall be kings." But Macbeth adds, with great satisfaction, to Banquo's remark ("you shall be king,") : "And thane of Cawdor, too ; went it not so?" Banquo replies most indifferently, and in an off-hand way, "To the selfsame tune and words. Who's here?"

That Macbeth has tempted the witches to tempt him, that they, in return, have set about stimulating and inflaming what has originated within his own breast, is evident enough from the scene up to this point. But the evidence is enforced by what follows. Upon Banquo's question, "Who's here," Rosse and Angus enter ; and after they inform Macbeth of the joy with which the King has received the news of his victory, and of the praises which have been showered upon his valor, and present their royal master's thanks, Rosse adds : "And for an earnest of a greater honor, he bade me, from him, call thee *thane of Cawdor ;* in which addition, hail, most worthy thane ! For it is thine." This almost immediate fulfilment of one of the salutations of the witches, " Hail to thee, thane of Cawdor " (and it must be inferred that they got their knowledge by being invisibly present at the time when the King commanded his ministers to pronounce the traitorous thane of Cawdor's immediate death, and with his former title to greet Macbeth, and thus were able to convey to Macbeth the information ahead of Rosse and Angus), is to Macbeth an assurance that the prophetic salutation, " All hail, Macbeth, that shalt be King hereafter," will also be fulfilled ; what Coleridge called the concatenating tendency of the imagination is fostered by the sudden coincidence ; and he soliloquizes : " Glamis, and thane of Cawdor ! the greatest is behind." And then thanking Rosse and Angus for their pains, he says, excitedly, to Banquo, " Do you not hope your children shall be kings, when those that gave the thane of Cawdor to me, promised no less to them ? "

The reply of Banquo, under the circumstances, makes him appear, as do, indeed, his speeches on all occasions, as the very spokesman of Macbeth's good angels, as the intermediate agency between them and Macbeth's soul, whose evil suggestions the powers of darkness are inciting. To Macbeth's question, " Do you not hope your children shall be kings, when those that gave the thane of Cawdor to me, promised no less to them," he replies, as one who is proof against the wiles of evil, " That trusted home [*i.e.*, fully, unreservedly trusted] might yet enkindle you unto the crown, besides the thane of Cawdor. But 'tis strange : and *oftentimes to win us to our harm, the instruments of darkness tell us truths, win us with honest trifles, to betray us in deepest consequence.*"

The entire moral of the tragedy is expressed in this speech.*

Banquo appears to have been specially designed by the poet, as a counter-agency to the agency of the weird sisters (if that can be

---

* Of like import is the following stanza from Wordsworth's " Peter Bell " :

"I know you, potent Spirits, well,
How, with the feeling and the sense
Playing, ye govern foes or friends,
Yoked to your will, for fearful ends."

called a counter-agency which proves entirely ineffective) ; or, as a support or encouragement to Macbeth's free agency, if he choose to assert it.

But the aside speech of Macbeth which follows, shows how impervious he is to any saving influence, by reason of his all-absorbing desire of sovereignty. He disregards what Banquo says, and soliloquizes : " Two truths are told, as happy prologues to the swelling act of the imperial theme." And then he interposes, " I thank you, gentlemen," as a bit of merely politic courtesy, and continues : " This supernatural soliciting [*i.e.*, incitement] cannot be ill, cannot be good : if ill, why hath it given me *earnest of success commencing in a truth ?*" To this question Banquo has already given a wholesome answer, which he disregarded. He continues : " I *am* thane of Cawdor : if good, why do I yield to that suggestion whose horrid image doth unfix my hair, and make my seated heart knock at my ribs, against the use of nature? Present fears are less than horrible imaginings : my thought, whose murder yet is but fantastical, shakes so my single state of man, that function is smothered in surmise, and nothing is but what is not" (A. I. Sc. iii. 137–142).

Here we have the first indication of that keenly imaginative temperament of Macbeth which will play so important a part in his murderous career, which will deceive his wife as to its true character, and which has misled many commentators. It is what will, at first, in his murderous career, shake his fell purpose, and may be easily mistaken for what Lady Macbeth calls " compunctious visitings of nature "; but a genuine compunction there is no evidence that he experiences : and his " horrible imaginings " are, in fact, only one mode in which his *selfishness* manifests itself. He has selfish fears from external dangers, intensified by a morbidly active imagination.

This is shown in his soliloquy (A. I. Sc. vii.) : " If it were done when 'tis done," that is (the word " done " having a double application), if the deed I am contemplating were done with, and there would be nothing more of it, after it is committed, "then 'twere well." " It were done quickly," without any hesitation and without any misgivings, "if the 'assassination could trammel up the consequence," *i.e.*, could catch up, as in a net, could shut out all bad results to myself (in *this* world, as the following lines show), "we'ld jump [risk] the life to come." This is explicit enough. The consequences of the act to his soul are nothing to him. The outside consequences of the act alone cause him to hesitate. Surely there are no moral scruples whatever exhibited in this soliloquy, but only selfish " imaginings."

To return from this digression to the scene before us, the 3d of the 1st Act. Banquo remarks, as Macbeth soliloquizes, " Look how our partner's rapt." Macbeth continues his soliloquy : " If chance will have me king, why chance may crown me, without my stir." Here's an implied admission (even supposing the weird sisters to be the original instigators) that he has received no warrant, no suggestion, of any kind, from without, to murder his King, in order that the " All hail, Macbeth, that shalt be King hereafter," be realized. Banquo remarks upon his rapt condition : " New honours come upon him, like our strange garments, cleave not to their mould but with the aid of use." But Macbeth still continues in soliloquy : " Come what come may, time and the hour runs thro' the roughest day." And then Banquo breaks in upon his musing : " Worthy Macbeth, we stay upon [await] your leisure. *Macb.* Give me your favour [that is, indulgence] : my dull brain was wrought with things forgotten." On this speech Coleridge well remarks : " Lost in the *prospective* of his guilt, he turns round alarmed lest others may suspect what is passing in his own mind, and instantly vents the lie of ambition : ' My dull brain was wrought with things forgotten ; ' and immediately after pours forth the promising courtesies of a usurper in intention : ' Kind gentlemen, your pains are registered where every day I turn the leaf to read them.' " Then, addressing Banquo, " Let us toward the King. Think upon what hath chanced, and, at more time, the interim having weighed it, let us speak our free hearts each to other."

The next scene wherein the witches appear, is the 5th of the 3d Act. "*A Heath. Thunder. Enter the three Witches, meeting Hecate.*" Hecate, in her reproof of the witches, represents herself as the mistress of their charms, and the secret contriver of all harms. She commands them to meet her in the morning at the pit of Acheron, where Macbeth will come to know his destiny. (By "the pit of Acheron" must be meant some secret and gloomy cavern near Macbeth's castle.) Hecate continues: "I am for the air; this night I'll spend unto a dismal and a fatal end: great business must be wrought ere noon: upon the corner of the moon there hangs a vaporous drop profound: I'll catch it ere it come to ground: and that, distilled by magic sleights, shall raise such artificial sprites as by the strength of their illusion shall draw him on to his confusion [destruction]: he shall spurn fate, scorn death, and bear his hopes 'bove wisdom, grace, and fear: and you all know security is mortals' chiefest enemy." ("Security" is here used in a subjective sense, and means as much as "recklessness," such recklessness as is expressed in the preceding lines, spurning fate, scorning death, and bearing hopes above wisdom, grace, and fear. When Macbeth is fairly started upon his murderous career, the "horrible imaginings" which deterred him at the outset, give place to the recklessness characterized in the speech of Hecate.)

In the banquet scene, the 4th of the 3d Act, after the guests have been unceremoniously dismissed by Lady Macbeth, by reason of her husband's overwrought condition, consequent upon the appearance of the ghost of the murdered Banquo, he says to her: "I will to-morrow, and betimes I will, to the weird sisters: more shall they speak, for now I am bent to know, by the worst means, the worst. For mine own good all causes shall give way: I am in blood stepp'd in so far that, should I wade no more, returning were as tedious as go o'er: strange things I have in head that will to hand, *which must be acted ere they may be scann'd.*"

(The last sentence indicates the stage he has reached since he first started upon his career. There's to be no more scanning of consequences. He is now in the firm grip of Fate. The free agency which he might have exercised at the outset, when he received the wise caution of Banquo, he has forfeited; his self-determination is lost; and he is now given over to the powers of evil.   And it should be noted that this speech is in the scene *before* that in which Hecate appears, and says "he shall spurn fate, scorn death, and bear his hope 'bove wisdom, grace and fear." She only *harps what is already in his mind and purpose.*   And this is true throughout the relations of the weird sisters to Macbeth. They *originate* nothing.   This is the great fact to be noted in the Play; but it has *not* been noted by many of the commentators.)

Lady Macbeth makes no other reply to the speech of her husband, last quoted, "I am in blood stepp'd in so far," etc., than "you lack the season of all natures, sleep." She is broken. The Lady Macbeth of the early part of the play is no more. The strong will, at first untrammelled by any considerations of consequences, by any of her husband's "horrible imaginings," gives place to remorse (capabilities of which, it becomes evident, she possessed in a high degree; but they were kept down by the terrific will which swept everything before it — a will *in the service of a wifely sympathy with her husband's o'ermastering desire for sovereignty, and not of an independent ambition;* and when that desire of her husband is realized, and she sees what its realization has brought with it, and also discovers that he is of a different nature from what she represents him to be, in the speech she utters after receiving his letter, her womanly nature (and her nature is *most* womanly) succumbs to the violation to which it is subjected.

The next witch scene is the 1st of the 4th Act: "*A cavern. In the middle, a boiling cauldron.   Thunder.   Enter the three witches.*

> " 1 *Witch*. Thrice the brinded cat hath mew'd.
>
> 2 *Witch*. Thrice, and once the hedge-pig whin'd.
>
> 3 *Witch*. Harpier cries. — 'Tis time, 'tis time.
>
> 1 *Witch*. Round about the cauldron go;
> In the poison'd entrails throw.
> Toad, that under cold stone,
> Days and nights has thirty-one

Swelter'd venom sleeping got,
Boil thou first i' the charmed pot.

All. Double, double, toil and trouble;
Fire burn, and cauldron bubble.

2 *Witch.* Fillet of a fenny snake,
In the cauldron boil and bake:
Eye of newt, and toe of frog,
Wool of bat, and tongue of dog,
Adder's fork, and blind-worm's sting,
Lizard's leg, and owlet's wing,
For a charm of powerful trouble;
Like a hell-broth boil and bubble.

All. Double, double, toil and trouble;
Fire burn, and cauldron bubble.

3 *Witch.* Scale of dragon, tooth of wolf;
Witches' mummy, maw and gulf
Of the ravin'd salt-sea shark;
Root of hemlock digg'd i' the dark;
Liver of blaspheming Jew;
Gall of goat, and slips of yew
Silver'd in the moon's eclipse;
Nose of Turk, and Tartar's lips;
Finger of birth-strangled babe
Ditch-deliver'd by a drab,
Make the gruel thick and slab;
Add thereto a tiger's chaudron,
For the ingredients of our cauldron.

All. Double, double, toil and trouble;
Fire burn, and cauldron bubble.

2 *Witch.* Cool it with a baboon's blood,
Then the charm is firm and good."

The loathsome ingredients of the hell-broth they are brewing to work the charm which will add fresh fuel to the sin-inflamed soul of Macbeth, and draw him on to his destruction, symbolize the relationship of these demons with the night side of nature — with the powers of darkness: poisoned entrails, the toad's sweltered venom, fillet of a fenny snake, maw and gulf of the ravined salt-sea shark, liver of blaspheming Jew, gall of goat, slips of yew slivered in the moon's eclipse, finger of birth-strangled babe ditch-delivered by a drab, and other revolting things.

Just before Macbeth enters, the 2d witch scents the approaching prey, and, as may be imagined, upturns her nostril wide into the murky air, sagacious of her quarry, and exclaims : "By the pricking of my thumbs, something *wicked* this way comes. Open locks, whoever knocks." A speech of deep significance, revealing, as it does, the nature of these horrible hags — their magnetic sensitiveness to whatever is akin to their own evil nature — their readiness to open to every one who knocks. "Knock, and it shall be opened unto you," is even more true where the determination of any one's nature is toward evil than where it is toward good.

What follows, in this scene, prefigures, in an *equivocal* way, what has become the *fated* career which Macbeth has to run, to its bitter end — fated, because he has not held on to himself. He has lost his free will and has drifted into the irresistible current of evil forces.

The several apparitions which are summoned to address him, are the "artificial sprites" which Hecate, in the 5th Scene of the 3d Act, says shall, "by the strength of their illusion, draw him on to his confusion."

The first apparition, "an armed head," is generally understood as prefiguring Macbeth's head, cut off and brought to Malcolm by Macduff. Macbeth begins to address it with the words, "Tell me, thou unknown power, — " but is interrupted by the 1st witch : "*He knows thy thought :* hear his speech, but say thou nought." Here it is again indicated that everything originates in Macbeth's own mind. "*1st App.* Macbeth ! Macbeth ! Macbeth ! beware Macduff; beware the thane of Fife. Dismiss me : enough. [*Descends.*] *Macb.* Whate'er thou art, for thy good caution thanks ; *thou hast harped my fear aright :* but one word more, — *1st Witch.* He will not be commanded : here's another, more potent than the first. *Thunder. 2d Apparition : a bloody child.*" The bloody child represents Macduff untimely ripped from his mother's womb, and is, in the words of the 1st witch, "more potent than the first," that is, Macbeth. "*2d App.* Be bloody, bold, and resolute;" just what Macbeth has already determined to be : "laugh to scorn the powers of man, for none of woman born shall harm Macbeth. *Macb.* Then live, Macduff: what need I fear of thee? But yet I'll make assurance double sure, and take a bond of fate : thou shalt *not* live ; that I may tell pale-hearted fear it lies, and sleep in spite of thunder."

It should be especially noted that after the witches vanish, Macbeth learns from Lenox that Macduff has fled to England. This fact the witches must be supposed to know, and they give Macbeth a gratuitous warning against Macduff, and thus secure for themselves his faith in their guardianship of him ; a *gratuitous* warning, because, Macduff being out of Macbeth's reach, the latter cannot make assurance double sure, by putting his dreaded enemy out of the way. This is a very shrewd dodge of the witches. Their warning is not for his safety, but for his destruction.

"*Thunder. Third Apparition: a child crowned, with a tree in his hand.*" This child prefigures the King's son, Malcolm, who, as he advances against Macbeth, will order every soldier hew him down a bough and bear it before him to Dunsinane, thereby to shadow the number of his forces, and make Macbeth's spies err in report of them.

"*3d App.* Be lion-mettled, proud, and take no care who chafes, who frets, or where conspirers are : Macbeth shall never vanquished be until great Birnam wood to high Dunsinane hill shall come against him."

Macbeth's confidence in the witches' protecting power has been strengthened by the predictions of the 1st and 2d Apparitions, who have warned him against the man whom he already knew was to be especially feared, and assured him that no one of woman born could harm him. The prediction of the 3d Apparition, that he never shall be vanquished until great Birnam wood to high Dunsinane hill shall come against him, clinches his confidence, as his speech in reply shows : " That will *never* be : who can impress the forest, [that is, press the forest into military service], bid the tree unfix his earth-bound root ? "   But now that he is assured that he "shall live the lease of nature, pay his breath to time and mortal custom," he is eager to know whether their predictions in regard to Banquo will be fulfilled : " Yet my heart throbs to know one thing : tell me, — if your art can tell so much, — shall Banquo's issue ever reign in this kingdom ? "   When he is told to "seek to know no more," his haughty and arbitrary imperiousness denounces them roundly, which they repay with "a show of eight Kings, the last with a glass in his hand : Banquo's Ghost following ; " — not the Banquo as he knew him in life, but the Banquo, blood-boltered, as he appeared to him in the banquet scene : " the blood-boltered Banquo smiles upon me, and points at them [the Kings] for his."

The witches are gleeful over their victim, whose eyeballs have been seared by what has been shown him.   The first witch says : " Come, sisters, cheer we up his sprights, and show the best of our delights : I'll charm the air to give a sound, while you perform your antic round, that this great king may kindly say our duties did his welcome pay."

There's a hellish sarcasm intended in the word " kindly."   And note especially the last sentence uttered by the witches, in the tragedy : " OUR DUTIES DID HIS WELCOME PAY."

It expresses implicitly all that has been set forth, in regard to the relation of the witches to Macbeth.   He was the first to *welcome* them as guests to his bosom, and they have done their duty by him, as agents of the devil.   They have originated nothing within him.   They have but *harped* what he has previously *desired* and *premeditated,* and have thus stimulated his evil propensities into acts.   In this last scene in which they appear, they urge him on in his career by flattering equivocations, and to these he will cling to the bitter end.   Each in turn proves a false reliance ; and, finally, he drops into the abyss which is yawning to receive him.

Verily the tragedy affords no support to the interpretation that the witches are the original instigators. If this interpretation were the true one, if Macbeth were a man "whose natural temper," according to one of his interpreters, " would have deterred him " from the murder of his King, and if he were subjected at the out-set, to an *irresistible* objective instigation (his free agency being destroyed by that instigation), to do such violence to his *better* nature, the tragedy would have no true dramatic merit, and should be consigned to the limbo of the so-called Heroic Plays of the Restoration Drama.

LADY MACBETH'S RELATIONS TO MACBETH.

IN the foregoing chapter, it is shown that Macbeth welcomed the Witches as guests to his bosom, and that they did their duty by him as agents of evil. They originated nothing within him, they but *harped* what he had previously *desired* and *meditated*, and thus stimulated his evil propensities into acts. In the last scene in which they appear, the 1st of the 4th Act, they urge him on in his career by flattering equivocations, each of which proves a false reliance; but he clings to them, to the bitter end, and finally drops into the abyss which is yawning to receive him.

It can be as plainly read that the part played by Lady Macbeth was *in the service of a wifely sympathy with her husband's o'ermastering desire for sovereignty and not of an independent ambition;* a desire with which, so far as the evidence goes, in the play, she had nothing originally to do.

Macbeth first reveals himself, after his victory over his country's foes, before he returns to his own castle, there to be sustained and urged on to the killing of his King, by his devoted wife, whose powerful and untrammelled will is set against his trammelled will — trammelled, not by compunctious visitings, as is supposed by many commentators and readers, but by considerations of *consequences;* not of consequences to his own soul (for he goes so far as to say that he'd risk the life to come, if his ambition could be realized with *outward* safety to himself).

After his victory, when he and Banquo return to the palace, the amiable King expresses, in the strongest terms, his gratitude for the great services which his two generals, Macbeth and Banquo, have rendered him. Macbeth replies in a speech informed apparently with the very soul of loyalty, but in which hypocrisy can no further go — an hypocrisy involving, under the circumstances, the basest dishonor, and the blackest ingratitude : " The service and the loyalty I owe, in doing it, pays itself [that is, is its own reward] : Your highness' part is to receive our duties ; and our duties are to your throne and state, children and servants ; which do but what they should, by doing everything safe toward your love and honor." The meaning of which is plain enough, if it be not considered too curiously. Duncan replies : " Welcome hither : I have begun to plant thee, and will labour to make thee full of growing. Noble Banquo that hast no less deserved, nor must be known no less to have done so, let me infold thee and hold thee to my heart."

How genuine and simple Banquo's reply ! " There if I grow, the harvest is your own."

But now comes the *immediate* motive for Macbeth's evil desire to go forth into act. Duncan, in the fulness of his joys, nominates his eldest son, Malcolm, as his successor to the throne : " My plenteous joys, wanton in fulness, seek to hide themselves in drops of sorrow. — Sons, kinsmen, thanes, and you whose places are the nearest, know we will establish our estate upon our eldest, Malcolm, whom we name hereafter the Prince of Cumberland ; which honour must not unaccompanied invest him only, but signs of nobleness, like stars, shall shine on all deservers. — From hence to Inverness, and bind us further to you." Macbeth replies in another hypocritical and traitorous speech : " The rest is labour, which is not used for you [that is, the rest which is not spent in the King's service, is like severe labor]. I'll be myself the harbinger and *make joyful the hearing of my wife with your approach ;* so, humbly take my leave. *Duncan.* My worthy Cawdor ! "

Before Macbeth goes out, he soliloquizes, the King and Banquo confer apart — the subject of their conference being, as appears from Duncan's speech, Macbeth's valiant conduct. Macbeth says aside : " The Prince of Cumberland ! that is a step on which

I must fall down, or else o'erleap, *for in my way it lies.* Stars, hide your fires! Let not light see my black and deep desires: the eye wink at the hand; yet let that be which the eye fears, when it is done, to see."

How prophetic the last sentence is! "Yet let that be, which the eye fears, when it is done, to see."

In the 2d Scene of the 2d Act, he says, after the murder: "I'll go no more: I am afraid to think what I have done; look on't again I dare not."

This soliloquy is an all-sufficient evidence that Macbeth's regicidal intent was entirely independent of any suggestions from his wife, as it was entirely independent of any suggestions from the weird sisters. Lady Macbeth's ambition is wholly sympathetic. It is not with her an independent passion at all. When she knows her husband's all-absorbing desire, she sets about, in her wifely devotion, to help him to its realization, although she's fully aware that she must do fatal violence to her woman nature.

In the face of this 4th Scene of the 1st Act, and, it may be said, in the face of the whole play, Hazlitt pronounces Macbeth "full of the milk of human kindness" (an expression used by Lady Macbeth, but not therefore true; for she overestimates her husband at the outset — she doesn't truly know him), "frank and generous. He is tempted to the commission of guilt by the instigations of his wife, and by prophetic warnings. Fate and metaphysical aid conspire against his virtue and his loyalty." This is an opinion substantially entertained by a large number of Shakespearian critics.

The temptation, on the contrary, was subjective. There's not a particle of evidence in the Play that the temptation originated from without, either with the witches or with Lady Macbeth. In their interview after his soliloquy, "If it were done when 'tis done," etc. (A. I. Sc. vii.), she says, in reply to his speech, "I dare do all that may become a man," "what beast was't then that *made you break this enterprise to me?*" That's sufficiently explicit, certainly.

Ambition for sovereignty and masterdom is the mainspring motive of Macbeth, but as Lloyd, in his "Critical Essays," more correctly puts it than critics generally, Lady Macbeth "participates in his ambition only by sympathy. No expression falls from her that indicates it as her independent passion, or hints that it was from her original suggestion that it was excited in her husband." Again he says, "Subjected to the doom, she has lost her own individuality in that of her husband, and in the necessity to occupy the nearest place in his interest and heart. She allies herself with his master passion, and becomes its minister. Ambition, therefore, is not in her absolute and self-dependent; it is the expression of *another* feeling which, with a different companion, might have taken any other turn; and hence her association of the direst acts with the offices and tenderness of maternity, is as truly consistent and natural as momentary compunction at the resemblance of the sleeping Duncan to her father."

In the 3d Scene of the 2d Act, Lady Macbeth enters in the confusion consequent upon the discovery and announcement, by Macduff, of the murder of the King, and inquires: "What's the business, that such a hideous trumpet calls to parley the sleepers of the house? speak, speak!" And when Macbeth returns from the chamber of the King, and, with the blackest hypocrisy, describes the horrid scene, including what Lady Macbeth herself had done, "the murderers steeped in the colors of their trade, their daggers unmannerly breached with gore," the strain is too much for her, and she faints, and is carried out. There's no reason for supposing that it's a sham faint. Her woman nature asserts itself, and she can hold out no longer. It is plain, from the next scene, that she's quite broken. When Macbeth enters, she says, "How now, my lord! Why do you keep alone, using those thoughts which should indeed have died with them they think on? Things without all remedy should be without regard: what's done is done."

She mistakes him here. He is not suffering from remorse for

what has been done, but from fears of what is before him. He replies to her last speech, " We have scotch'd the snake, not kill'd it. She'll close and be herself, whilst our poor malice remains in danger of her former tooth." The rest of this speech shows that Macbeth is ready to enter upon the course in which he will no longer need his wife. In reply to her speech, " you must leave this," he says : " Oh, full of scorpions is my mind, dear wife ! " This speech taken by itself may easily be understood as express-ing remorse ; but the next sentence explains it : " Thou know'st that Banquo, and his Fleance, lives." To her question, " What's to be done ? " he replies : " Be innocent of the knowledge, dearest chuck, till thou applaud the deed." He needs her no longer.

In the banquet scene, after the guests have been dismissed, Macbeth asks, " What is the night ? " To which she replies, " Al-most at odds with morning, which is which." Here is the point where she entirely breaks. She has made one additional effort to sustain her husband, and can do no more.

Charlotte Cushman, in her impersonation of Lady Macbeth, rendered " almost at odds with morning, which is which," with great effect. Right upon Macbeth's question, " What is the night ? " she dropped passively into a chair, and uttered the words with an intonation of entire hopelessness, which told the whole story.

All of Lady Macbeth's part in the tragedy, is reflected by her speeches in the night-walking scene, the 1st of the 5th Act. And it is affecting to note the contrasts which some of these speeches present to her earlier speeches. In A. I. Sc. v. she says : " Come thick night, and pall thee in the dunnest smoke of hell ! " In A. V. Sc. i. she says, evidently thinking herself in hell : " Hell is murky ! " In A. I. Sc. v. she says : " You shall put this night's great business into my dispatch ; which shall to all our nights and days to come, give solely sovereign sway and masterdom." In A. V. Sc. i. she says : " What need we care who knows it, when none can call our power to account ? " In the murder scene

(A. II. Sc. ii.) she says: "If he do bleed, I'll gild the faces of the grooms withal, for it must seem their guilt. In A. V. Sc. i. she says: "Yet who would have thought the old man to have had so much blood in him!" In A. II. Sc. ii. she says: "My hands are of your color: but I shame to wear a heart so white." In A. V. Sc. i. she says: "What, will these hands ne'er be clean?" In the banquet scene (A. III. Sc. iv.) she says: "Oh, these flaws and starts"—and "think of this, good peers, but as a thing of custom: 'tis no other; only it spoils the pleasure of the time." In A. V. Sc. i. she says: "No more o' that, my lord, no more o' that: you mar all with this starting." In the murder scene she says: "Go get some water, and wash this filthy witness from your hand." In A. V. Sc. i. she says: "Wash your hands, put on your nightgown; look not so pale." In the murder scene she says: "I hear a knocking at the south entry: retire we to our chamber: a little water clears us of this deed: how easy is it then?" In A. V. Sc. i. she says: "Here's the smell of the blood still: all the perfumes of Arabia will not sweeten this little hand. Oh, Oh, Oh!" In the murder scene she says: "Your constancy hath left you unattended.—Hark! more knocking. Get on your nightgown, lest occasion call us, and shew us to be watchers. Be not lost so poorly in your thoughts." In A. V. Sc. i. she says: "To bed, to bed! there's knocking at the gate; come, come, come, come, give me your hand."

In A. III. S. ii. she says: "Things without all remedy should be without regard: what's done, is done." In A. V. Sc. i. she says: "What's done, cannot be undone."

The artistic purpose of this night-walking scene appears to be, to reflect the real womanly nature of Lady Macbeth (to which she did such violence in the part she took upon herself to play that it suffered, for a time, a total eclipse), and her possibilities for great good or great evil (the latter in every man and woman being commensurate with the former). Her misfortune was that as a wife, she sunk her individuality in her husband; and terrible was the penalty she paid for this. If that individuality had rendered the same fealty to a noble nature, how different, with its great capabilities of love, would have been the result! As it was, she "knew how tender 'twas to love the babe that milked her." And she shows, in one of her speeches, that she had been a loving daughter: "Had he not resembled my father as he slept, I had done't."

The last we hear of the poor conscience-stricken queen is in the 5th Scene of the 5th Act. A cry within of women is heard. On which the Countess of Charlemont remarks: "She was not all evil. Her own sex and her servants mourned for her."

Macbeth asks, when the cry is heard, "What is that noise?" and Seyton replies, "It is the cry of women, my good lord," and goes out to learn the cause. When he re-enters, he says, "The queen, my lord, is dead." Whereupon Macbeth soliloquizes: "She should have died hereafter;" etc. (In uttering the words, "Out, out, brief candle," in this soliloquy, some actors strike their breasts, as if the reference were to Macbeth's own light of life, but they should certainly be understood as having reference to the candle of Lady Macbeth's life. Though commas are used in the First Folio, the words should be uttered with an interrogative intonation, united with that of surprise: "Out? out? brief candle?" [out so soon?] The latter meaning suits better, too, the reflections which follow.)

Dr. Furnivall says, in a note on a paper by the Countess of Charlemont, which was read before the New Shakspere Society of London, and which takes the view that Lady Macbeth's ambition was wholly sympathetic: "The notion that Lady Macbeth stirred, nay forced, Macbeth to his villanous murder, to gratify *his* ambition only, and not her own too, is so in the teeth of Shakespeare's authority, Holinshed, 'but especially his wife lay sore upon him to attempt the thing, as she that was very ambitious, burning in unquenchable desire to bear the name of queen,' that I don't think the point worth arguing."

On this it should be remarked (whether the theory that Lady Macbeth's ambition was sympathetic, be or be not correct), that the student of any play of Shakespeare, must not go to the history or novel from which the framework of the play was derived, for the interpretation of the characters of the play. But commentators have frequently done this, when they should have asked themselves the question, what saith the play? not, what saith the original history or novel on which it is based? Shakespeare always brought an independent dramatic purpose to the adopted story or history, by which dramatic purpose the movement of the play is determined and not by the adopted story or history. The latter has nothing whatever to do with the interpretation of any of the characters.

ANTONY AND CLEOPATRA.

THE date of the composition of Antony and Cleopatra is generally assigned to the year 1607 or 1608, when Shakespeare
was 43 or 44 years of age, in the full maturity of his powers, and
when "the profoundest concerns of the individual soul were press-
ing upon the imagination of the poet." The Play ranks with his
grandest productions, and perhaps surpasses them all. "The
highest praise," says Coleridge, " or rather form of praise, of this
Play, which I can offer in my own mind, is the doubt which the
perusal always occasions in me, whether the Antony and Cleopatra
is not, in all exhibitions of a giant power, in its strength and vigor
of maturity, a formidable rival of Macbeth, Lear, Hamlet, and
Othello. *Feliciter audax* is the motto for its style comparatively
with that of Shakespeare's other works, even as it is the general
motto of all his works compared with those of other poets. . . .
As a wonderful specimen of the way in which Shakespeare lives
up to the very end of this play, read the last part of the concluding scene. And if you would feel the judgment as well as the
genius of Shakespeare in your heart's core, compare this astonish-
ing drama with Dryden's ' All for Love,' which is based on it."

Antony and Cleopatra is, to all intents and purposes, a tragedy,
the moral interest predominating over the historical or political.
The latter is, indeed, entirely subservient to the former — constituting a background against which individualities are exhibited.
Even Coriolanus, though much stress has been laid by some critics
upon its politico-historical character (see especially Hazlitt), is,
strictly speaking, a tragedy. As Swinburne well puts it, "the whole
force of the final impression is not that of a conflict between patri-

cian and plebeian, but solely that of a match of passions played
out for life and death between a mother and a son. The partisans of oligarchic or democratic systems may wrangle at their will
over the supposed evidences of Shakespeare's prejudice against
this creed, and prepossession in favor of that: a third bystander
may rejoice in the proof established of his impartial indifference
towards either: it is all nothing to the real point in hand. The
subject of the whole play is not the exile's revolt, the rebel's repent-
ance, or the traitor's reward, but above all it is the son's tragedy.
The inscription on the plinth of this tragic statue is simply to
Volumnia Victrix." •

Prof. Denton J. Snider treats the play as "essentially a drama
of Political Parties. . . . Moreover, the warring principles of the
two parties are aristocracy and democracy — the conflict which
has always in History been most prolific of political strife. The
main characters are graded according to their partisan bias and
intensity, for the essence of the conflict is party versus country."

But it is a mistake, I think, to impute a doctrinal character
to any play of Shakespeare, whether that character be moral, political, religious, or philosophical. Everything is held more or less
in solution, in the Plays — there's comparatively little of precipi-
tation, and hardly anything at all of crystallization into opinions
or doctrines. (It's a marked characteristic of literary educational
processes in these days, that nothing is allowed to be held in
solution in a literary work, if it can be precipitated and crystal-
lized into ideas and opinions; in other words, if it can be brought
into the domain of the insulated intellect. The age would be
healthier if there were less of this.)

Shakespeare is always, and pre-eminently, and exclusively, the
dramatist; but as a dramatist, he is distinguished from all the
contemporary dramatists, in his working more strictly than any
of them, under the condition of moral proportion (and by moral
proportion I mean that which is in harmony with the permanent
constitution, with the eternal fitness, of things), and this he did,
because, as must be inferred, he *felt* more than did any other of

the contemporary dramatists, the constitution of things, and knew
that that constitution of things could not be violated with impunity. To unite moral proportion with a more or less unrestrained
play of the passions, is the great artistic achievement of Shakespeare, in his tragic masterpieces. And when a critic looks into
his Plays with an eye for the doctrinal, he can easily find it there,
because the best results of human philosophy in its several depart-
ments have been induced and deduced from careful observations
of the permanent constitution of things, and therefore correspond
more or less with the philosophy concretely embodied in the
Plays. The concrete philosophy and the abstract philosophy are
based on, or derived from, the same permanent constitution of
things.

Accordingly, it's easy for any one with philosophical tendencies
to mistake the artist, or creator, for the explicit teacher. The
great artist works within boundless nature, and in conformity with
nature ; and in his works may be found the same principles which
are found in nature. But we must not suppose that he first
educed these principles before he embodied them — that he
started with abstractions, and translated them into the concrete.
No ; the true artist uses the concrete as a native language, so
to speak ; and the abstract principles which may be found in his
work, are involved in the creative movement, and did not, in an
abstract form, predetermine that movement.

There's no partisanship in Shakespeare's Plays, political, religious, or any other, though he lived at a time when it was almost
impossible to be neutral in regard to many things, and especially
in regard to religion. The great body of the people was composed of two classes, — one strongly Roman Catholic and one
strongly Protestant. There must have been very few half and half
religious people in those days. Shakespeare's impartiality, as exhibited in his Plays, in regard to religion and government, could not
fairly be ascribed to a religious and political indifference — to his
having no strong feeling one way or the other ; it should rather be
ascribed to his affinities as an artist, a great creator, for the essen-

tial or the real, rather than for the phenomenal or the actual — for the permanent rather than for the conventional — for the spirit rather than for the letter, so to speak. He was too complete a man to take one-sided views of things ; and partisanship of any kind implies generally a more or less one-sidedness of view ; and the stronger, the more violent the partisanship, the more exclusive the one-sidedness of view. The impartiality of Shakespeare, in a religious point of view, is especially shown in his King John, as compared with the earlier play, "The Troublesome Reign of King John," whose general casting, but none of its moulding, religious spirit Shakespeare adopted in his play.

The question as to whether Shakespeare was Roman Catholic or Protestant has been more than sufficiently discussed, but with no conclusive results. And so the question as to whether he was aristocratic in his proclivities or democratic, cannot be answered with any more certainty than that in regard to his religious creed. If it could be answered at all, Coriolanus is the play to which we should go for the answer. But no conclusive answer can be got from this play as to his political creed. Its political character is a background for the exhibition of personal character. It's a drama of individuality, as are all of Shakespeare's dramas, more or less, whatever be their framework. It was never his aim, his *direct* aim, to embody abstract principles — although the profoundest principles are operative in his creations. His dramatic motive is individuality, personality, acting and exhibiting itself under outward conditions and collisions, those conditions or collisions being political, social, domestic, or what not. Shakespeare is, in one sense, and that the very highest, a moralist, and a social and political philosopher ; that is, he is *concretely* these ; he *embodies* the principles of morality and of social and political philosophy, and thus vitalizes and emphasizes them to a degree beyond what any abstract enunciation could do.* And it is all-important that

---

* Perhaps to say that he *embodies* the principles of morality, and of social and political philosophy, may convey a wrong idea. It is better to say that

the student of his works should come into as full a sympathy as possible with the concrete embodiment, which is the product of this creative energy (even if he have no consciousness of *any* immanent principle). If his mind be set in an abstract direction, and he aim to translate the word made flesh into the abstract word, he shuts himself off more or less from a vitalizing sympathy with the concrete.

Professor Delius, at the conclusion of his 2d paper " On Shakespeare's Use of Narration in his Dramas " (Transactions of the New Shakspere Society, 1875–6, Part I. p. 345), remarks : " In the two last Acts [of Antony and Cleopatra], Shakespeare evidently allows the psychological and personal interest attaching to the two principal actors in his drama to outweigh the historical interest. The further action up to the tragic end is scenically enacted before our eyes, within a narrower compass, so that the poet had no need to again make use of the epic element."

It seems to be assumed by Professor Delius, in the first of these sentences, that the historical interest is the dominant one in the first three Acts of the drama; and he asserts that "in the two last Acts, Shakespeare *allows* the psychological and personal interest attaching to the two principal actors *to outweigh the historical interest.*" Which would seem to mean that Shakespeare, after working through three Acts with a historical interest, was finally carried out of his course by a psychological and personal interest. But the fact is, that this latter interest is the dominant one from the beginning to the end of the Play, and outweighs the historical interest which is subsidiary to it. Shakespeare always strikes distinctly and unmistakably the keynotes of his Plays in the opening scenes.

The key note of Antony and Cleopatra is struck in the initial sentence. Philo says to Demetrius :

---

these principles were more or less unconsciously involved in the current of his creative energy — which creative energy must have been in the fullest harmony with the constitution of things.

" Nay, but this dotage of our general's
O'erflows the measure : those his goodly eyes,
That o'er the files and musters of the war
Have glow'd like plated Mars, now bend, now turn,
The office and devotion of their view
Upon a tawny front : his captain's heart,
Which in the scuffles of great fights hath burst
The buckles on his breast, reneges all temper,
And is become the bellows and the fan
To cool a gipsy's lust."

Here, announced by a flourish, enter Antony, Cleopatra, her
Ladies, the Train, with Eunuchs fanning her.   Philo continues his
speech aside to Demetrius :

" Look, where they come :
Take but good note, and you shall see in him
The triple pillar of the world transform'd
Into a strumpet's fool : behold and see."

In the 4th Scene of the 1st Act, the self-poised Octavius re-
counts to Lepidus, Antony's life in Alexandria :

" From Alexandria
This is the news : he fishes, drinks, and wastes
The lamps of night in revel ; is not more manlike
Than Cleopatra ; nor the queen of Ptolemy
More womanly than he ; hardly gave audience, or
Vouchsafed to think he had partners : you shall find there
A man who is the abstract of all faults
That all men follow."

Lepidus, who, with a sense of his weakness and insecurity in the
triumvirate, is ever disposed to smooth down all roughnesses, attempts a defence of his erring colleague :

" I must not think there are
Evils enow to darken all his goodness :
His faults in him seem as the spots of heaven,
More fiery by night's blackness ; hereditary,
Rather than purchased ; what he cannot change,
Than what he chooses."

Octavius replies :

> "You are too indulgent.   Let us grant, it is not
> Amiss to tumble on the bed of Ptolemy ;
> To give a kingdom for a mirth ; to sit
> And keep the turn of tippling with a slave ;
> To reel the streets at noon, and stand the buffet
> With knaves that smell of sweat : say this becomes him, —
> As his composure must be rare indeed
> Whom these things cannot blemish, — yet must Antony
> No way excuse his soils, when we do bear
> So great weight in his likeness.   If he fill'd
> His vacancy with his voluptuousness,
> Full surfeits, and the dryness of his bones,
> Call on him for't : but to confound such time,
> That drums him from his sport, and speaks as loud
> As his own state and ours, — 'tis to be chid
> As we rate boys, who, being mature in knowledge,
> Pawn their experience to their present pleasure,
> And so rebel to judgement."

Here a messenger enters and informs Octavius of Pompey's
strength at sea, that the malcontents are repairing to the ports,
that Menecrates and Menas, famous pirates, control the sea, and
make many hot inroads in Italy.   These bad news leads Octavius
to contrast Antony's present life of ruinous voluptuousness with the
heroic promise of his earlier life, when no kinds of hardship were
too much for him to endure :

> "Antony,
> Leave thy lascivious wassails.   When thou once
> Wast beaten from Modena, where thou slew'st
> Hirtius and Pansa, consuls, at thy heel
> Did famine follow ; whom thou fought'st against,
> Though daintily brought up, with patience more
> Than savages could suffer : thou didst drink
> The stale of horses, and the gilded puddle
> Which beasts would cough at : thy palate then did deign
> The roughest berry on the rudest hedge ;
> Yea, like the stag, when snow the pasture sheets,

The barks of trees thou browsed'st; on the Alps
It is reported thou didst eat strange flesh,
Which some did die to look on: and all this —
It wounds thine honour that I speak it now —
Was borne so like a soldier, that thy cheek
So much as lank'd not.*
  Lep.   'Tis pity of him.
  Cæs. Let his shames quickly
Drive him to Rome: 'tis time we twain
Did show ourselves i' the field; and to that end
Assemble we immediate council: Pompey
Thrives in our idleness."

---

* What Octavius says of Antony's former life, affords a good illustration of how closely Shakespeare follows his original, namely, North's Plutarch.

"Cicero on the other side, being at that time the chiefest man of authority and estimation in the city, he stirred up all men against Antonius: so that in the end he made the senate pronounce him an enemy to his country, and appointed young Cæsar sergeants, to carry axes before him, and such other signs as were incident to the dignity of a Consul or Prætor: and moreover, sent Hircius and Pansa, then Consuls, to drive Antonius out of Italy. These two Consuls, together with Cæsar, who also had an army, went against Antonius that besieged the city of Modena, and there overthrew him in battle: but both the Consuls were slain there.

"Antonius, flying from this overthrow, fell into great misery all at once: but the chiefest want of all other, and that pinched him most, was famine. Howbeit he was of such a strong nature, that by patience[1] he would overcome any adversity: and the heavier fortune lay upon him, the more constant showed he himself. Every man that feeleth want or adversity, knoweth by virtue and discretion what he should do: but when indeed they are overlaid with extremity, and be sore oppressed, few have the hearts to follow that which they praise and commend, and much less to avoid that they reprove and mislike: but rather to the contrary, they yield to their accustomed easy life, and through faint heart, and lack of courage, do change their first mind and purpose. And therefore it was a wonderful example to the soldiers, to see Antonius, that was brought up in all fineness and superfluity, so easily to drink puddle water, and to eat wild fruits and roots: and moreover it is reported, that even as they passed the Alps, they did eat the barks of trees, and such beasts as never man tasted of their flesh before."

[1] endurance.

In these speeches, artistically important in respect to Antony (for the poet's purpose is to emphasize his great possibilities), the character of Octavius is also reflected — the man before whom Sextus Pompeius and Antony and Lepidus must give way, and who is to effect a realization of the tendency of the time to imperialism. Octavius is the representative of the spirit of Cæsar which Brutus and Cassius, in the Play of Julius Cæsar, did not take sufficient account of when they planned and effected his assassination. They killed his body, but had no power over his spirit. This they both discovered on the plains of Philippi, Cassius's last words being, "Cæsar, thou art revenged, even with the sword that killed thee." And Brutus, when he learns of Cassius's death, exclaims, "O Julius Cæsar, thou art mighty yet! thy spirit walks abroad, and turns our swords in our own proper entrails."

This then is the dramatic situation: a man of extraordinary possibilities, altogether of colossal but unsymmetrical proportions, brought under the sway of a fascinating woman — fascinating in a sensuous direction — with all possible adventitious aids to her instrinsic fascination; but to induce a vigorous resistance to this sway under which he is brought, and to save him from becoming a helpless victim of her magic, the greatest possible demands are made upon his asserting his nobler self — demands which, if met, would enable him "to walk the earth with dominion," though wanting in the civic genius of his colleague in the triumvirate, Octavius. He is an unparalleled illustration of what Hamlet is made to give expression to (A. I. Sc. iv. 23–38):

> "So, oft it chances in particular men,
> That for some vicious mole of nature in them,
> As in their birth, — wherein they are not guilty,
> Since nature cannot choose his origin, —
> By the o'ergrowth of some complexion,
> Oft breaking down the pales and forts of reason,
> Or by some habit that too much o'er-leavens
> The form of plausive manners; that these men, —
> Carrying, I say, the stamp of one defect,

Being nature's livery, or fortune's star, —
Their virtues else — be they as pure as grace,
As infinite as man may undergo —
Shall in the general censure take corruption
From that particular fault; the dram of eale
Doth all the noble substance of a doubt
To his own scandal."

This passage expresses the very theme of Antony and Cleopatra as a tragedy; and when Shakespeare wrote it, he had
already, there can be little or no doubt, produced the play of
Julius Cæsar, and had seen in the character of Antony, notwithstanding all its great elements, the fatal consequences of a
"vicious mole of nature." Antony may have been in his mind
when he wrote this passage. Thomas De Quincey, in his volume
on "The Cæsars," credits Shakespeare with an insight into the
grand possibilities of Antony's nature, which the Romans themselves could not have had : "Shakespeare," he says, "had a just
conception of the original grandeur which lay beneath that wild
tempestuous nature presented by Antony to the eye of the undis-
criminating world. It is to the honor of Shakespeare that he
should have been able to discern the true coloring of this most
original character under the smoke and tarnish of antiquity. It is
no less to the honor of the great triumvir, that a strength of coloring should survive in his character, capable of baffling the wrongs
and ravages of time. Neither is it to be thought strange that a
character should have been misunderstood and falsely appreciated
for nearly two thousand years. It happens not uncommonly, especially amongst an unimaginative people, like the Romans, that
the characters of men are ciphers and enigmas to their own age,
and are first read and interpreted by a far distant posterity. . . .
Men like Mark Antony, with minds of chaotic composition —
light conflicting with darkness, proportions of colossal grandeur
disfigured by unsymmetrical arrangement, the angelic in close
neighborhood with the brutal — are first read in their true meaning
by an age learned in the philosophy of the human heart. Of this

philosophy the Romans had, by the necessities of education and domestic discipline, not less than by original constitution of mind, the very narrowest visual range. . . . Not man in his own peculiar nature, but man in his relations to other men, was the station from which the Roman speculators took up their philosophy of human nature. Tried by such standard, Mark Antony would be found wanting. As a citizen, he was irretrievably licentious, and therefore there needed not the bitter personal feud, which circumstances had generated between them, to account for the *acharnement* with which Cicero pursued him. Had Antony been his friend even, or his near kinsman, Cicero must still have been his public enemy. And not merely for his vices; for even the grander features of his character, his towering ambition, his magnanimity, and the fascinations of his popular qualities, — were all, in the circumstances of those times, and in *his* disposition, of a tendency dangerously uncivic.

"So remarkable was the opposition, at all points, between the second Cæsar and his rival, that whereas, Antony even in his virtues seemed dangerous to the state, Octavius gave a civic coloring to his most indifferent actions, and, with a Machiavelian policy, observed a scrupulous regard to the forms of the Republic, after every fragment of the republican institutions, the privileges of the republican magistrates, and the functions of the great popular officers, had been absorbed into his own autocracy. Even in the most prosperous days of the Roman state, when the democratic forces balanced, and were balanced by, those of the aristocracy, it was far from being a general or common praise, that a man was of a civic turn of mind, *animo civili*. Yet this praise did Augustus affect, and in reality attain, at a time when the very object of all civic feeling was absolutely extinct; so much are men governed by words."

The occasion of Antony's meeting with Cleopatra — an important artistic feature of the Play, as it strikes the keynote to the sensuous fascination of which Antony is to be the victim — Shakespeare found fully described in Plutarch; but while following Plutarch very closely, he gives additional touches to his prose original which heighten its coloring, and impart an imaginative glow to the whole picture.

The description, in the Play, is given by Enobarbus to Agrippa, in the 2d Scene of the 2d Act, beginning at the 196th line.

North's " Plutarch " reads : " . . . she disdained to set forward otherwise, but to take her barge in the river of Cydnus ; the poop whereof was of gold, the sails of purple, and the oars of silver, which kept stroke in the rowing after the sound of the music of flutes, howboys, cithernes, viols, and such other instruments as they played upon in the barge."

Shakespeare :

> " The barge she sat in, like a burnish'd throne,
> Burn'd on the water ; the poop was beaten gold ;
> Purple the sails, and so perfumed that
> The winds were love-sick with them ; the oars were silver,
> Which to the tune of flutes kept stroke and made
> The water which they beat to follow faster,
> As amorous of their strokes."

North :

" And now for the person of her self, she was laid under a pavilion of cloth of gold of tissue, apparelled and attired like the goddess Venus, commonly drawn in picture : and hard by her, on either hand of her, pretty fair boys apparelled as painters do set forth god Cupid, with little fans in their hands, with the which they fanned wind upon her."

Shakespeare :

> " For her own person,
> It beggar'd all description : she did lie
> In her pavilion — cloth-of-gold of tissue —
> O'erpicturing that Venus where we see
> The fancy outwork nature : on each side her
> Stood pretty dimpled boys, like smiling Cupids,
> With diverse colour'd fans, whose wind did seem
> To glow the delicate cheeks which they did cool,
> And what they undid did.
>   *Agr.* O, rare for Antony ! "

North :

" Her ladies and gentlewomen also, the fairest of them, were apparelled like the nymphs Nereids (which are the mermaids of the waters) and like the Graces ; some steering the helm, others tending the tackle and ropes of the barge, out of the which there came a wonderful passing * sweet savour of perfumes, that perfum'd the wharf's side, pestered † with innumerable multitudes of people."

Shakespeare :

> " Her gentlewomen, like the Nereides,
> So many mermaids, tended her i' the eyes,
> And made their bends adornings : at the helm
> A seeming mermaid steers ; the silken tackle
> Swell with the touches of those flower-soft hands,
> That yarely frame the office. From the barge
> A strange invisible perfume hits the sense
> Of the adjacent wharfs."

North :

" Some of them followed the barge all along the river-side : others also ran out of the city to see her coming in. So that in the end, there ran such multitudes of people one after another to see her, that Antonius was left post ‡ alone in the market-place, in his imperial seat, to give audience."

Shakespeare :

> " The city cast
> Her people out upon her ; and Antony,
> Enthroned in the market-place, did sit alone,
> Whistling to the air ; which, but for vacancy,
> Had gone to gaze on Cleopatra too,
> And made a gap in nature.
> *Agr.* Rare Egyptian ! "

North :

" And there went a rumour in the people's mouths, that the goddess Venus was come to play with the god Bacchus, for the general good of all Asia. When Cleopatra landed, Antonius sent to invite her to supper to him. But she sent him word again, he

---

    * surpassingly.   † crowded.   ‡ posted.

should do better rather to come and sup with her. Antonius, therefore, to shew himself courteous unto her at her arrival, was contented to obey her, and went to supper to her: where he found such passing sumptuous fare, that no tongue can express it."
Shakespeare:

> " Upon her landing, Antony sent to her,
> Invited her to supper: she replied,
> It should be better he became her guest;
> Which she entreated: our courteous Antony,
> Whom ne'er the word of ' No ' woman heard speak,
> Being barber'd ten times o'er, goes to the feast,
> And, for his ordinary, pays his heart
> For what his eyes eat only."

There should be noted, in the first place, the slight circumstantial omissions Shakespeare makes, which were not essential to his purpose. But what is chiefly remarkable, are the additions he makes to his prose original: his imagination projects itself into inanimate things and impassions them. For example, the winds are represented as love-sick with the perfumes from the sails; the water beat by the silver oars, follows faster, as if *amorous* of their strokes; the silken tackle *swell with the touches of the flower-soft hands that tend them;* the very air of the city, whose inhabitants had all gone out to gaze on Cleopatra, is represented as eager to go and gaze upon her too, but that it feared to make a gap in nature !

In such a highly-colored and richly-sensuous passage, the great artist creates the atmosphere in which the passion-fated pair are exhibited.

Now what moral problem was involved in the dramatic treatment of such a theme? It could be said, *a priori*, that the problem consisted in shutting off sympathy with moral obliquity, and inviting sympathy with moral freedom so far as the latter is asserted, on the part of the principal actors. And just this, it will be seen, Shakespeare has done. We are nowhere brought into a sympathetic relationship with the moral obliquity of either Antony

or Cleopatra. We are protected by the moral spirit with which
the dramatist works, from any perversion of the moral judgment.
And this protection is positive rather than negative; for the moral
judgment is stimulated to its best activity, throughout the play.

An interesting feature of the play, bearing on its moral spirit, is
that part of its narrated element which pertains to the hero and
heroine — what is *told* of Antony and of Cleopatra, instead of being brought dramatically forward. Professor Delius, in his valuable papers " On Shakespeare's Use of Narration in his Dramas,"
attributes too much, perhaps, of the narrated element, to the defi-
ciencies of the stage in Shakespeare's time, and not enough to
the perspective the artist aimed after, by his use of narration, and
to the moral proportion of a play. What is thrown into the background by narration often serves moral proportion by its being
thus kept apart from our sympathies. This is especially the case
with the tragedy of Antony and Cleopatra.

In the opening scene, when Cleopatra urges Antony to hear the
messengers who have brought news from Rome, he replies:

> " Let Rome in Tiber melt, and the wide arch
> Of the ranged empire fall! Here is my space.
> Kingdoms are clay: our dungy earth alike
> Feeds beast as man: the nobleness of life
> Is to do thus; when such a mutual pair   [*Embracing.*
> And such a twain can do't, in which I bind,
> On pain of punishment, the world to weet
> We stand up peerless." — A. I. Sc. i. 33-39.

When Cleopatra again urges him to hear the messengers, he
replies:

> " Fie, wrangling queen!
> Whom everything becomes, to chide, to laugh,
> To weep; whose every passion fully strives
> To make itself, in thee, fair and admired!
> No messenger, but thine." — A. I. Sc. i. 48-52.

In the 2d Scene, after having learned from the messenger, of
the death of Fulvia, Antony says in his temporary contrition, " I

must from this enchanting queen break off" (A. I. Sc. ii. 132).
Further on he says, "Would I had never seen her!" to which
Enobarbus replies, "O, sir, you had then left unseen a wonderful piece of work; which not to have been blest withal would have
discredited your travel" (A. I. Sc. ii. 155–158). In Act II. Sc. ii.
234–245, he says:

> "I saw her once
> Hop forty paces through the public street;
> And having lost her breath, she spoke, and panted,
> That she did make defect perfection,
> And, breathless, power breathe forth. . . . .
> Age cannot wither her, nor custom stale
> Her infinite variety: other women cloy
> The appetites they feed: but she makes hungry
> Where most she satisfies: for vilest things
> Become themselves in her; that the holy priests
> Bless her when she is riggish."

Scarus, speaking of the disastrous sea-fight, says (A. III. Sc. x.
18–21):

> "She once being loof'd,
> The noble ruin of her magic, Antony,
> Claps on his sea-wing, and, like a doting mallard,
> Leaving the fight in height, flies after her."

After his shameful flight from the engagement at sea, Antony
says to Cleopatra (A. III. Sc. xi. 51–71):

> "*Ant.* O, whither hast thou led me, Egypt? See,
> How I convey my shame out of thine eyes
> By looking back what I have left behind
> 'Stroy'd in dishonour.
> *Cleo.* O my lord, my lord,
> Forgive my fearful sails! I little thought
> You would have followed.
> *Ant.* Egypt, thou knew'st too well
> My heart was to thy rudder tied by the strings,
> And thou shouldst tow me after: o'er my spirit

Thy full supremacy thou knew'st, and that
Thy beck might from the bidding of the gods
Command me.
    Cleo.   O, my pardon!
    Ant.   Now I must
To the young man send humble treaties, dodge
And palter in the shifts of lowness; who
With half the bulk o' the world play'd as I pleased,
Making and marring fortunes. You did know
How much you were my conqueror; and that
My sword, made weak by my affection, would
Obey it on all cause.
    Cleo.   Pardon, pardon!
    Ant. Fall not a tear, I say; one of them rates
All that is won and lost: give me a kiss;
Even this repays me."

In the 4th Act, 14th Scene, when all is lost, and he believes
that Cleopatra has "pack'd cards with Cæsar, and false-play'd
his glory unto an enemy's triumph," the eunuch Mardian enters
and informs him (though falsely) that Cleopatra is dead. He at
once resolves to follow her to the shades:

    " I will o'ertake thee, Cleopatra, and
    Weep for my pardon. So it must be, for now
    All length is torture: since the torch is out,
    Lie down, and stray no farther: now all labour
    Mars what it does; yea, very force entangles
    Itself with strength: seal then, and all is done.
    Eros!—I come, my queen:—Eros!—Stay for me:
    Where souls do couch on flowers, we'll hand in hand,
    And with our sprightly port make the ghosts gaze:
    Dido and her Æneas shall want troops,
    And all the haunt be ours."—A. IV. Sc. xiv. 44–54.

The fascination which Cleopatra exercised upon Antony, could
hardly be more strongly expressed than it is here — a fascination
which, he imagines, will, even in the world of spirits, draw all
ghosts after them.

After he has stabbed himself, and has been borne to the monument wherein Cleopatra has shut herself with her attendants, he says to her :

> " I am dying, Egypt, dying; only
> I here importune death awhile, until
> Of many thousand kisses the poor last
> I lay upon thy lips." — A. IV. Sc. xv. 18–21.

And then the attachment and devotion unto death of her attendants, Charmian and Iras, reflect the mysterious charm which she wrought upon all that approached her. When she is attired for death in her royal robes, and crowned, she kisses her two women, and Iras thereupon falls and dies, she having, as must be supposed, secretly applied an asp to her arm. After Cleopatra dies from the bite of the asp, Charmian says :

> " So, fare thee well.
> Now boast thee, death, in thy possession lies
> A lass unparallel'd. Downy windows, close;
> And golden Phœbus never be beheld
> Of eyes again so royal! Your crown's awry;
> I'll mend it, and then play." — A. V. Sc. ii. 227–232.

There's a deep pathos in Cleopatra's crown being awry, as she lies dead, in her royal robes, upon the couch ; and in Charmian's last sentence, " I'll mend it," (that is, adjust it), " and then play." And when the guard rushes in, she applies to her arm an asp ; and, to the question of one of the guard, who sees that Cleopatra is dead, " Charmian, is this well done ? " she replies, " It is well done, and fitting for a princess descended of so many royal kings. Ah, soldier ! " and dies.

And when Octavius comes in, the first guard says to him :

> " O Cæsar,
> This Charmian lived but now; she stood and spake:
> I found her trimming up the diadem
> On her dead mistress : tremblingly she stood
> And on the sudden dropp'd." — A. V. Sc. ii. 343–347.

The astute Cæsar says, as he gazes upon the dead queen:

> " She looks like sleep,
> As she would catch another Antony
> In her strong toil of grace." — A. V. Sc. ii. 349–351.

These passages sufficiently indicate the fascination which the Egyptian queen exerted upon those about her. And before Antony came under her spell, the " broad-fronted Cæsar " and " great Pompey " were wrapped in the coils of this " serpent of old Nile." Cleopatra says (A. I. Sc. v. 29–34), — and she doesn't increase our admiration of her by saying it of herself:

> " Broad-fronted Cæsar,
> When thou wast here above the ground, I was
> A morsel for a monarch : and great Pompey
> Would stand and make his eyes grow in my brow;
> There would he anchor his aspect and die
> With looking on his life."

Now the point to be especially noted is, that Cleopatra's fascination is, in the passages quoted, *described* and *spoken of*, rather than brought dramatically to our feelings through what she herself says and does. These descriptions of her charms do not bring us into any sympathetic relationship with her personality. We simply *know of* her charms. The dramatist does but little more than the historian. Plutarch *tells* us of her fascination, and so does Dion Cassius. Both these writers emphasize it even more than Shakespeare does. But they narrate it as historians. They address the fact to our minds. But the drama, if it be within its purpose, should bring it, as far as possible, to our æsthetic appreciation, rather than simply acquaint us with the fact. But it does not do so. In some, indeed in all the scenes in which Cleopatra appears, she is not a very fascinating creature. Her treatment of the messenger who brings her the news of Antony's marriage to Octavia does not present her in a very attractive light; rather, in a very repulsive one (A. II. Sc. v.). In her rage she is simply irrational. She beats the innocent messenger, hales him up and down, and even prepares to kill him. She is almost divorced from the moral constitution of things. Her will is the wind's will. Her fascination, as represented by Shakespeare, is almost wholly a sexual one, exerted upon those who are in her bodily presence. But Plutarch attributes to her a moral fascination (I use the word "moral" as opposed to "physical") which is not, dramatically, at least, presented in the play: "Now her beauty (as it is reported) was not so passing as [to be] unmatchable of other women, nor yet such as upon present view did enamour men with her: but *so sweet was her company and conversation, that a man could not possibly but be taken. And besides her beauty, the good grace she had to talk and discourse, her courteous nature that tempered her words and deeds, was a spur that pricked to the quick. Furthermore, besides all these, her voice and words were marvellous pleasant: for her tongue was an instrument of music to divers sports and pastimes, the which she easily turned into any language that pleased her."*

Skottowe, in his "Life of Shakespeare; Enquiries into the Originality of his Dramatic Plots and Characters"; etc., remarks (Vol. II. p. 240): "Shakespeare has not been successful in conveying an idea of the elegance of Cleopatra's mind. Neither her manners, thoughts, nor language impress us with a conviction of her possessing those accomplishments which he ascribes to her. Mark the model which Shakespeare had before him." Skottowe then gives the passage quoted above from Plutarch. To say that "Shakespeare has not been successful in conveying," etc., is not the way to put it. He could have been "successful," if he had seen fit to be. It should rather be said that his art purpose did not demand that; it rather demanded that the "elegance of Cleopatra's mind" (supposing that an elegance of mind could be attributed to her) should not be brought to our æsthetic appreciation as, to use Plutarch's expressions, "a spur that pricked to the quick." The moral spirit with which the artist worked did not allow of it. This is one of the most important things to be noted in the play. Mrs. Jameson says (and Verplanck endorses her words by saying that "there are few readers who do not feel with her"), that "Shakespeare's Cleopatra produces exactly the same effect on us that is recorded of the real Cleopatra. She dazzles our faculties, perplexes our judgments, bewilders and bewitches our fancy; from the beginning to the end of the drama, we are conscious of a kind of fascination against which our moral sense rebels, but from which there is no escape." The poet Campbell more truly says, and with more justice to Shakespeare's dramatic art, that, "playfully interesting to our fancy as he makes this enchantress, he keeps us far from a vicious sympathy. The asp at her bosom, that lulls its nurse asleep, has no poison for our morality. A single glance at the devoted and dignified Octavia recalls our homage to virtue; but with delicate skill he withholds the purer woman from prominent contact with the wanton queen, and does not, like Dryden, bring the two to a scolding match."

Judging from the low estimate of woman, exhibited in the works of Dryden, he could not have had any appreciation of Shakespeare's Octavia. In the Preface to his "All for Love; or, The World well lost," he says: "They [the French poets] would not have suffered Cleopatra and Octavia to have met; or, if they had met, there must have only passed betwixt them some cold civilities, but *no eagerness of repartee*, for fear of offending against the greatness of their characters and the modesty of their sex. This objection I foresaw, and at the same time *contemned; for I judged it both natural and probable, that Octavia, proud of her new-gained conquest, would search out Cleopatra to triumph over her;* [!] and that Cleopatra, thus attacked, was not of a spirit to shun the encounter: and it is not unlikely that two exasperated rivals should use such satire as I have put into their mouths; for, after all, though the one was a Roman, and the other a queen, *they were both women!*"

Comment on such bosh is quite unnecessary.

When we read The Winter's Tale, we understand perfectly why Hermione has such a hold upon all about her. She sheds a fragrance through the whole Play. And the same may be said of Imogen in Cymbeline, of Isabella in Measure for Measure, and of others of Shakespeare's women. We understand the power which these women are represented as exerting, because the poet has brought it, through his dramatic art, to our æsthetic appreciation. But he has rather aimed to shut off Cleopatra's power from any such appreciation. The moral spirit with which he always worked, determined him in this. Perhaps no one of his Plays exhibits this moral spirit more distinctly than Antony and Cleopatra. There is one Shakespearian critic, however, who appears to have come under the fascination of the Cleopatra of the Play more completely than did Marc Antony under that of the living Cleopatra, namely, Algernon Charles Swinburne. In his "A Study of Shakespeare," pp. 188–191, he says :

"It would seem a sign or birthmark of only the greatest among poets that they should be sure to rise instantly for awhile above the very highest of their native height at the touch of a thought of Cleopatra. So was it, as we all know, with William Shakespeare : so is it, as we all see, with Victor Hugo. As we feel in the marvellous and matchless verses of Zim-Zizimi all the splendour and fragrance and miracle of her mere bodily presence, so from her first imperial dawn on the Stage of Shakespeare to the setting of that eastern star behind a pall of undissolving cloud we feel the charm and the terror and the mystery of her absolute and royal soul. . . .

"Never has he given such proof of his incomparable instinct for abstinence from the wrong thing as well as achievement of the right.* He has utterly rejected and disdained all occasion of setting her off by means of any lesser foil than all the glory of the world with all its empires. And we need not Antony's example to show us that these are less than straws in the balance.

> " ' Entre elle et l'univers qui s'offraient à la fois
> Il hésita, lâchant le monde dans son choix.'

---

* This is quite true, but not in the sense in which Mr. Swinburne would have it taken.

"Even as that Roman grasp relaxed and let fall the world, so has Shakespeare's self let go for awhile his greater world of imagination, with all its all but infinite variety of life and thought and action, for love of that more infinite variety which custom could not stale. Himself a second and a yet more fortunate Antony, he has once more laid a world, and a world more wonderful than ever, at her feet. He has put aside for her sake all other forms and figures of womanhood ; he, father or creator of Rosalind, of Cordelia, of Desdemona, and of Imogen, he too, like the sun-god and sender of all song, has anchored his eyes on her whom ' Phœbus' amorous pinches ' could not leave ' black ' nor 'wrinkled deep in time '; on that incarnate and imperishable 'spirit of sense,' to whom at the very last

> " ' The stroke of death is as a lover's pinch,
>   That hurts, and is desired.'

To him, as to the dying husband of Octavia, this creature of his own hand might have boasted herself that the loveliest and purest among all her sisters of his begetting,

> ' With her modest eyes
> And still conclusion, shall acquire no honour,
> Demurring upon me.'

To sum up, Shakespeare has elsewhere given us in ideal incarnation the perfect mother, the perfect wife, the perfect daughter, the perfect mistress, or the perfect maiden : here only once for all he has given us the perfect and the everlasting woman."

In what sense Mr. Swinburne uses the word " perfect," it would be hard to decide. Verily, nothing more crazy has ever been said in Shakespearian criticism.

If such rapture had a real basis — if Cleopatra, as *dramatically* presented, were to impress readers generally as she appears to have impressed the poet-critic, the moral spirit of the Play would be far below the Shakespearian standard. Shakespeare's art, exercised, as it evidently was, to shut Cleopatra off from our sympathies, has not been successful in Mr. Swinburne's ease. But the great artist could not have anticipated, with all his knowledge of human possibilities, any such susceptibility to female charms as he exhibits.

Antony must, by his very constitution, be subordinate to Octavius — though the range of his nature is far greater than that of Octavius, which is comparatively limited ; but its limitations are compensated for (so far, at least, as his civic abilities are concerned) by definiteness and positiveness. And he always knows " when to take occasion by the hand." The potentially great elements of Antony's nature are not organized into any practical effectiveness, and the strong sensual set of his nature induces a more and more chaotic condition of his powers. And, thus, it may be said, that his genius is rebuked by that of Octavius. There's a special dramatic exhibition of this in the 2d Scene of the 2d Act of the Play, and it is set forth by the Soothsayer in the 3d Scene of the 2d Act.

Octavius says to Antony (A. II. Sc. ii. 71) :

> " I wrote to you
> When rioting in Alexandria: you
> Did pocket up my letter, and with taunts
> Did give my missive * out of audience.
>   *Ant.*   Sir,
> He fell upon me ere admitted : then
> Three kings I had newly feasted, and did want
> Of what I was i' the morning: "

Here Antony admits his weakness.

>   " But next day
> I told him of myself; "

i.e., that he was under the influence of wine the day before.

>   " Which was as much
> As to have ask'd him pardon. . . .
>   *Cæs.*   You have broken
> The article of your oath, which you shall never
> Have tongue to charge *me* with."

* messenger.

Here Octavius speaks with warmth, and the would-be peace-maker, Lepidus, interposes:

> " Soft, Cæsar.
> *Ant.*   No,
> Lepidus, let him speak:
> The honour is sacred which he talks on now,
> Supposing that I lack'd it.   But on, Cæsar;
> The article of my oath.
>   *Cæs.*   To lend me arms and aid when I required them;
> The which you both denied.
>   *·Ant.*   Neglected, rather;
> And then when poison'd hours had bound me up
> From mine own knowledge."

Another admission of his bad habits, which weakens his position.

>   " As nearly as I may,
> I'll play the penitent to you: but mine honesty
> Shall not make poor my greatness, nor my power
> Work without it.*   Truth is that Fulvia,
> To have me out of Egypt, made wars here;
> For which myself, the ignorant motive, do
> So far ask pardon as befits mine honour
> To stoop in such a case."

Here Antony's real sense of his inferiority to his young colleague is brought distinctly out, by an affectation of a sense of honor.

> " *Lep.*   'Tis noble spoken.
>   *Mec.*   If it might please you to enforce no further
> The griefs between ye: † to forget them quite
> Were to remember that the present need
> Speaks to atone ‡ you.   .
>   *Lep.*   Worthily spoken, Mecænas."

These little interposed speeches of Lepidus very happily reveal the weak triumvir, who feels that it's best for himself that things be kept quiet.

---

* *i.e.*, without mine honesty.
† emphasize no further the grievances between you.
‡ bring you at one, reconcile you.

"*Eno.* Or, if you borrow one another's love for the instant, you may, when you hear no more words of Pompey, return it again: you shall have time to wrangle in when you have nothing else to do.

Ant. Thou art a soldier only; speak no more.

Eno. That truth should be silent I had almost forgot.

Ant. You wrong this presence; therefore speak no more.

Eno. Go to, then; your considerate stone."

A very pregnant expression: I shall be as silent as a stone, and have the honour to assure you of my high consideration.

"*Cæs.* I do not much dislike the matter, but
The manner of his speech; for't cannot be
We shall remain in friendship, our conditions *
So differing in their acts.   Yet, if I knew
What hoop should hold us stanch, from edge to edge
O' the world † I would pursue it."

It must evidently be understood by the last speech, that a "hoop," and a very politic one, has been already decided upon by Octavius and his crafty counsellor, Agrippa.   What follows shows this; and affords a special illustration, too, of Antony's genius rebuked by Octavius's:

"*Agr.* Give me leave, Cæsar.

Cæs. Speak, Agrippa.

Agr. Thou hast a sister by the mother's side,
Admired Octavia: great Mark Antony
Is now a widower.

Cæs. Say not so, Agrippa:
If Cleopatra heard you, your reproof
Were well deserved of rashness."

This speech seems meant to convey the impression that the proposal of marriage between Antony and Octavia, intimated in the last speech of Agrippa, was something new to Octavius.   But he evidently knows just what's coming from Agrippa.

---

* temperaments, dispositions.

† from one end of the world to the other.

"*Ant.* I am not married, Cæsar: let me hear Agrippa further
speak.

Agr. To hold you in perpetual amity,
To make you brothers, and to knit your hearts
With an unslipping knot, take Antony
Octavia to his wife; whose beauty claims
No worse a husband than the best of men;
Whose virtue and whose general graces speak
That which none else can utter. By this marriage,
All little jealousies, which now seem great,
And all great fears, which now import * their dangers,
Would then be nothing: truths would be tales,
Where now half tales be truths: her love to both
Would each to other and all loves to both,
Draw after her. Pardon what I have spoke;
For 'tis a studied, not a present thought,
By duty ruminated.

    Ant.   Will Cæsar speak?

    Cæs. Not till he hear how Antony is touch'd
With what is spoke already.

    Ant.   What power is in Agrippa,
If I would say, 'Agrippa, be it so,'
To make this good?

    Cæs.   The power of Cæsar, and
His power unto Octavia.

    Ant.   May I never
To this good purpose, that so fairly shows,
Dream of impediment! — Let me have thy hand;
Further this act of grace, and from this hour
The heart of brothers govern in our loves
And sway our great designs!

    Cæs.   There is my hand.
A sister I bequeath you, whom no brother
Did ever love so dearly; let her live
To join our kingdoms and our hearts, and never
Fly off our loves again!

    Lep. Happily, amen!

---

* carry with them.

Ant. I did not think to draw my sword 'gainst Pompey;
For he hath laid strange courtesies and great
Of late upon me: I must thank him only,
Lest my remembrance suffer ill report;
At heel of that, defy him.

Lep. Time calls upon's:
Of us must Pompey presently be sought
Or else he seeks out us.

Ant. Where lies he?

Cæs. About the mount Misenum.

Ant. What is his strength by land?

Cæs. Great and increasing: but by sea
He is an absolute master.

Ant. So is the fame.
Would we had spoke together! Haste we for it:
Yet, ere we put ourselves in arms, dispatch we
The business we have talk'd of.

Cæs. With most gladness:
And do invite you to my sister's view,
Whither straight I'll lead you.

Ant. Let us, Lepidus,
Not lack your company.

Lep. Noble Antony,
Not sickness should detain me.

What a mere cipher poor Lepidus is! To adopt a couplet from
Churchill's " Gotham," he " attends at councils which he must not
weigh, does what they bid, and what they dictate, say."

In the next scene, the subordination of the Genius of Antony
to that of Octavius, is set forth by the Soothsayer. This Shakespeare took from Plutarch and made the best use of. Plutarch
says: " With Antonius there was a soothsayer or astronomer of
Egypt, that could cast a figure, and judge of men's nativities, to
tell them what should happen to them. He, either to please Cleopatra, or else for that he found it so by his art, told Antonius
plainly that his fortune (which of itself was excellent good, and
very great) was altogether blemished and obscured by Cæsar's fortune; and therefore he counselled him utterly to leave his com-

pany, and to get him as far from him as he could. 'For thy
demon,' said he (that is to say, the good angel and spirit that
keepeth thee), 'is afraid of his: and being courageous and high
when he is alone, becometh fearful and timorous when he cometh
near unto the other.' Howsoever it was, the events ensuing proved
the Egyptian's words true: for it is said, that as often as they two
drew cuts for pastime, who should have anything, or whether they
played at dice, Antonius always lost. Oftentimes when they were
disposed to see cock-fight, or quails that were taught to fight one
with another, Cæsar's cocks or quails did ever overcome."

In the Play we have, A. II. Sc. iii., beginning at 10th line:

> *Ant.* Now! sirrah; you do wish yourself in Egypt?
> *Sooth.* Would I had never come from thence, nor you
> Thither!
> *Ant.*   If you can, your reason?
> *Sooth.*   I see it in
> My motion,* have it not in my tongue: but yet
> Hie you to Egypt again.
> *Ant.*   Say to me,
> Whose fortunes shall rise higher, Cæsar's or mine?
> *Sooth.* Cæsar's.
> Therefore, O Antony, stay not by his side:
> Thy demon, that thy spirit which keeps thee, is
> Noble, courageous, high, unmatchable,
> Where Cæsar's is not; but, near him, thy angel
> Becomes a fear, as being o'erpower'd: † therefore
> Make space enough between you.
> *Ant.*   Speak this no more.
> *Sooth.* To none but thee; no more, but when to thee.
> If thou dost play with him at any game,

---

* in the movement of my soul, intuitively.

† Macbeth says of Banquo:

> " There's none but he
> Whose being I do fear; and under him
> My Genius is rebuk'd, as it is said
> Mark Antony's was by Cæsar."

Thou art sure to lose ; and, of that natural luck,
He beats thee 'gainst the odds : thy lustre thickens∗
When he shines by : I say again, thy spirit
Is all afraid to govern thee near him ;
But, he away, 'tis noble.
    Ant.   Get thee gone ;
Say to Ventidius I would speak with him : [*Exit Soothsayer.*
He shall to Parthia.   Be it art or hap,
He hath spoken true : the very dice obey him ;
And in our sports my better cunning † faints
Under his chance : if we draw lots, he speeds ; ‡
His cocks do win the battle still of mine,
When it is all to nought ; § and his quails ever
Beat mine, inhoop'd, ‖ at odds.   I will to Egypt :
And though I make this marriage for my peace,
I' the east my pleasure lies."

Antony and Octavius have done what the keen-sighted Enobarbus foresaw they would do, and therefore proposed the same
(A. II. Sc. ii.), namely, " borrowed one another's love for the
instant," in order the better to dispose of the troublesome Sextus
Pompeius.   The reconciliation of the two triumvirs (the flimsiness
and purely politic character of which Pompey doesn't appear to
suspect), and the military operations which are on foot, against
him, dispose him to accept the offer made him by the triumvirate,
and the conditions involved therein.   His attitude as the son of
Cneius Pompeius Magnus, and as the feeble representative, or
relic, of the old republican constitution, and his evanescent relation to the historical movement of the play, are exhibited in the
6th Scene of the 2d Act.   Though regarding himself as the representative of the old republican constitution, he inconsistently agrees
with the triumvirate to accept a slice of the Roman world :

∗ thy brightness grows dim; "light thickens, and the crow makes wing to
the rooky wood." — Macbeth, A. III. Sc. ii. 50.
  † skill.   ‡ has success.
  § " When the odds are as everything to nothing."
  ‖ " Confined within a circle to keep them ' up to the scratch.' "

"*Pom.* Your hostages I have, so have you mine;
And we shall talk before we fight.

Cæs.   Most meet
That first we come to words; and therefore have we
Our written purposes before us sent;
Which, if thou hast considered, let us know
If 'twill tie up thy discontented sword,
And carry back to Sicily much tall youth
That else must perish here.

Pom.   To you all three,
The senators alone of this great world,
Chief factors * for the gods, I do not know
Wherefore my father should revengers want,
Having a son and friends; since Julius Cæsar,
Who at Philippi the good Brutus ghosted,†
There saw you labouring for him.   What was't
That moved pale ‡ Cassius to conspire; and what
Made the all-honour'd, honest Roman, Brutus,
With the arm'd rest, courtiers of beauteous freedom,
To drench the Capitol; but that they would
Have one man but a man? §   And that is it
Hath made me rig my navy; at whose burthen
The anger'd ocean foams; with which I meant
To scourge the ingratitude that despiteful Rome
Cast on my noble father.

---

* agents.   † appeared to, as a ghost.

‡ "*Cæs.*   Let me have men about me that are fat:
Sleek-headed men and such as sleep o' nights:
Yond Cassius has a lean and hungry look;
He thinks too much: such men are dangerous."
                        — Julius Cæsar, A. I. Sc. ii. 191–194.

§ " *Cæs.* When went there by an age, since the great flood,
But it was famed with more than with one man?
When could they say till now, that talk'd of Rome,
That her wide walls encompass'd but one man?
Now is it Rome indeed and room enough,
When there is in it but one only man."
                        — Julius Cæsar, A. I. Sc. ii. 143–148.

Cæs.   Take your time.

Ant. Thou canst not fear * us, Pompey, with thy sails ; †
We'll speak with thee at sea : at land, thou know'st
How much we do o'er-count thee.

Pom.   At land, indeed,
Thou dost o'er-count me of my father's house.‡
But, since the cuckoo builds not for himself, §
Remain in't as thou mayst.

 Lep.   Be pleased to tell us —
For this is from the present ‖ — how you take
The offers we have sent you.

Cæs.   There's the point.

Ant. Which do not be entreated to, but weigh
What it is worth embraced.

Cæs.   And what may follow,
To try ¶ a larger fortune.

Pom.   You have made me offer
Of Sicily, Sardinia ; and I must
Rid all the sea of pirates ; then, to send
Measures of wheat to Rome ; this greed upon,
To part with unhack'd edges, and bear back
Our targes undinted.

 Cæs. Ant. Lep. That's our offer.

---

* affright.   † ships, navy.

‡ "At land indeed thou dost exceed me in possessions, having added to
thy own my father's house. *O'er-count* seems to be used equivocally, and
Pompey perhaps meant to insinuate that Antony not only *outnumbered*, but
had *over-reached* him." Plutarch says: "When Pompey's house was put to
open sale, Antonius bought it ; but when they asked him money for it, he
made it very strange and was offended with them." Again : "Whereupon
Antonius asked him [Sextus Pompeius], ' And where shall we sup ? ' ' There,'
said Pompey ; and showed him his admiral galley, which had six benches of
oars : ' That,' said he, ' is *my father's house* they have left me.' He spake it
to taunt Antonius, because *he had his father's house*, that was Pompey the
Great." — Malone.

§ "Since, like the cuckoo, that seizes the nests of other birds, you have
invaded a house which you could not build, keep it while you can." — Johnson.

‖ apart from the present business.

¶ And what bad consequences may follow in trying for a larger fortune.

Pom.   Know, then,
I came before you here a man prepared
To make this offer: but Mark Antony
Put me to some impatience: though I lose
The praise of it by telling, you must know,
When Cæsar and your brother were at blows,
Your mother came to Sicily and did find
Her welcome friendly.
    Ant.   I have heard it, Pompey;
And am well studied for a liberal thanks *
Which I do owe you.
    Pom.   Let me have your hand:
I did not think, sir, to have met you here.
    Ant. The beds i' the east are soft; and thanks to you,
That call'd me timelier than my purpose hither;
For I have gain'd by't.
    Cæs.   Since I saw you last,
There is a change upon you.
    Pom.   Well, I know not
What counts harsh fortune casts upon my face; †
But in my bosom shall she never come,
To make my heart her vassal.
    Lep.   Well met here.
    Pom. I hope so, Lepidus. Thus we are agreed:
I crave our composition ‡ may be written,
And seal'd between us.
    Cæs.   That's the next to do.
    Pom. We'll feast each other ere we part; and let's
Draw lots who shall begin.
    Ant.   That will I, Pompey.
    Pom. No, Antony, take the lot: § but, first
Or last, your fine Egyptian cookery
Shall have the fame. I have heard that Julius Cæsar
Grew fat with feasting there.

---

* "a" used with reference to "thanks" as an abbreviated expression.

† "Metaphor from making marks or lines in casting accounts." — Warburton.   ‡ agreement

§ By metonymy for result of lot.

> *Ant.*　　　　　　　　You have heard much.*
> *Pom.* I have fair meanings, sir, . . .
> Aboard my galley I invite you all:
> Will you lead, lords?
> 　*Cæs. Ant. Lep.*　　Show us the way, sir.　　　.
> 　*Pom.*　　　　　　　　　　　Come."

Throughout this scene, Shakespeare follows his original in its minutest details. But of Pompey's entertainment on board his admiral galley, which is made by Shakespeare so dramatically important a scene in the Play, Plutarch simply says, " and there " (meaning on his galley) " he welcomed them and made them great cheer." But Shakespeare, knowing that wine reveals as well as disguises, that " *in vino est veritas*," made this banquet the means of characterizing and contrasting the triumvirs, and the poor relic of republican Rome, Sextus Pompeius. This scene exhibits that Shakespearian irony which plays so freely with all things, regardless of all conventional ideas of high and low, great and small.

What an affliction this scene, if he ever read it, must have been to Thomas Rymer, the author of " A Short View of Tragedy; it's Original Excellency and Corruption. With some Reflections on Shakespear, and other Practitioners for the Stage. 1693 "! He must have gone into a rage about the indignity with which Shakespeare treats the masters of the world, as if they were not different from common mortals. (See his criticisms of Othello and Julius Cæsar in his " Short View.") One great and common merit of all Shakespeare's characters, both men and women, is, that his men are men, and his women are women, before they are anything else — before they are kings or queens, princes or princesses, lords or ladies. They are not mounted on the stilts of rank, but tread the common mother earth. " One of the most formidable adversaries of true poetry," says Godwin,† " is an attribute which is generally

---

* There is implied in " much," that Antony thinks he has heard also of his excesses. Pompey, recognizing what is implied, says, " I have fair meanings, sir." 　　　　　　† " Life of Geoffrey Chaucer," 1803, Vol. I. p. 324.

miscalled dignity. Shakespeare possessed, no man in higher perfection, the true dignity and loftiness of the poetical afflatus, which
he has displayed in many of the finest passages of his works with
miraculous success. But he knew that no man ever was, or ever
can be, always dignified. He knew that those subtler traits of
character which identify a man, are familiar and relaxed, pervaded
with passion, and not played off with an eternal eye to decorum."

" Scene VII. *On board Pompey's galley, off Misenum.*

Music plays. Enter two or three Servants *with a banquet.**

First Serv. Here they'll be, man. Some o' their plants are ill-rooted
already ; † the least wind i' the world will blow them down.
Sec. Serv. Lepidus is high-coloured.
First Serv. They have made him drink almsdrink.‡
Sec. Serv. As they pinch one another by the disposition,§ he cries
out " No more ; " reconciles them to his entreaty,‖ and himself to the
drink.
First Serv. But it raises the greater war between him and his discretion.
Sec. Serv. Why, this it is to have a name in great men's fellowship : I had as lief have a reed that will do me no service as a partisan
I could not heave.
First Serv. To be called into a huge sphere, and not to be seen to
move in't, are the holes where eyes should be, which pitifully disaster
the cheeks."

---

* dessert.

† A play on the words " plants " and " ill-rooted "; they are unsteady on
their feet, from drinking.

‡ According to Warburton, " a phrase, amongst good fellows, to signify that
liquor of another's share which his companion drinks to ease him "; but perhaps it rather means, as Schmidt explains, " the leavings." Warburton adds,
" It satirically alludes to Cæsar and Antony's admitting him into the triumvirate, in order to take off from themselves the load of envy." But that's
attributing too deep a meaning to the servant's speech.

§ " try each other by banter."

‖ he is still disposed to be the peace-maker, even when drunk.

The last two speeches characterize well the position of Lepidus in the triumvirate, but they seem too wise for the servants to utter.

"*A sennet sounded. Enter* CÆSAR, ANTONY, LEPIDUS, POMPEY, AGRIPPA, MECÆNAS, ENOBARBUS, MENAS, *with other captains.*

Ant. [*To Cæsar.*] Thus do they, sir : they take the flow o' the Nile
By certain scales i' the pyramid ; they know,
By the height, the lowness, or the mean, if dearth
Or foison follow ; the higher Nilus swells,
The more it promises : as it ebbs, the seedsman
Upon the slime and ooze scatters his grain,
And shortly comes to harvest."

There's an air of solidity in this speech, which indicates a consciousness on the part of the speaker, that he has imbibed quite freely, and therefore assumes a solid tone of speech. But he is in pretty good possession of himself, as he has been well seasoned in Egypt, and can bear a great deal. Lepidus breaks in upon their talk :

" *Lep.* You've strange serpents there.
Ant. Ay, Lepidus.
Lep. Your serpent of Egypt is bred now of your mud by the operation of your sun : so is your crocodile.
Ant. They are so.
Pom. Sit, — and some wine ! A health to Lepidus !
Lep. I am not so well as I should be, but I'll ne'er out.*
Eno. Not till you have slept ; I fear me you'll be in † till then."

No incidental remarks divert Lepidus from the interest which has been awakened in his mind, in regard to Egypt, its serpents and crocodiles and pyramids. He continues :

" *Lep.* Nay, certainly, I have heard the Ptolemies' pyramises are very goodly things ; without contradiction, I have heard that."

He is too far gone to get the *d* into " pyramides." Charles Cowden Clarke well remarks : " His feeble attempt at scientific

---

* back out.   † "in for it."

inquiry, in the remark concerning ' your serpent of Egypt,' his
flabbily persistent researches touching ' your crocodile,' and his
limp recurrence to his pet expression, ' strange serpent,' are all
conceived in the highest zest of comic humour."

" *Men.* [*Aside to Pom.*] Pompey, a word.
Pom.   [*Aside to Men.*] Say in mine ear what is't?
Men. [*Aside to Pom.*] Forsake thy seat, I do beseech thee, captain,
And hear me speak a word.
Pom. [*Aside to Men.*] Forbear me till anon. This wine for Lepi-
dus ! "

But he'll not be turned aside from his interest in the crocodile,
and inquires :

" *Lep.* What manner o' thing is your crocodile?
Ant. It is shaped, sir, like itself; and it is as broad as it hath
breadth : it is just so high as it is, and moves with it own organs : it
lives by that which nourisheth it ; and the elements once out of it, it
transmigrates.
Lep. What colour is it of ?
Ant. Of it own colour too.
Lep. 'Tis a strange serpent.
Ant. 'Tis so. And the tears of it are wet.
Cæs. Will this description satisfy him?
Ant. With the health that Pompey gives him, else he is a very
epicure."

What contempt is shown, in these speeches of Antony and Octavius, for poor Lepidus, now that he is, through drink, far below
his weak, sober self !

" *Pom.* [*Aside to Men.*] Go hang, sir, hang! Tell me of that?
    Away !
Do as I bid you. Where's this cup I call'd for?
Men. [*Aside to Pom.*] If for the sake of merit thou wilt hear me,
Rise from thy stool.
Pom. [*Aside to Men.*] I think thou'rt mad. The matter?
                                        [*Rises, and walks aside.*
Men. I have ever held my cap off to thy fortunes.

Pom. Thou hast served me with much faith. What's else to say?
Be jolly, lords."

The attentive host is shown here. Withdrawn from his guests
by Menas, he interrupts his speech by calling to them, " Be jolly,
lords."

" *Ant.* These quicksands, Lepidus,
Keep off them, for you sink.
 Men. Wilt thou be lord of all the world?
 Pom.   What say'st thou?
 Men. Wilt thou be lord of the whole world? That's twice.
 Pom. How should that be?
 Men.   But entertain it,
And, though thou think me poor, I am the man
Will give thee all the world.
 Pom.   Hast thou drunk well?
 Men. No, Pompey, I have kept me from the cup.
Thou art, if thou darest be, the earthly Jove :
Whate'er the ocean pales, or sky inclips,
Is thine, if thou wilt ha't.
 Pom.   Show me which way.
 Men. These three world-sharers, these competitors,
Are in thy vessel : let me cut the cable ;
And, when we are put off, fall to their throats :
All there is thine."

Pompey's reply shows that he " would not play false, and yet
would wrongly win."

" *Pom.*   Ah, this thou shouldst have done,
And not have spoke on't ! In me 'tis villainy ;
In thee't had been good service. Thou must know,
'Tis not my profit that does lead mine honour ;
Mine honour, it. Repent that e'er thy tongue
Hath so betray'd thine act : being done unknown,
I should have found it afterwards well done ;
But must condemn it now. Desist, and drink.
 Men. [*Aside.*] For this,
I'll never follow thy pall'd fortunes more.

Who seeks, and will not take when once 'tis offer'd,
Shall never find it more.
 Pom.   This health to Lepidus!
 Ant. Bear him ashore. I'll pledge it for him, Pompey.
 Eno. Here's to thee, Menas!
 Men.   Enobarbus, welcome!
 Pom. Fill till the cup be hid.
 Eno. There's a strong fellow, Menas.
     [*Pointing to the Attendant who carries off* LEPIDUS.
 Men. Why?
 Eno. A' bears the third part of the world, man; see'st not?
 Men. The third part, then, is drunk: would it were all,
That it might go on wheels!
 Eno. Drink thou; increase the reels.
 Men. Come.
 Pom. This is not yet an Alexandrian feast.
 Ant. It ripens towards it. Strike the vessels, ho!
Here is to Cæsar!
 Cæs.   I could well forbear't.
It's monstrous labour, when I wash my brain,
And it grows fouler.
 Ant.   Be a child o' the time.
 Cæs. Possess it, I'll make answer:
But I had rather fast from all four days
Than drink so much in one."

Significant speeches. Antony is a child of the time in a much
fuller sense than he means — he is *possessed* by it; while Octavius
possesses it, is master of it.

 " *Eno.*   Ha, my brave emperor! [*To Antony.*
Shall we dance now the Egyptian Bacchanals,
And celebrate our drink?
 Pom.   Let's ha't, good soldier.
 Ant. Come, let's all take hands,
Till that the conquering wine hath steep'd our sense
In soft and delicate Lethe.
 Eno.   All take hands.
Make battery to our ears with the loud music:

The while I'll place you ; then the boy shall sing ;
The holding * every man shall bear as loud
As his strong sides can volley.

> [*Music plays*. ENOBARBUS *places them hand in hand*.

· THE SONG.

> Come, thou monarch of the vine,
> Plumpy Bacchus with pink eyne !
> In thy fats our cares be drown'd,
> With thy grapes our hairs be crown'd:
> Cup us, till the world go round,
> Cup us, till the world go round !

Cæs. What would you more?"

Every speech of Octavius in this scene shows that, though *in*
the revels, he is not *of* them. He simply endures them as a
necessary evil, for the time being. "What would you more?"
shows that he has been a reluctant but politic attendant, and is
impatient to have them over. After bidding Pompey good night,
he says to Antony :

> "Good brother,
> Let me request you off: *our graver business*
> *Frowns at this levity.* Gentle lords, let's part:
> You see we have burnt our cheeks: strong Enobarb
> Is weaker than the wine: and mine own tongue
> Splits what it speaks: the wild disguise hath almost
> Antick'd us all.† What needs more words? Good night.
> Good Antony, your hand.
> *Pom.*   I'll try you on the shore.
> *Ant.* And shall, sir: give's your hand.
> *Pom.*   O Antony,
> You have my father's house, — But, what? we are friends.
> Come, down into the boat."

Clarke calls this a " capital bit of maudlin, half lingering resentment, half drunken magnanimity of forgiveness."

---

      * burden.   † made antics or buffoons of us all.

" *Eno.*   Take heed you fall not.
                        [*Exeunt all but* ENOBARBUS *and* MENAS.
Menas, I'll not on shore.
    Men.   No, to my cabin.
These drums! these trumpets, flutes! what!
Let Neptune hear we bid a loud farewell
To these great fellows: sound and be hang'd, sound out!
                                [*Sound a flourish with drums.*
    Eno. Ho! says a'. There's my cap.
    Men. Ho! Noble captain, come."   [*Exeunt.*

Menas is a grand old representative servant of a time that has
passed away.

There is no other scene in all the Plays of Shakespeare, perhaps, which exhibits a more complete dramatic identification on
the part of the poet, than this banquet scene. There must have
been, at the time of his writing it, the fullest sympathetic reproduction within himself, of the several characters.

The reconciliation which has been patched up between the several leading actors in the drama, cannot last long, as it is based
merely on policy, and is quite inconsistent with the state of things,
with the irresistible drift of things — the drift toward imperialism.
Octavius is the only one who sees through this politic reconciliation,
and knows, with an assurance double sure, what the upshot will be.
He alone represents the main drift of things, in which the spirit
of Cæsar is the immanent controlling principle.

Antony goes back, as soon as he can, to the flesh-pots of Egypt,
and when the affairs of the Empire shall reach their flood tide
(which they very soon will), Antony, with all his moral sinews
severed, will be helplessly swallowed up in this flood tide, while
Octavius will be wafted upon it, to "solely sovereign sway and
masterdom." The two men unite in illustrating what Brutus says
in Julius Cæsar (A. IV. Sc. iii. 218–221):

> " There is a tide in the affairs of men,
>   Which, taken at the flood, leads on to fortune."

That is illustrated by Octavius.

> " Omitted, all the voyage of their life
> Is bound in shallows and in miseries."

That is illustrated by Antony.

In the Scene between Enobarbus and Eros, the 5th of the 3d Act, we learn what has been done, since the Triumvirate was restored to a provisional harmony, through the dexterous management of Octavius. The Scene is Athens, where Antony now is with Octavia.

" *Eno.* How now, friend Eros !

Eros. There's strange news come, sir.

Eno. What, man?

Eros. Cæsar and Lepidus have made wars upon Pompey.

Eno. This is old: what is the success?

Eros. Cæsar, having made use of him in the wars 'gainst Pompey, presently denied him rivality; * would not let him partake in the glory of the action: and not resting here, accuses him of letters he had formerly wrote to Pompey; upon his own appeal,† seizes him: so the poor third is up ‡ till death enlarge his confine.

Eno. Then, world, thou hast a pair of chaps, no more;
And throw between them all the food thou hast,
They'll grind the other.   Where's Antony?

Eros. He's walking in the garden — thus; and spurns
The rush that lies before him: cries ' Fool Lepidus ! '
And threats the throat of that his officer
That murdered Pompey.

Eno.   Our great navy's rigg'd.

Eros. For Italy and Cæsar.   More, § Domitius;
My lord desires you presently: ‖ my news
I might have told hereafter.

Eno.   'Twill be naught:
But let it be.   Bring me to Antony.

Eros. Come, sir."   [*Exeunt.*

---

* associateship, equality.   † impeachment.   ‡ shut up.
§ I've more to tell you.   ‖ immediately.

Enobarbus shows by his last speech, that he has no more hopes for Antony — that in desiring him immediately, he can have nothing to devise which will be worth anything. Antony makes Octavius's doings since he left Rome, the occasion of sending Octavia back to Rome as a mediator. In the east his pleasure lies, and he's glad to get rid of her. Poor Octavia is in a situation not unlike, but more pathetic than, that of Blanch of Castile, in King John. She says in the preceding scene, in reply to Antony's complaint of Octavius:

> "*Oct.*   O my good lord,
> Believe not all; or, if you must believe,
> Stomach * not all. A more unhappy lady,
> If this division chance, ne'er stood between,
> Praying for both parts :
> The good gods will mock me presently, †
> When I shall pray, 'O, bless my lord and husband!'
> Undo that prayer, by crying out as loud,
> 'O, bless my brother!' Husband win, win brother,
> Prays, and destroys the prayer; no midway
> 'Twixt these extremes at all.‡
>   *Ant.*   Gentle Octavia,
> Let your best love draw to that point, which seeks
> Best to preserve it: if I lose mine honour,
> I lose myself; better I were not yours
> Than yours so branchless. But as you requested,
> Yourself shall go between's; the meantime, lady,
> I'll raise the preparation of a war
> Shall stain § your brother: make your soonest haste;
> So your desires are yours.

---

* resent.   † immediately.

‡ Compare this speech with that of Blanch (King John, A. III. Sc. i. 331–336):

> " Husband, I cannot pray that thou mayst win;
> Uncle, I needs must pray that thou mayst lose;
> Father, I may not wish the fortune thine;
> Grandam, I will not wish thy wishes thrive:
> Whoever wins, on that side shall I lose;
> Assured loss before the match be play'd."

§ eclipse.

> *Oct.*　　　　　　　Thanks to my lord.
> The Jove of power make me most weak, most weak,
> Your reconciler! Wars 'twixt you twain would be
> As if the world would cleave, and that slain men
> Should solder up the rift.
> 　　*Ant.* When it appears to you where this begins,
> Turn your displeasure that way; for our faults
> Can never be so equal, that your love
> Can equally move with them. Provide your going;
> Choose your own company, and command what cost
> Your heart has mind to."　　　　　　　*[Exeunt.*

In the 6th Scene, Octavius gives expression to the grievances which Antony's conduct in Egypt is causing him, *if grievances they can be called which afford him a pretext for doing just what he desires to do.* He has got rid of Lepidus and Pompey, and his purpose is now to get rid of Antony and rule alone; and toward this end, Antony, in his crazy infatuation, is himself co-operating — is doing more than Octavius himself. Octavius's consummate skill as a politician is especially shown in his securing the willing co-operation of those who are in his way, toward the realization of his ambitious aims. They are entrapped into the belief that they are advancing their own individual interests while they are exclusively advancing his own.

> " *They* see the card that falls, — *he* knows
> The card that followeth." *

Octavius says to Agrippa and Mecænas:

> " Contemning Rome, he has done all this, and more,
> In Alexandria; here's the manner of 't:
> I' the market-place, on a tribunal silver'd,
> Cleopatra and himself in chairs of gold
> Were publicly enthroned: at the feet sat
> Cæsarion, whom they call my father's son,·
> And all the unlawful issue that their lust

---

* Adapted from Rossetti's "Card Dealer."

> Since then has made between them.   Unto her
> He gave the stablishment of Egypt; made her
> Of lower Syria, Cyprus, Lydia,
> Absolute queen.
> > *Mec.*   This in the public eye?
> > *Cæs.*   In the common show-place, where they exercise . . .
> The people know it; and have now received
> His accusations.
> > *Agr.*   Who does he accuse?
> > *Cæs.*   Cæsar: and that, having in Sicily
> Sextus Pompeius spoil'd, we had not rated him
> His part o' the isle: then does he say, he lent me
> Some shipping unrestored: lastly, he frets
> That Lepidus of the triumvirate
> Should be deposed; and, being, that we detain
> All his revenue.
> > *Agr.*   Sir, this should be answer'd.
> > *Cæs.*   'Tis done already, and the messenger gone."

Octavius is a man of dispatch.   He is always fully up to, if not
ahead of, time.   Keen-eyed ambition, such as his " on occasion's
forelock watchful waits." *

Octavia enters with her train.   Her brother expresses great
surprise at her having come as a market-maid to Rome.   The extravagance of his language is evidently designed to exhibit his
insincerity:

> " . . . the wife of Antony
> Should have an army for an usher, and
> The neighs of horse to tell of her approach
> Long ere she did appear; the trees by the way
> Should have borne men; and expectation fainted,
> Longing for what it had not; nay, the dust
> Should have ascended to the roof of heaven,
> Raised by your populous troops; but you are come
> A market-maid to Rome; and have prevented
> The ostentation of our love, which, left unshown

---

* "Paradise Regained," III. 173.

Is often left unloved ; * we should have met you
By sea and land ; supplying every stage
With an augmented greeting.

    Oct.   Good my lord,
To come thus was I not constrain'd, but did
On my free will. My lord, Mark Antony,
Hearing that you prepared for war, acquainted
My grieved ear withal ; whereon, I begg'd
His pardon † for return.

    Cæs.   Which soon he granted,
Being an abstract ‡ 'tween his lust and him.

    Oct. Do not say so, my lord.

    Cæs.   I have eyes upon him,
And his affairs come to me on the wind. §
Where is he now?

    Oct.   My lord, in Athens.

    Cæs. No, my most wronged sister ; Cleopatra
Hath nodded him to her. He hath given his empire
Up to a whore ; who ‖ now are levying
The kings o' the earth for war : . . .

    Oct.   Ay me, most wretched,
That have my heart parted betwixt two friends
That do afflict each other!

    Cæs.   Welcome hither :
Your letters did withhold our breaking forth ;
Till we perceived, both how you were wrong led,
And we in negligent danger.¶ Cheer your heart :
Be you not troubled with the time, which drives
O'er your content these strong necessities ;
But let determined things to destiny **

---

  * deprived of its character as love.

  † leave, permission, with the implied idea of apologizing for the same.

  ‡ As Schmidt explains, "the shortest way for him and his desires, the readiest opportunity to encompass his wishes." Most editors substitute "obstruct," suggested by Warburton.

  § A revelation of his keen-eyed ambition which "on occasion's forelock watchful waits."   ‖ "who" = and they.

  ¶ danger due to negligence.   ** things determined to destiny.

Hold unbewail'd their way.   Welcome to Rome;
Nothing more dear to me.   You are abused
Beyond the mark of thought: and the high gods,
To do you justice, make them ministers
Of us and those that love you.   Best of comfort; *
And ever welcome to us.
    Agr.   Welcome, lady.
    Mec. Welcome, dear madam.
Each heart in Rome does love and pity you:
Only the adulterous Antony, most large
In his abominations, turns you off;
And gives his potent regiment † to a trull, ‡
That noises it § against us.
    Oct.   Is it so, sir?
    Cæs. Most certain.   Sister, welcome: pray you,
Be ever known to patience: my dear'st sister!"   [*Exeunt.*

Octavius feigns a brotherly affection so well that the reader is apt to be deceived, and to lose sight of the fact that he is really only carrying out a purpose which he had when he gave his sister in marriage to Antony — that purpose being to have a plausible occasion for breaking with Antony and, by force of arms, getting him out of the way in the sovereignty of the Roman world.   Antony has acted just as he supposed he would, and Enobarbus, to whom the dramatic situation seems to be ever revealed, saw clearly what the result of the marriage would be.   He says to Menas (A. II. Sc. vi.) : " You shall find the band that seems to tie their friendship together will be the very strangler of their amity.   Octavia is of a holy, cold, and still conversation.   *Menas.* Who would not have his wife so?   *Enobarbus.* Not he that himself is not so; which is Mark Antony.   He will to his Egyptian dish again: then shall the sighs of Octavia blow the fire up in Cæsar; and, as I said before, that which is the strength of their amity shall prove the immediate author of their variance.   Antony will use

---

   * Optative: "best of comfort" be to you.   † rule, sway.
   ‡ harlot.   § Used indefinitely. Gr. 226.

his affection where it is; he married but his occasion here." Enobarbus is "as good as a chorus." The whole situation of things, in their successive stages, can be read in his speeches.

Shakespeare often, as does a cunning artist in color, produces effects by a few slight touches — places distinctly before us a personality with which we are brought into a sympathetic relationship, though that personalty says and does very little in a play. It must not be supposed that the dramatic artist defined to himself, with any distinctness, such a personality. By his artistic skill he was able to produce a certain *impression* upon the feelings, as a color artist produces a certain impression upon the eye.

Octavia is a signal illustration of this. How little she says and does! And yet through that little we are made so to feel the beauty of her womanhood, that it serves, along with the other dramatic agencies employed to that end, to deepen our sense of the ruin wrought by "fleshly lusts which war against the soul." This "gem of women" cannot withhold Antony from his "Egyptian dish." He returns to the poisonous food, which will now soon do for him its fatal work.

All things are now ready for the final conflict — a conflict which will not only bring the historical movement to its goal, namely, the "solely sovereign sway and masterdom" of Octavius, but (and this is really the leading purpose of the drama, the other being rather the dramatic background) the bondage of Antony will be exhibited, in this final conflict, in the boldest relief. But the great artist will not allow him to be entirely divorced from our sympathies. The nobler qualities of his nature which have, at times, suffered a total eclipse, will come out sufficiently to assure us that they are not altogether destroyed.

Against the advice of his lieutenant-general, Canidius, and the clear-sighted, sagacious Enobarbus, and the entreaty of a veteran soldier, he persists in his purpose of fighting by sea. The 7th Scene of the 3d Act exhibits this persistence, which has no other basis than the caprice of the woman to whom he is a slave.

"SCENE VII. *Near Actium.   Antony's camp.*

Enter CLEOPATRA *and* ENOBARBUS.

Cleo. I will be even with thee, doubt it not.

Eno. But why, why, why?

Cleo. Thou hast forspoke * my being in these wars,
And say'st it is not fit.

Eno.   Well, is it, is it?

Cleo. Is't not denounced against us? † why should not we
Be there in person? . . .

Eno. Your presence needs must puzzle Antony;
Take from his heart, take from his brain, from's time,
What should not then be spared.   He is already
Traduced for levity; and 'tis said in Rome
That Photinus an eunuch and your maids
Manage this war.

Cleo.   Sink Rome, and their tongues rot
That speak against us! A charge we bear i' the war,
And, as the president of my kingdom, will
Appear there for a man.   Speak not against it;
I will not stay behind.

Eno.   Nay, I have done.
Here comes the emperor.

Enter ANTONY *and* CANIDIUS.

Ant.   Is it not strange, Canidius,
That from Tarentum and Brundusium
He could so quickly cut the Ionian sea,
And take in ‡ Toryne?   You have heard on't, sweet?

Cleo. Celerity is never more admired
Than by the negligent.

Ant.   A good rebuke,
Which might have well becomed the best of men,
To taunt at slackness.   Canidius, we
Will fight with him by sea.

Cleo.   By sea! what else?

Can. Why will my lord do so?

---

* spoken against.   † "Is not the war declared against us?"   ‡ capture.

Ant.   For that he dares us to't.

Eno. So hath my lord dared him to single fight.

Can. Ay, and to wage this battle at Pharsalia,
Where Cæsar fought with Pompey: but these offers,
Which serve not for his vantage, he shakes off;
And so should you."

Antony gets the best advice from his advisers, but this best advice only serves to exhibit his crazy persistence in what will result in his ruin. His " wit's diseased."

" *Eno.*   Your ships are not well mann'd;
Your mariners are muleteers, reapers, people
Ingross'd by swift impress; * in Cæsar's fleet
Are those that often have 'gainst Pompey fought:
Their ships are yare; † yours, heavy: no disgrace
Shall fall you for refusing him at sea,
Being prepared for land.

Ant.   By sea, by sea.

Eno. Most worthy sir, you therein throw away
The absolute soldiership you have by land;
Distract your army, which doth most consist
Of war-mark'd footmen; leave unexecuted
Your own renowned knowledge; quite forego
The way which promises assurance; and
Give up yourself merely ‡ to chance and hazard,
From firm security.

Ant.   I'll fight at sea.

Cleo. I have sixty sails, Cæsar none better.

Ant. Our overplus of shipping will we burn;
And, with the rest full-mann'd, from the head of Actium
Beat the approaching Cæsar. But if we fail,
We then can do't at land.

Enter a Messenger.

          Thy business?

Mess. The news is true, my lord; he is descried;
Cæsar has taken Toryne.

---

* " got together by hurried impressment or levy."
† " light and manageable."   ‡ wholly, entirely.

> *Ant.* Can he be there in person? 'tis impossible;
> Strange that his powers should be."

Octavius's rapid movements are in strong contrast with Antony's dallying foolery.

>   " Canidius,
> Our nineteen legions thou shalt-hold by land,
> And our twelve thousand horse.   We'll to our ship."

And then, addressing Cleopatra, he says, "Away, my Thetis!" *i.e.*, my sea-nymph; in which is implied that he regards himself already as Neptune, god of the sea, and Cleopatra as his Thetis.

> " *Enter a* Soldier.
>
>   How, now, worthy soldier?
> *Sold.* O noble emperor, do not fight by sea;
> Trust not to rotten planks: do you misdoubt
> This sword and these my wounds?   Let the Egyptians
> And the Phœnicians go a-ducking: * we
> Have used † to conquer, standing on the earth,
> And fighting foot to foot.
> *Ant.*   Well, well: away!
>   [*Exeunt* ANTONY, CLEOPATRA, *and* ENOBARBUS.
> *Sold.* By Hercules, I think I am i' the right.
> *Can.* Soldier, thou art: but his whole action grows
> Not in the power on't; so our leader's led,
> And we are women's men.

---

* *i.e.*, as ducks on the water.

† been accustomed.   Shakespeare follows Plutarch closely here: "Now as he was setting his men in order of battle, there was a captain, a valiant man, that had served Antonius in many battles and conflicts, and had all his body hacked and cut; who, as Antonius passed by him, cried unto him and said: ' O noble emperor, how cometh it to pass that you trust to these vile, brittle ships?   What, do you mistrust these wounds of mine, and this sword?   Let the Egyptians and Phœnicians fight by sea, and set us on the main land, where we use [are accustomed] to conquer or to be slain on our feet.'   Antonius passed him by and said never a word, but only beckoned to him with his hand and head, as though he willed him to be of good courage, although indeed, he had no great courage himself."

Sold.   You keep by land
The legions and the horse whole, do you not?
    Can. Marcus Octavius, Marcus Justeius,
Publicola, and Cælius, are for sea :
But we keep whole by land.   This speed of Cæsar's
Carries beyond belief.
    Sold.   While he was yet in Rome,
His power went out in such distractions as
Beguiled all spies.
    Can.   Who's his lieutenant, hear you?
    Sold. They say, one Taurus.
    Can.   Well I know the man.

                Enter a Messenger.

    Mess. The emperor calls Canidius.
    Can. With news the time's with labour, and throes forth,
Each minute, some."   [*Exeunt.*

The calamitous result of the sea-fight is told in the 10th Scene.
Cleopatra's ship, "the Antoniad, the Egyptian admiral, with all
their sixty, fly and turn the rudder "; and "she once being loof'd,
the noble ruin of her magic, Antony, claps on his sea-wing, and,
like a doating mallard, leaving the fight in height, flies after her."
When Canidius, who has been commanding the land forces, learns
of the disaster, he says : "To Cæsar will I render my legions and
my horse ; six kings already show me the way of yielding." The
saddened but still faithful Enobarbus replies : "I'll yet follow the
wounded chance of Antony, though my reason sits in the wind
against me."

The disastrous consequences of his insane persistence to fight
at sea, in spite of all entreaty to the contrary, cause Antony to
rise to a deep and mortifying sense of his infatuation and enslave-
ment.   It is in representing the moral struggle which ensues that
he is kept within the pale of our sympathy.   He is not wholly
despicable.   He is capable of feeling the degradation of his situation.   To his attendants he says : "Hark ! the land bids me tread
no more upon't ; it is ashamed to bear me !"   He thinks of
Philippi, and what he showed himself there.   Octavius, he says,

> " Kept
> His sword e'en like a dancer, while I struck
> The lean and wrinkled Cassius ; and 'twas I
> That the mad Brutus ended : he alone
> Dealt on lieutenantry, and no practice had
> In the brave squares of war ; yet now — no matter."

But the "serpent of old Nile" soon has him again in her brilliant folds.   Weeping, she says :

> "O my lord, my lord,
> Forgive my fearful sails ! I little thought
> You would have follow'd.
>   *Ant.*   Egypt, thou knew'st too well
> My heart was to thy rudder tied by the strings,
> And thou shouldst tow me after : o'er my spirit
> Thy full supremacy thou knew'st, and that
> Thy beck might from the bidding of the gods
> Command me.
>   *Cleo.*   O, my pardon !
>   *Ant.*   Now I must
> To the young man send humble treaties, dodge
> And palter in the shifts of lowness ; who
> With half the bulk o' the world play'd as I pleased,
> Making and marring fortunes.   You did know
> How much you were my conqueror ; and that
> My sword, made weak by my affection, would
> Obey it on all cause.
>   *Cleo.*   Pardon, pardon !
>   *Ant.* Fall not a tear, I say ; one of them rates
> All that is won and lost : give me a kiss ;
> Even this repays me.* We sent our schoolmaster ;
> Is he come back ? Love, I am full of lead.
> Some wine, within there, and our viands ! Fortune knows
> We scorn her most when most she offers blows."   [*Exeunt.*

---

* "He holds a dubious balance : — yet *that* scale,
   Whose freight the world is, surely should prevail?
   No; Cleopatra droppeth into *this*
   One counterpoising orient sultry kiss."
— "Epigrams of Art, Life, and Nature." By William Watson. Ep. xviii.

At this point, when a kiss can counterpoise "that scale, whose freight the world is," the fatality of an overmastering passion has fully set in. Antony can withdraw from the sovereignty of the world, but cling to Cleopatra he must, till he die.

In the next Scene, his ambassador, Euphronius, presents his humiliating petition to Octavius :

> " Lord of his fortunes he salutes thee, and
> Requires * to live in Egypt: which not granted
> He lessens his requests ; and to thee sues
> To let him breathe between the heavens and earth,
> A private man in Athens : this for him.
> Next, Cleopatra does confess thy greatness ;
> Submits her to thy might ; and of thee craves
> The circle † of the Ptolemies for her heirs,
> Now hazarded to thy grace."

Octavius's reply expresses the attitude which the imperturbable victor will maintain to the end. Antony and he must not together "breathe between the heavens and earth."

> " For Antony,
> I have no ears to his request. The queen
> Of audience nor desire shall fail, so she
> From Egypt drive her all-disgraced friend,
> Or take his life there : this if she perform,
> She shall not sue unheard. So to them both."

Octavius, in the same scene, when the ambassador goes out, instructs Thyreus to try his eloquence to win Cleopatra from Antony :

> " Promise,
> And in our name, what she requires ; add more,
> From thine invention, offers : women are not
> In their best fortunes strong ; but want will perjure
> The ne'er-touch'd vestal : try thy cunning, Thyreus ;
> Make thine own edict for thy pains, which we
> Will answer as a law. . . .

---

* requests.   † crown.

> Observe how Antony becomes his flaw,*
> And what thou think'st his very action speaks
> In every power † that moves."

In the next Scene, to Cleopatra's question, " Is Antony or we in fault for this?" Enobarbus replies :

> " Antony only, that would make his will
> Lord of his reason.   What though you fled
> . . . why should he follow?
> The itch of his affection should not then
> Have nick'd his captainship; at such a point,
> When half to half the world opposed, he being
> The meered question: ‡ 'twas a shame no less
> Than was his loss, to course your flying flags,
> And leave his navy gazing."

When Antony learns from Euphronius the answer of Octavius to his petition, his feelings vent themselves in merely " wild and whirling words" about his victor's youth and resources; and he adds :

> " I dare him therefore
> To lay his gay comparisons § apart,
> And answer me declined,‖ sword against sword,
> Ourselves alone.   I'll write it : follow me."

When he goes out with Euphronius, Enobarbus comments on the emptiness of his words :

> " Yes, like enough, high-battled ¶ Cæsar will
> Unstate ** his happiness, and be staged †† to the show,

---

* " conforms himself to this breach of his fortune."
† " bodily organ."   See Troilus and Cressida, A. IV. Sc. v. 55–57.
‡ " he being the only cause and subject of the war."
§ " all things which are in his favor when compared with me."
‖ " fallen in fortune."
¶ " commanding proud armies."
** " Divest of state and dignity his good fortune."
†† " exhibited on the stage against a gladiator."

> Against a sworder! I see men's judgments are
> A parcel of their fortunes : * and things outward
> Do draw the inward quality after them,
> To suffer all alike. That he should dream,
> Knowing all measures, the full Cæsar will
> Answer his emptiness! Cæsar, thou hast subdued
> His judgment too. . . .
> Mine honesty and I begin to square.†
> The loyalty well held to fools does make
> Our faith mere folly."

But in the next sentence he shows the reluctance of his disaffection :

> " Yet he that can endure
> To follow with allegiance a fallen lord
> Does conquer him that did his master conquer,
> And earns a place i' the story."

Antony returns and comes upon Thyreus kissing the hand of Cleopatra. He is inflamed with jealous rage, and orders the messenger from Octavius to be soundly whipped. She for whom he has sacrificed a world he fears is untrue to him. He comes to a sense of his degradation :

> "When we in our viciousness grow hard
> (Oh misery on't) the wise gods seel our eyes,
> In our own filth drop our clear judgments, make us
> Adore our errors, laugh at's while we strut
> To our confusion." ‡

But he is soon overcome by Cleopatra's artful and lachrymose appeals. Her control over him is absolute. What remains of his moral sense goes for nothing. In his weak violence, or rather violent weakness, as her slave, he ejaculates :

> " I will be treble-sinew'd, hearted, breathed,
> And fight maliciously : for when mine hours

---

* " of a piece with their fortunes,"   † quarrel.   ‡ destruction.

> Were nice and lucky, men did ransom lives
> Of me for jests : but now, I'll set my teeth,
> And send to darkness all that stop me."

And see the preparation he proposes for all this !

>   " Come,
> Let's have one other gawdy night : * call to me
> All my sad Captains, fill our bowls once more :
> Let's mock the midnight bell.
>   *Cleo.*   It is my birth-day :
> I had thought to have held it poor : but since my lord
> Is Antony again, I will be Cleopatra."

There's an unconscious and pathetic if not ludicrous irony in
this speech : " but since my lord is Antony again," really means,
he has returned to his weak and sensual self; " I will be Cleopatra," that is, she will be again the fascinating serpent of old
Nile. When all go out but Enobarbus, we have from him again
a comment on the emptiness of Antony's words and on his
weak violence :

> " Now he'll outstare the lightning. To be furious,
> Is to be frighted out of fear ; and in that mood
> The dove will peck the estridge ; and I see still,
> A diminution in our Captain's brain
> Restores his heart ; when valour preys on reason,
> It eats the sword it fights with. I will seek
> Some way to leave him."

A second battle results in a temporary advantage to Antony's
forces on land — a mere " lightning before death " — which is followed by the utter destruction of the Egyptian fleet. Antony
believes, and perhaps truly, that Cleopatra has betrayed him.
(That she was not indisposed to do so, seems to be intimated in
her interview with Thyreus.)

>   " Betray'd I am :
> Oh this false soul of Egypt ! this grave charm,†

---

    * joyous, festive.   † fatal charmer.

Whose eye beck'd forth my wars, and call'd them home:
Whose bosom was my crownet, my chief end,
Like a right gipsy, hath, at fast and loose,*
Beguiled me to the very heart of loss.†

Enter CLEOPATRA.

Ah, thou spell? Avaunt!
    Cleo. Why is my lord enraged against his love?
    Ant. Vanish, or I shall give thee thy deserving,
And blemish Cæsar's triumph. Let him take thee,
And hoist thee up to the shouting plebeians:
Follow his chariot, like the greatest spot
Of all thy sex: most monster-like,‡ be shown
For poor'st diminutives, for dolts,§ and let
Patient Octavia plough thy visage up
With her prepared nails.   [*Exit* CLEOPATRA.
                        'Tis well thou'rt gone,
If it be well to live; but better 'twere
Thou fell'st into my fury, for one death
Might have prevented many. . . .
                        The witch shall die:
To the young Roman boy she hath sold me, and I fall
Under this plot; she dies for't."

Here it would appear that all the ties which have bound him to
Cleopatra have been severed. But it is not so, and Cleopatra proceeds to prove it not so. In the next Scene she instructs Mardian
to tell him she has slain herself:

" Say, that the last I spoke was 'Antony';
And word it, prithee, piteously: hence, Mardian,
And bring me how he takes my death."

What has become the mainspring of Antony's being in this
world, he feels is broken, and that, therefore, nothing now remains

---

* a cheating game.   † the extremity of loss.
‡ " as a monster, or monstrosity."
§ " be made a show for the lowest and stupidest of the people."

for him but to die. With a sense of the dispersion and fading out of all earthly things, a sense which shows the remains of a noble nature, he says, to the faithful Eros :

> " Sometime we see a cloud that's dragonish,
>   A vapour sometime, like a bear or lion,
>   A tower'd citadel, a pendent rock,
>   A forked mountain, or blue promontory
>   With trees upon't, that nod unto the world,
>   And mock our eyes with air: thou hast seen these signs;
>   They are black vesper's pageants.
>   *Eros.*   Ay, my lord.
>   *Ant.* That which is now a horse, even with a thought
>   The rack dislimns, and makes it indistinct,
>   As water is in water.
>   *Eros.*   It does, my lord.
>   *Ant.* My good knave Eros, now thy captain is
>   Even such a body: here I am Antony;
>   Yet cannot hold this visible shape, my knave.
>   I made these wars for Egypt, and the queen, —
>   Whose heart I thought I had, for she had mine,
>   Which whilst it was mine had annex'd unto't
>   A million moe, now lost, — she, Eros, has
>   Pack'd cards with Cæsar, and false-play'd my glory
>   Unto an enemy's triumph.
>   Nay, weep not, gentle Eros; there is left us
>   Ourselves to end ourselves."

But when he is told by Mardian that Cleopatra is dead, the love which has proved so fatal to him, reasserts itself, and the desire to be reunited to her determines him to follow her to the shades and there to weep for pardon.

> " I will o'ertake thee, Cleopatra, and
>   Weep for my pardon. So it must be, for now
>   All length is torture : since the torch is out,
>   Lie down, and stray no farther : now all labour
>   Mars what it does; yea, very force entangles
>   Itself with strength : seal then, and all is done.

Eros! — I come, my queen : — Eros ! — Stay for me :
Where souls do couch on flowers, we'll hand in hand,
And with our sprightly port make the ghosts gaze :
Dido and her Æneas shall want troops,
And all the haunt be ours. Come, Eros, Eros!

Re-enter EROS.

 Eros. What would my lord?
 Ant.   Since Cleopatra died,
I have lived in such dishonour, that the gods
Detest my baseness. I, that with my sword
Quarter'd the world, and o'er green Neptune's back
With ships made cities, condemn myself to lack
The courage of a woman; less noble mind
Than she which by her death our Cæsar tells
' I am conqueror of myself.' Thou art sworn, Eros,
That, when the exigent * should come, which now
Is come indeed, when I should see behind me
The inevitable prosecution † of
Disgrace and horror, that, on my command,
Thou then wouldst kill me : do't; the time is come :
Thou strikest not me, 'tis Cæsar thou defeat'st.
Put colour in thy cheek.
 Eros.   The gods withhold me!
Shall I do that which all the Parthian darts,
Though enemy, lost aim, and could not?
 Ant.   Eros,
Wouldst thou be window'd ‡ in great Rome and see
Thy master thus with pleach'd § arms, bending down
His corrigible ‖ neck, his face subdued
To penetrative ¶ shame, whilst the wheel'd seat
Of fortunate Cæsar, drawn before him, branded
His baseness that ensued? **
 Eros.   I would not see't.
 Ant. Come, then; for with a wound I must be cured.

---

* exigency.   † pursuit.   ‡ stationed at a window.   § folded.
‖ submissive to correction.   ¶ affecting the heart strongly.
** branded the baseness of him that followed.

Draw that thy honest sword, which thou hast worn
Most useful for thy country.

    Eros.   O, sir, pardon me!

    Ant. When I did make thee free, sworest thou not then
To do this when I bade thee?   Do it at once;
Or thy precedent services are all
But accidents unpurposed.   Draw, and come.

    Eros. Turn from me, then, that noble countenance,
Wherein the worship of the whole world lies.

    Ant. Lo thee!   *[Turning from him.*

    Eros. My sword is drawn.

    Ant.   Then let it do at once
The thing why thou hast drawn it.

    Eros.   My dear master,
My captain, and my emperor, let me say,
Before I strike this bloody stroke, farewell.

    Ant. 'Tis said, man; and farewell.

    Eros. Farewell, great chief.   Shall I strike now?

    Ant.   Now, Eros.

    Eros. Why, there then: thus I do escape the sorrow
Of Antony's death.   *[Kills himself.*

    Ant.   Thrice nobler than myself!
Thou teachest me, O valiant Eros, what
I should, and thou couldst not.   My queen and Eros
Have by their brave instruction got upon me
A nobleness in record: but I will be.
A bridegroom in my death, and run into't
As to a lover's bed.   Come, then: and, Eros,
Thy master dies thy scholar: to do thus
                           [Falling on his sword.
I learn'd of thee.   How! not dead? not dead?
The guard, ho!   O, dispatch me!

Dercetas and Guard enter.   They refuse to do his bidding and go out.   Diomedes enters, sent by Cleopatra to say,

            " She had a prophesying fear
Of what hath come to pass: for when she saw —
Which never shall be found — you did suspect

> *She had dispos'd with Cæsar*, and that your rage
> Would not be purg'd, she sent you word she was dead ;
> But, fearing since how it might work, hath sent
> Me to proclaim the truth, — and I am come,
> I dread, too late."

A message in which one deception is admitted, and another substituted.

Antony is borne by the guard to the monument where Cleopatra has locked herself. She heaps upon him expressions of her affection, in words and kisses. He enjoins upon her to seek of Cæsar her honor with her safety, and to trust none about Cæsar but Proculeius. In regard to himself, he reposes overmuch, for our full sympathy, upon his past :

> " The miserable change now at my end
> Lament nor sorrow at ; but please your thoughts
> In feeding them with those my former fortunes
> Wherein I lived, the greatest prince o' the world,
> The noblest ; and do now not basely die,
> Nor cowardly put off my helmet to
> My countryman, — a Roman by a Roman
> Valiantly vanquish'd. Now my spirit is going ;
> I can no more.
> *Cleo.*   Noblest of men, woo't die?
> Hast thou no care of me? shall I abide
> In this dull world, which in thy absence is
> No better than a sty? Oh see, my women, [ANTONY *dies.*
> The crown o' the earth doth melt. My lord?
> Oh withered is the garland of the war,
> The soldier's pole * is fall'n : young boys and girls
> Are level now with men ; the odds is gone,
> And there is nothing left remarkable †
> Beneath the visiting moon.   [*Faints.*
> *Char.*   Oh quietness, lady !
> *Iras.* She is dead too, our sovereign.
> *Char.*   Lady !

---

 * "loadstar," Schmidt.   † worthy of consideration,

Iras.   Madam !
Char. O madam, madam, madam !
Iras.   Royal Egypt,
Empress !
   Char.   Peace, peace, Iras !
   Cleo. No more, but e'en a woman, and commanded
By such poor passion as the maid that milks
And does the meanest chares.*   It were for me
To throw my sceptre at the injurious † gods ;
To tell them that this world did equal theirs
Till they had stol'n our jewel.   All's but naught ;
Patience is sottish,‡ and impatience does
Become a dog that's mad : then is it sin
To rush into the secret house of death,
Ere death dare come to us?   How do you, women?
What, what ! good cheer !   Why, how now, Charmian?
My noble girls?   Ah, women, women ! look,
Our lamp is spent, it's out !   Good sirs,§ take heart :
We'll bury him ; and then, what's brave, what's noble,
Let's do it after the high Roman fashion,
And make death proud to take us.   Come, away ;
This case of that huge spirit now is cold :
Ah, women, women ! come ; we have no friend
But resolution, and the briefest end."

The 5th Act belongs to Cleopatra.   All in it is relative to her.
If her love for Antony had become the mainspring of her being,
as Antony's love for her had become the mainspring of *his* being,
the 5th Act would hardly have been needed.   " The difference
between her and Antony," says Denton J. Snider, "is seen in the
fact that she is willing to survive him, but he was not willing to
survive her ; separation does not mean death in her case.   There
is, however, no doubt about her love for Antony, but there is as
little doubt about her readiness to transfer it to another person.

---

   * turns of work; A. S. cyrr, *a turn.*
   † acting against justice or right.   ‡ Endurance is foolish.
   § For this use of " sirs," see Love's Labor's Lost, A. IV. Sc. iii. 211.

She has been making provision for the future — she has been laying plans to catch Octavius in her toils. He comes into her presence, but he is not charmed; his cool head cannot be turned by sensuous enchantment. This seals her fate. She has met her master; she has found the man who is able to resist her spell. The proof is manifest — she learns that Octavius intends to take her to Rome to grace his triumph. This secret is confided to her by Dolabella, who seems to be the last victim of her magical power. That power is now broken; nothing remains except to die. Still, she shows signs of a better nature in this latter part — misfortune has ennobled her character :

" 'My desolation begins to make a better life.

"The heroic qualities of Antony, now that he is gone, and she can captivate no new hero, fill her imagination ; she will go and join him in the world beyond. · Her sensual life seems purified and exalted as she gives expression to her 'immortal longings.' Her deepest trait is, however, conquest through sensual love ; she will live as long as she can conquer ; when her spell is once overcome she will die, dwelling in imagination upon the greatest victory of her principle, and upon its most illustrious victim."

JOTTINGS ON THE TEXT OF HAMLET.

(First Folio *versus* "Cambridge" Edition.)

———•◦•———

O F the First Folio, J. Payne Collier remarks ("Memoirs of the Principal Actors in the Plays of Shakespeare," pp. 69, 70), "The book does credit to the age, even as a specimen of typography: it is on the whole remarkably accurate, and so desirous were the editors and printers of correctness, that they introduced changes for the better, even while the sheets were in progress through the press."

This, perhaps, is too strongly stated. It *is* too strongly stated. But the typographical errors with which the book swarms have led many editors to put too low an estimate on its authority, and to prefer many quarto texts. The editors of the "Cambridge" edition say, "In Hamlet we have computed that the Folio, when it differs from the Quartos, differs for the worse in forty-seven places, while it differs for the better in twenty at most." The following "Jottings," I am bold to say, show this statement to be very wide of the mark. The punctuation, too, of the First Folio, faulty as it frequently is, is often better than theirs.

In the present unsettled and irregular use of the note of interrogation and the note of exclamation, I do not expect that all who take the trouble to read these "Jottings" will, in every case where the Folio has a ? and the "Cambridge" an !, agree with me in my preference for the ? of the Folio. But I claim that, as both are rhetorical, the general rule laid down by Wilson, that, "after words to which an answer is expected or implied, the note of interrogation is added; and after those, though apparently denoting inquiry, where no answer is intended by the writer to be given, the note of exclamation is the proper and distinctive mark," cannot be justified; and more than that, its observance, in pointing the text of Shakespeare, often leads to a misconception of the meaning. When, in expressing a feeling of surprise, a mental question is involved as to the truth or possibility of what occasions the surprise ; as, for example, when Horatio tells Hamlet that he thought he saw his father the previous night, and Hamlet replies, "The King my father," the note of interrogation should most certainly be used. The note of exclamation would tend to mislead the reader. " Indeed !" represents a different feeling, and, consequently, a different elocution, from " Indeed?" Given in reply to something that has been said, " Indeed ! " would indicate an unquestioning surprise, — the information occasioning it being accepted as the truth. " Indeed !" should, in such case, be read with a direct downward inflection of the voice. " Indeed?" on the other hand, while also indicating surprise, indicates, at the same time, a question in the mind of the speaker as to the truth or the possibility of the information occasioning it, and should be read with a strong interrogative movement of voice — the unequal upward wave, the upward inflection of the wave passing through a considerably wider interval than the downward. This distinction in the use of these two rhetorical notes (for I claim that they are strictly rhetorical, the authorities to the contrary notwithstanding), is observed in the Folio with a remarkable uniformity.

I am ready to admit the frequent faultiness of the punctuation of the Folio, — a faultiness extending sometimes to absurdity ; for example, " Making the Greene one, Red," which has, however, had its defenders ; but I am persuaded, after a careful study of the Folio in respect to the punctuation, that, whoever did the pointing, whether the author, in the original manuscript, the editors, which is not very likely, or the proof-reader, if there was one, or the printer, it was done with a remarkable regard to the spoken language. And this is especially true in respect to the notes of interrogation and of exclamation. On the other hand, I am persuaded, after an equally careful study of the punctuation and numerous other features of the "Cambridge" text, that the editors were not in the habit of voicing the language — that they studied it through the eye, and, in regard to punctuation, followed certain prescribed rules ; and thus went astray in many particulars.

It is remarkable how many features of Elizabethan English, exhibited by the early texts of Shakespeare's Plays, are eliminated in modern "critical" texts. Exact reprints of the First Folio text would be much better for students of the language of the time, than the texts presented in school editions of the Plays, in which subjunctives and their subjects are often converted, by punctuation, into imperatives and vocatives, respectively ; pure infinitives, after certain verbs, into imperatives ; word forms and contracted forms of the time, changed to those of the present, etc., etc.

These "Jottings" were privately printed some years ago to set forth some of the unrecognized merits of the First Folio text of Hamlet, and to help to induce a conservativeness on the part of Shakespeare students and editors. Dr. Horace Howard Furness has incorporated most of them in the notes to his New Variorum edition of Hamlet.

EDITIONS OF HAMLET REFERRED TO IN THE NOTES.

THE

Tragicall Historie of

HAMLET

Prince of Denmarke.

By William Shake-speare.

As it hath beene diuerse times acted by his Highnesse seruants in the Cittie of London: as also in the two V-niuersities of Cambridge and Oxford, and else-where.

At London printed for N. L. and Iohn Trundell.
1603.

Referred to as the 1st Quarto. Two copies only are known to exist; one is in the Library of the Duke of Devonshire, and wants the last leaf containing the 22 concluding lines; the other is in the British Museum, and is without the title-page.

"The edition of 1603 is obviously a very imperfect reproduction of the play, and there is every reason to believe that it was printed from a manuscript surreptitiously obtained." — Editors Cambridge edition.

THE

Tragicall Historie of

HAMLET,

Prince of Denmarke.

By William Shakespeare.

Newly imprinted and enlarged to almost as much againe as it was, according to the true and perfect Coppie.

AT. LONDON,

Printed by I. R. for N. L. and are to be sold at his shoppe vnder Saint Dunstons Church in Fleetstreet. 1604.

Referred to as the 2d Quarto; is of chief authority among the Quarto editions.

The 3d Quarto, printed from the same forms as the 2d, was published in 1605; the 4th, in 1611; the 5th is without date, but the Cambridge editors are of the opinion that it was printed from the edition of 1611; the 6th, printed from the 5th, was published in 1637.

Editions known as Players' Quartos, were published in 1676, 1685, 1695, and 1703. The variations which their texts exhibit from the earlier editions, are without any known authority. But the Cambridge editors state "that many emendations usually attributed to Rowe and Pope are really derived from one or other of these Players' Quartos."

The 1st Folio was published under the following title:

Mr. WILLIAM

SHAKESPEARES

COMEDIES,
HISTORIES, &
TRAGEDIES.

Published according to the True Originall Copies.

LONDON
Printed by Isaac Iaggard, and Ed. Blount. 1623.

In this volume, "The Tragedie of Hamlet, Prince of Denmarke," occupies, in the division of Tragedies, pages 152 to 156, then the numbering passes to 257 and continues to the end of the play, page 282 (but pages 279 and 282 are misprinted 259 and 280) ; page 278 copies vary.

The Editors were two of Shakespeare's personal friends and fellow actors, John Heminge and Henry Condell, whose long professional experience, dating back to the beginning of Shakespeare's theatrical career, and probably earlier, and continuing some years after his death, must have made them familiar with the authorized texts of his plays, and with their renderings on the stage of the time.

Our positive knowledge of Heminge's connection with theatrical affairs extends back to 1596, twenty years before the death of Shakespeare, when, it appears, he was already of some consideration as an actor. He survived his great friend more than fourteen years, dying in October, 1630. Our earliest knowledge of Henry Condell is, that in 1598, he sustained a part in Ben Jonson's "Every Man in his Humour"; according to Collier's conjecture, he was the Captain Bobadill of that comedy. His connection with the stage continued up to the time of his death in December, 1627. He appears to have been held in high esteem by his theatrical associates.

The wills * of these two men show them to have possessed considerable property, to have had strict business habits and great uprightness of character, and to have been affectionate husbands and fathers. Shakespeare honored them with an expression of his regard, in the following item of his will:

"I gyve and bequeath . . . *to my fellowes John Hemynges, Richard Burbage, and Henry Cundell, xxvj.ᵃ· viij.ᵈ· a peece to buy them ringes."*

They express their regard for their "Friend and Fellow" in their Dedication of the First Folio edition of his plays, wherein they say, " *We haue but collected them, and done an office to the dead, to procure his Orphanes, Guardians; without ambition either of selfe-profit, or fame: onely to keepe the memory of so worthy a Friend, & Fellow aliue, as was our* SHAKESPEARE, *by humble offer of his playes, to your most noble patronage."*

The Dedication is addressed

TO THE MOST NOBLE

AND

INCOMPARABLE PAIRE

OF BRETHREN.

WILLIAM

Earle of Pembroke, &c.   Lord Chamberlaine to the

Kings most Excellent Maiesty.

AND

PHILIP

Earle of Montgomery, &c.   Gentleman of his Maiesties

Bed-Chamber.   Both Knights of the most Noble Order

of the Garter, and our singular good

LORDS.

---

* Published in " Memoirs of the Principal Actors in the Plays of Shakespeare." By J. Payne Collier, Esq., F.S.A. London: printed for the Shakespeare Society, 1846.

"The text of Hamlet given in the Folio of 1623 is not derived from any of the previously existing Quartos, but from an independent manuscript. Many passages are found in the Folio which do not appear in any of the Quartos. On the other hand many passages found in the Quartos are not found in the Folio. It is to be remarked that several of those which appear in the Folio and not in the Quarto of 1604 or its successors, are found in an imperfect form in the Quarto of 1603, and therefore are not subsequent additions. Both the Quarto text of 1604 and the Folio text of 1623 seem to have been derived from manuscripts of the play curtailed, and curtailed differently, for purposes of representation." From Preface to Volume VIII. of "Cambridge" edition.

The 2d, 3d, and 4th Folios were published in 1632, 1663, and 1685, respectively. The 3d was reissued in the following year (1664), with a new title-page, and seven additional Plays, not now regarded as by Shakespeare, though they may all have received some touches from his hand. They were repeated in the 4th Folio. These editions are of no special authority in the matter of the text.

JOTTINGS ON THE TEXT OF SHAKESPEARE'S HAMLET.

The three numbers used designate, respectively, the Act, Scene, and Line. F. stands for First Folio, C. for "Cambridge" edition.

Where readings of the First Folio and of the "Cambridge" are given without remarks, it will be understood that the former are considered obviously preferable.

I. I. 30.   Sit downe a-while, And let vs F.   Sit down awhile; And let us C.   The meaning is, Sit down and let us etc.

I. I. 40.   Looke where it comes againe. F.   Look, where etc. C.

I. I. 49.   By Heauen I charge thee speake. F.   by heaven I charge thee, speak ! C.   "speak" is an infinitive after "charge," and not an imperative as the C. makes it by the use of the comma. In line 51, it is an imperative, and is preceded in **F.** by a comma.

1. 1. 53. How now *Horatio?* You tremble & look pale : **F.** How now, Horatio ! etc. **C.** The **?** of the **F.** represents the elocution better ; "Horatio" should be uttered with an unequal upward wave, expressing the triumph of the speaker in the confirmation of his report of the appearance of the ghost.

1. 1. 70. Good now sit downe, & tell me he that knowes **F.** Good now, sit down, etc. **C.** "Good" may be a vocative, and "now" may belong to "sit down." But see Abbott, § 13.

1. 2. 11. With one Auspicious, and one Dropping eye, **F.** With an auspicious and a dropping eye, **C.**

1. 2. 50. Dread my Lord, **F.** My dread lord, **C.**

1. 2. 76. Seemes Madam? **F.** Seems, madam ! **C.** The **?** represents the elocution again better than the !

1. 2. 85. passeth show ; **F.** passes show ; **C.** The older form not only suits the tone of the passage better, but the two *s's* and the *sh* in "pa*ss*es *sh*ow" coming together are very cacophonous.

1. 2. 127. the Heauens shall bruite againe, **F.** the heaven etc. **C.** The plural form is the better here.

1. 2. 132. O God, O God ! **F.** O God ! God ! **C.** The verse doesn't scan so well in the **C.** In the **F.**, the ending *er* of "slaughter" should be read as an internal extra syllable : His can | non 'gainst | Selfe-slaught | er. | O God, | O God ! | And every reader would feel the want of the second "O" on which to dwell before uttering "God" with a strong aspiration.

1. 2. 135. Fie on't? Oh fie, fie, **F.** Fie on't ! ah fie ! **C.** "ah" doesn't express the feeling of the speaker so well.

1. 2. 135. 'tis an vnweeded Garden That growes to Seed : **F.** 'tis an unweeded garden, That grows to seed : **C.** There should be no comma after "garden," as the relative clause is not used simply as an *additional* characterization of an unweeded garden, but as an inseparable part of the whole characterization — an important distinction that should be made in pointing.

1. 2. 153. Within a Moneth? Ere yet the salt etc. **F.** Within

a month; Ere yet the salt etc. C. The meaning is, Within a
month [did I say]? [Yea] Ere yet etc.

I. 2. 159. But breake my heart, for I must hold my tongue. F.
But break, my heart, for I must hold my tongue ! C. "break" is
a subjunctive, not an imperative, as it is made by the C. punctuation, and "heart" is a subject, not a vocative.

I. 2. 170. I would not haue your Enemy say so ; F. I would
not hear your enemy say so, C. cet. par., "have" is more euphoni-
ous than "hear," by reason of "ear" in next line, Nor shall you
doe mine eare that violence,

I. 2. 171. mine eare F. my ear C.

I. 2. 177. I pray thee doe not mock me (fellow Student) F.
I prethee, etc. C. The F. reading suits the required deliberateness
of the expression better.   There is an earnest entreaty meant.

I. 2. 183. Ere I had euer seene that day *Horatio.* F. Or ever
I had seen etc. C. The F. reading is better again for the preceding reason.

I. 2. 191. The King my Father? F. The king my father ! C.
This should be uttered with an inquiring wonder, which is better
expressed by the ?

I. 2. 204. Whilst they bestil'd Almost to Ielly F. whilst they,
distill'd Almost to jelly C. "bestil'd" seems to be used as a strong
form of 'still'd," as the next line, "Stand dumbe and speake not
to him," shows. I get no meaning out of the other word.

I. 2. 232. Pale, or red? F. Pale or red? C. The absence of
the comma in the C. mars the meaning. Hamlet must be supposed to utter "Pale" as a thing of course, paleness being the
conventional idea attached to a ghost. The word should be
uttered with a falling inflection, and then "or red" added, after
a pause, with a certain anxious impatience : Pale, was he? or red ;
how was it?   In other words, he hasn't the two ideas, "pale" and
"red" in his mind at once ; when he first speaks, he has only that
of "Pale" upon which his voice rests. He then adds, somewhat
impatiently, "or red?"   A semicolon would mark the division
better than a comma.

I. 2. 239.   His Beard was grisly? no.   F.   His beard was griz-zled? no?   C.   Hamlet is subjecting his friends to a searching examination, and when he asks the question, "His Beard was grisly?" he adds, with decision, "no," as though he had caught them on this point.   "no" should be read with a strong down-ward inflection.   To show that he has not been caught, Horatio gives a specific reply, "It was as I have seen it in his life, *A sable silver'd.*"

I. 2. 241.   Ile watch to Night; F.   I will watch to-night; C. The "I" is strongly emphatic here, and it can be better made so in "I'll" than in "I will."   It seems, too, that the abbre-viated form suits better Hamlet's off-hand mode of speech with his friends.

I. 2. 242.   I warrant you it will.   F.   I warrant it will.   C.

I. 2. 252.   *All.* Our duty to your Honour.   *Ham.* Your loue, as mine to you: F.   Your loves, etc.   C.   "loue" is better, being used as opposed to "duty:" "love" should be uttered with a slow and deliberate downward wave: your love, I ask; I don't wish you to act from a sense of duty alone, I ask your love in the matter.   The old Quarto of 1603 throws light on the true mean-ing: "Our duties to your honor.   *Ham.* O your loues, your loues."   There is something similar in the 162d and 163d lines of this scene: *Hor.* The same my Lord, And your poore Seruant euer.   *Ham.* Sir my good *friend,* Ile change *that* name with you: F.   The italics are mine.   Hamlet, though always princely, is impatient of certain conventional courtesies.

I. 2. 254.   My Fathers Spirit in Armes?   F.   My father's spirit in arms !   C.   Here the ? is again better than the !   "Arms" should be uttered with a strong interrogative intonation, expressive of an *inquiring* wonder.

I. 2. 257.   foule deeds will rise, Though all the earth orewhelm them to mens eies.   F.   foul deeds will rise, Though all the earth o'erwhelm them, to men's eyes.   C.   It is questionable as to whether the phrase, "to men's eyes," should be connected with "rise" in the preceding verse, or with "o'erwhelm."   A reader finds it awkward to connect it with "rise." The omission of the comma in the F. after "them," thus connecting "to men's eyes" with "o'erwhelm," makes equally good sense and adapts the construction of the sentence better to its vocal expression.

I. 3. 1.   My necessaries are imbark't; F. embark'd: C. There is no authority in the old editions for "embark'd." The 2d, 3d, and 4th Quartos read "inbark't;" the 5th and 6th, imbark't; the 1st and 2d Folios, "imbark't," the 3d and 4th, "imbark'd." As applied to things, "imbark't" or "inbark't" seems preferable to "embark'd."

I. 3. 5.   For *Hamlet,* and the trifling of his fauours, F. favour, C.

I. 3. 8.   Froward, not permanent; F. Forward, C.

I. 3. 10.   No more but so. F. No more but so? C. Here the C. follows Rowe's pointing. The Quartos and Folios all have a period. This speech of Ophelia is certainly meant to express her submissiveness to her brother's opinion and not to question the correctness of it.

I. 3. 12.   his Temple F. this temple C. "his," in the F. stands for "nature:" as nature's temple grows, the service within widens. There is a metaphor implied. Nature does not grow only in thews and bulk, but as nature's temple waxes in thews and bulk, the inward service of the mind and soul grows wide withal.

I. 3. 21.   The sanctity and health of the weole State. F. The safety and health of this whole state, C. "sanctity" is better than "safety," and "the" than "this," "state" being used abstractly.

I. 3. 34.   And keepe within the reare of your Affection; F. And keep you in the rear of your affection, C. "within" as opposed to "without," or outside of.

I. 3. 40.   the buttons F. their buttons C.

I. 3. 46.   watchmen F. watchman C. The plural seems better as referring to the several particulars of Laertes's advice.

I. 3. 55.   Yet heere *Laertes ?* F. Yet here, Laertes ! C. The

? is better. The speech should be uttered to express an inquiring surprise.

1. 3. 57. The winde sits in the shoulder of your saile, And you are staid for there : my blessing with you ; F. And you are stay'd for. There ; my blessing with thee ! C. The punctuation of the C. is Theobald's, who in accordance with his understanding of "there," added the stage direction, "Laying his hand on Laertes's head." But " there " certainly means at the port, where the ship is all ready to sail, and the attendants are waiting for him. In the 83d line, Polonius says : " The time inuites yoû, goe, your seruants tend."

1. 3. 59. See thou Character. F. Look thou character. C.

1. 3. 62. The friends thou hast, and their adoption tride, Grapple them to thy Soule, with hoopes of Steele : F. Those friends thou hast, C. The use of "them" in next verse, makes " The " preferable to "Those" which serves to strengthen the pleonasm.

2. 3. 68. thine eare ; F. thy ear, C.

1. 3. 106. That you haue tane his tenders for true pay, F. these tenders C. "his" is decidedly better in the connection.

1. 3. 109. Tender your selfe more dearly ; Or not to crack the winde of the poore Phrase, Roaming it thus, you'l tender me a foole. F. Running it thus — C. The C. reading is after Dyce (Collier conj.). It is not authorized by any of the Quartos, all of which read "Wrong," or of the Folios, all reading "Roaming," which is probably right, Polonius having reference to his varying the application of the word " tender."

1. 3. 120. For this time Daughter, Be somewhat scanter of your Maiden presence ; F. From this time be something scanter, etc. C. It may be that " For this " = For[th] this, the final *th* of " Forth " being absorbed, in pronounciation, in the initial *th* of " this," a kind of absorption not unfrequent in Shakespeare. The F. verse, moreover, scans better : You must | not take | for fire. | For this | time Daught | er, In the scanning of the C. verse, " fire " must be made dissyllabic, and " From " a

heavy syllable : You must | not take | for fi | re.   From | this
time.   It will be observed, too, that the speech in which the verse
occurs, is characterized by the double endings, and the F. verse
is more in keeping therewith.

  I. 3. 127–131.

> " Doe not beleeue his vowes ; for they are Broakers,
> Not of the eye, which their Inuestments show :
> But meere implorators of vnholy Sutes,
> Breathing like sanctified and pious bonds,
> The better to beguile." F.

Not of that dye which their investments show, C. The reading
of the C. is after the 6th Quarto, 1637. The 2d, 3d, 4th, and
5th, Quartos read " that die," the Folios, " the eye," which is
most probably right, " eye " being used, by metonymy, for " aspect," " hue," " shade of colour."

  I. 3. 130.   Breathing like sanctified and pious bawds, C. after
Pope, ed. 2 (Theobald). The Quartos and Folios all agree in
reading " bonds," which makes good sense. The general term
" bonds," suggested, no doubt, by " brokers," is used for the more
special term, " vows." " Breathing " refers back to " they," standing for " vows " ; " bonds," involving the idea of " vows," should
not receive the stress, in reading, which should be given to
" pious."

  I. 4. 5.   Indeed I heard it not : then it drawes neere the season, Wherein the Spirit held his wont to walke. F.   Indeed ? I
heard it not : it then etc. C. The ? of the C. is after Capell ;
the 2d, 3d, 4th, and 5th, Quartos read " Indeed ; I " the 1st
Quarto and all the Folios, " Indeed I " the 6th Quarto, " Indeed,
I " The use of the ? after " Indeed " imports an inquiring surprise which is not intended.

  I. 4. 17–38.   Omitted in F. The last three lines of this passage, which all the commentators have regarded as corrupt, the
editors of the C. have left unaltered " because," as they say, Note
VI., " none of the conjectures proposed appear to be satisfactory."

> " the dram of eale
> Doth all the noble substance of a doubt
> To his own scandal."

" eale," whether it be a corrupt form of " ill " or " evil," or whatever it be, stands, as a general term, for " some vicious mole in
nature," the " habit that too much o'er-leavens the form of plausive
manners," the " one defect," just alluded to by Hamlet. All the
difficulty of the passage is removed, I think, by understanding
" noble," not as an adjective, as all the commentators have understood it, qualifying " substance," but as a noun opposed to " eale,"
and the object of " substance," a verb of which " doth " is auxiliary. Thus : "the dram of eale doth all the noble, substance
of" [*i.e.,* "with," a sense common in the English of the time,] "a
doubt " [which works] " to his own scandal." " Substance " is
used in the sense of " imbue with a certain essence " ; " his " is a
neuter genitive, standing for " noble," and = " its." The dram of
ill *transubstantiates* the noble, *essences* it to its own scandal. In
regard to the uses of " of " and " to," see Abbott's " Shakespearian
Grammar," rev. and enl. ed., §§ 171 and 186.

The use of " substance," in the sense of " essence," was, of
course, sufficiently common, and had been for more than two centuries, to justify the interpretation given. In Macbeth, 1. 5. 48,
we have " sightless substances " = " invisible essences," " sightless" being used objectively. " Being of one substance with the
Father." — " Book of Common Prayer." Chaucer, in " The Pro-
loge of Nonne Prestes Tale " (l. 14,809 of Tyrwhitt's edition, l.
16,289 of Wright's) uses the word to express the *essential* character or nature of a man. The Host objects to the Monk's Tale, as
being too dull for the occasion ; and, that the fault may not be
thought to lie in himself, says,

> " And wel I wot the substance is in me,
> If eny thing schal wel reported be."

That is, I am so *substanced*, so constituted, so tempered, such is
my *cast* of spirit, that I can appreciate and enjoy, as well as the

next man, a good story well told. Whether "substance" can ɔe found, in this sense, as a verb, matters not. The free functional application of words which characterized the Elizabethan English, allowed, as every English scholar knows, of the use of any noun, adjective, or neuter verb, as an active verb.* See Abbott's "Shakespearian Grammar."

1. 4. 42. Be thy euents wicked or charitable, F. Be thy intents C. "events" = issues. The meaning is, not that Hamlet attributes any *intents* to the ghost, but that the ghost's appearance is to him the prognostic of certain *issues* or events ; "thy" is the personal, and not the possessive adjective, pronoun ; in other words, it is used objectively.

1. 4. 63. then will I follow it. F. then I will C.

1. 4. 78. It wafts me still : F. It waves me still. C. "Whom Fortune with her Iuory hand wafts to her," Timon of Athens, 1. 1. 73.

1. 4. 80. Hold off your hand. F. hands. C.

1. 4. 84. Still am I cal'd? F. Still am I call'd : C. The ? is better. Am I still called and do I trifle here? unhand me, gentlemen ; By heaven, I'll make a ghost of him that lets me.

1. 5. 22. list Hamlet, oh list, F. List, list, O, list ! C.

1. 5. 26. Murther? F. Murder ! C.

1. 5. 35 and 59. mine Orchard, F. my orchard, C.

1. 5. 40. O my Propheticke soule : mine Vncle? F. my uncle ! C. The ? better represents the proper elocution.

1. 5. 75. Of Life, of Crowne, and Queene at once dispatcht ; F. Of life, of crown, of queen, C.

1. 5. 80. Oh horrible, Oh horrible, most horrible : F. O, horrible ! O, horrible ! most horrible ! C. The "Cambridge" editors make no distinction between the emotional interjection, "Oh," and the "O" vocative, but print both "O." It can be seen, I think, that the distinction was intended to be made in the F. ; the use

---

* This interpretation I communicated, in the main, to "Notes and Queries," some years ago. But I did not then recognize an important element in it that the pronoun "his" is a neuter genitive, standing for "noble" used as a noun.

of " Oh " and " O " is, however, quite irregular there. But in a modernized text, consistency requires that the distinction should be made, as it is one that is observed in modern orthography. It is a distinction, too, not merely factitious, as might be supposed, but based on good ground. "There is a difference between 'O sir!' 'O King!' and 'Oh! sir,' 'Oh! Lord,' both in sense and pronunciation. As to the sense, the *O* prefixed merely imparts to the title a vocative effect; while the *Oh* conveys some particular sentiment, as of appeal, entreaty, expostulation, or some other. And as to the sound, the *O* is enclitic;[*] that is to say, it has no accent of its own, but is pronounced with the word to which it is attached, as if it were its unaccented first syllable. The term Enclitic signifies 'reclining on,' and so the interjection *O* in 'O Lord' reclines on the support afforded to it by the accentual elevation of the word 'Lord.' So that 'O Lord' is pronounced like such a dissyllable as *alight, alike, away ;* in which words the metrical stroke could never fall on the first syllable. *Oh !* on the contrary, is one of the fullest of monosyllables, and it would be hard to place it in a verse except with the stress upon it. The example from Wordsworth illustrates this.

> "'But she is in her grave, — and oh
> The difference to me!'"

—Earle's "Philology of the English Tongue," 2d ed. pp. 191–92.

1. 5. 91. Adue, adue, *Hamlet :* remember me. F. Adieu, adieu, adieu ! remember me. C. The addressing his son by name at the conclusion of his speech is more effective from its familiarity, than the third repetition of "adieu."

1. 5. 95 and 97. Remember thee? F. Remember thee ! C.

1. 5. 114–116. *Hor.* Heauen secure him. *Mar.* So be it. *Hor.* Illo, ho, ho, my lord. *Ham.* Hillo, ho, ho, boy; come bird, come. F.

Hor. Heaven secure him ! *Ham.* So be it ! *Mar.* Illo, ho, ho, my lord ! *Ham.* Hillo, ho, ho, boy ! come, bird, come. C.

---

[*] "Proclitic" would be the better word here.

The disposition of the speeches in the F. is the best.   Marcellus seconds Horatio's " Heaven secure him," with his "So be it " ; Horatio, then, as Hamlet's bosom friend, uses the falconer's call, which would have been too familiar on the part of Marcellus, and Hamlet, in his excitement, responds in the same language.

I. 5. 119.   *Ham.*   No you'l reueale it.   F.   No ; you will reveal it.   C.   The more off-hand "you'll " is preferable here.

I. 5. 129.   desires F.   desire C.

I. 5. 130.   For euery man ha's businesse F.   hath C.

I. 5. 135–6.   *Hor.*   There's no offence my Lord.   *Ham.*   Yes, by Saint *Patricke,* but there is my Lord, F. . . . but there is, Horatio, C.   The " my Lord " in Hamlet's speech is a retort to the "my Lord" in Horatio's speech, and it has an effect which is lost in the C. reading ; " is " should receive a strong accent, " my Lord" being uttered enclitically.

I. 5. 137.   And much offence too, touching this Vision heere : It is an honest Ghost, that let me tell you : F.   And much offence too.   Touching this vision here, It is an honest ghost, that let me tell you : C.

The punctuation of the C., a period after " too," has no Q. nor F. authority, all the editions having a comma after "too," except the 6th Quarto, which has a colon.   Horatio, of course, means that he intended no offence to Hamlet, in saying "These are but wild and hurling words, my Lord " ; and Hamlet, in his reply, flies off, and speaks with reference to the offence or wrong which, he has just learned, has been done to his father: "Yes, by Saint *Patricke,* but there is my Lord, And much offence too, touching this Vision heere : " he then adds, " It is an honest Ghost, that let me tell you " : but more than that he'll not tell : " For your desire to know what is betweene vs, O'remaster't as you may."

I. 5. 154.   Neuer to speake of this that you haue seene. Sweare by my sword. F.   The C. has a comma after " seen," thus subordinating the clause, " Never . . . seen," to " swear by my sword."   In the first place such an inversion of the construction is awkward ; and in the second place, the speech doesn't hitch on to the preceding speech so well.   Horatio asks Hamlet to propose the oath, which he does, namely, " Never to speak of this that you have seen," and then, having proposed the oath, he tells them to swear by his sword, which is additional.

I. 5. 157–160. " Come hither Gentlemen, And lay your hands againe vpon my sword, Neuer to speake of this that you haue heard : Sweare by my Sword." F. " Come hither, gentlemen, And lay your hands again upon my sword : Never to speak of this that you have heard, Swear by my sword." C. Here the C. construes again, as in line 154, the clause " Never to speak of this that you have heard," with " Swear by my sword." But the true meaning is certainly that indicated by the punctuation of the F. : "lay your hands again upon my sword, never to speak of this that you have heard." The "Swear by my sword" is but a repetition of the same idea.

I. 5. 162. "Well said old Mole, can'st worke i' th' ground so fast?" F. "Well said, old Mole ! canst work i' the earth so fast?" C. " ground " seems preferable with reference to " mole."

I. 5. 167. "There are more things in Heauen and Earth, *Horatio*, Then are dream't of in our Philosophy" F. your philosophy. C. Hamlet and Horatio had been fellow-students at the University; this may explain the use of " our." Or it would be better, perhaps, to understand Hamlet as using it in the general sense of *human* philosophy, which is limited in its scope. Why he should say " your," does not appear; but it may be ethical.

I. 5. 173. That you at such time seeing me, F. That you, at such times seeing me, C. " time " suits the context better, and " such time seeing " is less harsh than " *such* time*s* *s*eeing."

I. 5. 174. neuer shall With Armes encombred thus, or thus, head shake ; F. never shall, With arms encumber'd thus, or this head-shake, C. The Quartos 1–5 have " this head shake." The hyphen of the C. is after Theobald ; the 6th Quarto reads " head thus shak't." The construction of the C. reading is imperfect, " shall " having no verb connected with it ; according to the F., " shake " is a verb, having " shall " as its auxiliary : never shall, with arms encumbered thus, or thus, (suiting the action to the word,) head shake.

2. 1. 70.   Good my Lord. F.   Good my lord ! C. after Dyce.
The Quartos and Folios all have a period after " Lord." This
speech seems to express the simple assent of Reynaldo to what
Polonius has said. The ! is not required. To the next item of
Polonius's advice, he replies, " I shall my Lord "; and to the
next, " Well, my Lord."

2. 1. 99.   helpe ; F.   helps, C.

2. 2. 5.   so I call it, F.   so call it, C.

2. 2. 10.   I cannot deeme of. F.   I cannot dream of : C.

2. 2. 12.   so Neighbour'd to his youth, and humour, F.   so
neighbour'd to his youth and haviour, C.   More force in the F.
word " humour " which must be taken in its earlier sense of " temper of mind," " disposition."

2. 2. 16.   Occasions F.   occasion C.

2. 2. 43.   Assure you, my good Liege, F.   I assure my good
liege, C.   Feeble.

2. 2. 111, 112.   but you shall heare these in her excellent white
bosome, these. F.   but you shall hear.   Thus : " In her excellent
white bosom, these, &c."   C.   It would seem that the first " these "
in the F. is right, the second being a mere repetition for emphasis ;
so that all that is wanting in the F. is a colon after " heare."
" These in her excellent white bosom, these : "   The expression
is evidently directive or optative, and given as an introduction to
" *Doubt thou, the Starres are fire,*" etc.   There is a studied odd-
ness in the letter, as is shown by the subscription, " *whilst this
Machine is to him,* Hamlet."

2. 2. 151.   Do you thinke 'tis this? F.   Do you think this? C.
The F. reading suits better what precedes, and the reply of the
queen that follows, " It may be very likely."

2. 2. 173.   Excellent, excellent well : y'are a Fishmonger. F.
Excellent well ; you are a fishmonger. C.   The repetition of
" excellent " in the F. seems to express better the impatient,
don't-trouble-me mood of the speaker.   In 5. 2. 173. when the
obsequious courtier, Osric, whom he despises, takes leave of him,
there is a repetition of " yours " with the same contemptuous

coloring : *"Osr.* I commend my duty to your Lordship. *Ham.* Yours, yours ; " [*Exit Osric. Then turning to Horatio,*] "he does well to commend it himself, there are no tongues else for's turn."

2. 2. 175.   Honest, my Lord ? F.   Honest, my lord ! C.

2. 2. 180, 181.   *Ham.* For if the Sun breed Magots in a dead dogge, being a good kissing Carrion —— Haue you a daughter? F.   *Ham.* For if the sun breed maggots in a dead dog, being a god kissing carrion — Have you a daughter ? C.

The C. gives the following collation of readings (Qq standing for the Quartos but not including the 1st Q., 1603, Ff, the Folios) :

180.   Ham.] Ham. [reads].   Staunton.

181.   *god kissing carrion*] Hanmer (Warburton). *good kissing carrion* Qq Ff.   *god-kissing carrion* Malone conj.   *good, kissing carrion* Whiter conj.   *carrion-kissing god* Mitford conj.   *carrion* —]Ff.   *carrion.* Qq.

Dyce's note : P. 136 (57)   *"For if the sun breed maggots in a dead dog, being a good kissing carrion,"*

This passage is not in the quarto 1603. — The other old eds. have " —— *being a good kissing carrion.*" — I give Warburton's emendation, which, if over-praised by Johnson, (who called it a "noble" one,) at least has the merit of conveying something like a meaning. — That not even a tolerable sense can be tortured out of the original reading, we have proof positive in the various *explanations* of it by Whiter, Coleridge, Caldecott, Mr. Knight, and Delius. ("The carrion," says Mr. Knight with the utmost gravity, "the carrion is good at kissing — ready to return the kiss of the sun — 'Common kissing Titan,' and in the bitterness of his satire Hamlet associates the idea with the daughter of Polonius. Mr. Whiter, however, considers that *good,* the original reading, is correct ; but that the poet uses the word as a substantive —— the GOOD principle in the fecundity of the earth. In that case we should read 'being a good, kissing carrion.' " —— Equally outrageous in absurdity is the interpretation of Delius, which (translated for me by Mr. Robson) runs thus : "Hamlet calls the dog,

in which the sun breeds maggots, a good, kissing carrion ; alluding to the confiding, fawning manner of the dog towards his
master.   If the sun breeds maggots in a dead dog, which during
its lifetime was so attached, — what, says Hamlet, in his bitter
distrust [Misstrauen], and to annoy Polonius, might not the sun
breed in the equally tender Ophelia, who ought therefore not to
expose herself to the sun.") — "The Works of William Shakespeare.   The text revised by the Rev. Alexander Dyce.   In nine
Volumes.   Vol. VII.   Second edition.   London: 1868."   p. 223.

In "The Shakespeare Society's Papers.   Vol. II.   London:
printed for the Shakespeare Society.   1845."   Art. VII. — Conjectures on some of the corrupt or obscure passages of Shakespeare.   By Barron Field, Esq., pp. 41, 42, the author remarks :

"And we are indebted to Bishop Warburton, the most arbitrary,
but the most sagacious of critics, . . . for reading in 'Hamlet,'
'If the sun breed maggots in a dead dog, being a *God*-kissing carrion,' instead of a '*Good*,' as the old copies have it: 'a noble
emendation (Dr. Johnson calls it) which almost sets the critic on
a level with the author.'"

In a foot-note he adds (p. 42) :

"Mr. Collier and Mr. Knight retain 'good,' and understand the
dead dog to be the good kissing carrion ; but this seems to me
somewhat too much meaning for the words to be licensed to carry.
That the sun is the osculist, and not the dog, is confirmed by the
following passage from 1 Hen. IV. 2. 4. [113] : 'Didst thou
never see Titan kiss a dish of butter?' and by the phrase, 'common-kissing Titan,' in Cymbeline, 3. 4. [164]."

One thing can with certainty be assumed at the outset, namely,
that the Sun, "common-kissing Titan," is the "osculist," to use
Mr. Field's word, and not the carrion dog; "and now remains
that we find out the cause of the effect, or rather say, the cause of
the defect," in the several attempted explanations of the passage
in question.   That defect is due to one thing, and one thing only,
and that is, to the understanding of "kissing" as the present active
participle, and not as the verbal noun.   It is well known to all

English scholars that, in the early period of our language, there were distinct forms for the present active participle and the verbal noun, the former ending in Anglo-Saxon in -*ende,* and the latter in -*ung,* which endings became, respectively, -*end* (-*ende*), and -*ing* (-*inge*), in Middle English. This distinction between the participle and the verbal noun continued to be quite strictly observed until near the end of the 14th century. It is so observed in the earlier text of the Wycliffite versions of the Scriptures, and in Gower's " Confessio Amantis," the present participle terminating almost invariably in -*ende,* a few cases only occurring of the latter form in -*inge* (-*ing*). In Chaucer's works, which represent the most advanced stage of the language in his time, the present participle terminates, with very rare exceptions, in -*ing* or -*yng* (-*inge* or -*ynge*). Soon after the close of the 14th century, -*ing* became the common ending of the participle and the verbal noun. But it is often important to determine which is which, in reading an author of so contriving a spirit of expression as Shakespeare exhibits.

In the following passages, for example, the present active participle is used : " Life's but a walking shadow," Macbeth, 5. 5. 24 ; " Look, here comes a walking fire." King Lear, 3. 4. 110 ; " the dancing banners of the French." King John, 2. 1. 308 ; " my dancing soul doth celebrate This feast of battle with mine adversary." Richard II. 1. 3. 91 ; " labouring art can never ransom nature From her inaidable estate ; " All's Well that Ends Well, 2. 1. 116 ; " more busy than the labouring spider " 2 Henry VI. 3. 1. 339 : " And let the labouring bark climb hills of seas Olympus-high " Othello, 2. 1. 184 ; " thy parting soul ! " 1 Henry VI. 2. 5. 115 ; " parting guest " Troilus and Cressida, 3. 3. 166 ; " a falling fabric." Coriolanus, 3. 1. 247 ; " this breathing world," Richard III. 1. 1. 21 ; " O blessed breeding sun," Timon of Athens, 4. 3. 1.

But in the following passages the same words are verbal nouns used adjectively :

" a palmer's walking-staff," Richard II. 3. 3. 151 ; " you and I are past our dancing-days ; " Romeo and Juliet, 1. 5. 29 ; " you ought not walk Upon a labouring day " Julius Cæsar, 1. 1. 4 ; " ere I could Give him that parting kiss " Cymbeline, 1. 3. 34 ; " And say, what store of parting tears were shed ? "   Richard II. 1. 4. 5 ; " he hath the falling sickness."   Julius Cæsar, 1. 2. 252 ; " Cannot be quiet scarce a breathing while," Richard III. 1. 3. 60 ; " it is the breathing time of day with me ; " Hamlet, 5. 2. 165.

And now we are all ready for " kissing " :   In the following passages it is the participle :

" A kissing traitor."   Love's Labour's Lost, 5. 2. 592 ; " the greedy touch Of common-kissing Titan," Cymbeline, 3. 4. 164 ; " O, how ripe in show, Thy lips, those kissing cherries, tempting grow ! "   A Midsummer Night's Dream, 3. 2. 140.

" Kissing," in the last passage, might be taken for the verbal noun, meaning, for kissing, or, to be kissed ; but it must here be understood as the participle.   Demetrius speaks of the lips of Helena, as two ripe cherries that kiss, or lightly touch, each other. But to say of a pair of beautiful lips that they are good kissing lips, would convey quite a different meaning, — a meaning, however, which nobody would mistake :   " Kissing " in such expression, is the verbal noun used adjectively, and equivalent to " for kissing." And so the word is used in the passage in question :

" For if the sun breed Magots in a dead dogge, being a good kissing Carrion " —

That is, a dead dog being, not a carrion good *at* kissing, as Mr. Knight and others understand it, and which would be the sense of the word, as a present active participle, but a carrion good *for* kissing, or, to be kissed, by the sun, that thus breeds a plentiful crop of maggots therein, the *agency* of " breed " being implied in " kissing."   In reading this speech, the emphasis should be upon " kissing " and not upon " carrion," the idea of which last word is anticipated in " dead dog"; in other words, " kissing carrion " should be read as a compound noun, which in fact it is, the stress of sound falling on the member of the compound which bears the burden of the meaning.   The two words might, indeed, be hyphened, like " Kissing-comfits," in The Merry Wives of Windsor, 5. 5. 19.

The fact that all the Quartos and Folios perfectly agree in the expression "a good kissing carrion," is quite conclusive evidence that it is the correct reading, and that its meaning was plain to early readers and hearers. Had it been obscure, so obscure that "not even a tolerable sense," to use Dyce's words, could have been "tortured out of the original reading," it would no doubt have been tinkered into variations before Bishop Warburton made "the noble emendation which almost sets the critic on a level with the author." !

2. 2. 183–185. Conception is a blessing, but not as your daughter may conceive. Friend look too't. F. conception is a blessing; but as your daughter may conceive, — friend, look to't. C. The sentence is complete in the F. and the "not" is essential to Hamlet's obvious meaning. He says what he does to make the old man uneasy, meaning, that though conception is a blessing, in the legitimate way, it wouldn't be as his daughter might conceive — out of wedlock. Polonius, with his fossilized prudential wisdom, has had no living organs of discernment to perceive Hamlet's sensibility of principle and chastity of honor, and has feared that his daughter's relations with the prince "out of her star," would result in her shame. Hamlet's penetrating sagacity has revealed to him the old man's fears, and he accordingly plays upon them.

2. 2. 188. he is farre gone, farre gone : F. he is farre gone : C. The repetition in the F. is more effective, and very natural, too, for one speaking in Polonius's assured state of mind. There is, also, more of the old man in it.

2. 2. 197. their eyes purging thicke Amber, or Plum-Tree Gumme : F. . . . thick amber and plum-tree gum, C.

2. 2. 201. For you your selfe Sir, should be old as I am, if like a Crab you could go backward. F. for yourself, sir, shall grow old as I am, if like a crab you could go backward. C. It is not likely that the poet meant that Hamlet should talk nonsense in this passage, but rather that he should express himself in a way to puzzle the old man. As it stands in the F. it would seem that

"old" is used, not as opposed to "young," but as denoting age in general. So that the expression really means, "you yourself, sir, should be *young* as I am, if, like a crab, you could go backward." The sense is further obfuscated by speaking of the purely ideal going backward in time under the purely literal image of going backward like a crab.

2. 2. 205. *Pol.* will you walke Out of the ayre my Lord? *Ham.* Into my grave? F. Into my grave. C. There can be no question of the correctness of the ? in the F. Hamlet's speech, paraphrased, would be, "You ask me to walk out of the air : would you have me walk into my grave?" Hamlet's replies to those persons of the play whom he dislikes or despises, the King, Polonius, and the courtiers, are characterized by their literalness. When the King asks, "How fares our cousin Hamlet?" Hamlet replies, "Excellent, i' faith ; of the chameleon's dish : I eat the air, promise-crammed : you cannot feed capons so." When he asks Osric, "What's his [Laertes's] weapon?" and Osric replies, "Rapier and dagger," Hamlet replies, "That's two of his weapons."

2. 2. 206. Indeed that is out o' th' Ayre : F. Indeed, that's out of the air. C. The proper elocution requires that "is" be made emphatic, which it cannot be if contracted as in the C.

2. 2. 217. *Polon.* You goe to seeke my Lord Hamlet ; there he is. F.   . . . the Lord Hamlet ; C.

2. 2. 219–222. *Guild.* .Mine honour'd Lord? *Ros.* My most deare Lord? *Ham.* My excellent good friends? How do'st thou *Guildensterne ?* Oh, *Rosincrane ;* good Lads : How doe ye both? F. *Guil.* My honoured lord ! *Ros.* My most dear lord ! *Ham.* My excellent good friends ! How dost thou, Guildenstern? Ah, Rosencrantz ! Good lads, how do you both? C. The ? of the F. represents the elocution better than the ! of the C. It would appear from the F. reading, that Hamlet, when addressing Rosencrantz and Guildenstern, gives his attention to the latter, saying, after the common address, "How dost thou Guildenstern?" before recognizing Rosencrantz ; the "Oh," in

" Oh Rosincrane " involves a friendly apology. There seems to
be a certain playfulness in the " How do *ye* both? " of the F.,
which is not in the " How do *you* both ? " of the C.

2. 2. 229. *Ham.* Then you liue about her waste, or in the
middle of her fauour? F. Then you live about her waist, or in
the middle of her favours? C. There is a word play intended in
the use of " favour " which is precluded by the plural form of the
C.; " favour " is used equivocally in the sense of " face," " countenance," for which the plural " favours " could not be used, and in
the sense of " propitiousness."

2. 2. 238. *Guil.* Prison, my Lord? F. Prison, my lord ! C.

2. 2. 336. (as it is like most if their meanes are no better) F.
— as it is most like, if their means are no better, — C. This passage does not occur in the Quartos. The change of "like most "
to " most like " adopted by the C., was made by Pope. But
" like most " may be what the poet wrote, in the sense of " like-
liest," " most " being used as a suffix, as in " foremost," " mid-
most," ".inmost," etc.

2. 2. 238. there ha's bene much to do on both sides : F.
there has been much to do on both sides, C. In a modernized
edition, " to do " should be hyphened, the two words being used
together as a substantive. " In place of this *to-do* the King's
English accepted a composition, part French, part English, and
hence the substantive *ado.*" — Earle's " Philology of the English
Tongue," 2d ed. p. 420. But see Skeat's " Etymological Dictionary," *s.v.* " ado," where the correct etymology is given of the
word.

2. 2. 354. Let me comply with you in the Garbe, F. This
garb, C. " the " is used in the F. generically, and makes the
better sense.

2. 2. 369. for a Monday morning 'twas so indeed. F. o'Monday morning ; 'twas so, indeed. C. " o' " is after Capell ; the
Quartos read " a," the 1st, 2d, and 3d, Folios, " for a," the 4th,
" for on." The 2d and 3d Quartos have a comma after " morning," the 4th, 5th, and 6th, and the Folios, have no point.

2. 2. 376. Vpon mine Honor. F.   Upon my honour, — C.
In the use of the dash, the C. follows Rowe. But the sense is
apparently complete.   All the Quartos and Folios have a period.

2. 2. 381–3. *Seneca* cannot be too heauy, nor *Plautus* too
light, for the law of Writ, and the Liberty.   These are the onely
men. F. Seneca cannot be too heavy, nor Plautus too light.
For the law of writ and the liberty, these are the only men. C.
The pointing of the C. is Theobald's.   The 2d, 3d, 4th, and 5th,
Quartos have no point after "light" and a colon after "liberty";
the Folios all have a comma after "light" and a period after
"liberty"; the 6th Quarto and Quarto (1676) have no point
after "light" and a semicolon after "liberty."   All the Quartos
and Folios, therefore, connect in construction, "for the law of
writ and the liberty," with Seneca and Plautus, and not with
"these are the only men," which evidently refers to the actors
he's talking about.   "Liberty" should be construed with "law":
the law and the liberty of writ [writing].   And "law" and "liberty"
seem to refer, respectively, to "heavy" and "light."   This respective construction is frequent in Shakespeare.   See Macbeth, 1. 3.
60, 61 ; Hamlet, 3. 1. 151 ; Winter's Tale, 3. 2. 160–162 ; Antony and Cleopatra, 3. 2. 15–18 ; 4. 15. 25, 26 ; Comedy of Errors,
2. 2. 112–117 ; The Tempest, 1. 2. 335, 336 ; Midsummer Night's
Dream, 3. 1. 98–101.

2. 2. 401. For looke where my Abridgements come. F. . . .
my abridgement comes. C.   The singular is used in all the
Quartos, and the plural in all the Folios, and it would seem that
they were used with a different understanding of their meaning;
"my abridgement," they who will cut short my talk, "my" being
used objectively ; "my Abridgements," they who are, as Hamlet
calls them further on in the Scene, ll. 501, 502, "the Abstracts
and breefe Chronicles of the time," "my" being ethical.

2. 2. 403. O my olde Friend? F.   O, my old friend! C.   The
? is better. The speech should be uttered with an interrogative
intonation expressive of a pleasant surprise.   So 405, 406. What,
my young Lady and Mistris? F.   The C. employs a ! again.

2. 2. 406. neerer Heauen F. nearer to heaven C.

2. 2. 424. One cheefe Speech in it, I cheefely lou'd, F. One speech in it I chiefly loved: C.

2. 2. 438. a tyrannous, and damned light F. a tyrannous and a damned light. C. The repetition of "a" makes two distinct lights.

2. 2. 501. the Abstracts and breefe Chronicles of the time, F. the abstract and brief chronicles of the time: C.

2. 2. 503. while you liued. F. while you live. C.

2. 2. 506. and who should scape whipping: F. and who shall 'scape whipping? C. The conditional "should" is better after the postulate "use every man after his desert."

2. 2. 521. *Rosin.* Good my Lord. F. Good my lord! C. The period is better. Rosencrantz simply assents to what Hamlet has just said, "I'll leave you till night."

2. 2. 526. whole conceit, F. own conceit C.

2. 2. 558. I [*i.e.*, Ay] sure, this is most braue, F. This is most brave, C. The "I sure" of the F. adds to the irony of the expression.

3. 1. 63. That Flesh is heyre too? 'Tis F. That flesh is heir to, 'tis C. The punctuation of the F. is preferable. After the reflection that death is no more than a sleep, the question arises in Hamlet's mind as to whether by a sleep we shall end the heart-ache, and the thousand natural shocks that flesh is heir to. On which he reflects, "'Tis a consummation Devoutly to be wish'd."

3. 1. 71. the poore mans Contumely, F. the proud man's contumely, C. The Quartos all read "proud," the Folios, "poor." In the two expressions, the genitive is differently used: in the first, it is objective, "the poor man's contumely," meaning the contumely or contemptuous treatment the poor man suffers; in the second, it is subjective, "the proud man's contumely" meaning the contumely or contemptuous treatment the proud man exercises.

3. 1. 72. The pangs of dispriz'd Loue, the F. The pangs of despised love, the C. "dispriz'd" is the reading of the Folios ; 2d and 3d Quartos, "despiz'd"; 4th and 5th Quartos, "office, and the"; "mispriz'd" Collier MS. (erased). It would be hard to decide as to the relative force of the two words "dispriz'd" and "despised." But, perhaps, a disprized or undervalued love, a love that is only partially appreciated and responded to, would be apt to suffer more pangs than a despised love.

3. 1. 76. Who would these Fardles beare F. who would fardels bear, C. "these Fardles" is the reading of all the Folios; according to the C. reading, which is that of the Quartos, "fardels" means something additional to what Hamlet has enumerated in the six preceding lines, "the whips and scorns of time," "the oppressor's wrong," "the poor man's contumely," etc.; but according to the F. reading, "fardels" represents all these. It would seem that, having said, ll. 70 *et seq.,* "who would bear," (the several things he *specifies,*) he repeats "who would bear," with the *general* object, "fardels," (representing all the special ones,) for the purpose of introducing the exceptive clause, "But that the dread of something after death, . . . puzzles the will," etc. Besides, the general term "fardels" when not identified in meaning, by the use of "these," with the preceding specifications, comes in somewhat flat. The F. reading seems altogether the best.

3. 1. 86. And enterprizes of great pith and moment, F. . . . of great pitch and moment C. Independently of the authority for "pith," namely, all the Folios and the players' Quartos of 1676, 1683, 1695, 1703, "pitch" and "moment" haven't the congruity that "pith" and "moment" have, more especially, too, if "moment" be understood as retaining some of its original force of "momentum." The greater congruity of "pith" and "moment" than of "pitch" and "moment" will be seen by Shakespeare's uses of these words in the following passages : "that's my pith of business 'Twixt you and your poor brother." Meas. for Meas. 1. 4. 70 ; "Perhaps you mark'd not what's the pith of all." T. of the S. 1. 1. 161 ; "grandsires, babies, and old women, Either past

or not arrived to pith and puissance;" Hen. V. 3. 1. Chorus, 21;
"The pith and marrow of our attribute." Ham. 1. 4. 22; "For
since these arms of mine had seven years' pith," Othel. 1. 3. 83;
"pithy and effectual," T. of the S. 1. 1. 66; "An oath is of no
moment, being not took Before a true and lawful magistrate," 3
Hen. VI. 1. 2. 22; "I have seen her die twenty times upon far
poorer moment:" A. and C. 1. 2. 137. And does not "pith"
suit the idea of "currents" better, in the next line? The editors
of the C. remark, Note XVI., "In this doubtful passage we have
retained the reading of the Quartos, although the players' Quartos
of 1676, 1683, 1695, 1703, have, contrary to their custom, followed the Folios, which may possibly indicate that 'pith' was the
reading according to the stage tradition."

3. 1. 87. their Currants turne away, F. their currents turn
awry C. "turn away" expresses more of an entire *change* of
current, which is Hamlet's idea, than does "turn awry."

3. 1. 89. The faire *Ophelia ?* F. The fair Ophelia ! C.

3. 1. 94. I pray you now, receiue them. F. I pray you, now
receive them. C. Having longed long to re-deliver his remembrances, she, now that the opportunity is afforded, prays him to
receive them. The pointing of the F. is the more correct. Even
the very different reading of the First Quarto indicates the bearing
of "now": "My Lord, I haue sought opportunitie, which *now* I
haue, to redeliuer to your worthy handes, a small remembrance."

3. 1. 97. I know right well you did F. you know right well
you did; C. The F. reading is the more significant. Ophelia's
meaning is, the remembrances you gave me, may have been trifles
to *you*, such trifles as left no impression on your mind of your
having given them; but *I* know right well you did, as they were
most dear to me at the time, accompanied as they were with
expressions of affection. "I" should be read with a strong upward circumflex.

3. 1. 158. Like sweet Bels iangled out of tune, and harsh, F.
Like sweet bells jangled, out of tune and harsh; C. All the
Quartos and Folios agree in having a comma after "tune" (Qq

time) ; the pointing of the C. is Capell's.   The phrase " out of
tune " is certainly an adverbial element to "jangled" and not an
adjective element to " sweet bells."   The two ideas attached to
" bells " are 1. "jangled out of tune "; 2. " harsh," which expresses to what extent "jangled out of tune."

3. 1. 178.   How now *Ophelia?* F.   How now, Ophelia ! C.

3. 1. 183.   To shew his Greefes : F.   To show his grief : C.
" Greefes " is used here in the sense of grievances.   So further on
in the play,   3. 2. 323, "if you deny your greefes to your Friend."

3. 2. 8.   to see a robustious Pery-wig-pated Fellow, teare a
Passion to tatters, F.   to hear . . . C.   The tearing of a passion
to tatters by a robustious periwig-pated fellow, is more addressed
to the eye than to the ear.   His robustiousness and his periwig-
patedness are *seen* alone, as are also the distortions through which
he endeavors to exhibit the passion ; it is only what he *says* that
is addressed to the ear.

3. 2. 12.   I could haue such a Fellow whipt F.   I would
. . . C.

3. 2. 51.   O my deere Lord. F.   O, my dear lord,— C.   The
Quartos and Folios all agree in having a period after " Lord."
The dash of the C., indicating an interrupted speech, is after
Rowe.   The context shows that no interruption is intended.
Horatio must be supposed to say " O my dear Lord " in a way
expressive of a feeling of being flattered by what Hamlet has just
said, " Horatio, thou art e'en as just a man As e'er my conversation coped withal," uttering " O " and " Lord " with a downward
circumflex, and Hamlet replies, " Nay, do not think I flatter : "
etc.

3. 2. 59, 60.   Since my deere Soule was Mistris of my choyse,
And could of men distinguish, her election Hath seal'd thee for
her selfe. F.   The C. follows the pointing of the F. in having a
comma after " distinguish."   The Quartos read, " distinguish her
election, S'hath " (Shath Quartos 4th and 5th, Sh'ath Quarto 6th) ;
" distinguish her election " is decidedly Shakespearian, and may
be what the poet wrote.   The use of a cognate accusative is a

marked feature of Shakespeare's diction. "of men," too, joins
better to "election" than to "distinguish." The C. reads "her
choice," after the Quartos.

3. 2. 60–63. For thou hast bene As one in suffering all, that
suffers nothing. A man that Fortunes buffets, and Rewards Hath
'tane with equall Thankes. F. . . . Hast ta'en with equal thanks:
C. The C. follows the Quartos here in spite of the solecism in
the use of "Hast." Though the subject-nominative "thou" is 2d
person, the predicate-nominative "man" is 3d person, and being
the antecedent of the relative "that," determines the person of
the verb to which "that" is the nominative or subject.

3. 2. 72. the Circumstance Which I haue told thee, of my
Father's death. F. The C., following the Quartos, omits the
comma after "thee"; it serves to show that the phrase "of my
father's death" is connected with "circumstance" and not with
"told," and, in neat pointing, should not be omitted.

3. 2. 73–75. I prythee, when thou see'st that Acte a-foot, Euen
with the verie Comment of my Soule Obserue mine Vnkle: F.
. . . comment of thy soul Observe my uncle: C. after the Quartos.
The F. reading is the more expressive: Hamlet's meaning is, I
would have thee so enter into my feelings, so identify thyself with
me that, when thou seest that act a-foot, even with the very comment of *my* soul, thou wilt observe my uncle. The use of "my"
also gives force to "Even with the very," which has less force in
the other reading.

3. 2. 79, 80. Giue him needfull note, For I mine eyes will
riuet to his Face: F. "For" depends, for its force, on what
Hamlet says in the 74th and 75th lines, "Even with the very comment of my soul Observe mine Uncle:" then having again enjoined Horatio to "Give him needful note," or as the Quartos
have it, which the C. follows, "heedful note," he adds, "For I
mine eyes will *rivet* to his face:"

3. 2. 81, 82. And after we will both our iudgments ioyne, To
censure of his seeming. F. . . . In censure of his seeming. C.
after the Quartos. In the F. reading, "censure" is a noun, as it

is in the C.   For the force of "To," see Abbott's Shakespearian Grammar, rev. and enl. ed. § 186.

3. 2. 92–96.   *Ham.* . . . you plaid once i' th' Vniuersity, you say?   *Polon.* That I did my Lord, and was accounted a good Actor.   *Ham.* And what did you enact?   F.   What did you enact?   C. after the Quartos.   The F. reading has a touch of the contemptuous imparted to it by the initial word "And:"   "What, I pray, or forsooth, did *you* enact?"

3. 2. 194, 195.   The great man downe, you marke his fauourites flies, The poore aduanc'd, makes Friends of Enemies: F.   . . . you mark his favourite flies; C.   The plural "favourites" suits the context better; it is, in fact, demanded; and in regard to "flies," see Abbott's "Shakespearian Grammar," § 333, where this passage is quoted.

3. 2. 220.   *Qu.* The Lady protests to much me thinkes. F. The lady doth protest too much, methinks. C.   The more familiar "protests" is better here than "doth protest."

3. 2. 240.   *Ophe.* Still better and worse.   *Ham.* So you mistake Husbands. F.   So you must take your husbands. C.   So you must take your husband, 1st Quarto; the other Quartos, mistake your husbands.   The other Folios like the 1st.   There is a quibble evidently intended : so you mistake, or take amiss, husbands, *i.e.*, for better and worse.

3. 2. 250.   writ in choyce Italian. F.   This may be a case of absorption : the *-en* of the participle being present in "in."   But it's not necessary to understand it so.   The C. reads, after the Quartos, "written in very choice Italian:"

3. 2. 251.   Murtherer F.   This form of the word it would be well to retain; "murther," noun and verb, and "murtherer" were the usual forms of the English of the time.

3. 2. 262.   So runnes the world away. F.   Thus runs the world away. C. after the Quartos.   The more general and indefinite "So" seems preferable here to the formal "Thus."

3. 2. 292.   Your wisdome should shew it selfe more richer, to signifie this to his Doctor : F.   the doctor; C.

3. 2. 301–303. If it shall please you to make me a wholsome answer, I will doe your Mothers command'ment : if not, your pardon, and my returne shall bee the end of my Businesse. F . . . if not, your pardon and my return shall be the end of my business. C. Do the editors of the C., by omitting the comma after " pardon," mean to construe it with " return " ? That would certainly not give Rosencrantz' meaning, which the F. shows to be, " if you cannot give me a wholesome answer, pardon me for having troubled you, and my return shall be the end of my business."

3. 2. 322, 323. You do freely barre the doore of your owne Libertie, if you deny your greefs to your Friend. F. you do surely bar the door upon . . . C. " freely " = " of your own free will," perhaps as much as " wilfully."

3. 2. 329. to withdraw with you, why do you go about to re-couer the winde of mee, as if you would driue me into a toyle? F. To withdraw with you : — C. the rest like F. ; the Quartos all have a comma after "you," except the 6th, which has a semicolon. Taking the F. reading as it stands, it appears that Hamlet, after receiving the recorder from the attendant, steps aside, and as he does so, says to Guildenstern, " To withdraw with you," as an intimation of his wish to speak to him apart, and then continues, " why do you go about " etc. A similar example of this absolute use of the infinitive occurs, 4th Scene of this Act, l. 216 : " Come, sir, to draw toward an end with you."

3. 2. 341. *Ham.* 'Tis as easie as lying : F. It is as easy as lying : C.

3. 2. 343. it will discourse most excellent Musicke. F. most eloquent music. C. after the Quartos. I feel a certain seriousness — that's hardly the word — about " eloquent," not in keeping ; whereas, in the use of " excellent," there seems to be implied the idea, that the music that can be got out of the little instrument, is superior to what one would suspect. The word " excellent " should be pronounced with a downward circumflex on " ex-," imparting a patronizing tone.

3. 2. 347, 348. Why looke you now, how vnworthy a thing you

make of me : F. . . . you make of me ! C. The colon is used
in the F. as it quite uniformly is, before a specification when for-
mally introduced. The sentence is not exclamatory. Hamlet
simply invites Guildenstern's attention to what he is about to state.
The use of " now " seems also to indicate this.

3. 2. 352. There is much Musicke, excellent Voice, in this
little organe, yet cannot you make it. F. . . . yet cannot you
make it speak. C. The C. reads better, but the F. is not imperfect without " speak : " " it " stands for " music " or " voice."

3. 2. 354, 355. though you can fret me, you cannot play vpon
me. F. . . . yet you cannot play upon me. C. after the First
Quarto ; all the others, and the Folios, omit " yet." The use of
" yet " as the correlative of " though," adds to the formalness, and
takes away from the plain *decisiveness,* of the speech.

3. 2. 359, 360. Do you see that Clowd? that's almost in shape
like a Camell. F. Do you see yonder cloud that's almost in shape
of a camel? C.

3. 2. 361. By th' Misse, and it's like a Camell indeed. F.
By the mass, and 'tis like a camel, indeed. C. " Misse " may
have been a form of " Mass " in use, or an abbreviation of " Mis-
sal " ; *Lat.* missa.

3. 2. 381, 382. How in my words someuer she be shent, To
giue them Seales, neuer my Soule consent. F. soever C. never,
my soul, consent ! C. The absence of the commas in all the
Quartos and Folios, is correct, " consent " being, not an imperative, but a subjunctive, and " soul," a nominative, not a vocative.
See Abbott's "Shakespearian Grammar," §§ 364, 365. The pointing of the C. is after Capell.

3. 3. 5–7. The termes of our estate, may not endure Hazard
so dangerous as doth hourely grow Out of his Lunacies. F. *i.e.,*
Hazard as doth hourly grow so dangerous. The C. reads, Hazard
so near us etc.

3. 3. 14. That spirit vpon whose spirit depends and rests The
liues of many, F. That spirit upon whose weal depends and rests
The lives of many. C. after Quartos. Though the repetition of

" spirit " in the F. is somewhat awkward, there seems to have been a reason for departing from the reading of the Quartos. In the 3d line below, majesty is spoken of as a massy wheel, Fixt on the summit of the highest mount, etc. The clashing of the words " weal " and " wheel " may have led to the change.

3. 3. 77. I his foule Sonne, F. I, his sole son, C. after Quartos.

3. 3. 81. With all his Crimes broad blowne, as fresh as May, F. The metaphor involved is that of fresh, full-blown flowers in Spring; as flush as May; C. after Quartos; " flush " is, perhaps, the more forcible term.

3. 3. 91. At gaming, swearing, F. At game, a-swearing, C.

3. 4. 4. Ile silence me e'ene heere: F. I'll sconce me even here. C. "sconce " has no authority, while "silence," which makes excellent sense, is the reading of all the Quartos and Folios. The editors of the C. say, note XX.: " We have adopted Hanmer's correction ' sconce ' for ' silence ' because in the corresponding passage of the First Quarto Polonius says : ' I'le shrowde my selfe behinde the Arras.'" That really seems to be reaching very far after a reason for the adoption of "sconce," in opposition to all the authorities.

3. 4. 13. Why how now *Hamlet?* Why, how now, Hamlet! C.

3. 4. 29. *Ham.* . . . almost as bad good Mother, As kill a King, and marrie with his Brother. *Qu.* As kill a King? The Queen's speech should be uttered with a strong inquiring surprise. The C. has an !

3. 4. 38. That it is proofe and bulwarke against sense. F. That it be C. The indicative " is " is more correct here than the subjunctive " be."

3. 4. 55. See what a grace was seated on his Brow, F. this brow; C.

3. 4. 95. mine ears. F. my ears ; C.

3. 4. 104. What would you gracious figure? F. What would your gracious figure? C. after Quartos. With a comma after " you," making " figure " vocative, the F. is the better reading,

Knight has adopted it, so pointed. " figure " doesn't make, logically, a very good subject to " would."

3. 4. 139. Extasie? F. Ecstasy ! C.

3. 4. 145. Lay not a flattering Vnction to your soule, That, F. Lay not that flattering unction to your soul, That C.

3. 4. 152. And do not spred the Compost or the Weedes, F. . . . on the weeds, C. The "or" of the F. may be for "ore" or "o'er." Knight has " o'er."

3. 4. 159. mine Vnkles bed, F. my uncle's bed; C.

4. 1. 1, 2. There's matters in these sighes. These profound heaues You must translate ; F. There's matter in these sighs, these profound heaves : You must translate : C. The better pointing of the Folio here is unquestionable. According to the pointing of the C., "heaves " is construed with "sighs " and " You must translate " stands detached in construction. Furthermore, the King uses " profound " equivocally, as it may mean, "deep," literally, and " deep " in significance ; and upon the latter meaning, " translate " bears. The king then adds, " 'tis fit we understand them," This is lost in the C. pointing.

4. 1. 4. Bestow this place on us a little while.

[*Exeunt* ROSENCRANTZ *and* GUILDENSTERN. C.

This line and the stage direction are not in the F. and it was, perhaps, found best, in the representation, not to have Rosencrantz and Guildenstern enter until they were wanted. According to the Quartos, they enter with the King and Queen, only to be immediately dismissed. In the F. they are made to enter at the 32d line of the Scene, where the King calls them in and gives them orders about Hamlet and they then go out.

4. 1. 11. And in his brainish apprehension killes The vnseene good old man. F. And in this . . . C. The idea of " brainish apprehension " has not been anticipated, so that " his " is preferable to " this " of the Qq.

4. 1. 19–23. But so much was our loue, We would not vnderstand what was most fit, But like the Owner of a foule disease, To keepe it from divulging, let's it feede Euen on the pith of life. F.

. . . But, like the owner of a foul disease, To keep it from divulging, let it feed Even on the pith of life. C. " let" after the Quartos ; the 1st, 3d, and 4th, Folios read "let's," the 2d reads, "lets." In the reading both of the Quartos and of the Folios, the comparison is somewhat mixed with the leading thought. In the F. reading, " it " in "To keep *it* from divulging," and in "lets *it* feed Even on the pith of life," properly refers to " foul disease " ; but in the C. reading, it would seem to refer, rather incongruously, to " love." The meaning, however, is perfectly plain, to which the reading of the F. comes nearest : " We would not understand what was most fit, but [were] like the owner of a foul disease, [that,] to keep it from divulging, lets it feed even on the pith of life." The application of the comparison is left mental.

4. 2. 12, 13. Besides, to be demanded of a Spundge, what replication should be made by the Sonne of a King F. Besides, to be demanded of a sponge ! what replication should be made by the son of a king? C. The ! of the C. is after Steevens, who added also a dash. The Quartos and Folios have all a comma after " sponge," which is, no doubt, right. The sentence is not meant . to be exclamatory, as the pointing of the C. makes it ; " to be demanded of " = " in being demanded by." The modern English of the whole sentence would be, " in being demanded by a sponge, what reply should be made by the son of a king ? " · In regard to the force of " to " before, and of " of " after, " be demanded," see §§ 356 and 170, respectively, of Abbott's " Shakespearian Grammar," rev. and enl. ed. pp. 256 and 112.

4. 3. 19. At Supper? F. At Supper ! C.

4. 3. 44. Th' Associates tend, and euery thing at bent For England. F. and everything is bent For England. C. " at bent " is the more forcible, expressing, as it does, the *suspended* readiness indicated by what precedes, " the bark is ready," " the wind at help," " th' associates tend."

SCENE v. *Elsinore. A room in the castle. Enter* QUEEN, HORATIO, *and a* Gentleman. C. the numbering of the Scene, after Pope, the Scene, after Capell, the Enter after Pope. The F., without any designation of Scene, has the stage-direction, *Enter Queene and Horatio.* The 2d and 4th speeches of the Scene, in reply to the 1st and 3d, which are spoken by the Queen, are given by the C., after the Quartos, to the Gentleman. It would appear that the Gentleman was afterwards dispensed with as a superfluity, and his speeches given to Horatio. Lines 14–16, which are given in the Quartos to Horatio, are, in the F., given, more appropriately, to the Queen, along with the four following lines which are no doubt meant as an *Aside,* and are so designated by the C. The C. gives ll. 14 and 15, " 'Twere good she were spoken with, for she may strew Dangerous conjectures in ill-breeding minds," to Horatio, and begins the Queen's speech with "Let her come in." The whole speech, as it stands in the F., is as follows :

> " *Qu.* 'Twere good she were spoken with,
> For she may strew dangerous conjectures
> In ill breeding minds.   Let her come in.
> To my sicke soule (as sinnes true Nature is)
> Each toy seemes Prologue, to some great amisse,
> So full of Artlesse iealousie is guilt,
> It spill's it selfe, in fearing to be spilt."

It would be better to regard the whole speech as an *Aside,* except "Let her come in."

4. 5. 112, 113.   *Qu.* Calmely good *Laertes.   Laer.* That drop of blood, that calmes Proclaimes me Bastard : F.   That drop of blood that's calm C. after Quartos.   The F. reading is the better. Laertes is under the wildest excitement, with not a calm drop of blood in his veins, and when the Queen entreats, "Calmly, good Laertes," be, or become, calm, he replies, "That drop of blood that calms," that is, that grows calm, or, will calm, " proclaims me bastard ; " " calms " and " proclaims " are both future in force.

4. 5. 124.   *Laer.* Where's my Father ? F.   Where is my father ? C.

4. 5. 146.   And am most sensible in greefe for it, F. sensibly C.

4. 5. 150.   Oh heate drie vp my brains, F. C. puts a (,) after

" heat," converting it into a vocative, and " drie " into an imperative. And "Oh " is the emotional form.

4. 5. 152. By Heauen, thy madnesse shall be paid by waight,
F. with weight, C.

4. 5. 160–162. *Ophe. They bore him bare fac'd on the Beer,
Hey non nony, nony, hey nony: And on his graue raines many a
teare,* F. And in his grave rain'd many a tear, — C. The F.
reading is more significant : They bore him barefaced on the bier,
and many a tear [now] rains on his grave. According to the C.
reading, " rain'd " is used transitively, the subject being "They,"
and the reference is to the shedding of tears at the burial.

4. 5. 196. Do you see this, you Gods? F. . . . O God? C.

4. 5. 197. *King. Laertes,* I must common with your greefe,
F. commune C.

4. 7. 38. From *Hamlet ?* F. From Hamlet ! C.

4. 7. 153–155. therefore this Project should haue a backe or
second, that might hold, If this should blast in proofe : F. did
blast C.

4. 7. 185. *Laer.* Alas then, is she drown'd? *Queen.* Drown'd,
drown'd. F. Alas, then she is drown'd ! *Queen.* Drown'd,
drown'd. C. It would appear from the Queen's reply, that Laertes's
speech must have been meant to be interrogative. If exclamatory,
as the C. makes it, after Pope, " Alas, then she is drown'd ! " the
iteration thereupon of the Queen, " Drown'd, drown'd," is almost
ludicrous, and makes one feel that the poor girl has had indeed,
as Laertes says in the next speech, " too much of water."

5. 1. 76. It might be the Pate of a Polititian which this Asse
o'er Offices : F. The old lout of a grave-digger, in the discharge
of his office, lords it over the once scheming pate of the state-
official who felt himself able, in the exercise of his state-craft, to
circumvent God himself.

which this ass now o'er-reaches ; C. " o'er-reaches " is used with
a literal reference to the grave-digger, and a metaphorical reference
to the circumventing politician. " Office " is used as a verb in
Coriolanus, 5. 2. 59 : " you shall perceive that a Jack guardant

cannot office me from my son Coriolanus ; " and in All's Well that
Ends Well, 3. 2. 124 : " although The air of paradise did fan the
house, and Angels officed all : "   Knight adopts the reading of the
F., " oer-offices ; " and it is, without doubt, the more expressive
term of the two.

5. I. 77.   one that could circumuent God, F.   one that would
C. " could " is better, referring to the politician's craftiness in
getting the better of others.

5. I. 93.   why might not that bee the Scull of a Lawyer? F.
Why may C.

5. I. 140.   hee that was mad, and sent into England. F.   he
that is mad, C.   " was " suits better what follows : " *Ham.* Ay,
marry, why was he sent into England ?   *Clo.* Why, because he
was mad ; "

5. I. 169, 170.   This same Scull Sir, this same Scull sir, was
Yoricks Scull, F.   The C., after the Quartos, gives the expression
but once.   The repetition in the F., serves to exhibit the grave-
digger's sense of his official importance as he turns the skull over
in his hands.

5. I. 201.   Imperiall *Cæsar*, F.   Imperious Cæsar, C.

5. I. 206, 207.   Who is that they follow, And with such maimed
rites ? This doth betoken F.   who is this they follow ?   And with
such maimed rites ?   This doth betoken C.   " that " is, *per se,*
better than " this," Hamlet and Horatio being supposed to be at
some distance from the procession ; and then " this " occurring in
next line, referring to " maimed rites," adds to the preferableness
of the F. reading.

5. I. 209.   Fore do it owne life ; F.   its own life ; C.   " it "
should be retained for its historical significance.   All the Quartos
and the 2d Folio have " it " ; the 6th Quarto has " its " and the
3d and 4th Folios have " it's," this neuter gentive form, which
had been for some time struggling for admission into the written
language, having, at the dates of their publication, begun to be in
general use.   But Shakespeare must have used the tentative form
" it."

5. 1. 230.   What, the faire *Ophelia?* F.   What, the fair Ophelia ! C.

5. 1. 234.   I thought thy Bride-bed to haue deckt (sweet Maid) And not t'haue strew'd thy Graue. F.   And not have C.

5. 2. 224.   Who does it then? His Madness? If't be so, *Hamlet* is of the Faction that is wrong'd, F.   Who does it then? His madness : C.

5. 2. 284.   Come for the third. *Laertes*, you but dally, F. Come, for the third, Laertes : you but dally ; C.

The 2d Scene of the 5th Act, is less correctly printed in the F. than any other portion of the play.

MISCELLANEOUS NOTES.

(CHIEFLY IN SUPPORT OF FIRST FOLIO READINGS.)

THE SPELLING OF THE POET'S NAME.

IT is desirable that a name used as frequently as is that of Shakespeare, at the present day, should be uniformly spelt. The three forms now most in use, or, it may be said, exclusively in use, are Shakespeare, Shakspeare, and Shakspere. The tendency seems to be, to settle upon the first of these, though the New Shakspere Society, of London, has adopted the last. The authority of the original editions is decidedly in favor of the first.

There were 16 undoubted plays printed in quarto, some of them more than once, during the poet's lifetime, the date of the first, Romeo and Juliet, being 1597, and that of the last, Pericles, being 1609. The tragedy of Othello was printed in quarto, in 1622, six years after the poet's death, and the year preceding the publication of the First Folio. Of these 17 quarto editions of separate plays, some were printed with, and some without, the author's name. But on all the title-pages where it appears, it is spelt, with but two exceptions, Shakespeare (the two parts of the name being sometimes hyphened and sometimes not). The exceptions are, Shakespere, on the title-page of the first edition of Love's Labor's Lost, 1598, and Shak-speare, on that of the first edition of King Lear, 1608. In the first edition of the Sonnets, to which "A Louers complaint. By William Shake-speare.", is appended, the name occurs three times, being spelt each time Shake-speare. The name as attached, in the first editions, to the two dedicatory letters to the Earl of Southampton, prefixed to the

Venus and Adonis, and The Rape of Lucrece, (1593 and 1594,) the only letters of the author known to exist, is spelt Shakespeare. These are, probably, the only two of his works which the author himself saw through the press. They are printed with remarkable accuracy. The author's name doesn't appear on the title-pages. In 1616, the year of the author's death, The Rape of Lucrece was reissued, with his name, spelt Shakespeare; again, in 1624, with the same spelling of the name. The Passionate Pilgrim was first printed in 1599, the name of the author being given on the title-page, as W. Shakespeare. An edition of the Poems was issued in 1640, with "Written by Wil. Shake-speare. Gent." on the title-page.

In "The Workes of Beniamin Jonson," published in folio, 1616, the name appears in the list of "the principall Comœdians" who acted in "Euery Man in his Humour" (p. 72), and in the list of "the principall Tragœdians," who acted in "Seianvs his Fall" (p. 438). In the first, the name is given, "Will. Shakespeare," and in the second, "Will. Shake-Speare."

The first edition of the collected Plays, known as the First Folio, was published in 1623. The editors were John Heminge and Henry Condell, who had been associated professionally with Shakespeare for twenty years or more. In this first edition, the name of Shakespeare appears, altogether, 19 times : once, in Ben Jonson's lines "To the Reader," once, on the title-page, twice in "The Epistle Dedicatorie," 13 times in the Verses to his Memory, by Ben Jonson, Hugh Holland, L. Digges, and I. M., once in the title repeated over the List of Names of the principal Actors, and once in the List, and it is invariably spelt Shakespeare.

As to the spelling adopted by the New Shakspere Society, Dr. Furnivall remarks (Prospectus, p. 5, note 1) : "This spelling . . . is taken from the only unquestionably genuine signatures of his that we possess — the three in his will, and the two in his Stratford conveyance and mortgage. None of these signatures have an *e* after the *k*, four have no *a* after the first *e;* the fifth I read *eere*."

In Ingleby's "Shakespeare's Centurie of Prayse," which contains, exclusive of documentary notices, all the known allusions to

Shakespeare, in the original spellings, from 1592, when he was 28
years of age, to 1693, that is, 77 years after his death, the name is
spelt Shakespeare, 153 times; Shakespear, 96 times; Shakspeare,
9 times; Shakspear, 3 times; Shakespeere, twice; Shackspeer,
twice; Shakspeer, once; Shack-Spear, once; Shakspere, once;
Shacksperus (in a Latin Tractatulus), twice; and Shakesphear
(evidently advisedly, *quasi* Shake-sphere), twice.   The form
Shakespeare is, therefore, considerably in the majority over all the
other forms, and is used, too, by the best writers.   And this form
is chiefly used in the more important modern editions, — English,
German, and American,— of the poet's works, and in Shakespearian
literature generally.   And so it would seem best to conform to that
spelling of the poet's name which has the greater weight of authority on its side.

" BAYTED LIKE EAGLES."

" All furnisht, all in Armes,
All plum'd like Estridges, that with the Winde
Bayted like Eagles, hauing lately bath'd,
Glittering in Golden Coates, like Images,
As full of spirit as the Moneth of May,
And gorgeous as the Sunne at Mid-summer,
Wanton as youthfull Goates, wilde as young Bulls.
I saw young *Harry* with his Beuer on,
His Cushes on his thighes, gallantly arm'd,
Rise from the ground like feathered *Mercury*,
And vaulted with such ease into his Seat,
As if an Angell dropt downe from the Clouds,
To turne and winde a fierie *Pegasus*,
And witch the World with Noble Horsemanship."
— 1 Henry IV. 4. 1. 97–110.

l. 98, *that with*] *that wing* Rowe.   *and with* Hanmer.   *that
whisk* Tyrwhitt conj.   *wind*] *wind are fann'd* Keightley conj.
98, 99. *plum'd . . . Winde Bayted*] *plum'd! . . . wind Bated:*
Johnson conj.
99 *Baited*] Q1 Q2 Q3 Q4 F3 F4.   *Bayted* Q5 Q6 F1 Q7 Q8

F2. *Baiting* Hanmer. *Bated* Malone. — *Var. Lect.*, as given in "Cambridge" ed.

> " All plum'd like estridges that wing the wind;
> Bated like eagles having lately bath'd; " — Third Variorum text.

The "Cambridge" editors, in their note, say, " We leave this obscure passage as it stands in the old copies. Possibly, as Steevens suggested, a line has dropped out after *wind*. The phrase 'wing the wind' seems to apply to ostriches (for such is unquestionably the meaning of 'estridges') less than to any other birds. . . ."

Malone, agreeing with Steevens that a line might have been lost, suggested the following :

> " All plum'd like estridges, that with the wind
> *Run on, in gallant trim they now advance :*
> Bated like eagles, etc."

The whole difficulty which the passage presents, as the many notes written on it, show, centres in " Bayted." To bait or bate means, as Dr. Schmidt defines it, " to flap the wings, to flutter (a term in falconry) : " Fr. *battre*, Lat. *batuere.*

If "Bayted " is understood as a past participle, the relative " that " is left without a verb; if it is understood as a verb, the tense presents a difficulty — it should properly be present tense.

As all the original editions agree in the word, from the 1st Quarto to the 4th Folio, inclusive, the only difference being, as noted above, in the two spellings, " baited " and " bayted," I feel quite certain that the word was originally written as the ear took it in, and that it represents " bait it," the " it " being used, as it frequently was, indefinitely, and with an enlivening effect, after the intransitive verb.

See Abbott's " Shakespearian Grammar," rev. and enl. ed. p. 150, § 226; Hales's " Longer English Poems," Notes, p. 236; Schmidt's " Shakespeare-Lexicon," *s.v.* " it."

The meaning therefore is, " all plumed like ostriches, that run with, or before, the wind, flapping their wings (*remigio alarum*) like newly-bathed eagles." Steevens, in his note on the passage, says, " They (ostriches) are generally hunted on horseback, and the art of the hunter is to turn them from the gale, by the help of which they are too fleet for the swiftest horse to keep up with them."

I suspect, too, that " vaulted," l. 107, represents " vault it," to be construed with the infinitive " rise " after " saw." Malone suggests this, and it is somewhat remarkable that he didn't see the other ear-word, " bayted."

" An Anthony it was."

In Antony and Cleopatra, 5. 2. 86–88, Cleopatra says of Antony :

> " For his Bounty,
> There was no winter in't. An *Anthony* it was,
> That grew the more by reaping : "

This is the reading of the First Folio, 1623, in which the Tragedy, so far as is known, appeared for the first time. The name of Antony is spelt in the title and throughout the Play, Anthony. The " Cambridge " editors adopt Theobald's " emendation," " an autumn 'twas."

If " An Anthony it was " is not right, " an autumn 'twas " is certainly wrong. It is too tame for the intensely impassioned speech in which it occurs, or, rather, into which it has been introduced by the editors. Again, if " autumn" could, by metonymy, be wrenched to mean the crops of autumn, it could hardly be said that an autumn *grows* the more by reaping. But this reading of Theobald has been silently adopted by all subsequent editors, without any consideration of its tameness or of the resultant incongruity.

I think the Folio is right, as it sometimes is, and that there is a *quibble* in the speech, that has been overlooked. It is a patent fact in regard to the manifold and multiform quibbles in the plays of Shakespeare, that they are often indulged in by his characters while in the highest intensity of mind and feeling. The poet has been blamed for this, especially by the critics of the " correct " school, and his defenders have found some excuse for it in the general quibbling propensity of the writers of his time. But the best excuse for it is that it is true to nature, although I would not explain it on the theory set forth by Bucknill in his "Psychology of Shakespeare," namely, that "when the mind is wrought to an excessive pitch of emotion, the instinct of self-preservation indicates some lower mode of mental activity as the one thing needful."

To return now to the passage in question: "An *Anthony* it was,"; "it" stands, of course, for "Bounty." His Bounty was an *Anthony*, "that grew the more by reaping."

Now, could not the "less Greek" which, Ben Jonson tells us, Shakespeare possessed, have led him to see in "Anthony" the word ἄνθος? and to quibble on the word as meaning a flower garden? His bounty had no winter in it; it was a luxuriant, ever-blooming flower garden.

"Center" *versus* "Cincture."

> "Now happy he, whose cloake and center can
> Hold out this tempest." — King John, 4. 3. 155, 156.

This passage is contained in the Bastard's speech, the concluding one of the 4th Act, in which he predicts the many calamities that are to follow the violent death of the little prince, whose body has just been found by the courtiers outside the castle walls, from which he leapt down to make his escape. The above reading is that of the Folio of 1623, in which the play was printed for the first time. Pope, in his edition of Shakespeare, not understanding the meaning of "center" made a meaning, as he frequently did, and changed the word to "cincture," supposing the word as it stands in the Folio, to owe its form to the French *ceinture*. This change has been followed, so far as I know, by all subsequent editors, not excepting Knight, the most loyal to the Folio, and the editors of the "Cambridge Shakespeare," William George Clark and William Aldis Wright; and Aug. Wilh. Schlegel translates the passage: "Nun ist der glücklich, dessen *Gurt* und Mantel Diesz Wetter aushält."

I claim that the original word " center," is right, and I should do so, even if there were no confirmatory uses of it elsewhere in the Plays, for the simple reason that it is Shakespearian, while "cincture," in such connection, is not. The sentence is, of course, metaphorical, and it would not be in the poet's manner to speak of a cloak *and* its girdle, or a coat *and* its buttons, or a hat *and* its securing string, holding out against a tempest. His mind was always too full and too vigorous, to move in that way. But all *a priori* argument can be dispensed with in the face of other and similar uses, in the Plays and Sonnets, of the word " center." For literal uses of the word, see the following passages, in some of which it is used with qualifications, in others, absolutely, for the centre of the earth, etc., or for the earth as the centre around which the planets move, according to the Ptolemaic system of the heavens : M. N. D. 3. 2. 54 ; W. T. 2. 1. 102 ; Hen. V. 1. 2. 210 ; 1 Hen. VI. 2. 2. 6 ; Rich. III. 5. 2. 11 ; T. & C. 1. 3. 85; 3. 2. 186 ; 4. 2. 110 ; T. A. 4. 3. 12 ; Ham. 2. 2. 159 ; metaphorically, it is used for the soul or the indwelling spirit, — the centre of the earthly body, — as in the following passages :

> " *Rom.* Can I goe forward when my heart is here?
> Turne back dull earth, and find thy Center out."
> — R. & J. 2. 1. 2.

This seems to be one of the many instances of Shakespeare's apparent intuitive feeling, for correcter views than were current in his day.   The idea suggested is of the earth — symbol of the earthly body — at its aphelion, or the point of its orbit most remote from the sun, returning to it again by the force of gravitation to the common centre of gravity. — Singer (2d edition 1856), as given by Furness in his New Varr. ed. of R. & J.

> " Poor soul, the center of my sinful earth." — Sonnet 146.

In the following passage from the W. T. 1. 2. 138, " may't be Affection? thy Intention stabs the Center.", the word is generally understood to mean the soul ; but it means rather the centre of the thing aimed at. The punctuation is faulty in the Folio. "Affection" is vocative. Leontes is addressing his own affection or imagination : "May it be, Affection," (that) thy intention (used in literal Latin sense,) stabs the centre, intuitively pierces the very heart, hits the white, touches the root of the matter?

To return now to the passage from King John. The Bastard's meaning is, that such dire calamities will sweep over the land that they will not only act disastrously upon the outward circumstances of men's lives, but will penetrate to their inmost being, and happy he who can stand out against them.

"MEANE IT."

"*Lor.* . . . How dost thou like the Lord *Bassiano*'s wife?
Iessi. Past all expressing, it is very meete
The Lord *Bassanio* liue an vpright life
For hauing such a blessing in his Lady,
He findes the ioyes of heauen heere on earth,
And if on earth he doe not meane it, it
Is reason he should neuer come to heauen?"
—The Merchant of Venice, 3. 5. 77–83.

The last two lines of Jessica's speech read in the "Roberts Quarto" of 1600, . . . "meane it, then In" . . . and in the "Hayes Quarto" of 1600, . . . "meane it, it In" . . . the other Folios, as the First, the 3d and 4th Quartos, . . . "meane it, In" . . . Pope, not understanding "mean it," changed it to "merit it," in his edition of Shakespeare, and began the next line with "In," and his reading has been followed by a number of prominent editors, some of them among the latest. The editors of the "Cambridge Shakespeare," in their note on the passage, in the "Clarendon Press Series" edition of the Play, 1874, pronounce the Folio reading "evidently a conjectural emendation," and add "There is some corruption in this passage for which no satisfactory emendation has been proposed. That of Pope, 'merit it,' for 'mean it, then,' is perhaps the most plausible. 'Earn it, then,' or 'merit them,' might be suggested. But we rather require a

word with the sense of 'appreciate.'" Dyce reads, after Pope,
. . . "merit it, In " . . . and says in a note, "So Pope ; and so
Walker, except that he reads ''*Tis* reason,' etc., 'Crit. Exam.,'
etc. Vol. III. p. 110," and adds "He evidently did not know
that Pope had anticipated him in reading ' merit it.'" Hudson
also adopts Pope's reading. Staunton conjectured "moan, it is
In " . . .

It is quite apparent that all to whom the subject has presented
a difficulty have overlooked the force of "mean " understanding
it in the usual sense of "purpose," "intend." b_ "mean " is
the noun in the sense of middle between two extr�‍es, as in
"golden mean," (as a noun it occurs in M. of V. 1. 2. } "it is
no smal happinesse therefore to bee seated in the meane,") _d in
the passage before us is used as a verb (in the Elizabethan English,
any part of speech was freely used as any other part of speech.
See Introduction to Abbott's "Shakespearian Grammar"), and
the pronoun "it" is used indefinitely, as was very commonly
done after intransitive verbs, and *especially after nouns used as
verbs.* For this use of "it," see Abbott's "Shakespearian Grammar," rev. and enl. ed. p. 150, § 226. See also Hales's "Longer
English Poems," Notes, p. 236, and Schmidt's "Shakespeare-
Lexicon," *s.v.* "it." And see, for numerous examples of the use
of nouns as verbs, Appendix to Bartlett's "Familiar Quotations,"
6th ed. 1871, p. 613. Marlowe's Plays abound with nouns used
as verbs and followed by the indefinite "it."

The passage from the M. of V. means, then, "it is very meet
the Lord Bassanio live an upright life, for, having such a blessing
in his lady, he finds the joys of heaven here on earth ; and if on
earth he do not observe a mean in his pleasures, it is reason that
he should never come to heaven."

Clark and Wright, though they see a difficulty in the passage,
and consider it corrupt, follow, in the "Cambridge edition," the
reading of the "Roberts Quarto," . . . "mean it, then In " . . .
Though the sense is the same as in the Folio, the reading of the
latter shows a nice revision, as by the substitution of "it " for

"then," the more formal conclusive character which the latter word imparts to the impression, is advantageously got rid of.

"An Unstained Shepherd with Wisdom."

"*Perd.* O *Doricles*,
Your praises are too large: but that your youth
And the true blood which peepes fairely through't,
Do plainly giue you out an vnstain'd Sphepherd [*sic*]
With wisedome, I might feare (my *Doricles*) ᾽
You woo'd me the false way."
—The Winter's Tale, 4. 4. 146–151.

All modern editors of Shakespeare, so far as I know, pervert the true meaning of the 4th and 5th lines of this passage, by changing the punctuation of the First Folio: that is, by putting a comma after "Shepherd," and omitting that after "wisdom," thus connecting the phrase "With wisdom," with "I might fear." But it is properly, as indicated by the Folio punctuation, connected with "unstain'd," the meaning being "a shepherd unstain'd with wisdom," that is, an unsophisticated shepherd, who, according to Perdita's meaning, says what he thinks, frankly, and without reserve, and also without flattery. This construction had its origin in the inflected period of the language. For example, the Anglo-Saxon version of John, Chap. I. v. 9, reads: "Sóth Leóht wæs, thæt onlyht ælcne cumendne man on thysne middan-eard," that is, "True light [it] was, that lighteth each coming man into this mid-earth," instead of "each man coming into this mid-earth."

In present English, whose syntax is almost wholly logical, and, consequently, positional, when a participle or adjective qualifies a noun, and is itself qualified by a phrase, it is placed after the noun in order to bring it immediately before the phrase which qualifies it, and to the preposition of which it is the antecedent term.

For numerous examples, both from Shakespeare and other authors, of the construction in the above passage from The Winter's Tale, see Abbott's "Shakespearian Grammar," § 419 a.

Professor Child, in his " Observations on the Language of Chau-

cer," § 110, notes the following examples : . . . "whan these tres-
pasours and repentynge folk of here folies . . . hadden herd
what the messangeres sayden," . . . C. T. "Melibeus," Harl. text,
3d par. from end ; *i.e.*, folk repenting of their follies ; . . . "doth
digne fruyt of penitence," . . . C. T., "The Persones Tale," 6th
par. from beginning ; *i.e.*, fruit digne (worthy) of penitence ; "With
kempe heres on his browes stowte ;" C. T., 2136; *i.e.*, with hair
combed on his brows ; " oure grounde litarge eek on the porfurye,"
C. T., 12,703 ; *i.e.*, litharge ground on the porphyry ; so in Gower's
C. A., Pauli's ed., V. I. p. 189, " o dampned man to helle," *i.e.*, a
man dampned (condemned) to hell.

I have said that this construction had its origin in the inflected
period of the language. But more may be said of it. The writers
of the age of Elizabeth and James, and this is especially true of
Shakespeare, wrote more synthetically and less analytically, wrote
with less literary consciousness, than it is now the custom to do,
and many of the peculiarities of their diction can be explained on
this ground.

ABSORPTION OF COGNATES IN THE FIRST FOLIO.

There is an abundance of evidence in the First Folio that the
poet, or, which is more likely, the scribe in writing from dictation,
wrote by ear, and, consequently, omitted to represent to the eye
certain elements that are more or less or altogether absorbed in
pronunciation. William Sidney Walker, in his work on Shakespeare's Versification, notices this in the case of *s*, but it does not
appear that he carried his observations beyond the sibilant. Dr.
George Allen, Greek Professor in the University of Pennsylvania,
in a valuable note he contributed to Horace Howard Furness's
New Variorum edition of Romeo and Juliet, pp. 429–31, cites
entirely confirmatory examples of the absorption of gutturals,
nasals, and dentals, especially of the latter, and shows, quite conclusively, that "we see defects in the original text where none
exist, and proceed to amend them by thrusting words into the

supposed gaps, when we should fully meet all the demands even of the modern eye by merely indicating [by the apostrophe] the actual presence of what has been treated as absent."

I would cite the following from a very large number of such cases I have noted in my reading of the First Folio text:

> "better I were not yours
> Then your [= yours] so branchlesse." — A. & C. 3. 4. 24.

> " His face was as the Heau'ns, and therein stucke
> A Sunne and Moone, which kept their course and lighted
> The little o' th' earth [= O o' th' earth]" — A. & C. 5. 2. 81.

> " But, when the splitting winde
> Makes flexible the knees of knotted Oakes,
> And Flies fled [=Flies 've fled] vnder shade," . . . — T. & C. 1. 3. 51.

The following all occur in one Scene of The Winter's Tale:

> " But that our Feasts
> In euery Messe, haue folly; and the Feeders
> Digest [=Digest it] with a Custome, I should blush
> To see you so attyr'd : " — 4. 4. 12.

> " The Mary-gold, that goes to bed with ' Sun [= with the Sun],
> And with him rises, weeping : " — 4. 4. 105.

Here the absorption is indicated in the First Folio by the apostrophe.

> " Your praises are too large : but that your youth
> And the true blood which peepes [= peepes so] fairely through't,
> Do plainly giue you out an vnstain'd Sphepherd [*sic*]
> With wisedome," . . . — 4. 4. 148.

> " The selfe-same Sun, that shines upon his Court,
> Hides not his visage from our Cottage, but
> Lookes on alike [= on all alike]." — 4. 4. 457.

> " She's as forward of her Breeding, as
> She is i' th' reare' our Birth [= reare o' our Birth]." — 4. 4. 592.

Here the absorption is again indicated by the apostrophe.

> " For [=Forth] this time Daughter,
> Be somewhat scanter of your Maiden presence ; " — Ham. 1. 3. 120.

> " Dis-mantle you, and (as you can) disliken
>   The truth of your owne seeming, that you may
>   (For I do feare eyes ouer) to Ship-boord
>   Get vndescry'd." — 4. 4. 668.

i.e., " For I do fear eyes overt," open or watchful.

" Over," followed by a " t," also represents " overt," in the following passage, according to the First Folio :

> " To vouch this, is no proofe,
> Without more wider, and more ouer [= overt] Test
> Then these thin habits, and poore likely-hoods
> Of moderne seeming, do prefer against him." — Oth. 1. 3. 107.

i.e., without more open, evident test.

In the first citation, the " s " of " yours " is absorbed in the following " s " ; in the 2d, the " O " in the following " o' " ; in the 3d, the " v " in the following cognate " f " ; in the 4th, the " it " in the preceding " t " ; in the 5th, the " th " in the preceding " th " ; in the 6th, the " so " in the preceding " s " ; in the 7th, the " all " in the following " al " ; in the 8th, the " o' " in the following " ou " ; in the 9th, the " th " in the following " th " ; and in the 10th and 11th, the final " t " of " overt," in the following " t."

These examples, and I have noted hundreds of others equally conclusive, will suffice to illustrate an important feature of the First Folio text.

The Ethical Dative in Shakespeare.

The idiom familiar to classical scholars, known as *Dativus Eth-icus* or Ethical Dative, is of most common occurrence, in English

Literature, in the Dramas of Shakespeare and of his contemporaries. It occurs not unfrequently in Anglo-Saxon, Semi-Saxon, and early English, and it crops out occasionally in the literature subsequent to the Shakespearian era, even down to the present day. Mätzner gives examples of it from Bulwer's " Rienzi " and Carlyle's " Frederick the Great " ; and there are instances of it in the novels of George Eliot, and in the poetry of Robert Browning.

The susceptible reader, whenever he meets with it, feels at once its force, as àn enlivening touch to the expression in which it occurs ; but its *rationale* he would be, perhaps, at a loss to set forth. Mätzner in his " Englische Grammatik," 2ter Th. p. 213, puts it quite satisfactorily : " Dieser ethische Dativ im engeren Sinne tritt als persönliches Fürwort der ersten oder zweiten Person auf, wodurch die vertrauliche, gemüthliche oder lebhafte Rede das subjektive Interesse des Sprechenden oder des Angeredeten bei der Erwähnung einer Thatsache hervorkehrt, welche nach ihrer objektiven Erscheinung unabhängig von jenem Interesse vollzogen gedacht wird."

Dr. Johnson, in his Dictionary, says ot the ethical dative " me," " Me is sometimes a kind of ludicrous expletive " ; and " It is sometimes used ungrammatically for *I; as methinks*."/ The latter is, of course, the A. S. *me thincth* = mihi videtur, *it seems to me ;* so, methought, A. S. me thuhte, *it seemed to me,* and in early English, him thought, her thought, hem thought, it seemed to him, her, them. Rossetti, in his " Blessed Damosell," uses " Her seemed."

Doctor Schmidt, in his " Shakespeare-Lexicon," *s.vv.* " I " and " you," presents quite an exhaustive list of passages in which the ethical " me " and " you " occur in Shakespeare ; and *s.v.* " your," he gives numerous examples of the word used indefinitely, that is, " not with reference to the person addressed, but to what is known and common," a use not unlike the ethical ; in fact hardly distinguishable from it. Two or three examples of each must suffice here :

. . . " he steps me to her Trencher, and steales her Capons-leg :

. . . Hee thrusts me himselfe into the company of three or foure gentleman-like dogs, vnder the Duke's table : " — T. G. V. 4. 9. 18. [Said by Launce of his dog.]

"The skilfull shepheard pil'd me certaine wands, And . . . stucke them vp before the fulsome Ewes," . . . — M. of V. 1. 3. 85.

"Thou art like one of these fellowes, that when he enters the confines of a Tauerne, claps me his Sword vpon the Table, and sayes, God send me no need of thee : " — R. & J. 3. 1. 6.

"I will roare you as gently as any sucking Doue ; " — M. N. D. 1. 2. 84.

"Ile be sworne 'tis true, he will weepe you an 'twere a man borne in Aprill." — T. & C. 1. 2. 188.

. . . "he will last you some eight yeare, or nine yeare. A Tanner will last you nine yeare." — Ham. 5. 1. 183.

"Your Serpent of Egypt, is bred now of your mud by the operation of your Sun : so is your Crocodile." — A. & C. 2. 7. 29–30.

"I will discharge it, in either 'your straw-colour beard, your orange tawnie beard, your purple in graine beard, or your French crowne colour'd beard, your perfect yellow." — M. N. D. 1. 2. 95.

In the following humorous passage from the Taming of the Shrew, A. I. Sc. ii. 8 *et seq.*, it would seem that the use of the ethical dative was already beginning to come to the consciousness as an odd superfluity in speech; Petruchio uses "me" ethically, and his man Grumio understands it, or pretends to understand it, as pertaining personally to his master :

"*Petr.* . . . I trow this is his house : Heere sirra *Grumio*, Knocke I say. *Gru.* Knocke sir ? whom should I knocke ? Is there any man ha's rebus'd your worship ? *Petr.* Villaine I say, Knocke me heere soundly. *Gru.* Knocke you heere sir ? Why sir, what am I sir, that I should knocke you heere sir. *Petr.* Villaine I say, Knocke me at this gate, And rap me well, or Ile knocke your knaues pate. *Gru.* My M^r is growne quarrelsome : I should knocke you first, And then I know after who comes by the worst. . . . *Enter Hortensio. Hor.* How now, what's the matter ? . . . *Gru.* . . . He bid me knocke him, and rap him soundly sir. . . . *Petr.* A sencelesse villaine : good *Hortensio,* I bad the rascall knocke vpon your gate, And could not get him for my heart to do it. *Gru.* Knocke at the gate? O heauens : spake you not these words plaine? Sirra, Knocke me heere : rappe me heere : knocke me well, and knocke me soundly? And come you now with knocking at the gate?"

From a large number of examples of the ethical dative I have noted in the dramatic and other literature of the Shakespearian era, I select the following from Marlowe, as being quite curious :

"I went me home to his house, . . . I . . . took him by the leg, and never rested pulling till I had pulled me his leg quite off ; " . . . "Doctor Faustus," 4. 6. Cunningham's ed., 1870.

> "A lofty cedar-tree, fair flourishing,
> On whose top-branches kingly eagles perch,
> And by the bark a canker creeps me up,
> And gets into the highest bough of all."
> — Edward II. 2. 2.

> "Even now as I came home, he slipt me in,
> And I am sure he is with Abigail."
> — "Jew of Malta," 2. 2. 331.

"With that hee takes me the pensill, and with another colour drew within the same line a smaller than it." — "Pliny's Nat. Hist.," Holland's transl., Book xxxv. p. 538, ed. of 1634.

Abbott, in his "Shakespearian Grammar," does not seem to recognize an exclusively moral use of "me" and "you," but endeavors to explain them always on a logical or thought basis. He makes no allusion, even, to the *dativus ethicus* or ethical dative, of the grammars. His suggested explanations may be accepted as covering certain cases of what are generally considered as ethical, but they certainly do not cover them all nor any considerable part of them.

RESPECTIVE CONSTRUCTIONS IN SHAKESPEARE AND WRITERS OF HIS TIME.

There is a construction of language much affected by writers of the Shakespearian era, which may be characterized as a *respective* construction; that is, a series of phrasal adverbs qualifies, respectively, a series of adjectives; a series of adjectives qualifies, respectively, a series of nouns; a series of verbs is governed, respectively, by a series of subject-nouns; a series of object-nouns complements, respectively, a series of verbs; a series of subject-nouns or object-nouns governs, respectively, a series of nouns in the genitive case; a relative pronoun, representing two or more antecedents, governs verbs referring, respectively, to those antecedents, etc., etc. The following are good examples :

> "Faynt, wearie, sore, emboyléd, grievéd, brent,
>   With heat, toyle, wounds, armes, smart, and inward fire."
>> — Spenser's "Faerie Queene," B. I. c. xi. St. 28, ll. 1, 2.

That is, faint with heat, weary with toil, sore with wounds, emboiled with arms, grieved with smart, and brent [burnt] with inward fire.

> " For this, this head, this heart, this hand and sword,
>   Contrives, imagines, fully executes
>   Matters of import aiméd at by many,
>   Yet understood by none."
>> — Marlowe's " Massacre at Paris," I. 2.

That is, this head contrives, this heart imagines, this hand and sword fully executes, etc.

> " And he that shall arrive at so much boldness,
>   To say his mistress' eyes, or voice, or breath,
>   Are half so bright, so clear, so sweet as thine,
>   Hath told the world enough of miracle."
>> — " The Traitor," by Shirley.

That is, his mistress's eyes are half so bright, or voice so clear, or breath so sweet, etc.

" Yet will I weep, vow, pray to cruel she :
   Flint, frost, disdain, wears, melts, and yields, we see."
                                 — Daniel's " Sonnets to Delia," XI.

That is, flint wears, frost melts, and disdain yields, etc.

" They move their hands, stedfast their feet remain,
   Nor blow nor foin, they struck or thrust in vain."
                                 — Fairfax's " Tasso," 7. 55.

That is, nor blow they struck, nor foin they thrust, in vain.

" Virtue, beauty, and speech, did strike, wound, charm,
   My heart, eyes, ears, with wonder, love, delight ; "
                                 — Sir Philip Sidney.

That is, Virtue did strike my heart with wonder, beauty did
wound my eyes with love, and speech did charm my ears with
delight. The sonnet from which these two verses are taken exhibits this trick of construction throughout, which, when carried
to such an extent, becomes mere ingenious trifling, wholly inconsistent with any sincerity of feeling on the part of the poet.

Shakespeare occasionally employs this respective construction,
as he does, with an easy success, all the peculiarities, affectations,
and euphuisms, of the diction of his time :

" If you can looke into the seedes of Time,
   And say, which Graine will grow, and which will not,
   Speake then to me, who neyther begge, nor feare
   Your fauors, nor your hate." — Macbeth, 1. 3. 58–61.

That is, who neither beg your favors nor fear your hate.

" though I with Death, and with
   Reward, did threaten and encourage him,
   Not doing it, and being done : "
                                 — Winter's Tale, 3. 2. 164–166.

That is, though I did threaten him with death, and encourage
him with reward, etc,

> " Sometime a horse Ile be, sometime a hound :
> A hogge, a headlesse beare, sometime a fire,
> And neigh, and barke, and grunt, and rore, and burne,
> Like horse, hound, hog, beare, fire, at every turne."
> — A Midsummer Night's Dream, 3. 1. 111–114.

That is, sometimes a horse I'll be, and neigh; sometimes a hound, and bark; a hog, and grunt; a headless bear, and roar; sometimes a fire, and burn, etc.

> " The time was once, when thou vn-vrg'd wouldst vow,
> That neuer words were musicke to thine eare,
> That neuer obiect pleasing in thine eye,
> That neuer touch well welcome to thy hand,
> That neuer meat sweet sauour'd in thy taste,
> Vnlesse I spake, or looked, or touch'd, or caru'd to thee."
> — The Comedy of Errors, 2. 2. 115–120.

Here, "unless I spake" is respective to the 2d line of the passage, "(unless I) looked," to the 3d, " (unless I) touched," to the 4th, and " (unless I) carved to thee," to the 5th.

> " and teach me how
> To name the bigger Light, and how the lesse,
> That burne by day, and night : "
> — The Tempest, 1. 2. 334, 335.

Here the two phrasal adverbs, " by day" and " (by) night," qualify " burn," with a respective reference to the two antecedents of the relative " That," " the bigger light " and " the less (light)."

> " So Bees with smoake, and Doues with noysome stench,
> Are from their Hyues and Houses driuen away."
> — 1 Henry VI., 1. 5. 23, 24.

That is, bees are driven away from their hives with smoke, and doves, from their houses, with noisome stench.

> " But he loues *Cæsar* best, yet he loves *Anthony* :
> Hoo, Hearts, Tongues, Figure[s],

Scribes, Bards, Poets, cannot
Thinke [,] speake, cast, write, sing, number: hoo,
His loue to *Anthony*." — Antony and Cleopatra, 3. 2. 15–18.

That is, hearts cannot think, tongues speak, figures cast, scribes write, bards sing, poets number.

" if Knife, Drugges, Serpents haue
Edge, sting, or operation, I am safe."
                    — Antony and Cleopatra, 4. 15. 25, 26.

Here, "sting" and "operation" are *inversely* respective to "drugs" and "serpents," the meaning, of course, being, if knife have edge, drugs operation, serpents sting, I am safe. The order of both series of nouns was determined by the rhythm.

" O what a Noble minde is heere o're-throwne?
The Courtiers, Soldiers, Schollers: Eye, tongue, sword."
                    — Hamlet, 3. 1. 158, 159.

Here, again, "tongue" and "sword" are *inversely* respective to "soldier's" and "scholar's," the meaning being, "courtier's eye, soldier's sword, scholar's tongue." Either the words "soldier's" and "scholar's," or "tongue" and "sword," might change places, without disturbing the rhythm. But Shakespeare wrote synthetically, and the derangement was purely accidental.

" They are apt enough to dislocate and tear
Thy flesh and bones." — King Lear, 4. 2. 65, 66.

Here "flesh" and "bones" are *inversely* respective to "dislocate" and "tear": to dislocate thy bones and tear thy flesh.

" And will to Eares and Tongues
Be Theame and hearing euer."
                    — Cymbeline, 3. 1. 3, 4.

"Theme" and "hearing" are *inversely* respective to "ears" and "tongues."

EXAMINATION QUESTIONS.

1. Our meagre knowledge of Shakespeare's personal history, how explained? Comment thereupon.

2. How does it compare with our knowledge of contemporary dramatists and poets? What does Halliwell-Phillipps say on this subject, in his "Outlines"?

3. Evidences afforded by Dr. Ingleby's "Shakespeare's Centurie of Prayse," of the appreciation of Shakespeare in his own time and in the subsequent half-century or more.

4. What higher knowledge can we have of the man Shakespeare, than any knowledge which might have been delivered to us, of his outer life?

5. How may the Plays be said to be, in the deepest sense, autobiographic in their character?

6. What testimony to the estimation of Shakespeare is afforded by the "Palladis Tamia" of Francis Meres?

7. When was the "Palladis Tamia" published, and what Plays are mentioned in it?

8. Analyze, and trace the sequence of the thought of, Ben Jonson's lines, in the First Folio, "To the Memory of . . . Shakespeare: and what he hath left us."

9. Sketch the life and the personal character of Ben Jonson. The evidence we have of the sincerity of his expressed admiration of Shakespeare.

10. Comment on "He was not of an age, but for all time."

11. What is properly meant by universality? What does Ruskin say, in his "Modern Painters," of the universality of great authors and painters?

12. Comment on the opinion expressed by Gerald Massey, in his "Secret Drama of Shakespeare's Sonnets," in regard to the contemporary estimate of Shakespeare.

13. Who was the great impersonator, of the time, of the leading characters of Shakespeare's Plays?

14. Comment on the idea expanded by Whipple, in "The Literature of the Age of Elizabeth," that "the measure of a man's individuality is his creative power."

15. The favorableness of the age for the exercise of great dramatic genius. Expatiate on what Rev. James Byrne says of this.

16. The part played by the circumstances of time and place, in the creative activity of a great genius.

17. Comment on the education of Shakespeare, exhibited by the Plays, as distinguished from mere scholarship. Give De Quincey's definition of a great scholar.

18. Comment on the passage on study, in Love's Labor's Lost, A. I. S. 1, 55–93.

19. What makes Shakespeare the greatest of the world's teachers?

20. Shakespeare's knowledge of the classical unities of action, time, and place. Which of these can alone be regarded as an absolute dramatic-art principle? To what were the others originally due?

21. In which of his Plays has Shakespeare strictly observed all the unities?

22. How are the unities departed from in "The Suppliants" of Euripides, and in the "Heautontimoroumenos" (the Self-Tormentor) of Terence?

23. What is the period of time covered by The Tempest? By the Comedy of Errors? Give a time-analysis of the plots of these plays.

24. Give the periods of time covered by the several plays included in "A Time-Analysis of the Plots of Shakspere's Plays," by P. A. Daniel (Transactions of the New Shakspere Society, 1877–9. Series I. Part II).

25. In which Play has Shakespeare utterly disregarded the unities in an actual sense? What higher unity is realized in this Play? Contrast organic and mechanical unity. From what does the higher vital unity of Shakespeare's Plays result?

26. Characterize the dramatic time-scheme which has been shown to be present in the Plays.

27. To whom were the discovery and exposition of this time-scheme originally due?

28. Which of the two was the earlier discoverer? In what work did

he set forth the scheme? Where was the other's exposition of the scheme published? and through what Plays did he set it forth?

29. What feature of the Plays contributes to the dramatic perspective, and constitutes the still background to what is dramatized? Give examples of this feature, in addition to those given in the text.

30. By whom has this feature been specially treated? Present it in all the Plays which he has treated.

31. Comment on the heterogeneous character of the Romantic Drama, so far as its material is concerned, and on its unity in variety.

32. Comment on Shakespeare's employment of Contrast. Give examples of it from various plays.

33. Comment, in this respect, on the following scenes: Henry VIII. A. V. S. 3; Romeo and Juliet, A. IV. S. 5, 96 *et seq.*; Macbeth, A. II. S. 3, 1–45; Hamlet, A. V. S. 1; Othello, A. III. S. 1; Antony and Cleopatra, A. V. S. 2, 241–281. Comment on other scenes of your own selection, wherein contrast is effectively employed.

34. Comment on the natural evolution of Shakespeare's dialogue; on Julius Cæsar, A. II. S. 1, 86–112. What does DeQuincey say of Shakespeare's dialogue, and of the dialogue of the French and the Italian Drama?

35. Comment on the "Crossing Speeches" given in "The Shakespeare's Key," by Charles and Mary Cowden Clarke, pp. 69–73.

36. What appears to have been assumed at the outset of the Shakespeare-Bacon controversy?

37. What had learning to do, or, rather, what had learning not to do, with the composition of the Plays?

38. Shakespeare's learning as distinguished from his knowledge and wisdom. His direct perception of truth. Conditions of this direct perception. Character of the learning which the Plays exhibit. The anachronisms. The jumble of times, and events, and persons, exhibited in The Winter's Tale. The ideal unity of this jumble. What characters of subsequently remote times are mentioned in Coriolanus? Give other anachronisms of your own noting.

39. What evidence is there in the works of Francis Bacon that he possessed the *kind* of powers demanded for the composition of the Plays?

40. What is meant by the *artistic* physiology of human passion?

41. What is meant by the fatalism of passion?

42. Wherein consists the moral proportion of the Plays? To what must this moral proportion have been due?

43. What *must* the greatest physiologist of human passion, as the author of the Plays certainly was, himself have been?

44. To what do the Works of Francis Bacon bear an emphatic testimony?

45. Characterize his Essay, " On Love "; his " Translation of certain Psalms into English Verse." What Psalms are included? When was the Translation published, and what was Bacon's age at the time?

46. Give the title of the First Folio edition of the Plays. Who engraved the portrait, and what other portraits of the time are by him? What value may be ascribed to Ben Jonson's lines " To the Reader," facing the title-page? The evidence that the plate on which the portrait was engraved, was tampered with before it was used for printing. What of the proof-impression contained in the collection of rarities made by the late James Orchard Halliwell-Phillipps?

47. Sketch the lives and characters of the dedicatees, and comment on the Dedication.

48. What other works were dedicated to the Earl of Pembroke? and to what do all the dedications bear testimony? Ben Jonson's dedication of his " Catiline his Conspiracy." Chapman's Sonnet to the Earl of Pembroke.

49. The evidence adduced by Charles Armitage Brown, in his " Shakespeare's Autobiographical Poems, being his Sonnets clearly developed," that the dedicatee, " Mr. W. H.," was William Herbert, Earl of Pembroke.

50. What does Hallam say of Brown's hypothesis, in his " Introduction to the Literature of Europe "?

51. Where are the Sonnets first alluded to, and in what terms?

52. What do we know of the lives and characters of the editors of the First Folio?

53. Comment on their Address " To the great Variety of Readers." What internal evidence is there that Ben Jonson had a hand in this Address? What does he say in his " Timber; or, Discoveries," as to the statement of the Players, that Shakespeare " never blotted out a line "?

54. Which of the Plays were published during Shakespeare's lifetime? How are they alluded to in the Address " To the great Variety of Readers "?

55. Name the Plays which appeared for the first time, so far as is known, in the First Folio.

56. What do we know of the lives and characters of Hugh Holland, Leonard Digges, and I. M., whose commendatory verses follow the Address? Comment on the verses.

57. What evidence is afforded that the monument in the Stratford Church was erected before the publication of the First Folio? By whose order was it, without question, erected?

58. The importance of determining the chronological order of the Plays.

59. What period is covered by Shakespeare's authorship?

60. The kinds of evidence which have been brought to bear upon the dates of the composition of the Plays.

61. What was done by Edmund Malone, in the last century, toward determining the chronology of the Plays? To what extent did he take note of the verse test?

62. What was the first contribution to the special study of the verse, as a chronological test? What chronological verse characteristics are therein presented?

63. Characterize the blank verse of Lord Surrey's translation of the 2d and 4th Books of Virgil's Æneid. When was the translation published?

64. Characterize the blank verse of the Tragedy of Gorboduc. When and by whom was it written? What improvement does the verse show upon Surrey's?

65. What is the most marked characteristic of all the earlier blank verse in the language?

66. What advance does Marlowe's blank verse show upon all that was previously produced? Characterize it as specially as you can, and read examples of it of your own selection.

67. To what extent does Marlowe's blank verse support the eulogies bestowed upon it by a writer in The Cornhill Magazine, Vol. XV.? Comment on the extract given in the text, and on the passages the writer selects from Doctor Faustus, Edward the Second, Tamburlane, and the Jew of Malta.

68. To what extent was Shakespeare indebted for his verse, to his predecessors and contemporaries, beyond its generic form?

69. What is the nature of the general development of Shakespeare's verse, from the earliest to the latest period of his authorship?

70. What is an indispensable condition of pause-melody?

71. Comment on the pause-melody of Milton's verse, and give

numerous examples, other than those given from Masson, of varied cæsuras.

72. What does Cowper say of variety of pause, and what all-important thing does he omit to say?

73. What scheme of *emphasis* melody is noticeable in the verse of Paradise Lost? Give examples.

74. The demands of the most effective dramatic movement of blank verse as contrasted with the most effective epic movement.

75. The different elocution demanded by the earliest and by the latest forms of Shakespeare's verse. What change must have been wrought, along with the change in the verse, in the stage-elocution of the time?

76. What appears to have been the style of Burbadge's elocution?

77. Which of Shakespeare's characters did he impersonate, according to "A Funeral Elegy on the death of .... Richard Burbadge"? What is said of this Elegy in "Shakespeare's Centurie of Prayse"?

78. The advantage which Shakespeare and Burbadge must have derived from each other.

79. Define the terms, Recitative and Spontaneous, as applied to Shakespeare's earlier and later verse.

80. What relation has the use of Rhyme to the chronology of the Plays?

81. The rhymes in Love's Labor's Lost, A Midsummer Night's Dream, Romeo and Juliet, Richard II.; and in Cymbeline, Coriolanus, Antony and Cleopatra, The Tempest, and the Winter's Tale.

82. The relation of the place of a pause or break in a verse (whether in the middle or at the end of a foot) to the current of the feeling.

83. In which Plays does the Recitative form of verse reach its highest degree of freedom, and thus realize its fullest dramatic capabilities?

84. What are the most obvious characteristics of the Spontaneous form of Shakespeare's blank verse?

85. By what means is the metre, in the Spontaneous form, more or less sunk? Comment at length on these means.

86. Give examples of the Spontaneous form of verse, in which the melody fusion is reduced, and the standard measure is sunk in the varied measures.

87. Comment on Shakespeare's organic use of extra end-syllables. Cite examples of their organic use, other than those given in the text.

88. What is their value, in Shakespeare's Plays as a chronological

test? Their value as determining the joint authorship of Henry VIII. See the treatment of this subject in the Publications of the New Shakspere Society.

89. Comment on Shakespeare's freedom from normal restrictions, and on his being, more or less, a law to himself.

90. Fletcher's use of extra end-syllables. Give examples from his Plays of their use as a monotonous mannerism.

91. What does Sir Henry Taylor say of the verse of the Elizabethan era (Correspondence, edited by Dowden)?

92. Comment on Shakespeare's distinctive use of verse and prose. What classes of character speak generally in prose?

93. What development is shown in the Plays, of Shakespeare's sense of the peculiar domains of verse and prose?

94. Give examples from Richard II. and other early Plays, of speeches in verse which, later, Shakespeare would have written in plain prose.

95. Hamlet's distinctive use of verse and prose.

96. On what occasions does Falstaff use verse?

97. Comment on the distinctive use of verse and prose in the 3d Scene of the 1st Act of The Merchant of Venice, and in the 3d Scene of the 1st Act of Othello. Give other examples of this distinctive use.

98. The two characteristics of legitimate verse by which it is especially differentiated from prose. Give as many examples of these characteristics as you can note.

99. What do a poet's epithets and metaphors reveal?

100. What is the signification of the transference of epithets, from words to which they properly belong to those to which they are logically inapplicable? Give examples from Shakespeare and other poets.

101. Give an example, and comment thereupon, of how Shakespeare raised the prose of appropriated material into glowing and luxuriant poetry.

102. Shakespeare's prose as compared with that of Bacon's Essays.

103. Comment on the prose of the 2d Scene of the 5th Act of The Winter's Tale.

104. The distinctive domains of the Latin and the Anglo-Saxon elements of the English Language, as defined by Thomas De Quincey. Cite examples from Shakespeare of these distinctive domains.

105. The large Latin element of Troilus and Cressida, and what it

indicates. What does Dryden incorrectly say of the chronology of this Play?

106. The monosyllabic character of the Anglo-Saxon element of the English language, and its subserviency to the expression of strong feeling of every kind. Give examples from Shakespeare and other authors.

107. The different vowel elements attracted to themselves by different feelings.

108. The part played by the abrupt vowels of words in expressing the more violent feelings of anger, hate, detestation, scorn, etc. Give examples.

109. The part played by prolongable vowels in expressing the gentler feelings of love, or admiration, or of the beautiful. Give examples.

110. What passage in King Lear would serve as a motto to Romeo and Juliet? or what passage in the Sonnets would be equally appropriate?

111. How is love represented in Romeo and Juliet?

112. Comment on the Prologue as an exposition of the dramatic motive of the Play. Where does it first appear, and in what form? Where does it first appear in its complete form? What epithet gives the key-note of the Play?

113. What is characteristic of all the opening Scenes of Shakespeare's Plays?

114. What interpretation of the Play does the opening Scene testify against?

115. State at length the dramatic situation and the dramatic motive.

116. What relation has Romeo's first love to the subsequent dramatic action? Misinterpretation of this first love. What does Ulrici say of it? What does Kreyzig say of it? Mrs. Jameson?

117. How is Shakespeare's creative power shown by what he adopts from his originals? How is it shown in Romeo's first love?

118. What old English poem was the original of Romeo and Juliet, and when was it published?

119. In what two important particulars has Shakespeare modified what is said of Romeo's first love, in the original poem? and what bearing has the modification upon the dramatic motive?

120. Give the points of difference in the presentation of Romeo's first love, in the poem and in the play.

121. What has Shakespeare specially emphasized in Romeo's character? How is he contrasted with Tybalt?

122. Juliet's situation and surroundings before she meets with
Romeo.

123. Comment on Juliet's reply to her mother, in regard to her marrying Paris: " I'll look to like, if looking liking move," and " But no
more deep will I endart mine eye than your consent gives strength to
make it fly." What is indicated by these speeches?

124. In what respect do Romeo and Juliet differ, in their first love for
each other?

125. What modifications of the relations of Romeo and Tybalt in
the poem, are made in the Play, and what is the dramatic motive of
these modifications?

126. How is the justification of Romeo's slaying of Tybalt enforced
in the Play? What point is to be especially noted in the act which
proves such a misfortune to Romeo? Its bearing upon the dramatic
motive.

127. Give Halpin's interpretation of "runnaway's eyes," and of
Juliet's epithalamic monologue (Act III. S. 2).

128. Note where Juliet passes into a self-sustained, heroic womanhood.

129. The dramatic purpose of Juliet's dread imaginings before taking the sleeping-potion. Upon what does a dramatic interest in the
situation depend? What does Lord Lytton say of Miss Anderson's
acting in the potion scene?

130. Comment on the 4th Scene of the 4th Act, as exhibiting Shakespeare's use of Contrast.

131. Note the point where Romeo attains to self-poised, self-reliant
manhood.

132. What support, if any, does the Play afford to the charges of
rashness made against Romeo by numerous commentators? Cite some
of these charges from English and German commentators. Show how
Romeo is, throughout the play, protected from such charges.

133. Comment on the view entertained by various critics, English,
French, and German, that Friar Laurence voices the moral of the Play;
and on the view that the tragic consequences of the loves of Romeo
and Juliet are due to subjective causes (to causes existing within themselves), rather than to objective causes (to causes outside of themselves).
What does the Play especially emphasize? How should the prudential

maxims of Friar Laurence be taken? What does Bodenstedt say of them, in the Introduction to his translation of Romeo and Juliet?

134. To what artistically satisfying end, so far as they themselves are concerned, are the ardent loves of Romeo and Juliet dramatically brought?

135. Distinguish Shakespeare's moral spirit from a moralizing spirit.

136. A moralizing spirit as contrary to a true artistic, creative spirit.

137. What is meant by poetic justice? How did the playwrights of the Restoration period understand it?

138. How many English historical Plays did Shakespeare write, and in which is the historical connection preserved? How is the break in the series partly supplied? Which two may be regarded as the Prologue and the Epilogue to the series?

139. What circumstances favored the writing of English historical Plays, in the reign of Elizabeth?

140. What made the time, in its general character, especially favorable for the production of a great Drama?

141. When was King John, so far as is known, first published? Approximate date of its composition.

142. What may be said to be the informing spirit of the Play? In what speech is the spirit of the whole Play voiced?

143. Characterize the earlier Play of "The Troublesome Raigne of John King of England." When was it first published? The attribution of its authorship, in subsequent editions, to Shakespeare, how explained?

144. Characterize this earlier Play, in regard to its strong partisan spirit. Where is this spirit especially shown? What must have secured for the Play, a great popularity, at the time of its first appearance? What is known of its authorship?

145. What were Shakespeare's obligations to the Play? Dr. Ingleby's view.

146. Comment on the violent anti-papal spirit of the old Play, and on the entire absence of religious partisanship in Shakespeare's Play. Does such absence imply religious indifference on his part? What does it rather bear testimony to?

147. The relation of the narrated element in Shakespeare's Play to its non-partisan spirit.

148. On what unhistorical assumptions is King John based? Where did Shakespeare get his history in his other English historical Plays?

149. Comment on the opening scene as striking the key-note of the whole action.

150. The ignoring of authentic history, as shown in the characters of Constance and Arthur. The bearing of their characters, as given in the Play, upon the dramatic motive.

151. What special dramatic purpose is served by the beauty of person, and the sweetness and loveliness of character, which the poet has given to Arthur?

152. Comment on the view entertained by many critics, and on what has especially, but unwarrantably, favored that view, that personal ambition is the ruling motive of Constance. What may be said to be her ruling motive and her dominant passion?

153. The estimate to be attached to the opinions which characters, whether hostile or not, in Shakespeare's Plays, express of each other. The reliableness of those opinions to be tested as in real life.

154. How are Elinor's expressions in regard to Constance, to be taken?

155. What does Ulrici say of Constance and Arthur? Comment thereupon. What does Gervinus say of Constance? Does the Play in any way support what he says? How would the artistic symmetry and the moral tone of the Play be impaired if the views of these commentators were correct?

156. How do the unhistorical assumptions on which the Play is based, exclude the idea of personal ambition on the part of Constance?

157. Comment on the dramatic situation in A. III. S. 1, which has been led up to by the marriage of the Dauphin and Blanch.

158. Comment on Faulconbridge's soliloquy on the broken faith of the two kings, and on "commodity."

159. Comment on the capture of Arthur and his conveyance to England, as the turning-point in John's fortunes.

160. The current of fatalism into which John is finally borne.

161. Characterize Faulconbridge as voicing the national spirit of the Play.

162. The non-recognition of Shakespeare's moral proportion, on the part of the dramatists and dramatic critics of the Restoration period. The testimony borne by the *rifacimenti* of some of his Plays, perpetrated by Dryden, Davenant, Tate, *et al*.

163. When was Much Ado about Nothing first published? Date of its composition. State of the text.

164. What pun does Richard Grant White see in the title, and what is its relation to the action of the Play? Ellis's view of it, in his Early English Pronunciation. Where has Shakespeare repeated the pun in the Play? In what other Play does it occur?

165. Contemporary testimony to the popularity of the Play, and also to that of other Plays of Shakespeare over Ben Jonson's best plays.

166. Under what various forms is the story found on which the Play is based? Which appears to have been Shakespeare's original?

167. How is the essential originality of a Play of Shakespeare especially shown, when compared with the original story on which it was founded? The independent principle of movement shown by The Winter's Tale, when compared with the novel on which it was based (Robert Green's "Pandosto, or, the Triumph of Time").

168. Which characters in Much Ado about Nothing appear to have been entirely original with Shakespeare?

169. In what attitudes toward each other are Benedick and Beatrice presented in the opening scene, and to what were those attitudes previously due?

170. In what earlier Play are these two characters faintly sketched?

171. How is Beatrice characterized by the poet Campbell and by Mrs. Jameson? What of the imperious character attributed to her by Mrs. Jameson? Comment on the views of these critics.

172. What is the real purpose of the stratagem practised upon the pair by their friends, and how has this stratagem been misunderstood by some critics?

173. What do the soliloquies of Benedick and Beatrice, after the stratagem has been practised upon each, reveal of their real selves? What essentially constitutes the comedy of the situation?

174. What is the dramatic problem after the stratagem has been successfully carried out?

175. How does the rejection of Hero by Claudio, in the church, afterwards contribute to the solution of this problem? Comment at length on the art with which Shakespeare has raised Benedick and Beatrice to the height required for a mutual avowal of love, after all that has passed between them.

176. Comment on the part played by Friar Francis.

177. To what end do the color and the word artist employ, the one, physical darkness, and the other, moral darkness?

178. What must be the ultimate end of all true art, whatever be the material employed by the artist?

179. Comment at length on the three kinds of testimony afforded by the Play, corroborative of Hamlet's sanity, his keen intuition and high reasoning powers.

180. What is involved in the injunction imposed upon Hamlet by the ghost of his father, to "revenge his foul and most unnatural murder."

181. What is the subjective theory in regard to Hamlet, as set forth by Goethe and by Coleridge, and followed by most of the subsequent critics of the Play? Give summaries of the interpretations of these two critics.

182. What *dramatic* interest could there be in Hamlet, if Coleridge's characterization of him were correct?

183. What is the objective theory in regard to Hamlet, as presented by Klein, and afterwards more fully developed by Werder? By what English critic was this theory previously indicated?

184. Give a summary of Werder's interpretation, so far as it is presented in the extracts from his "Vorlesungen über Shakespeare's Hamlet," given in Dr. Furness's New Variorum edition of Hamlet.

185. Up to what point is Hamlet solving the objective problem, and what causes the action of the drama to pass into the hands of fate? Trace the current of fatalism to the catastrophe.

186. What increased interest is imparted to the subjective Hamlet by a recognition and understanding of the objective problem? What is the condition of a dramatic interest?

187. Approximate date of the composition of Macbeth, how determined? Relation of the Play to the accession of James I. to the English throne.

188. The two all-important things to be considered, in the Tragedy.

189. How is the agency of the witches to be understood; in other words, is the power of the "metaphysical" agency employed, to be understood as absolute to any extent, or as wholly relative?

190. Give the views of Hazlitt, Lamb, Thomas Whately, and others, as to their agency. The inconsistency of these views with a true dramatic interest, and with the general theory of Shakespeare's dramatic art. What is essential to a dramatic interest?

191. At what stage in the evolution of a great passion does its fatalism set in, in all Shakespeare's tragedies?

192. Compare the weird sisters with Milton's Sin and Death.

193. Note the correspondences which distinguish this Play, of the natural with the moral world, and how the toning of the play is largely induced by these correspondences.

194. From the place in the Play the speech occupies, what moral significance may be attached to "The west yet glimmers with some streaks of day" (A. III. S. 1)?

195. What does Fanny Kemble say of lines 40–53 of A. III. S. 3?

196. What did Shakespeare mean by the weird sisters, as shown in Lady Macbeth's soliloquy (A. I. S. 5, 41–51)?

197. What does Gervinus say of Shakespeare's spirit-world? What basis has this opinion?

198. What especially rendered Shakespeare the greatest poet of the race?

199. Explain "So foul and fair a day I have not seen." What seems to be intimated by the epithets "foul" and "fair"?

200. To what was the establishment of the relationship between the powers of evil in Macbeth's soul primarily due?

201. How are Macbeth and Banquo dramatically contrasted in their interview with the witches (A. I. S. 3)?

202. In what speech of Banquo is the entire moral of the tragedy expressed?

203. Comment on Macbeth's imaginative temperament.

204. How is Lady Macbeth's characterization of her husband, after reading his letter (A. I. S. 5), to be taken?

205. What is the true import of Macbeth's "horrible imaginings," and of what Lady Macbeth misunderstands as "compunctious visitings of nature"?

206. What revelation does Macbeth make of himself, in his soliloquy, "If it were done, when 'tis done" (A. I. S. 7)?

207. Summarize Lady Macbeth's relations to Macbeth's career. When do those relations cease, and what are the consequences to her when they cease? How do those consequences reflect her true nature which she at first repressed in the service of her husband's ambition? Comment on the 1st Scene of the 5th Act, as testifying to her womanly nature.

208. What does the Countess of Charlemont say of the "cry within of women" when Lady Macbeth dies? What does Dr. Furnivall remark on her view of Lady Macbeth? What has the original story to do with the interpretation of any character in a Play of Shakespeare?

209. The date of the composition of Antony and Cleopatra?

210. How does the Play rank among the Plays of Shakespeare? How does Coleridge characterize it?

211. Why should the Play be regarded as a tragedy rather than as a politico-historical play? What is properly an historical play? and what is properly a tragedy? How should Coriolanus, for example, be classed? What is, throughout, its dominant interest?

212. How does Denton J. Snider regard the Play of Antony and Cleopatra?

213. What stage in his development had Shakespeare reached when he composed the Play?

214. Can a doctrinal character be imputed to any play of Shakespeare?

215. In what way can a great work of art be said to *teach*?

216. What is meant by great truths being held in solution in a work of art?

217. How is Shakespeare, as a dramatist, distinguished from all the contemporary dramatists?

218. What is meant by moral proportion?

219. What is the great artistic achievement of Shakespeare, in his tragic masterpieces?

220. Why can the critic, with philosophical tendencies, always find the doctrinal in a great work of art, if he look for it?

221. Although the profoundest abstract principles may be operative in a work of art, is it the aim of the artist, as artist, to embody these principles? And are they necessarily in his intellectual consciousness during the exercise of his creative power?

222. What is always the business of Shakespeare's dramatic art?

223. In what high sense is Shakespeare a moralist, and a social and political philosopher?

224. What does Professor Delius seem to assume in regard to the character of the Play of Antony and Cleopatra?

225. What is the dominant interest from the beginning to the end of the Play?

226. In what speech is the key-note of the Play distinctly struck?

227. Present at length the dramatic situation of the Play, as a tragedy.

228. What passage in Hamlet is remarkably illustrated by the character of Antony?

229. What does Thomas De Quincey say of Shakespeare's insight, which the Romans themselves could not have had, into the possibilities of Antony's nature?

230. In the description of the first meeting of Antony and Cleopatra, how has the poet impassioned his prose original, and created the atmosphere in which the passion-fated pair are exhibited?

231. What was the moral problem involved in the dramatic treatment of the theme of Antony and Cleopatra?

232. How does the poet avoid any perversion of the moral judgment? and, further, how is the moral judgment stimulated to its best activity?

233. Comment at length on the narrated element of the Play as bearing on its perspective and on its moral spirit and moral proportion.

234. Comment on Skottowe's remark that " Shakespeare has not been successful in conveying an idea of the elegance of Cleopatra's mind." Was such a success demanded by the dramatic motive? rather, would not such a success have defeated the dramatic motive?

235. Comment on what Mrs. Jameson says of the fascination of Shakespeare's Cleopatra.

236. What does Dryden say of his bringing Cleopatra and Octavia together, in his " All for Love; or, the world well lost " ?

237. Comment on Swinburne's rapture over Shakespeare's Cleopatra.

238. Comment on the inevitable subordination of Antony to Octavius.

239. Comment on the dramatic significance of the Scene on Pompey's Galley (A. II. S. 7); and on the Shakesperian irony which it exhibits.

240. What is the one great and common merit of all Shakespeare's characters, both men and women? What does Godwin say of this?

241. Comment on Antony's speech to Octavius, " Be a child o' the time," and Octavius's reply, " Possess it, I'll make answer."

242. Comment on Octavius's subsequent speech, " What would you more."

243. Comment on the reconciliation which has been patched up between the several leading actors of the drama.

244. The illustrations which Octavius and Antony afford of Brutus's speech in Julius Cæsar (A. IV. S. 3, 218–221).

245. Compare the situation of Octavia with that of Blanch of Castile, in King John.

246. How is Octavius's consummate skill as a politician especially shown?

247. Comment on the speech of Enobarbus, " You shall find the band that seems to tie their friendship together will be the very strangler of their amity."

248. Comment on Shakespeare's dramatic skill in placing before us an impressive personality, by a few slight touches. Illustrate through Octavia, and Cordelia in King Lear.

249. Comment on the final conflict which brings the historical movement to its goal, and exhibits, in the boldest relief, the bondage of Antony.

250. Comment on Antony's love for Cleopatra, as the mainspring of his being (as shown in A. IV.), and on Cleopatra's love (as shown in A. V.). What does Denton J. Snider say of Cleopatra's love, after the death of Antony?

251. Comment on the merit of the Folio's readings (in some cases punctuations), of the following passages in Hamlet, as compared with the readings of the 2d Quarto, or, in some cases, "emended" readings given in modern editions :

I. 2. 11; I. 2. 76; I. 2. 170; I. 2. 191; I. 2. 239; I. 3. 10; I. 3. 57; I. 3. 109; I. 3. 120; I. 3. 127–131; I. 5. 135–137; I. 5. 154; I. 5. 157–160; I. 5. 174; 2. 2. 180, 181; 2. 2. 183–185; 2. 2. 201; 2. 2. 381–383; 3. 1. 63; 3. 1. 72; 3. 1. 76; 3. 1. 97; 3. 1. 158; 3. 2. 8; 3. 2. 60–63; 3. 2. 73–75; 3. 2. 301–303; 3. 2. 329; 3. 2. 347, 348; 3. 2. 354, 355; 3. 4. 4; 4. 1. 1, 2; 4. 1. 19–23; 4. 2. 12, 13; 4. 3. 44; 4. 5. 112, 113; 4. 5. 160–162; 4. 7. 185; 5. 1. 76; 5. 1. 77; 5. 1. 169, 170.

252. Comment on the use of the interrogative in the First Folio, and on its use in the "Cambridge" edition.

253. Explain whatever calls for explanation in the following passages in Hamlet :

I. 1. 42: Thou art a scholar; I. 1. 72: So nightly toils the subject of the land, I. 1. 94: And carriage of the article designed, I. 2. 37: more than the scope of these dilated articles allow. I. 2. 147: or ere I. 2. 182: dearest foe I. 4. 9: keeps wassail, and the swaggering upspring reels; I. 5. 77: Unhousel'd, disappointed, unanel'd,

254. 2. 1. 65: With windlasses and with assays of bias, 2. 2. 183:

being a good kissing carrion, — 2. 2. 337 : the clown shall make those laugh whose lungs are tickle o' the sere ; 2. 2. 354: an aery of children, little eyases, that cry out on the top of question, and are most tyrannically clapped for't, 2. 2. 388 : the appurtenance of welcome is fashion and ceremony : let me comply with you in the garb, lest my extent to the players, which, I tell you, must show fairly outward, should more appear like entertainment than yours. 2. 2. 396: I am but mad north-north-west : when the wind is southerly I know a hawk from a handsaw.

255. 3. 2. 15 : I could have such a fellow whipt for o'erdoing Termagant ; it out-Herods Herod : 3. 2. 131 : You are merry, my lord. . . . Oh God, your only jigmaker. 3. 2. 136: let the devil wear black, for I'll have a suit of sables. 3. 2. 286: Would not this, sir, and a forest of feathers — if the rest of my fortunes turn Turk with me — with two Provincial roses on my razed shoes, get me a fellowship in a cry of players, sir? 3. 3. 360: to withdraw with you, why do you go about to recover the wind of me, as if you would drive me into a toil? 3. 3. 401 : They fool me to the top of my bent. 3. 4, 89: such black and grained spots As will not leave their tinct.

256. 4. 3. 22 : Your worm is your only emperor for diet : 4. 5. 41 : Well, God 'ild you ! They say the owl was a baker's daughter. Lord, we know what we are, but know not what we may be. 4. 5. 83 : we have done but greenly, In huggermugger to inter him : 4. 5. 146 : And like the kind life-rendering pelican, Repast them with my blood. 4. 5. 180 : There's fennel for you, and columbines : there's rue for you ; and here's some for me : we may call it herb-grace o' Sundays. Oh, you must wear your rue with a difference.

257. 5. 1. 148 : How absolute the knave is ! we must speak by the card, or equivocation will undo us. 5. 2. 5 : methought I lay Worse than the mutines in the bilboes. 5. 2. 19 : an exact command, Larded with many several sorts of reasons Importing Denmark's health and England's too, 5. 2. 23 : on the supervise, no leisure bated, 5. 2, 30 : Ere I could make a prologue to my brains, They had begun the play — 5. 2. 39 : As England was his faithful tributary, As love between them as the palm should flourish, As peace should still her wheaten garland wear And stand a comma 'tween their amities, And many such like ' As 'es of great charge,

258. Comment on the spelling of the poet's name.

259. Comment on the following passages : I Henry IV. 4. 1. 97–110 ;

Antony and Cleopatra, 5. 2. 86–88; King John, 4. 3. 155, 156.　The Merchant of Venice, 3. 5. 77–83; The Winter's Tale, 4. 4. 146–151.

260. Comment on the absorption of cognates in the First Folio; on the ethical dative; on respective constructions in Shakespeare and writers of his time.

Lightning Source UK Ltd.
Milton Keynes UK
UKHW041611291219
356009UK00001B/79/P